PHILIPPIANS RIDICULOUS JOY!

By

Bruce Guckelberg, Ph.D.

ISBN: 9781983255847

In gratitude to God for my loving wife Carol

Table of Contents

Recommendations

In this book, scholar and pastor Bruce Guckelberg provides readers with a good exegetical treatment of Paul's tiny but powerfully inspiring epistle to the Philippians. Bruce shows how the apostle uses his own prison experience—and the attitude he maintains in spite of it—to show the Philippians the difference a Christ-formed mind makes in the way believers respond to adversity, rivalry, conflict, vanity, and any other circumstance they encounter in fundamentally different ways.

This is a good book for stimulating sermon preparation, for teaching, and even devotional reading that takes you straight to the text. This book is a resource all Christians will benefit from.

Dr. Saul Ebema
Sr. Pastor, Lombard Bible Church, Lombard, IL.

Dr. Guckelberg has written a commentary on Philippians that takes you into the culture of Philippi and uncovers many things that enhance our understanding of this letter. He writes in a manner that provides his readers with depth of insight regarding the text, while supplying many illustrations and applications that make it relevant to today. He provides comments on many Greek words that bring out the rich nuances of the original language which amplifies our understanding of the text. This commentary will be a benefit to anyone who wants to study Philippians.

Rev. David J Phillips
Interventionist, District Superintendent in the Christian & Missionary Alliance, Interim Pastor, Coach to Pastors

I found that Bruce's work is a concise and yet comprehensive commentary of Philippians for the student who is serious about seeing and applying what joy in Jesus Christ really is!

Dr. Darren Lim
Professor of Applied Theology, Bay Cities Bible College, Berkley, CA. Pastor, Fremont Asian Christian Church, Fremont, CA.

Bruce takes the New Testament call to joy seriously and makes the practice of it easy to grasp. His writing is refreshing, readable, realistic to life. *Ridiculous Joy* is a winsome study of orthopraxy for the modern reader. Bruce has a *"let's sit down with a cup of coffee and talk about this"* style that will make the reader want to personally apply Paul's message to the Philippians.

Dr. Marty Wilhelm, Professor William Jessup University, Rocklin, CA. Missionary, Associate Pastor Mountain Christian Fellowship, Arnold, CA.

Author's Preface

There have been many commentaries written on Philippians, so why have I chosen to undertake this writing project and add another commentary to the long list that already exists? This short letter Paul wrote over 2,000 years ago speaks to the modern reader in a very practical way. It's application for today's Christian is very powerful and life impacting. Paul wrote this letter when he was in prison and had a rough go of things for a long time. Many people today live in a prison, of sorts, and could use some instruction on rising above their dire circumstances that life may present them. In this season of Paul's life, he learned to be joyful, content, and experience God's peace, which is amazing when you consider what he's been through.

Studying Philippians can help the modern reader up his level of joy, contentment, and peace, which will improve the quality of his mental disposition. There are a lot of things to stress over these days, so God's peace can be a welcomed relief from all the anxieties of life. For these reasons, Philippians is a high value letter that is worth investing one's time in because it will pay huge spiritual dividends. A journey through Philippians can change your outlook on life, by showing you ways of processing both good and troubling things that happen to you in a spiritually and emotionally healthy way. You will be much better off for drinking from the deep well of Philippians.

In writing this commentary I take the reader back to the First Century in order to understand why Paul wrote this letter. It is necessary to understand the rhetorical nature of Paul's letter writing, and the social conventions of Greco-Roman culture to gain the full picture of Philippians, which I develop throughout this commentary.

I've chosen the World English Bible (WEB) as the translation I use in this commentary, which is a literal translation of the Greek text and is very accurate. However, literal translations don't always read smoothly like every day conversational English. For this reason, to make some passages more readable and understandable I offer my own translation, while keeping it as close to the WEB as possible.

I cite Greek words throughout the commentary, describing some of the nuances of the words to fill out, and color the meaning of the text, which will enhance our understanding of each passage. In the body of the commentary all the Scripture is in bold text, which sets it apart from my comments.

Some commentaries are written by scholars for scholars, which makes it difficult and out of reach for many people to read. Such is not the case here. While interacting with other scholars I deal with all the pertinent issues, in a way that is fluid and understandable for the reader. This commentary explores each passage in depth, and at the end of each unit I have a section for applications, insights, and life lessons to make the text relevant and show people how they can apply it to their lives. This brings the commentary home to the reader, because after studying Philippians one must live Philippians. Each person must try to make the Philippian narrative their own. All the stories I tell are totally truthful, but I've changed the names of the people to protect their identity.

I want to thank my wife Carol for giving me the freedom to undertake this project. I also want to thank those with whom I've dialogued about certain matters in Philippians and have served as a sounding board to me. Special thanks go to my valued colleagues in ministry Dr. Darren Lim, Rev. David Phillips, Dr. Marty Wilhelm, and Dr. Saul Ebema for reading through the book and offering me their comments and insights. I hope this journey through Philippians will enrich your walk with the Lord Jesus as it has enriched mine.

INTRODUCTION

The Author

It is generally agreed by scholars that Paul is the author of this inspired text of Scripture. He names himself as the author (1:1), plus the church fathers agreed that Paul wrote Philippians. What is known of the circumstances behind the founding of the church in Philippi, Paul's imprisonment, and the trial all seem to fit in Philippians. Reading through the letter leads one to believe that it is Paul, it sounds like Paul, the style is Pauline, and theology is consistent with Paul's other writings.

Who would have ever thought that a former Pharisaic Jew, converted to Christianity, would have taken some papyrus and begin to write a letter to his friends in Philippi, while under house arrest in Rome, that would survive twenty-one centuries and be cherished by Christians around the globe. Today's world-wide distribution of his letter to the church at Philippi would blow Paul away. Translated in multiple languages and found in many countries, this letter has been a huge success, for it has been a source of comfort and encouragement to followers of Christ for millennia. Drinking from the well of Philippians has provided much refreshment to its readers and will continue to do so. The letter consists of only four short chapters in our English Bibles, but it packs a punch.

Paul died in obscurity, but his legacy continues forever. People worship God in churches and large ornate cathedrals that bear the name St. Paul. His letters, especially Philippians, is a personal favorite of many disciples of Christ. If Paul walked into a Christian book store in today's modern world and went to the section titled "Bibles" and started paging through the New Testament, how would he respond to seeing his letters? If he grabbed a commentary on Philippians off the shelf and started skimming it, what would he think? I'm sure Paul would be astounded that the letter he wrote to the church at Philippi is alive and well thousands of years after he perished. If he were in our modern-day world, which is so different from his culturally, technologically, linguistically, and so on, he would be amazed at how relevant his letter to the church at Philippi is for today's Christian.

The Location

That Paul mentions the Praetorian Guard, and Caesar's household support Rome as the location from which he wrote the letter around AD 62. There have been attempts to place Paul, at the writing of Philippians in Ephesus (Acts 19:35–41; 1 Cor 15:32), Philippi (Acts 16:19–34), and Caesarea (Acts 23:23–26:32), but the data best supports the place of writing as Rome (Acts 28). Therefore, the traditional view is maintained in this commentary that Paul was in Rome when he wrote this letter.

The primary reason Rome is questioned by some scholars as the place of origin of the letter is because the distance between Rome and Philippi, about 740 miles, is too far to allow for all the visits required. The reconstruction of the visits would look something like this:

The first trip: the Philippians heard from somebody, through the grapevine, that Paul was incarcerated in Rome.

The second trip: the Philippians sent Epaphroditus to Rome to give Paul the money they raised for him, and to minister to his needs. (2:25)

The third trip: somebody went back to Philippi and informed them that Epaphroditus was sick. (2:26)

The Fourth trip: the Philippians sent word back to Rome to express their concern for him. (2:26)

It was then that Paul wrote Philippians. Afterwards, Paul sent Epaphroditus back to Philippi to deliver the letter (Philippians) to them (2:25-30), Timothy would follow shortly after Paul's day in court (2:19-23), then upon Paul's release (if he is released) he intended to make a visit to Philippi (2:24).

The distance between Rome and Philippi is too far to account for all four visits in the two-year imprisonment. It would take between four and seven weeks to make the trek of around 740 miles on foot. However, imperial couriers could travel 50 miles in a day. The messengers could travel in a carriage, or on horseback, which would greatly reduce the travel-time. The road system in the Roman Empire was very advanced and facilitated traveling distances. Plus, Paul had a network of people in his churches that most likely communicated with each other and may have made trips from Rome to Philippi and vice versa. Therefore, the argument that the distance between Rome and Philippi negates Rome as the place of writing the letter is unconvincing. The traditional view that Paul wrote the letter while under house arrest in Rome best supports the data.

The City of Philippi

Philippi is located in central Macedonia about 16 kilometers inland from the seaport of Neapolis. This city was originally founded by Greek colonists from the island of Thasos in 360 BC, and was given the name Krenides, which means "the little fountains" named because of nearby springs. The city was taken over by Philip of Macedon in 356 BC, who was Alexander the Great's father. He then renamed it after himself—Philippi "the city of Philip." There was great strategic significance attached to the city because it was next to the large fertile plain of Datos, it was well protected by its acropolis, and it was near Mount Panagaion, which was rich in mineral deposits including gold. Philippi was also the gateway to Asia Minor. For these reasons the city was important to Philip, who annexed the region and began to fortify the city that now bore his name.

In Paul's time the Via Egnatia ran through the city, which was an important roadway that greatly facilitated travel. All Macedonia was under Roman control in 168 BC thus ending the Macedonian dynasty. They created a Roman province, which they divided into four parts. Luke informs us that Philippi was the leading city of that part of Macedonia (Acts 16:11). The area lingered in obscurity for more than a century until one of the most important battles in Roman history occurred there in 42 BC.

The battle of Philippi featured the army of Antony and Octavian (Caesar Augustus) who defeated the forces of Brutus and Cassius—the assassins of Julius Caesar. This marked the end of Rome as a republic and established the Roman Empire. Another important battle occurred when Octavian defeated Antony and Cleopatra at the battle of Actium in 31 BC. The senate declared Octavian emperor in 29 BC and Philippi was given the status of a Roman colony. Octavian settled many of his soldiers there giving them land grants, which caused them to be fiercely loyal to Rome. The retired combat vets who lived in the area were given the prized possession of Roman citizenship, so the city was very much pro Roman, and patriotic. Philippi was also a Roman garrison city, which made it safe and secure, so seeing Roman soldiers roaming about the city was common.

Given the special status they enjoyed as a Roman colony the city was exempt from certain taxes, they weren't subject to the provincial governor, and enjoyed the same legal status as cities in Italy. Therefore, Roman law was used in local affairs, the legal disposition of the colonists in respect to ownership of land, payment of taxes, local administration, and law was executed as if they were on Italian soil. Their architecture was Roman, as was their clothing, they spoke Latin as the official language, and their coins bore Roman inscriptions. Philippi was a pro Roman city that demonstrated civic pride and was truly a "little Italy."

By the time the apostle Paul arrived in Philippi it had become an urban political center populated by Romans and Greeks, with about 10,000 inhabitants. Although Latin was the official language, Greek was the predominant language of commerce and everyday conversation, which shouldn't be surprising since Philippi is a city located in Greece. Additionally, there was a small Jewish population present (Acts 16:13), consisting of women that met for prayer, who were most likely God-fearers, not full converts to Judaism. There is no mention of a synagogue, or men, that were praying with the women. It was to these women that Paul first preached Jesus. A woman named Lydia responded positively to the gospel and two other women mentioned by name are Euodia and Syntyche (Phil 4:2-3), all

Greek names. Clement is also mentioned, which is a Roman name, so it appears that most of the people coming into the Philippian church are Gentiles. There were probably some slaves that attended the church, there may have been some Jews, but we don't know how many people were in the church after Paul left Philippi. Perhaps 50 – 100, but it's only a guess.

The Founding of the Church at Philippi (Acts 16:6-40)

When Paul and his companions (Silas, Timothy, and Luke) were on their second missionary journey he wanted to go into the province of Asia and introduce the gospel there, but the Holy Spirit redirected their footsteps. They tried to enter Bithynia, but the Holy Spirit gave them a detour and they couldn't enter that area either. How the Spirit prevented them from going into those places is unknown, but they knew it was the Holy Spirit who was directing their travels. In response to a vision that Paul had during the night, where he saw a man from Macedonia saying, "Come over to Macedonia and help us," Paul geared-up and went there to preach the gospel. He felt that was the call of God to preach the Good News about Jesus and plant churches in that area. The Holy Spirit directed them to that location, which would be a major benchmark in Paul's ministry because this would be the start of the gospel going into Greek territory.

They boarded a ship that set sail to Neapolis, then by land they went to Macedonia where Philippi was located. Paul's normal practice was to visit a synagogue on the Sabbath and preach the gospel, however there doesn't appear to be a synagogue in Philippi, so Paul went to the river to find a place of prayer where he came upon some women, who were presumably Jewish. He shared the gospel with them which resulted in his first convert to the Christian faith in Macedonia (and Europe) being Lydia, a Gentile God-fearer (not a full convert to Judaism), and business woman who was a dealer in purple cloth. Paul baptized her and the members of her household, then accepted her invitation to stay in her home.

As a side note, Lydia sold purple cloth (Acts 16:14) that was made from the madder root, which was found in Thyatira where she was from. The high-end purple, the royal purple dye came from the murex shell, and was closely controlled by the emperor and members of his household. They licensed its use to a few high-status business people and clients, one of which may have been Lydia. She may have been contracted to make purple cloth and work with members of Caesar's household. If this is so, she probably had contacts in Caesar's household that she directed to Paul when he was under house arrest in Rome. She appears to be a woman of high status that may have attracted other women of status to the church, possibly Euodia and Syntyche (4:2), who had the means to be Paul's coworkers in Philippi.

For several days, a slave girl followed Paul around who had a spirit of divination, which enabled her to make huge profits for her owners by fortune-telling. She kept saying, "These men are servants of the Most High God, who are telling you the way to be saved." Paul was uncomfortable with this and discerned there was an evil spirit in her, so he commanded the spirit to leave and she was set free. She may have been the second convert to Christianity, but we don't know that for sure. Her owners' profit margin dropped to zero since she could no longer do her fortune-telling, so their lucrative enterprise was over. They grabbed Paul and Silas, brought them to the authorities, accusing "these Jews" of causing an uproar in the city by advocating things that are unlawful for Romans to do. Apparently, there weren't many Jews in Philippi and they didn't have a good reputation.

The magistrate ordered Paul and Silas to be stripped and severely beaten, then threw them in prison and locked their feet in the stocks. During the night God intervened: there was an earthquake, the doors were opened, and their chains came off. When the jailer saw this, he drew his sword and was ready to take his own life, but they called out to him in the nick-of-time. Paul shared the gospel with him and the rest of his family, resulting in them becoming believers in Christ, then baptized them.

The magistrates released Paul and Silas, but when Paul informed them that he was a Roman citizen the officials became afraid, because it was illegal to treat a citizen of Rome as they treated Paul. They escorted them out of the prison then Paul and Silas made one last visit to Lydia's house, where they met with the brothers and sisters. The church had humble beginnings, a business woman named Lydia was the first Christian convert in Macedonia, then her household became believers in the Lord Jesus. She became a leading lady in the church, which presumably met in her home, and she appears to have been a successful entrepreneur and person of means. Possibly the slave girl that had the demon cast out of her by Paul worshiped in the newly founded church at Philippi, along with the Philippian jailer and his family who were the next converts to Christianity. We don't know how long Paul stayed in Philippi, but it doesn't appear to be a long time because the authorities requested that he leave the city.

The church is born, there is a gospel presence in Philippi, but it was costly to Paul and Silas because they felt the sting of the rods on their backs and were left with scares for their ministry in Philippi. He mentioned to the Thessalonians how he was mistreated and suffered when he was in Philippi, so it must have made a lasting impression on him (1 Thess 2:2). Others that came to know Jesus in Philippi may have seen Paul and Silas beaten, so we are left wondering what kind of impression that made on them. We know the Philippians were persecuted at times (1:28), and apparently knew that becoming a Christian could be a costly enterprise involving physical suffering.

Emperor Worship

With the Roman influence in Philippi there was a layer of Roman culture imposed over the indigenous Greek Hellenistic culture. What the Roman presence introduced into the religious culture in Philippi was the worship of the Emperor. In the middle of the First Century the emperor cult was becoming important to the composition of Greco-Roman religion. The emperor was thought to be a deified human being, but he didn't displace the other gods that were worshiped. The problem that Christianity and Judaism had was their belief in one God, which was viewed as a denial of the whole pantheon of Greco-Roman gods. It wasn't that people had a hard time with Christians' belief in Jesus, it was that Christians didn't worship the gods of Rome. That's one reason why Christians were persecuted.

Disciples of Christ believe that Jesus Christ is a divine man, but Christianity was the new religion in town, and may have been viewed as if it was in competition with emperor worship. The similarity must be seen between the belief that Jesus is the divine man, and the emperor is the divine man, so the two may have been headed on a collision course. This may have put the believers in Philippi in an uncomfortable position, especially those who were retired military. They may have felt conflicted about where their loyalties should lie. They were proud of their Roman heritage, and service to their country and Emperor, but Jesus was their Lord. Christianity wasn't an approved state religion as Judaism was, so there was no recognition or protection offered by the government.

The Purpose of Writing the Letter

Why did Paul write the letter to the church at Philippi? After the Philippians became aware that Paul was imprisoned in Rome, they took up a collection and sent Epaphroditus as their trusted emissary to hand deliver the money to Paul and attend to his needs. When he arrived in Rome he would have informed Paul about how things were going in Philippi, giving him a status report on the church. Paul would have asked him questions about how they were progressing, how so-and-so was doing, what challenges they were facing, and things of that nature. This conversation would have influenced the content of Paul's letter to the church.

He informed them of the travel itinerary of Epaphroditus and Timothy. Epaphroditus became sick, almost to the point of death, but the Lord raised him up giving him a full recovery. Paul wrote to inform them why he sent Epaphroditus back to Philippi, that it was his decision involving no fault of Epaphroditus. Paul would have him hand deliver this letter to the church upon his arrival, and it would be read out loud to the congregation in a worship setting. Then he would send Timothy after the verdict was rendered, to help them sort through their issues, and report back to Paul. If he is released he hopes to make a trip to Philippi and be reunited with them as well (2:19; 23-24).

Paul also wrote to let the Philippians know how he was doing. They hadn't seen each other for a while and he knew they were deeply concerned about him. They knew he was waiting for his trial, so he wanted to let them know how things were going with that situation. He reported to them that even though he was under house arrest the gospel was advancing in the Pretorian Guard and Caesar's household. Because of his imprisonment many of the brothers had gained confidence to preach the word of God with more boldness (1:12-20), although some had improper motives.

He wanted them to know that he was doing very well, even though he faced the possibility of execution. He has thought through the matter very carefully and shares with the Philippians how he has arrived at the conclusion that either way, life or death, it was a win-win situation for him. If he lives that means more ministry which people would benefit from. If he is executed that means being ushered into the presence of Jesus. It seems that he wants to arrest any fears and anxiety that the Philippians may have about his situation, so he writes with an incredible sense of calm that God is control of his life. Although he was conflicted about what the outcome would be, he seems confident that he would be released and one day reunited with the Philippians (1:21-26).

Most likely Epaphroditus informed him about their issues of internal strife, disunity, and conflict that was beginning to pick up steam, so Paul addressed that situation (1:27-30), which is the central part of the letter. It wasn't to the point where the church had one foot in the grave, but if the strife continued it would have serious effects down the road. Paul could see where it was heading, so he had to address the lack of unity. Specifically, he singles out Euodia and Syntyche and solicits the help of the entire church to help them work out their differences so there could be unity (4:2).

He wrote to encourage them in their spiritual development, to work out their salvation (sanctification) with fear and trembling (2:12-13). He wants them to shine like stars and have an effective witness to their city (2:14-16). Paul provides them with several positive examples for them to follow, the primary one being Christ (2:5-11), along with Timothy, Epaphroditus, and himself (2:19-30). He wants them to keep going down the right path by following the right examples, and avoiding harmful ones, which will enable them to make progress in their sanctification.

Paul was also concerned that false teachers might show up and lead the brothers and sisters astray, so he issued a warning to watch out for the dogs (Judaizers)—those who advocated one must convert to Judaism in addition to believing in Christ for salvation (3:2; possibly 3:18-19). It doesn't appear that they were there in Philippi at the writing of this letter, but Paul was anticipating that if they did appear the church should be on guard, and not duped into believing their toxic brew of false teaching. In issuing this warning

Paul reveals some things about his life as a Pharisaic Jew and the drastic turnabout he went through after he became a Christian (3:4-11). He reveals his deep personal passion to know Christ (3:10-14).

Paul wants the Philippians to know that he is doing well, so he gives them a glimpse into his emotional health. He offers the Philippians many things about his personal walk with Christ, such as his joy, his journey toward contentment, his ability to cope with anxiety and realize God's peace (4:4-9). In Christ, Paul was content and could cope with whatever came his way, which is why the letter is filled with shouts of joy, is upbeat, and incredibly positive.

One primary reason Paul wrote to the Philippians was to acknowledge the unsolicited gift of money they sent him (4:10-20). He thanks them for the gift but makes it clear that the more important things are that their relationship is renewed, they are making progress in their faith, and growing in Christ. The secondary matter was the money they sent to Paul, for which he was grateful. He didn't want them to send any more money, because he wanted to break the cycle of giving and receiving, which was virtually mandatory in that culture. He wanted to avoid any type of patron-client relationship with the church, which was so common in those days. If he overly expressed his gratitude for the money they could easily interpret Paul as requesting more. If he doesn't sufficiently thank them for the gift of money they could view him as ungrateful, which could damage the relationship. Therefore, Paul had to breach this topic with great sensitivity and diplomacy.

The Opponents

There were people giving Paul and the Philippians a hard time. Identifying these groups is somewhat problematic. One group is clearly seen in 1:15; 17, and possibly 2:21, where Paul identifies those who preach Christ out of rivalry and selfish ambition. These are Christians in Rome who are preaching the gospel, but are doing so to spite Paul and make things more difficult for him then they already were. Paul describes them as preaching Christ with improper motives, but they appear to be presenting the gospel accurately, so he can cope with that situation and even rejoice that the gospel is advancing.

A second group of opponents would be the nonbelievers in Philippi that were persecuting the church (1:27-30). It appears that this persecution wasn't a full-scale continuous one but broke out on occasion. When Paul founded the church he was beaten, flogged, and thrown in the slammer. The church was born in persecution, but it wasn't continuous.

A third group is the Judaizers that were advocating one had to be a convert to Judaism in addition to believing in Christ for salvation (3:2). It doesn't appear that they were present in Philippi at the writing of this letter, but Paul warns them that if they show up to be on guard. Paul has had the Judaizers follow him around presenting their false gospel to his churches for a decade, so he wouldn't be surprised if they showed up in Philippi and tried to lead the believers astray. They were an annoyance to Paul, and a clear and present danger to his churches.

A fourth group could be, but not with certainty, mentioned in 3:18-19. Traditionally it was felt that 3:2-3, and 3:18-19 were descriptions of the Judaizers. It was felt that Paul was using irony in his description of them, for instance, when he says "their god is their stomachs" he is thought to be speaking ironically about their food laws. However, some interpreters, such as Grant Osborne, suggest this isn't referring to the Judaizers, rather it better fits a description of Gentiles. He proposes this is a description of proto-gnostics, Gentiles that advocated a libertine, sensual lifestyle, similar to those mentioned in 1 John. That their god is their stomachs reflects their hedonistic liberties.[1]

Therefore, we have three groups that can be identified with certainty, and possibly a fourth. We must be careful not to read too much back into the text and find groups that aren't there.

The Theology of Paul's Letter to the Philippians

Paul gives us information on practical matters regarding the Christian life. One of the appealing features of reading through Philippians is that readers

---

[1] Osborne, Loc. 169

of any era of history can connect with such themes as joy, contentment, and peace. Even a cursory reading of Philippians reveals that joy is a key theme. I'm a big fan of Beethoven's music, especially his ninth symphony, the "Ode to Joy," which is a choral symphonic masterpiece. Reading through Philippians is like a spiritual choral symphony—Paul's "Ode to Joy." Paul gives us many insights into his personal walk with Christ that believers can learn much from. Who wouldn't cherish having a consistent level of joy, being content in whatever circumstances appear in their life, and realizing God's peace during anxious moments? Paul shows us how we can realize these desirable assets through our relationship with Christ.

Growing in Christ - Sanctification

Every believer is in the process of growing into a mature disciple of Christ, which is referred to as sanctification. Paul wants the Philippians to make progress in their journey of sanctification, so he commands them to "work out your salvation with fear and trembling" (2:11-12). He provides them with positive examples to follow in doing this, the biggest of which is Christ (2:6-11). He frames their spiritual development in the context of the entire body working out their sanctification together, not just as individuals. This includes bringing unity to their fellowship, propping up their testimony to their city, working through their conflicts, and standing firm in the Lord. Paul challenges them to shine like stars as they are good witnesses to their community (2:12-16), which can only be done by working out their salvation together.

Paul also deals with an issue that has presented itself throughout church history, which is the belief that perfection is attainable this side of heaven (3:12-16). He made it clear that he hasn't attained perfection, but he continues to progress by knowing more of Christ, and sees perfection only occurring at the resurrection. There may have been an element of this teaching that infiltrated the church, or Paul may have just cautioned them against that teaching since it was a commonly held belief in pagan religions and made its way into the church at Corinth. By looking at Paul's reckless abandon in his pursuit of knowing Christ, it gives believers an indication of how hard he worked at growing in the Christian life. His passionate pursuit of knowing Jesus should be duly-noted and emulated by the Philippians.

Fellowship

Reading Philippians expands our horizon about the meaning of fellowship, which is a translation of the Greek word *koinonia*. This is one Greek word that many Christians are familiar with, because quite often ministries are given this name. For instance, the preservice coffee time may be referred to as "koinonia coffee," or the potluck after church is called the "koinonia luncheon." Maybe the women's ministry is called "koinonia women," and so on. Any time Christians are socializing or gathering together informally they usually think of good fellowship—*koinonia*. Christians are called into fellowship with one another as members of the body of Christ. The Philippians' fellowship with Paul included being partners with him in his ministry, their financial support, being in fellowship with Christ's sufferings, and the relationship of giving and receiving (1:5; 2:1; 3:10; 4:15). Reading through the different uses of *koinonia* in Philippians will cause us to rethink and expand our concept of fellowship.

A Thinking Person's Letter

God has given us 66 books of the Bible that span two Testaments, so there is a lot to read and become familiar with. For this reason, I consider Christianity a thinking person's faith. One interesting characteristic of Philippians is that Paul calls for much reflection. He's telling the Philippians that they should give much thought to his teaching regarding living the worthy life of the Good News (1:27). The call to thinking about the attitudes that Christ displayed, and adopting them as their own comes out clearly in 2:1-5. Thinking about the very character of God and adjusting our thought-life to be in line with the Triune God is a must for Paul.

Lynn Cohick astutely observes that seventeen times Paul calls for a mindset that reflects the character of God. Ten times in this letter Paul uses the verb *phroneo,* which means: to think rightly, be wise, comprehend, or purpose such and such things (1:7; 2:2 [2x], 5; 3:15 [2x], 19; 4:2, 10 [2x]). Paul uses *hegeomai*, which means: to consider or regard (2:3, 6, 25; 3:7, 8). Finally, he uses *logizomai,* which means: to count, think, or reason (3:13; 4:8).[2]

Therefore, Philippians is a letter that should be "thought through" with much theological reflection, meditation, analysis, and contemplation so a believer develops the mind of Christ (2:5). This is a key emphasis in Philippians. Paul is challenging his audience to develop a *Christ-formed thought-process*, through which they filter the events that take place in their lives—both good and bad. Most importantly, having the mindset of Christ will radically transform their behavior such that they live as good citizens of heaven (1:27; 3:20).

The Gospel

Paul had a sense of urgency regarding the forward movement of the gospel, or the Good News. He brings to the foreground the partnership the Philippians had with him in the gospel ministry (1:5; 4:15). He was concerned about the progress the gospel made with the Philippians (1:25), with the gospel advancing through his incarceration in Rome (1:12), and with defending and confirming the gospel (1:7; 16). Paul was concerned that the Philippians live a lifestyle that is worthy of the Good News (1:27, 2:12-16), thus he sees the gospel having a transformative effect on those who believe. To preach the gospel is to preach Jesus. When someone enters a relationship with Christ they begin the process of sanctification, which is a key theme in Philippians.

The gospel is the Triune God's plan for the salvation of mankind and to create a people for himself. God sent his Son to die on the cross as punishment for man's sin, he rose from the dead, ascended into heaven and sits at the right hand of God. He sent the Holy Spirit to live in the hearts of his people and empower them for godly living and to fulfill the Great commission.

---

[2] Cohick, Loc. 612

God

The central player in Paul's theology is the Trinity. God is mentioned 24 times in this short letter to the Philippians. Although Jesus' death and resurrection are the basis for man's salvation, Christ's work must be viewed through the activity of the Triune God. God the Father sent his Son, who died and rose from the dead, he ascended into heaven, then the Holy Spirit was sent. This is the core of Pauline theology and his worldview.

God initiated the plan of salvation (1:6; 3:9; 14) and will bring it to completion (1:6). He is at work in believers to bring to them to greater levels of maturity (2:13) and works all things to the praise of his glory (1:11). He has called his people to realize perfection at the end of the age (3:14), they are his children in the family of God (2:15), and he supplies his people with all their needs according to his glorious riches in Christ (4:19). He gives peace to those who call on him (4:6-7), and his presence as the God of peace is available in times of need (4:19).

The work of the Holy Spirit is a work of close cooperation of the members of the Godhead working together to accomplish man's redemption. We can't isolate the work of one from the interaction with the others, for God is Triune.

Christology

Christ is mentioned 39 times in this short letter, thus occupying a central place in Paul's thinking. The preaching of the gospel, which is really preaching Christ, is paramount to Paul. His main thesis for the Philippians is to live as citizens of heaven, conducting themselves in a manner worthy of the Good News of Christ (1:27). Embracing the gospel is embracing Jesus and must transform those who believe it. Thus, knowing Christ is tied to the emphasis on sanctification that is so obvious in Philippians. The gospel is Christ's gospel, which in its very design is created to transform believers into his image. Philippians has much to say about living the Christian life.

The Christology is high and lofty in Philippians with the Christ Hymn being a theological nugget of gold—a literary masterpiece (2:6-11). Paul speaks of Christ in his incarnation, as a teaching device to demonstrate what humility looks like, which provides them with an example to follow. He is challenging them to have the same mindset that Christ has (2:5), which can help them resolve their differences and bring unity to their church. Therefore, Paul's primary purpose in the Christ Hymn is not theoretical, but practical in providing the Philippians with Jesus as a role model to emulate. The teaching is rich and speaks to the humanity of Jesus, his death on the cross, and his subsequent exaltation.

Timothy, Epaphroditus, and Paul, himself, are people who do a good job at emulating Christ, therefore, they can be living models of Jesus to imitate. In chapter three Paul speaks to how he gave up everything so that he could know more of Christ. His personal passion to go deeper in his relationship with Christ comes out clearly in this chapter serving as another example to follow. If he is executed his concern is that he will glorify Christ in death, by setting forth a good testimony, or if he lives it's for Christ's glory as well. Therefore, life was all about Christ for Paul. He states what could be considered the mission statement for his life, which is to know Christ (3:10), and considers all his accomplishments in Judaism to be rubbish, literally dung, compared to the surpassing greatness of knowing the Lord Jesus. Christians are called to be in fellowship with his suffering, to know Christ is to know his sufferings, to be called for salvation is to be called for suffering (1:28-30; 3:10; 4:14).

A watershed moment for Paul occurred when he discovered a righteousness not of his own, but through faith in Christ (3:9). Once a sinner becomes a believer they are "in Christ" thus they are being found "in him" with a new righteousness that is inherent in the gospel. The righteousness that is imputed to the believer at his conversion is the bedrock of justification by faith (Rom 3-4). Paul placed this understanding of righteousness alongside his previous attempt at being righteous through Torah observance, which he discovered was a fruitless activity (3:3-9). All the blessings of God are distributed in Christ, which means he is the basis of the believer's confidence (2:24), hope (2:19), and joy (3:1; 4:4).

The Holy Spirit

Paul doesn't have much to say about the Holy Spirit in Philippians, but not because he views the Spirit as having a diminished role in their community of faith. He does make several important references to the Holy Spirit that mustn't be glossed over. The boundary marker of God's people in the New Covenant community is possession of the Holy Spirit, in contrast to the marker of circumcision under the Old Covenant (3:3). This is a crucial point for Paul in that true worship of God isn't through Torah observance, and adherence to the traditions that were handed down through the elders, it is found in life in the Spirit. The believer boasts in Christ because he worships by the Spirit (3:3), who also assists him in magnifying Christ in his life. Hence, Paul is concerned that through the Spirit's help Christ will be glorified either by life or death (1:20), and the Holy Spirit will assist him in his defense of the gospel (1:19). The Holy Spirit is the agent who supplies believers with the strength to cope in troublesome times, and Paul saw the Spirit of Jesus as effecting his deliverance from prison. Paul also saw the Holy Spirit as the source of unity between all believers (1:27; 2:1). It is the work of the Spirit that enables believers to progress in their sanctification, becoming more conformed to the image of Jesus (2:13).

Eschatology

Philippians has a robust emphasis on the end times (eschatology). Paul frames the present age we live in as an "already" but "not yet" phenomenon, which means that with the resurrection of Christ, his ascension, the beginning of the church, and the sending of the Holy Spirit a new age has begun. Salvation is an "already" experience for God's people, however the consummation of the age is "not yet." Therefore, believers live in tension in that they have the Spirit of God within them, but an active propensity to sin still exists. They live in hope, with the expectation that Jesus will return and finalize their adoption as sons and daughters as he brings them into the glorified state in resurrection bodies (3:20-21).

Paul is confident that the work God began will come to completion on the Day of Christ (1:6), which is the day of his return, the same as the day of the Lord, often referred to in the Old Testament. Thus, Paul expresses his confidence that God can keep these believers on the right path such that they will endure to the final day. Paul prays that the Philippians will continue to grow and improve in their ability to discern and make good choices that will facilitate their sanctification, such that they will be pure and blameless until the day of Christ (1:10).

In the Christ hymn (2:6-11), Christ's resurrection isn't mentioned, rather it is assumed, for Christ has ascended and taken his place at the right hand of God. One day in the future he will have total reign over the universe, such that all creation will be completely submitted to his Lordship (2:10-11). This passage shows us where the entire created order is going—into submission to Christ. Even the demonic realm will acknowledge his Lordship and bow the knee. Of importance, is the fact that Jesus first humbled himself, thus demonstrating that the pathway to glorification is through suffering.

Paul believes that the way one lives her life on this earth is correlated with the way she spends eternity. Once someone becomes a believer, it truly matters how they live. He brings this out in 2:16, where he is encouraging the Philippians to progress in their sanctification, so that on the Day of Christ he may boast and find that his efforts were worth it, and not in vain. This suggests that Paul sees the Day of Christ as the day all accounts are settled, for it is judgment day.

Paul sees himself as being called heavenward in Christ, and the resurrection of the body as connected to Jesus. The purpose for which Jesus has taken hold of Paul is the transformation of his life which ends in resurrection. However, resurrection is something that believers can know experientially in the present (3:10), but it is also a future event that will occur at the coming of Christ (3:20-21).

Paul eagerly anticipates the second coming of Christ when believers will receive glorified bodies, by way of resurrection if they have already died, or by translation if they are still living at his return. Either way their bodies will be glorified to be like Jesus' glorious body. "Our citizenship is in heaven" (1:27; 3:20), which means believers are just passing through on this earth for a short time, but better things are in store for the future because they will spend eternity in the glorified state. That Paul mentions citizenship must be seen in contrast to the Roman citizenship many of the Philippians had and were very proud of. Christians have dual citizenship in Christ.

Because the Lord is near they should let their gentleness be evident to all people (4:5). There is some question as to whether the nearness of the Lord refers to the Lord's presence for comfort and encouragement, or nearness regarding his second coming. It is likely that both ideas can be present in this verse (see comments on 4:5). Because of the Lord's imminent second coming, it should have an ethical effect on the way one lives his life. Considering that Christ could return at any moment, should provide incentive to disciples to elevate their game when it comes to providing a godly witness to the community and progressing in their sanctification. The anticipation of Christ's coming must impact the believer's life.

God's Sovereignty

Because Paul has been imprisoned for over four years most people would conclude that nothing is happening with his ministry—he's off the grid and out of commission. He hasn't planted any new churches, nor has he traveled to the churches he's already established and provided more teaching to strengthen them. However, concluding Paul's ministry is unproductive wouldn't be supported by the data.

The fact is that he is right where God wanted him to be. He wasn't there by coincidence, happenstance, or random chance, it was the sovereignty of God that led him to be under house arrest in Rome, for the Lord told Paul that he would testify in Rome (Acts 23:11). During his incarceration in Caesarea Maritima, Paul had the opportunity to testify to people in places of power such as: Governor Felix, his wife Drusilla, Tertullus the lawyer, Jews from the Sanhedrin, Governor Porcius Festus, King Agrippa, and his wife Bernice (Acts 23:23-26:32). He isn't Missing in Action (MIA), he is testifying to people in high places about Jesus Christ.

When transferred to Rome, because he appealed to Caesar, he had opportunities to witness to the Praetorian Guard, because he was always guarded by a Praetorian that was chained to him at the wrist. He presumably witnessed to members of Caesar's household, which means his testimony about Jesus came very close to the Emperor. The believers in Rome became bolder and more fearless in sharing the gospel because of Paul's imprisonment (1:14).

During his incarceration, Paul wrote Ephesians (AD 61), Colossians (AD 61), Philemon (AD 62), and of course, Philippians (AD 62). These letters are cherished by Christians around the world and are some of the most often read books of the Bible. While Paul was in prison he could reflect on matters of theology, further develop his network of churches, and utilize his faithful colleagues to advance the gospel. It is amazing to consider that Paul ran the entire operation to the Gentile world from the slammer (prison). Even in chains Paul was still being used by God and was advancing the Good News.

The lesson we learn from this is that God is totally in control of all situations, even when it may look otherwise. No matter how hard Satan tries to stop the gospel from going forward, God ensures that it gains ground. Eventually, Paul had his day in court and it turned out well for him, because he was released from prison and continued with his ministry (1:24-26). God had Paul right where he wanted him when he wrote Philippians.

The Methodology in Analyzing Philippians – Understanding the Horizons

In writing a commentary on any book of the Bible it is essential to uncover the author's intent in writing, which can only be done by stepping out of today's world and going back in time to the world of the author. In reading this commentary you will be escorted back into Paul's world, with the objective of getting inside his head so one can understand what he was thinking, and what the circumstances were that led him to write his letter to the Philippians. Grasping the *author's intent* is the primary objective in understanding any book of the Bible and is one primary objective of this commentary. The author's intent will henceforth be referred to as the *author's horizon.*

It is also important to place ourselves in the Philippians' shoes and understand their horizon. When Paul's letter was read out loud to the congregation in one of their gatherings, how did they understand the content? After all, the letter was written to them, not to believers in the

Twenty First Century. Therefore, as the reader travels back in time he must step into the Philippians' shoes, and seek to understand how they would understand Paul's words. This is referred to as the *recipients' horizon* or the *Philippians' horizon*.

Once those horizons have been examined it is necessary to travel back to today's world, so it can be determined how Philippians applies to modern-day Christians, which is referred to as *our horizon*. The last interpretive task in understanding any Biblical text is to come up with meaningful applications, so the Scriptures can be lived out in one's daily experience. This is done by identifying principles that can easily be transferred from Paul's day to ours. There are some things that are timeless truths, that are transcultural, and have direct relevance to believers in all eras of history. For instance, Paul's exhortation to adopt the same attitude of Christ, and consider others more important than yourself is a timeless truth that is transferable from one culture to another, and from one historical era to another (2:1-5).

Some things that Paul writes about in Philippians have no cultural equivalent in the modern world. For instance, believers aren't incarcerated in the United States because of their faith in Christ as Paul was. His imprisonment has no cultural equivalent in American society because the government grants people freedom to worship as they choose. There is no one-to-one corresponding situation, which means principles from his incarceration must be identified and taken back into the modern-day world, so they can be applied to believer's lives. An example of a principle from Paul's imprisonment is his boldness and courage that he displayed in setting forth a good testimony for Christ, as he faced the possibility of being executed (1:20). He was in a life or death situation and faced it with amazing courage. Today's believer can apply this principle to their own life by setting forth a bold and brave testimony for Christ as opportunities arise.

The aim of this commentary is to understand Paul's intent in writing Philippians, and how the Philippians would have understood it when they heard it read to them. After each section applications, illustrations, life lessons, and a summary of each passage are provided, so that the text is relevant and meaningful to today's believer. The goal of any Biblical text is understanding how a believer can live it out in her experience. As James said, we should not just be hearers of the word, but doers of the word (Jam 1:22).

Grasping the Context

In being escorted back into Paul's world it is imperative to uncover the *historical context* of the letter to the church at Philippi, which includes such things as the date, where Paul was when he wrote the letter, what his relationship was with the church, Philippi as a Roman colony, what was happening in the church, and so forth. Included in the historical context would be understanding the culture of the Greco-Roman world, which is drastically different than today. Dissecting these factors will contribute to a clear understanding of Paul's intent in writing the letter (the author's horizon).

In addition to grasping the historical context the *literary context* of Paul's letter must be considered. This deals with the relationship of the words as they appear on the page, including grammar, syntax, chapter breaks, context, and the meaning of the Greek words. There are some Greek words that don't have English equivalents, which makes translation challenging. Greek is a colorful language that often conveys ideas in pictures, that the English translation doesn't capture. To provide the reader with insights regarding the nuances of the Greek, words will be cited then their range of meaning will be explained. This gives the reader more insights into the original words that the author used to convey his ideas and enhances the reading of Philippians.

Therefore, in interpreting Philippians this commentary will bring to light the following things:

- The author's horizon (Paul's intent in writing)
- The recipients' horizon (How the Philippians would have understood Paul's words)
- The modern-day horizon (How we can apply Philippians to our situation)
- The historical context (The historical and cultural circumstances behind Paul's writing to Philippi)

- The literary context (The relationship of the words as they appear on the page and the nature of letter writing in the ancient world)

Reading through Philippians with these things in mind will greatly facilitate understanding this amazing book of the Bible, and will be a safeguard against reading it with Twenty First Century Western eyes.

The Teaching Methodology in Paul's Day

Another critical factor to understand about Paul's world was the educational methodology that was commonly used. Being taught by example was a dominant part of learning in First Century culture. Virtues weren't taught in their pagan religions they were taught in schools of philosophy. Students were given positive examples to follow and negative ones to avoid. A teacher's oral instruction was important, but the example he provided through his lifestyle was an equally important part of the educational experience of the student.

He was to follow his teacher's example in developing into a person of high character and integrity. In the First Century world students would live in close proximity to their teacher, so they wouldn't just receive his instruction, they would examine his life and imitate his virtuous character. This is vastly different than our modern situation where we may sit in a classroom and listen to a professor wax eloquently to his students, but not have a clue how he lives his life. This puts Paul's exhortation to "imitate me" (3:17), as well as Timothy, and Epaphroditus in a different light. As modern readers we may think it arrogant and prideful for a teacher to command people to imitate him, but that is how it was done in the First Century. Considering that 85% of people couldn't read in the ancient world, following the example of positive role models was crucial to their personal development.

The Nature Letter Writing in Paul's Day

In stepping back into Paul's world without accounting for the nature of letter writing and their teaching methods, critical factors will be overlooked that will skew the reader's understanding of his letter. If these two important elements of First Century culture are bypassed, Paul's letter will be read with modern-day Western eyes, which will cause one to miss many things that Paul wished to convey. It will be as if the reader has one foot in the First Century, and the other foot in the present.

Today's world is a digital society with computers, kindles, nooks (and other *e* readers), books are readily available on every topic under the sun, and most people can read. With the advent of the internet information on any subject is at one's finger-tips—just do a google search and countless articles on any subject are available. Today's culture is a digital, text-driven, literate culture with knowledge increasing exponentially. Such was not the case in Paul's day. In the First Century Roman Empire approximately ten to fifteen percent of the people could read, which means that teaching methods had to account for vast numbers of people that were illiterate. *The dominant methodology in teaching was oral, rhetorical, and learning through the examples of people's lives.*

One important factor that is often overlooked in analyzing a Biblical text is the nature of letter writing in the First Century. Letter writing back then is a far cry from what it is today. In fact, writing letters in today's culture has been replaced by texting, emailing, phone calls, face booking, and is seldom done any more. In journeying back into the First Century world it must be understood how complex letter writing was in that culture, which will give the reader further insights into Philippians. About 85% of the people in the Roman Empire couldn't read, so letters were written to be read out loud to a group. They weren't crafted to be inspected by scholarly eyes under a microscope. Letter writing had a huge *rhetorical* aspect to them, which means that *letters were written to persuade people to action*. The spoken word was dominant in that culture, because of the massive illiteracy of the day, so philosophers were trained in the art of rhetoric—the art of persuasion. How to present an argument in a polished way and persuade one's audience was an art form that was taught in schools of philosophy.

Paul's letters are much different than letters written in the modern world. There were handbooks in the ancient world about letter writing, which described different types of letters that could be written. Schools of philosophy had as part of their curriculum teaching about the conventions of letter writing. Ben Witherington's observation is crucial to understanding Paul's letters:

> ...the more I have learned about the dominant rhetorical character of Paul's world and cultures, the more I have realized that what we are dealing with in Paul's documents are rhetorical discourses with some epistolary features at the beginning and conclusion because they had to be sent from a distance. We are not primarily dealing with letters that use occasional rhetorical devices such as rhetorical questions. Paul's letters are hybrid vehicles, but the epistolary framework only provides the outer body of the letter. The hybrid engine which empowers and drives the vehicle is rhetoric. It is high time that the emphasis is placed in the right spot when analyzing Paul's documents, and the analysis should be done primarily on the basis of rhetorical paradigms and conventions.[3]

Understanding the above statement is crucial in correctly analyzing Paul's letter. Philippians must be examined through First Century eyes by understanding the importance of rhetoric, and the nature of letter writing in Paul's day, not today. Paul was a product of that culture and was obviously familiar with the many types of letters that were written in that time, which poses the question: what type of letter is Philippians?

A Friendship Letter

One type of letter that was commonly written in the ancient word is a friendship letter, which is what Philippians is. It is necessary to understand how important friendship was to the Greeks and Romans in business, politics, and social aspects of their culture. It became a topic of importance in schools of philosophy where letter writing was part of their curriculum. Philosophers such as Aristotle, Cicero, Seneca, and Plutarch wrote extensively about friendship. Aristotle, who taught in Macedonia long before Paul ever arrived there, taught three different types of friendship: the first was friendship between virtuous people, the second was friendship based on pleasure, and

---

[3] Witherington, Loc. 424

the third was friendship based on need, in that it was utilitarian. It is the first type of friendship that is reflected in Paul's letter to the Philippians—friendship between virtuous people.

The core values of friendship included virtue, loyalty, and affection in the form of mutual goodwill toward the other. This is especially true in the matter of mutual "giving and receiving" (4:15), which includes benefits, such as goods, services, and expressions of gratitude that were of extreme importance. Reciprocity was a crucial element of friendship in that there was a sense of obligation to reciprocate to a friend when given a gift, service, gesture, and so on. Failure to do so would damage the relationship, cause a deep offense, and even severe the friendship. It was difficult to understand friendship apart from benefits, which could be abused and even cause a sense of one up-manship—a sort of competitive aspect in a friendship. Because friendship entailed reciprocity there was a sense of obligation, and necessary expressions of gratitude. For the modern person to understand this type of friendship is difficult because it was essentially a contractual arrangement.

Friendship was also *agonistic* in the sense that friendship was often in the context of having enemies. If you have friends that means you automatically have enemies, such that paying attention to your friends also meant paying attention to and being watchful of enemies.[4] The agonistic aspect comes into play with the opposition the Philippians were facing, which they also saw in Paul and were experiencing the same suffering he went through (1:28-30). He also identifies false teachers that must be avoided if they should show up in Philippi, so he issued a warning about them (3:2).

The core virtues of friendship mentioned above can be seen in Philippians. The church's relationship with Paul is about the mutual goodwill of each other. They are partners in spreading the gospel in their evangelism, and through their gifts to Paul. As partners, they were engaged in mutual suffering and persecution for the sake of the gospel (1:28-30), thus Paul uses deeply emotional language to describe his feelings for his friends in Philippi (1:7; 8; 4:1). His letter is also full of language of mutuality and reciprocity, such as: his longing to see them again, his concern for their progress in the

---

[4] Fee, p. 5

faith (1:25-26), and his praying for them (1:4), as they pray for him (1:19). The acknowledgement of the gift Paul received from them (4:10-20) is filled with language of giving and receiving (mutual reciprocity). He makes it clear that he is deeply grateful (4:10), has received enough (4:18), and God will reciprocate on Paul's behalf by supplying all their needs (4:19). Philippians has all the indicators that this is a friendship letter.

A Letter of Exhortation

Paul also had to address some issues to help them work through such as: their lack of unity, dissension among the leaders, handling persecution, and making progress in their sanctification. It was thought that good character couldn't be developed without having examples to follow, or what we would call "role models" in our modern situation. Ethical instruction belonged to philosophy not religion in the Greco-Roman world, and instruction of this type often took place in the context of friendship, where a superior taught an interior, often by means of letters (where distance separated them).

In proceeding with the analysis of Philippians this letter will be identified as a *friendship letter of exhortation*. However, what separates this letter from others written in the First Century is that it is a *Christian* letter of friendship and exhortation. It isn't a letter that is written between two friends—the Philippians and Paul. There is a third party that takes precedence over the other two—namely Jesus Christ. Although Paul and the Philippians are partners in the gospel, their partnership revolves around their mutual relationship with the Lord Jesus. Therefore, Philippians is a *Christian friendship letter of exhortation.*[5]

The Legacy of the Church at Philippi

The church at Philippi bears the distinction of being the one and only church that entered into a partnership of *giving and receiving* with Paul (4:15). That was very special to the apostle who was dependent upon support, even though he was a skilled tent-maker and worked to provide a good example

---

[5] Fee offers an excellent analysis of Philippians as a friendship letter (p. 2-14)

to some churches and not be a burden to them (Corinth and Thessalonica). However, his tent-making work took time away from preaching the gospel. The Philippians sent him money on several occasions, which benefited Paul and enabled him to devote more time to ministry.

The Macedonian churches were very poor, but their legacy is that they were the most generous churches mentioned in the Bible. They gave above and beyond the call of duty, given their poverty. They set forth a stellar performance in contributing to the collection for the impoverished church in Jerusalem (2 Cor 8:1-5). Their example of giving out of their poverty should cause today's believer to take-a-look at his approach to giving as people in the prosperous West. It isn't always the richest people who give the most in supporting their church or missionaries, often it is the people who make middle class wages, or even the poor that are the most generous.

The church at Philippi lays the groundwork with concepts that can be utilized in forming gospel partnerships, while providing insights into how modern-day churches can be more supportive of their missionaries. Paul had a special place in his heart for this church, and their relationship was unique among all the other churches because of their partnership in the gospel. Through the good times and the bad times, they never wavered in supporting Paul. When he was imprisoned some churches may have taken the position that it would be a better investment of their funds to direct them to someone else who is producing. Paul couldn't plant any churches for four years and running, but they stuck with him and continued their support. Some churches may not have done that.

The Timeline of Paul's Imprisonments

Paul first visited Philippi on his second missionary journey and founded the church (about AD 50). About five years later, on his third missionary journey, he appears to have visited Philippi (Acts 20:1-2). He set out for Macedonia, which is where Philippi is, and stayed there for three months then left for Syria and returned to Macedonia. He later set sail from Philippi, so he would have presumably visited them at that time (Acts 20:5-6). He was imprisoned in Rome from AD 60-62, so when he wrote Philippians he would have known some of them for over a decade.

One of the things that is often overlooked in reading through Philippians is Paul's detainment in Caesarea, which preceded his incarceration in Rome. Most people know that Paul was incarcerated in Rome when he wrote Philippians along with Ephesians, Colossians, and Philemon, which have been commonly referred to as Paul's *prison epistles*. However, Paul's imprisonment in Caesarea is often overlooked (AD 58-60). Acts 21 reveals that Paul was arrested in Jerusalem for creating a public disturbance. It was an ugly scene, because Jews from Asia arrived and stirred up the crowd making accusations against Paul. They thought he had taken a Gentile into the Temple area, which was forbidden, so they turned into an angry mob that almost tore Paul to pieces. Had it not been for the intervention of the Roman soldiers it would have been all over for Paul. The Romans felt it was best to send Paul to Caesarea because they had uncovered a plot to assassinate him. They sent him with an escort of two hundred soldiers, seventy horsemen and two hundred spearmen to go to Caesarea, which was under the jurisdiction of governor Felix. Paul was kept under guard in Herod's palace. Governor Felix met with Paul to discuss things with him, but basically forgot about him.

After two years Felix was succeeded by Porcius Festus. The Jews pressed Festus to have Paul stand trial in Jerusalem, but he had them come to Caesarea. They made many accusations against Paul that they couldn't substantiate, so the Jews convinced Festus to have Paul go to Jerusalem to answer the charges there. At that point Paul appealed to Caesar, so he would go to Rome and stand before the Emperor, which was the right of any Roman citizen. Had he not appealed to Caesar he would have been released, but the Lord told him he would testify there (Acts 23:11).

Paul was handed over to a centurion and boarded a ship to Rome, but because of severe weather the journey went slowly. They sought a place to harbor for the winter but sailed into a violent Northeaster and were shipwrecked. After three months they boarded another ship and headed for Rome, where he was detained for two more years, chained to a member of the Praetorian Guard around the clock (Acts 28:16-31). This makes the time of Paul's detainment over four years, maybe closer to four and a half years. The reader of Philippians must consider the effects of this imprisonment on Paul. His life was filled with hardship, persecution, physical beatings, and emotional abuse. In reading Philippians, it is imperative to grasp the strain

Paul was under from being incarcerated for over four years and facing every kind of trial imaginable.

With the threat of execution hovering over him and being unable to travel around the Mediterranean world to plant churches, that must have had a taxing effect on him. While under house arrest in Rome he could have visitors, which was a comfort to him, especially having Timothy there with him. He waited for his trial, but he didn't know if he would be executed or set free. All he could do was wait patiently to appear before the Emperor and have him render the verdict—life or death. Paul had that hanging over his head, plus he was burdened with the status of the churches that he had planted and wondered how they were doing.

No doubt, this period of somewhere between four and five years, must have been emotionally draining for him to be essentially off the grid from traveling and planting churches. One can only imagine what his emotional state was, which makes Philippians all the more meaningful. That Paul targeted joy as one of the major themes of his letter is amazing considering the sequence of events he went through. Paul doesn't present himself in Philippians as a man who is beaten down, at the end of his rope emotionally and spiritually, quite to the contrary, Paul seems to be filled with faith and is rejoicing that the gospel is advancing. The Lord told him he would testify in Rome (Acts 23:11), and he is fulfilling his mission there, but there is no trace of complaining or grumbling from Paul whatsoever. What Paul went through in the previous four plus years before he wrote Philippians makes the content of the letter even more incredible.

Understanding Paul's timeline of imprisonment gives more meaning to his words about learning the secret of being content in every and any set of circumstances. It causes one to marvel at his ability to cope with his life, considering his dire circumstances. Of course, he learned to depend on the Lord Jesus who strengthened him, so that he could not just survive, but thrive spiritually realizing joy, contentment, and God's peace during his grim circumstances.

The timeline of Paul's imprisonment has been placed at the end of the introduction, so it will be fresh in the reader's mind as she goes into the body of the letter. Now that these important issues have been discussed in the introduction, this will make the reading of Philippians much more meaningful. It is time to dive into the deep waters of Philippians and discover its treasures.

Outline

1. The Greeting, 1:1-2

2. Exordium – Paul's Connection With the Philippians, 1:3-11
   - A Paul's Deep Love for the Philippians, 1:3-8
   - B Paul's Prayer for the Philippians, 1:9-11

3. Narratio – Paul's Narrative About His Circumstances, 1:12-26
   - A. The Progress of the gospel, 1:12-18
   - B. Contemplating Life or Death, 1:19-26

4. Propositio – Living the Worthy Life for the Good News, 1:27-30

5. Probatio – Theology by Way of Examples, 2:1-4:3
   - A. The example of Christ, 2:1-11
   - B. The application of Christ's example, 2:12-18
   - C. The Example of Timothy, 2:19-24
   - D. The Example of Epaphroditus, 2:25-30
   - E. The Example of Paul Against the False teachers, 3:1-4:1
   - F. The Example of Euodia and Syntyche, 4:2-3

6. Peroratio – Virtuous Living Leading to Peace, 4:4-9
   - A. Coping with Anxiety, 4:4-7
   - B. The Christ-formed Mind, 4:8-9

7. Denouement – A Postscript on Giving and Receiving, 4:10-20

8. Closing with Grace, 4:21-23

CHAPTER ONE

* * *

"The Greeting"
Philippians 1:1-2

Much can be learned by examining the greetings of Paul's letters. It would be unwise to gloss over the greeting to quickly get to the heart of his letter, thinking that the greeting is just a mere formality lacking any theological content. His greetings often set the stage for the body of his letter in that he introduces themes that he will develop as he writes. Such is the case here.

Paul and Timothy, slaves of Christ Jesus. To all the holy people in Christ Jesus who are at Philippi, with the overseers and deacons: [2]Grace to you, and peace from God, our Father, and the Lord Jesus Christ. (Author's Translation, 1:1-2)

Paul and Timothy were together as he wrote this letter. Timothy occupied a special place in Paul's heart because he describes his relationship with him as a father and son (2:22). Paul met Timothy on his second missionary journey and he became of member of his leadership team (Acts 16:1-4). Timothy was with Paul and Silas when they traveled to Philippi, so the Philippians already knew him and were probably very fond of him (Acts 16:12-40). Paul wanted them to know that Timothy had a part in writing the letter, in fact, Paul may have dictated the letter to Timothy as he wrote it down. It's possible that Timothy may have made suggestions to Paul, and they may have discussed the content. Paul had great confidence in him because he urged the

Philippians to take note of Timothy's lifestyle and follow his example (2:19-22). The younger Timothy was Paul's protégé and was the recipient of two letters that Paul wrote to him that bear his name. That Timothy was there with Paul was a great source of encouragement to him during his imprisonment.

Paul identifies himself and Timothy as **slaves of Christ Jesus.** Many translations of the Bible water down the meaning of the Greek word *doulos* by translating it "servants" rather than "slaves." This weakens the meaning of the term and is an unfortunate translation of the word. A slave had no rights other than those given him by his master. He was mere property, such that his master could dispose of him by putting him to death if he was unpleased with him. Slavery was common in the First Century with half the people in the Roman Empire living in that condition. It was common to see slaves regularly bought and sold in the market place throughout the Empire.

By identifying himself and Timothy as slaves of Christ, in no way is Paul using this term in a pejorative or demeaning way. He considers it an honor to be the slave of Jesus. All Christians belong to Jesus because they have been bought and paid for by his sacrifice, so just as a slave in the natural realm was property of his master, Christians are property of the Lord Jesus Christ in the spiritual realm (1 Cor 6:19-20). As Paul considers his imprisonment by the Romans, he knows he is in chains as a prisoner of Christ—not the Emperor (Eph 4:1). His imprisonment was part of his service to Christ, and much good was being accomplished as the gospel was spreading throughout the Praetorian guard and Caesar's household, plus more of the Christians were boldly preaching the gospel because of Paul's example (1:12-14). To serve the Lord Jesus as his slave was considered by Christians to be a badge of honor—something to be proud of.

Paul is an apostle, which is a high and lofty position of leadership in the early church. He became a believer on the road to Damascus and was commissioned by the Lord Jesus to be the apostle to the Gentiles (Acts 9:1-16). His position is infused with authority directly from Christ, yet he doesn't mention his apostolic calling as he does in some of his other letters. Why is this? Paul was on good terms with the Philippian church such that his apostolic credentials weren't being questioned, so he didn't need to remind them that he is an apostle of Christ. Instead, he deliberately identifies himself and Timothy as Christ's slaves, which is a demonstration of his humility to the Philippian church. Later in his letter Paul urges them to be like Christ who humbled himself taking the form of a *slave* and was obedient to death (2:7-8). The Philippians needed to demonstrate humility in their relationships with one another to ratchet up their unity and resolve some conflicts in their fellowship. Paul is providing an example for them to follow by identifying himself and Timothy as Christ's slaves, rather than asserting his apostolic authority.

Paul addresses the letter **to all the holy people in Christ Jesus who are at Philippi.** The word **holy** is a translation of the Greek word *hagios*, which means to be "separate" or "set apart from something." It is the word that is translated in our English Bibles as: saint, holy ones, holy people, sacred, or consecrate. It is related to the word sanctification, which is the Greek word *hagiosmos*.

The moment the Philippians placed their faith in Jesus they were "set apart" to serve him. They are now property of the Lord Jesus and are to live in a way that honors their Master. Much of Paul's letter deals with the sanctification of the Philippian church. He is reminding them that they are set apart to Christ and should live accordingly. He is informing them of what their position is with Christ: they are his **holy people**. Thus, their church relationships should reflect their holy status with Christ. This is where they were lacking. Their sanctification as a body of believers, in relationship with one another, needed a boost. That Paul addresses his letter to **all** the holy people sets the stage for his appeals to prop up their solidarity and unity.

Paul identifies them as being **in Christ Jesus.** This is an important identity marker for Christians because it refers to the believer's union with Jesus, and his incorporation into his body—the church. Once someone becomes a believer in Christ they are said to be "in him," which is their spiritual location because they are now one with him. They are united with Christ in an inseparable union. Paul uses this terminology throughout his writings, especially his prison letters (Ephesians, Colossians, Philemon, and Philippians). Being "in Christ" is to be a member of the new Messianic community that Jesus created when the Spirit was poured out on the day of

Pentecost. Since Christians' spiritual address is "in Christ" and they are set apart to serve him, they must live a life that is worthy of their Master, not just as individuals, but as a body of believers.

Christians enjoy a privileged status of being Christ's holy people, and being united with him, but they must recognize the responsibility that goes along with their privileged position. Their status of being Christ's holy people must be reflected in their lifestyle. This doesn't always happen as was the case with the Corinthian church. The rest of Paul's letter has a great deal to say about how to live a sanctified life. One of Paul's purposes in writing his letter was to encourage the Philippians to make progress in their walk with Christ, so that they can live in a manner that is worthy of the Good News (1:27). Every believer is in the process of growing into a mature believer, which means that their lifestyle must be moving in the direction of holiness. The believer's *behavior* should be consistent with his *status* of being one of Christ's holy people (1 Thess 4:3). There should not be a vast disparity between the two.

Paul links their special status as holy people, in Christ, to their location in the city of **Philippi** (see introduction). With the founding of the church on Paul's second missionary journey, there is now a gospel presence in that city, where previously there was none. Prior to Paul's visit there were no Christians in that city of about 10,000 people, so they have an opportunity to introduce thousands of people to the life-saving gospel of Jesus Christ. The church at Philippi was just a small handful of people, maybe topping out at 100 members, that now had the mission of sharing with their fellow Philippians the benefits of being in a relationship with the Lord Jesus Christ. The Philippian church is comprised of Christ's holy people that need to demonstrate their holiness to the rest of the population, by setting forth good behavior that makes the gospel and fellowship of believers look attractive.

Paul singles out the **overseers and deacons**, who were the leaders of the church. Perhaps, Paul identifies them because they were the ones that were responsible for sending him the monetary gift delivered by Epaphroditus.[6] Paul may have mentioned them because he trusted that they would carry out

[6] This view goes back as early as Chrysostom.

his instructions, set forth in this letter, by helping the church work through some of their issues.

The overseer (or bishop) is synonymous with the term elder and pastor. These terms are used interchangeably in Scripture.[7] The emphasis here is on the function that overseers have, presumably the oversight of the church, administration, and caring for the people. To conclude that since Paul doesn't mention elders that there were none at Philippi would be incorrect. The overseers are elders and the deacons are another office of the church that serve in helping roles to free the apostles of menial tasks, so they can devote more time to the word of God and prayer (Acts 6:1-3). The qualifications for these offices are very high and are set forth in 1 Timothy three, and Titus chapter one. This indicates that Paul did have a leadership structure for the churches he planted, and he worked hard at developing these leaders and nurturing them, for the obvious reason that if the church was to thrive and continue in the next generation it had to have capable leaders equipped for service.

Perhaps the reason Paul uses the word overseer (*episkopos*), rather than elder, is because it would resonate more with his Roman audience. In secular usage, the term overseer refers to the commissioner, or administrator of a new colony, which is what Philippi is—a new colony of Rome. Later in the letter Paul says "our citizenship is in heaven" (3:20), in contrast to the prized possession of Roman citizenship, which many of the Philippians had. It was the Lord Jesus who was the founder of the Christian colony in Philippi through Paul—not Caesar. Just as secular Philippi had commissioners to *oversee* the city, the Christian colony in Philippi had *overseers* to provide administration and oversight of Christ's people.

Since Paul mentions overseers (plural) there may have been one assigned to each house church. The first place of worship in Philippi was Lydia's house because there were no church buildings at that time (Acts 16:15; 40). The spread of Christianity was a house church movement, where small gatherings of believers met in people's homes. All the house churches may have met together at times, in a public place, such as the river for prayer (Acts 16:13;

---

[7] See: Acts 20:17; 28; Titus 1:6-7; 1 Pet 5:1-2

16), but buildings that we call "churches" or "cathedrals" didn't exist until after Constantine's conversion in AD 312, when the church became Romanized.

It's possible that Lydia, Euodia, Syntyche, and Clement (4:2-3) are to be included in the leadership of the church—the overseers and deacons. That Paul mentions **all the holy people in Christ,** depicts the unity of status that all Christians share. Then he mentions the overseers and deacons, which presumably include Euodia and Syntyche who are not in unity with each other. This anticipates what Paul says in 4:2-3 to help them come together and be of one mind, thus ending their disagreements.

Paul is acknowledging the leaders of the Philippian church by their title, whereas he omits his title of apostle and calls himself and Timothy Christ's slaves. This is Paul's way of considering others more important than himself (2:3). He is demonstrating how to give preference to one another in humility and preparing them for the Christ Hymn (2:6-11), where Jesus presents the ultimate example of humility.

Paul offers them: **Grace to you, and peace from God, our Father, and the Lord Jesus Christ** (v. 2). What Paul says here goes way beyond just a formal greeting. **Grace** brings to the foreground an essential quality of the gospel—God's unmerited favor which he demonstrated by sending his Son to die on the cross (Eph 1:5-7; 2:8-9). Our salvation in Christ has nothing to do with our own personal goodness, it is strictly rooted in God's grace. That Paul says **Grace to you** is his way of reminding the Philippians that God's posture toward his creation is through grace. God is benevolent, good, and loving toward the objects of his affection. The total of all God has done, every blessing distributed, is an act of grace given through Jesus Christ. All God does for us is undeserved, but he withholds nothing from us in his Son. He has given us every spiritual blessing through Christ, which is all grace (Eph 1:3). **Grace to you** is plural so Paul is extending grace to the entire church, which should remind the Philippians of God's love and goodness, eliciting a symphony of thanks as they *all* recognize *together* that their salvation is a gift from God. Thus, Paul is giving them another reason why they should be in unity with one another.

Along with grace Paul offers the Philippians **peace from God**, which is an allusion to the Hebrew word *shalom*, also used as a greeting. The word means peace, wellness, wholeness, or prosperity. When someone becomes a believer in Christ they have peace with God in the sense that they are reconciled to him through his Son (Rom 5:1). The result of this new standing with God is eternal life and everlasting peace, along with wholeness and wellness. Paul seems to be using words that were common in the Old Covenant (*shalom*), and New Covenant (*grace*), bringing them together in the church of Jesus Christ.

Peace is extended to the Philippians from **God, our Father, and the Lord Jesus Christ.** The term "God" can sound impersonal but referring to God as **our Father** becomes deeply personal to each believer. Once someone becomes a believer in Christ, they are reconciled with God (have peace with him) and are adopted into his family. The church at Philippi consisted of people that were God's adopted sons and daughters, with God occupying the role of their loving heavenly Father who cares for them, having a vested interest in the wellbeing of each of his children. The church at Philippi is one part of the family of God.

The provision of grace and peace is from God our Father, **and the Lord Jesus Christ**. Grace and peace are extended to believers from both persons. The Christian life begins with the reception of God's grace and peace but continues for the duration of the believer's life. God the Father graciously initiated salvation by sending his Son to offer salvation for humanity. God shares his essential nature with the Son, which means that Jesus is fully God. The deity of Christ is one of the foundational beliefs of the Christian faith. This text points to the fact that in Paul's mind the Son is fully God, working in cooperation with the Father for the salvation of mankind. Later in Paul's letter he will develop his Christology in a glorious hymn (2:6-11) and explain how Jesus existing in "very nature God" should be viewed as "equality with God" (2:6).

Obviously, this simple greeting is loaded with theological content that has implications for the Philippians to mull over. To gloss over this and quickly get to the body of the letter, where the meatier teaching can be found, would be to miss a little nugget of spiritual gold. Furthermore, many of the things

Paul has mentioned in his greeting will be developed at length throughout his letter, thus the greeting sets the stage for much of the content to follow.

Insights, Applications, and Life Lessons

Today's world is far removed from the ancient practice of slavery, making it difficult to comprehend life as a slave in the Roman Empire. Slaves were regularly bought and sold in the marketplace, so it was a common sight to see. Over half the people living in the Empire were slaves with no rights, they were property, things, objects, commodities to be bought or sold, and could be disposed of by their masters if they weren't pleased with them. Masters had the legal right to put a slave to death if they so desired. Slaves occupied the lowest place in Greco-Roman society, having no special status whatsoever. Roman culture was all about status, honor, and recognition from their community. People sought after honor and status for it was something to be cherished in the ancient world. That Paul identifies himself and Timothy as slaves, strips them of any special status and places them at the bottom of the barrel in the social peaking order of that culture. Seeing slaves bought and sold in the market was commonplace throughout the Mediterranean world. That they identify themselves as slaves, with no status, is a true demonstration of their humility before the Philippians. That must have made an impression on them when the letter was read out loud in one of their gatherings.

By calling themselves the slaves of Christ, Paul is demonstrating his humility, which sets the tone for his letter. Rather than presenting his official title of "apostle of Jesus Christ" he identifies himself and Timothy as Jesus' slaves. He could have dropped all kinds of lofty titles on the table to impress his readers in Philippi, such as:

- Paul, an apostle who has seen the risen Christ
- Paul, who received his apostleship directly from Christ
- Paul, educated in the finest institutions of the day
- Paul, given authority from Christ
- Paul, who received his gospel directly from Jesus Christ
- Paul, successful church planter

- Paul, founder of the church at Philippi
- Paul, successful evangelist
- Paul, successful apologist of the gospel of Jesus Christ
- Paul, author of God's word

The list could go-and-on, for Paul was certainly a multi-talented individual, but that kind of boasting goes against the grain of Jesus' example of leadership, and what he was trying to teach the Philippians. In leadership, it isn't uncommon to see people who are governed by pride, who like to throw their authority around, and let everybody know that they're in charge. Paul displayed none of that, for behavior of that type was unacceptable to him, and not fitting for one who follows the Lord Jesus. Prideful leaders not only appear in the secular world, unfortunately, they are also in Christ's church. On more than one occasion the disciples were arguing among themselves about who would be the greatest in the Kingdom of heaven (Mark 9:33-35; Luke 9:46-48). Excessive pride, jockeying for power, and desiring to be in the limelight can be a problem with leaders in the Christian community, just as it is in secular culture.

Every Christian, regardless of their position in the church they attend, should consider that they are slaves of Christ, bought by his blood and belong to him. Jesus is the Master Christians serve. In no way is Paul belittling himself and Timothy in this designation, on the contrary, they consider it a great honor to be the slave of Christ. This truth should lead to humility and serve as a check against pride, for all believers are in the same position with Jesus, regardless of their title or status in church. All believers are slaves of the Lord Jesus, so they should humbly serve their Master.

Leading by Example

There has been a plethora of material written about leadership in recent years. One of the common clichés we hear about positive leadership is that good leaders lead by way of example. Some leaders lead from the top down and issue forth directives to those underneath them. They rarely, if ever, have any contact with their subordinates, because they lock themselves up in their office and are busy shuffling papers, looking at spreadsheets, emailing, skyping, and so on.

There are other leaders who are hands-on in their approach to leadership and won't ask anybody to do something that they themselves wouldn't do. They lead by example and earn the respect of those they lead. Something that each person needs to ask himself regarding the way he relates to those underneath him is: "Am I willing to do what I'm asking of everyone else?" This should cause people to pause and think about how they use their position(s) of authority. If I'm calling for people to make greater sacrifices with their time, am I going to lead the way by making greater sacrifices with my time? If I'm calling for people to be more generous with their money, am I going to lead the way by demonstrating my generosity? If leaders ask people to do things that they aren't willing to do themselves, then they have a double standard and make themselves out to be hypocrites. They don't earn the respect of those whom they lead.

Paul will be exhorting the Philippians to demonstrate humility as the pathway to unifying their church, so right out of the gate in his greeting he demonstrates his humility by calling himself the slave of Christ, while calling the Philippian leaders by their proper titles of overseers and deacons. This is his way of lowering himself before the Philippian leaders, while giving them preference by recognizing them by their official titles. What impression did this make on the Philippians? They knew Paul as "Paul the apostle" who had seen the risen Christ, but Paul lowered himself by choosing the title "Paul the slave" showing the Philippians how to be humble. Paul is leading by example.

Holy Status Must Lead to Holy Living

All believers are Jesus' holy people, set apart to serve him which should be a reminder that God saved people not just to go to heaven, but to do his work here on earth. Christians are "in Christ" which refers to their inseparable union with him—it is their spiritual address. This is an awesome privileged status, but Christians must be mindful of the responsibility that goes along with this position. Christians are set apart from the world and are positioned "in Christ" to live "on mission" for him. When thinking of the spiritual status believers have before God, it is imperative to live like his holy people, in a manner that is worthy of the Good News (1:27). Much of Paul's letter focuses on the practical matter of living in a way that reflects Christians' status as God's holy people in Christ, as they make progress in their sanctification.

A Christian Revision in Letter Writing

The normal greeting in ancient letter writing was *charein*, the infinitive of rejoice, but when used in the context of a letter it simply meant *greetings!* With the pen in Paul's hand, he put a uniquely Christian twist to this word and wrote *charis*, which means "grace." Therefore, Paul Christianized the typical greeting in ancient letter writing. That Paul offers them grace should be an instant reminder that all God has given to believers is his gift, having nothing to do with man's good works or efforts to please him. Our salvation in Christ is totally an act of God's benevolence to undeserving people. Whenever a believer thinks that he has merited God's favor or done something worthy enough to earn a favorable position with God, he needs to review the word *grace* in his mind. Grace should be a humbling concept for believers because there is nothing that could be done to procure one's own salvation—it's all God's grace freely given to sinners. Additionally, thinking of God's grace should cause believers to praise God for his goodness, and evoke a deep sense of humility.

Peace is also a loaded concept. Once someone becomes the recipient of God's grace the result is peace with God (Rom 5:1). The new believer is reconciled with God and is in a condition that can't be improved upon, because of Christ's redemptive work. Being at peace with God is the place everybody needs to be with him, and certainly, God desires all people to come to him through faith and repentance in his Son (2 Pet 3:9). But peace means more than just reconciliation with God, it also carries with it the benefits of being in relationship with him such as: wholeness, wellness, and prosperity. Grace and peace bring together terms from the New and Old Covenants respectively.

Grace and peace continue to be extended to believers throughout their lives, so the flow of grace and peace keep coming like a mighty river. This short greeting has terms that are loaded with theological grit and mustn't be glossed over, rather they should be meditated on for they will enrich one's soul:

- Holy ones (or saints): indicates what we are spiritually
- In Christ: indicates where we are spiritually
- Slaves: indicates who we serve (Jesus)
- Grace: indicates what we received but didn't deserve
- Peace: indicates what we have with God

The first three describe what believers are before God, whereas the last two describe what they have received from God. These terms are worthy of meditating on because their comprehension will have a deep spiritual impact on everyone.

Summary

Paul began his letter to the church at Philippi by presenting themes that he will develop in the body of his letter such as: unity, humility, and sanctification. He gave preference to the Philippians by recognizing them by their official titles of overseers and deacons, while identifying himself and Timothy as slaves of Jesus. This is Paul's way of leading by example and demonstrating the humility that he wants the Philippians to develop. Timothy was with Paul in Rome and had a part in writing the letter, which is something that he wants them to know because Timothy was with Paul when he founded the church there, so they already knew him, and were presumably fond of the young man. His presence was certainly comforting for Paul who considered Timothy his son in the faith. In this short greeting, Paul has set the stage for the body of the letter.

In the next section, Paul will thank God for the Philippians regarding the special partnership they have with him in the Good News. That he reveals his deep feelings for them indicates that his relationship wasn't superficial, it was intensely personal and caring.

CHAPTER TWO

* * *

"A Gospel Partnership"
Philippians 1:3-8

Normally in ancient letter writing at this point the author wishes the recipient good health, but Paul goes in a different direction. He thanks God for the Philippians, whom he regards as his friends and family members in Christ. These verses are not a prayer, rather they are descriptive of the way Paul prays for the Philippians. In classical rhetoric, this part of the letter is the *exordium*, the introductory part of an argument in which the writer establishes credibility and introduces the subjects of the discourse. Paul's words are overwhelmingly positive in tone and are filled with emotional content, for these people are near and dear to his heart. He establishes a good rapport with his friends through these words and reaffirms the partnership in the Good News that already exists between them. This *exordium* (1:3-11) is short and sweet, it addresses his audience in good terms such that he gains their undivided attention. Their ears will be wide open to Paul's words that follow in the next section of the letter, the *narratio* (1:12-26).

Being under house arrest one had to provide for his own expenses, so it isn't difficult to understand how deeply Paul appreciated the monetary gift the Philippians sent him. Their gift enabled Paul to pay the rent and eat. He is overwhelmed with joy at the Philippians concern they showed him and for standing by him when he was "off the grid" under house arrest.

I thank my God whenever I remember you, [4]always in every prayer of mine for all of you, I am making my requests with joy, [5]for your partnership in the Good News from the first day until now; [6]being confident of this very thing, that he who began a good work in you will complete it until the day of Christ Jesus. [7]It is even right for me to think this way about all of you, because I have you in my heart, both in my chains and in the defense and confirmation of the Good News, you all are partakers with me of grace. [8]For God is my witness, how I long after all of you in the tender mercies of Christ Jesus. (Author's Translation, 1:3-8)

There is a translation issue in v. 3 that needs to be addressed at the outset. There are two viable ways that v. 3 can be translated according to the Greek, so context must determine which is the best option:

Option 1: I thank my God whenever I remember you

Option 2: I thank my God for you remembering me

Most translations of the Bible favor the first option and say it is Paul who remembers the Philippians and thanks God for them. According to this translation throughout Paul's day as thoughts of the Philippians pop into his mind he thanks God for these faithful believers and prays for them.

Regarding the second option, it is the Philippians that remembered Paul by sending Epaphroditus with the money they raised for him. When they became aware that Paul was in Rome, under house arrest, they swung into action and took up a collection for him, so it was the Philippians that remembered Paul in his suffering and dire circumstances. One reason Paul wrote the letter was to thank them for the generous financial gift, which may tip the scales in favor of this translation. Paul is thanking God because they remembered him, and he is indirectly implying a "thank you" to the Philippians for their gift.

This translation seems to make more sense and better fits the context of the letter. It also solves a dilemma that has faced interpreters of Philippians in that if the first translation is correct, Paul seems to virtually ignore mentioning his appreciation of their financial gift until the end of the letter

(4:10), which appears to be rude and out of character for him. Thus, at the outset of his letter he is expressing his deep-seated appreciation for their caring concern for him by saying: "I thank God that you have remembered me, (and implying) and by the way, thanks for the gift of money."

As Paul thought of the Philippians he turned to God and prayed for them with a thankful heart because he says: **always in every prayer of mine for all of you.** Paul regularly prayed for the churches under his oversight and seems to have excelled in the discipline of prayer. Being under house arrest he couldn't visit the churches, but he could stand by them in prayer and commit them to God's loving care. The things he was unable to say to them, because of the distance separating them, he brought to God in prayer. No doubt, he prayed for the Philippians' spiritual maturity, and the issues that he will bring before them in this letter.

Paul describes his emotional disposition as he prays for the Philippians: **I am making my requests with joy**. One of the outstanding features of Philippians is Paul's experience of joy. As he prayed for them he did so with joy in all the requests he made for them, for reasons that will unfold in the passage. Praying for them wasn't a tedious matter that Paul found boring and monotonous, rather it brought joy to Paul's heart as he thought about them and prayed for them. This may have been a therapeutic practice for Paul which made life a little easier as he languished under house arrest.

Paul mentions joy (*chara*) and rejoicing (*chairein*) 16 times in Philippians, which is more than any other of his letters. Given the importance of this theme in Philippians it is worth spending some time on the theological understanding of joy. One of the fruit of the Spirit is joy (Gal 5:22). It is a virtue that is cultivated by the Spirit and is something that Jesus imparts to his disciples (John 15:11), thus spiritual joy stands in stark contrast to the world's understanding of joy. When favorable circumstances exist in one's life the world would say this is reason for being joyful. However, spiritual joy isn't based on one's circumstances in life. It is other-worldly in nature, which is why Paul could experience a high degree of joy in the dire circumstances he was in. Joy is a byproduct of being in relationship with Jesus. His mantra in Philippians seems to be "rejoice in the Lord" (3:1; 4:4; 10).

"Hence, for Paul joy is more than a mood or an emotion. Joy is an understanding of existence that encompasses both the elation and depression, that can accept with submission events that bring delight or dismay, because joy allows one to see beyond any particular event to the sovereign Lord who stands above all events and ultimately has control over them."[8]

Believers experience joy through the presence of the Holy Spirit. The world can't take away the joy Christians have because it is supernatural—it is not of this world. Joy is a general feature of the Christian life for Paul, and Philippians gives the reader a glimpse into how Paul retained his joy in the Lord, despite less than favorable circumstances.

One of the reasons Paul prays for the Philippians with joy is stated in v. 5: **for your partnership in the Good News from the first day until now.** The Greek word *koinōnia* is translated **partnership**. The meaning of the word refers to something that is "shared in common," so the word can be translated: fellowship, participation, partnership, community, or sharing. Examples of this are believers sharing money and possessions with those in need (Acts 4:32). Believers being called into fellowship with Jesus (1 Cor 1:9), with one another and the Father (1 John 1:3), and the Spirit (2 Cor 13:14). Of course, all believers are sharing a common faith in Christ and are in fellowship with each other in their church (the fellowship, Acts 2:42) and participate in the advancement of the Good News in their location.

The Philippians weren't passive bystanders, or spectators regarding the advancement of the gospel. They were in **partnership** with Paul in his apostolic ministry, which they expressed through their financial gifts to him. They put their money where their mouth was, and demonstrated their commitment to Paul, and the gospel, by supporting him when he was imprisoned. They stood with him regardless of his circumstances. Their partnership was in the **Good News** (gospel), which is the Greek *euaggelion*, literally translated *Good News*. Throughout this commentary I use both terms, gospel and Good News, interchangeably.

---

[8] Hawthorne, p. 21

The timeframe of their partnership with Paul is: **from the first day until now. The first day** must refer to Paul's visit to the city of Philippi when he preached the gospel and established the church. This is quite a complimentary view of the Philippians, because from the very beginning of their Christian experience they were faithful partners with Paul in his ministry. Any missionary would covet having a relationship with a church that was so faithful and generous in financial support. This gives Paul a sound reason for praying with joy in all his prayers for the Philippians. He always prays for them, from the beginning of his relationship with them, up to, and including the present.

Paul states another reason why he prays with such incredible joy in v. 6: **being confident of this very thing, that he who began a good work in you will complete it until the day of Christ Jesus.** God began a work in the Philippians when they received Jesus into their hearts by faith and became born again believers, but God's work doesn't stop there. Throughout the believer's life she goes through the process of sanctification, where she is separated from sin and becomes more-and-more like the Lord Jesus. Sanctification was certainly an issue for the Philippians, which is one of the themes that occupies a central place in this letter. Not everything was what it should be in the relationships that existed in the church, for there were divisions and conflicts between leaders (4:2-3), as well as improper attitudes that were out of character for Christians to maintain (2:1-5). Additionally, the Philippians may have had some misunderstandings about the process of sanctification regarding how they can grow into mature Christians, which may very well be why Paul wrote 3:10-17.

Paul's confidence is in God's ability to complete the process in the Philippians and bring them into the perfected state when Jesus returns. It is then that they will have their glorified bodies, and their spiritual maturity comes to fruition (3:20-21). They will be fully conformed to the moral perfection of Christ at that time (Rom 8:29). God takes the believer all the way to the finish line, which gives Paul another reason to pray with joy for the Philippians. Believers wait expectantly for the day of Christ Jesus (his return), because it is the source of their hope, in that sin will be a thing of the past and they will receive their glorified bodies. As Paul considers the problems that existed with the Philippians' sanctification he is encouraged because God is at work in them, so they will realize the perfected state. In Paul's mind, it is not a likelihood, no, it is a certainly. However, the Philippians must tighten things up and do their part in growing in the Christian faith.

Verse six paves the way for 2:12-13, where Paul points to the believer's role in his sanctification. It is because God is at work in believer's lives, undergirding everything they do, that Paul is so confident that as they "workout their salvation" God is working in them to bring them to perfection at Christ's return. There are two days mentioned in vv. 5-6: **the first day** (v. 5) refers to the day they heard the Good News and became believers in Christ. The second day is the **day of Christ Jesus** (v.6), when he returns, and their spiritual journey is completed. In between those two days, believers are to focus their efforts on growing in the faith, advancing the gospel, and making themselves ready for Christ's return.

One of the striking features of Paul's letter is the expression of love that he had for the Philippians, which was mutually shared. This love was a two-way street because the relationship was strong on both ends, so Paul expresses his intense feelings for them right at the outset of his letter.

It is even right for me to think this way about all of you, because I have you in my heart, because, both in my chains and in the defense and confirmation of the Good News, you all are partakers with me of grace. (1:7)

How else could Paul feel about the Philippians? This is the only justifiable way that Paul could think about these beloved supporters of his. He has no reason to think otherwise about them, so he says: **It is even right for me to think this way about all of you.** The word translated **think** is the Greek word *phronein,* which is written as a present infinitive, denoting nonstop action. The word refers to a focused thinking and reflection on something. The significance of this word is that Paul continuously reflected on the Philippians and has arrived at the conclusion that this is how he should feel about these dear Christians, who have been so faithful to him. He gave a great deal of thought to his relationship with the Philippians and always arrived at the conclusion that these are dear brothers and sisters in Christ, for whom he is grateful. He had a lot of time on his hands, so he must have invested much thought in this matter.

Paul reveals why he thinks about the Philippians as he does: **because I have you in my heart**, which in Biblical terms is the essence of a person. The heart is the locus of a person's mind, will, emotions or the core of his very existence. Believers are to love the Lord with all their *heart* (Deu 6:4-6; Matt 22:37) which is another way of saying love the Lord with everything you have, or with your entire being. Paul carried the Philippians right in the core of his being because he cared so deeply about them.

Another reason Paul is certain that his conclusions about the Philippians are right is that: **both in my chains and in the defense and confirmation of the Good News, you all are partakers with me of grace.** Being in chains refers to his present condition of being under house arrest in Rome. He was a prisoner because of his stand for Jesus and the gospel. However, Paul considered himself to be the Lord's prisoner (Eph 4:1), but not in a disparaging way, rather he considered it an honor to be the Lord's prisoner. He was in jail because of his apostolic ministry and the stand he took for Jesus. He was chained to a Roman soldier in the praetorian guard, around the clock, which was standard practice for those who were under house arrest.

Paul had been in Rome for nearly two years waiting for the verdict regarding whether he would be released or executed, but his purpose for being there was in **defense and confirmation of the Good News,** which are both legal terms. The Greek word *apologia*, translated **defense**, is the word from which our English words apology and apologetics is derived. This word refers to speaking in defense of something, which in this case is Paul speaking in defense of the gospel. The second Greek term is *bebaiósis* which means to confirm, establish, or ratify something. Paul confirmed the truth of the gospel, which is something that Paul did not just in his present circumstances in Rome, but throughout his ministry he would regularly defend and confirm the truth of the gospel. Christians throughout all eras of history are to defend and confirm the truth of the gospel to their culture.[9]

---

[9] Witherington understands this differently. He applies these two terms to the judicial process in the Roman Empire: I take them to refer here to an apologia in a Roman court during the primo actio, Paul's first meeting with the judge, which has apparently already transpired, following the Roman process of fact-finding called cognitio. In this first part of the legal process, the facts of the case would be agreed on to provide the basis or so-called "formula" for the judgment. It would seem that

Paul affirms that the Philippians stood by him through the tough times he faced offering him encouragement, financial support, and by sending Epaphroditus to alleviate his suffering. He saw them as partners in his ministry and affirms that **you all are partakers with me of grace.** It is true that both Paul and the Philippians have received the grace of God when they became believers in Christ, but here the thought Paul seems to have in mind is that they share in his apostolic ministry. Paul understood that his calling as an apostle to the Gentiles was entirely by the grace of God (Acts 9 :15-16; 1 Cor 15:10), and through the Philippians dedicated support they shared in his apostolic ministry. For this reason, Paul saw them as **partakers of grace** with him. **Partakers** translates the Greek word *synkoinōnia*, which is the second occurrence of *koinonia* with the prefix *syn* attached to it. *"Syn"* carries the idea of "with" thus intensifying the meaning of being **partakers with me** of grace. This could also be translated: "you are fellowshipers with me of grace," which causes us to stretch our understanding of fellowship going beyond socializing with other Christians.

Paul's calling as an apostle was a gift of the Lord's grace given to him. By sowing into his ministry through their prayers, financial support, their visits to Paul, and more, they share in his ministry, thus they are partakers of grace with Paul, and will be rewarded accordingly by the Lord on judgment day.

That they showed such loyalty to Paul is amazing considering their high sense of civic duty, their pride in their Roman citizenship, and their status as a Roman colony. Paul is being shamed by the Roman authorities, yet the Philippians are reaching out to Paul and supporting him. This says a lot about how they feel about Paul, especially in a culture of honor and shame such as theirs. Their loyalty to Paul could be considered shameful behavior and disrespectful to the Emperor.

---

under Nero the necessary personal jurisdiction of the Emperor, such as the trial of capital cases on appeal, was delegated to other persons, and the sentences confirmed by him afterwards. Nero was notably uninterested, at least before the fire in Rome in A.D. 64, in spending hours and hours in court settings, when he could be off composing his newest poem, sponsoring some athletic contest, acting, or engaging in some other leisure activity that pleased him better. (Witherington, Loc. 1082)

This is another reason Paul is so grateful to the Philippians. One might think that they had greater loyalties to Rome than to Paul and the gospel, but that wasn't the case. Their support of Paul could cause people to question their loyalty to Rome and view the Philippians' conduct to be unacceptable as good citizens of Rome.

For God is my witness, how I long after all of you in the tender mercies of Christ Jesus. (1:8)

Paul was so convicted about his deep feelings for the Philippians that he says: **For God is my witness.** This is Paul's way of saying: "God knows how I really feel about you. He bears witness to my thoughts and knows my heart for you Philippians." Paul is very serious about how he feels toward them, in fact, by calling God as his witness he can't get any more serious than he is. His feelings for them are no laughing matter.

Paul says: **how I *long* after all of you**, which is a translation of the Greek word *epipotheó*, a compound word consisting of *epi* meaning "on" or "upon" and *potheó* meaning "yearning affectionately" or "longing for with great affection." Putting the two words together intensifies the level of yearning, and it is written in the present tense which denotes continuous action on Paul's part. In other words, he keeps on *passionately, affectionately longing* to be with his friends in Philippi. It is difficult to imagine how someone can express their feelings in a deeper way than Paul is for the Philippians.

He longs after them **in the *tender mercies* of Christ**, which translates the Greek word *splagchnon,* literally referring to the bowels and internal organs. Figuratively it refers to the capacity to feel deep emotions such as sympathy, empathy, and compassion. It's like getting your stomach tied up in a knot or feeling gut-level compassion. One can't help thinking that Paul would love to see them in person because of his deep feelings, but all he can do is reach out to them through his prayers, letters, and representatives.

Paul has described his relationship with the Philippians in deep emotional terms, almost as if he feels about them the same way the Lord Jesus feels about them, because he longs after them with the tender mercies **of Christ**.

This was no shallow relationship that Paul had with his dear friends in Philippi. Make no mistake about it, Paul's heart is fully engaged with the Philippians.

If you're on the receiving end of this letter you couldn't miss the emotional content, and the love that Paul is pouring out on you. I wonder if some of the Philippians got emotional as they heard the letter read out loud to them. He is making it crystal clear that he loves them deeply, just as Christ loves them. It can't get any more real than that! At this point in his letter he has their attention, he has a captive audience because he has spoken to them in such favorable terms that he has prepared them for the body of his letter.

Insights, Applications, and Life Lessons

One characteristic of a true friend is loyalty, which the Philippians demonstrated to Paul. You might think that with Paul being imprisoned they might have reconsidered their financial support of the apostle. After all, he isn't producing in that he hasn't founded any churches for four years. Perhaps, the Philippians should get their missions committee together and begin to look elsewhere for someone to support. The Philippians never went there, they always stuck with Paul—he was their man! We can see why Paul had such joy as he thought about them.

Friendship in the ancient world took on a different dimension than today. It isn't uncommon to be in relationship with someone that you consider a friend, but it's a one-sided relationship. Whenever he needs something from you, you extend friendship by being there for him, but if you need something from him a litany of excuses will be presented as to why he can't help you out. This makes you feel like you're being used. From his end, it's a relationship of convenience—his convenience at your expense. You are loyal to him, but he is disingenuous toward you. That isn't true friendship. The relationship Paul had with the Philippians was infused with loyalty on both ends.

Genuine Friendship is a Source of Joy

I have come to see that the most precious gifts I have are the people that God has brought into my life. People who love me and stand by my side through good and bad times are reasons for me to be joyful and thankful. Thinking about friends who have contributed to my development by investing their time, energy, encouragement, and resources along the way causes me to thank God and brings joy to my heart.

Terry Bradshaw played quarterback for the Pittsburg Steelers and led them to four Super Bowl victories. He once commented on TV that his success was due to the people that invested in him throughout his career. Along the way, he realized had it not been for those people he may not have had the success that he did. He looked back on those people and thanked them for their support, in full realization that the four Super Bowl victories he had may not have happened without them.

It honors God to be thankful for the loyal people he brings into one's life who are always there when needed, whether it's a best friend, coach, spouse, pastor, parent, etc. Where would we be without them? Where would Paul have been without the Philippians partnering with him? No doubt they made his life much easier. Imagine how Paul felt being in his rented quarters chained to a Roman soldier of the Praetorian Guard around the clock. He hasn't heard from the Philippians for quite a while, then his dear friend Epaphroditus shows up. That must have been a moment of pure joy for Paul and Epaphroditus to see each other. They probably gave each other a big hug and a holy kiss, then started talking about life. Paul asked him how the journey went, Epaphroditus asked him how he was doing, and what the status of his trial was. Timothy was there so he would have embraced Epaphroditus as well. It must have a been a moment of pure joy for good friends to reunite.

Then Epaphroditus presents him with the money the church raised for him. I wonder what Epaphroditus said: "Paul, we love you and were concerned about you being locked up, so we took up this collection for you to cover your expenses. I'm going to stay here and attend to your needs and help you in any way I can to make your life more comfortable. We miss you back in

Philippi and we love you." Now Paul can eat and pay the rent. Imagine the sense of gratitude Paul must have felt and how joyful he was that the Philippians remembered him. This is loyal friendship at its best.

For this reason, Paul was thankful to God and prayed for the Philippians with joy. It's good to express gratitude to people and let them know how much their efforts are appreciated. They are the most valuable resource God brings into one's life. Reading this portion of Philippians has made me think of people that have been a huge blessing to me, which brings a glowing sense of joy to my heart, and a deep appreciation for their friendship. Think of the people in your life that have made a difference for you and have been there when you needed them. In your prayer time give thanks to God for them and pray with joy in the process. Make sure from time-to-time you tell them how much they mean to you! Don't let them think that you take them for granted. Don't assume that they know how you feel, give them a call every-so-often and express yourself. Nobody responds well to ingratitude!

Summary

Paul is deeply grateful to God for the Philippians and prays for them with an overwhelming sense of joy. They are special to Paul because of their partnership with him in the gospel which began when he visited Philippi and introduced them to Jesus. Paul identifies this as "the first day" for the Philippians because that was the day they placed their trust in Jesus. He is confident that God will complete the work he began in them right up to the day Christ returns, which is when believers will be in the glorified state. This is the second day Paul mentions.

Paul expresses his deep feelings for the Philippians and concludes this is the only justifiable way that he can think about them. He longs to see them with the tender mercies of Christ. So certain is he of how he feels about the Philippians that he calls God as witness to his feelings. I wonder if Paul shed a tear as he was writing this, or if Timothy was writing as Paul dictated to him and Paul had to stop, grab some tissue and regain his composure because he got emotional. When Paul thought about them he had gut-level emotion. The Philippians brought joy to Paul as he languished in prison.

In the next section, Paul will offer up a prayer for the Philippians that is short and sweet but filled with rich content.

CHAPTER THREE

* * *

"Potent Praying"
Philippians 1:9-11

Paul mentioned how he prays with joy for his cherished Philippians, now he reveals what he is specifically praying for them. This prayer is short and sweet but loaded with rich content and theological implications. It is a potent prayer of Paul's, one that is worth praying for ourselves, other believers, and entire churches.

This I pray, that your love may abound yet more and more in knowledge and all discernment; [10]so that you may approve the things that are excellent; that you may be sincere and without offense to the day of Christ; [11]being filled with the fruit of righteousness, that is through Jesus Christ, to the glory and praise of God. (Author's Translation, 1:9-11)

Paul's prayer focus is on their **love**, which is a translation of the Greek word *agápē,* used sparingly by Greek writers. It was chosen by the writers of the Septuagint (the Greek translation of the Hebrew Bible) to translate Hebrew words for God's love for his people (Deu 7:7), and in the two love commands for people loving God (Deu 6:5), and people loving their neighbor (Lev 19:18). The Christian writers gave the word a new potent meaning. "This usage, which thus fills an otherwise empty word full of theological grist, is unquestionably the source of its usage among the early Christians, for whom it became the ultimate theological word both to describe God's character and to articulate the essence of Christian behavior."[10]

The word *agápē* is God's deep love he gives to mankind and is cultivated in believers. It is a distinguishing feature of believers that the world takes note of (John 13:34-35) and is the greatest of all commands that the law and prophets hinge on (Mat 22:37-40). Thus, love is a primary virtue of disciples of Christ and is a fruit of the Spirit (Gal 5:22). But to whom should the Philippians' love be directed? In 1 Thessalonians 3:12 Paul prayed that their love would abound toward one another, which seems to be the sense in which Paul is praying for the Philippians. Their relationships needed some help, so Paul restates this in 2:2: "having the same love for another."

His concern is that their love will not become sterile and grow cold toward one another, meaning those on the inside—in the family of God. Relationships in a church setting can't be characterized by bad attitudes that are harmful to the unity of the body, such as those mentioned in Philippians 2:3-4: *doing nothing through rivalry or through conceit*, but in humility, each counting others better than himself; [4]*each of you not just looking to his own things*, but each of you also to the things of others (Italics Mine). Family love shared among God's people should always be overflowing and flooded with expressions of good deeds, compassion, and kindness for this is the essence of *agápē* (love). This love is primarily descriptive of the relationships in the family of God, secondarily with those outside the community of faith, for Jesus calls us to love (*agápē*) even our enemies (Mat 5:44).

Divine love and secular love are polar opposites. Secular culture views love as a sexual escapade—let's make love tonight, or love is a warm and fuzzy feeling that is based on emotions that change from moment-to-moment, or situation-to-situation. Worldly love is far removed from divine love. God's love is his self-giving for the benefit of others. "This attribute of God shows that it is part of his nature to give of himself in order to bring about blessing or good for others."[11] "His love expresses itself in actively seeking the benefit

[10] Fee, p. 98
[11] Grudem, p. 198

of the one so loved."[12] The objects of God's affection receive his benevolence for their benefit. He demonstrated his love in sending his Son to atone for man's sins through his death on the cross and extend uncountable blessings to those who believe.[13]

Therefore, the love that Paul is describing isn't the "tender mercies" or "longing for them" mentioned in 1:8. What Paul has in mind here is a sober love that is well thought out, placing a high value on the one toward whom it is directed. Paul prays **that your love may abound yet more and more. Abound** is a translation of the Greek word *perisseuó,* which has the idea of going beyond the measure, overflowing, or exceeding. Since Paul prays that their love will abound "more and more," this indicates that Paul desires to see in the Philippians' fellowship such a manifestation of God's love that they experience it in an overflowing capacity that is beyond containment. God's love is to be shared among believers in such an abundant capacity, that it is much like the excessive rainfall California experienced in 2017 that required opening the dams and letting mass quantities of water flow out. Images I saw on the news where mighty torrents of water were let out of the Oroville dam are still fresh in my mind. This is the type of overflowing love Paul wants to see cultivated in believers and shared with each other. Church should be a place of divine expressions of love.

Paul desires that their love overflows in their congregation, but **knowledge and all discernment** must accompany the super abundance of love. The **knowledge** (*epígnōsis*) Paul mentions here is experiential and personal, not theoretical, abstract, or conceptual knowledge. As the disciple studies God's word, it must become personal and experiential, so that it isn't study for the sake of filling one's mind with Bible content, it must go from the head to the heart and become personal. Thus, as love grows in the disciple knowledge must grow proportionately, so love and knowledge seem to be linked together.

Abounding love must also be accompanied by all **discernment**, a translation of *aisthésis,* a word that occurs only here in the New Testament. This word

---

[12] Fee, p. 99

[13] See: Rom 5:6-8; 1 John 4:10; Eph 1:3

describes a high level of spiritual discernment, understanding, perception, moral, and ethical insight. The word is virtually synonymous with wisdom or insight/understanding.[14]

One can see how knowledge and discernment are complementary in nature. Discernment will assist the disciple in properly applying the Biblical knowledge he has acquired. Discernment gives one the wisdom to live out God's word in her daily experience such that she lives in a way that is worthy of the gospel (Eph 4:1; Phil 1:27). Love accompanied by knowledge and discernment enables disciples to make good choices that promote godliness and optimizes the way they express love toward others. Paul said in 1 Corinthians 13:2: "if I have all *knowledge* but no *love* I am nothing," thus establishing a link between knowledge and love. One must exist with the other. If a disciple has love that isn't founded on knowledge of God's word, with no discernment, it is inevitable he will make some bad choices that may have dire consequences.

Without knowledge and discernment love may be expressed in a way that tolerates sin, overlooks immorality, and begins compromising with the world's value system which is dishonoring to Christ. Therefore, Paul is calling for the Philippians to express their abundance of love in a well thought out, wise, and intelligent way, rather than expressing love that is based on a whim driven by emotion and spontaneity. Where knowledge and discernment exist, but love is lacking, a person may exhibit behavior that seems harsh, insensitive, overly critical, and manipulative. Love must be balanced by knowledge and discernment, and knowledge and discernment must be balanced by love. They are complementary in nature.

Having love abound more and more in knowledge and discernment has a purpose: **so that you may approve the things that are excellent** (v. 10). **Approve** is the translation of the Greek word *dokimázō,* a word used to describe testing, examining, or approving something after it stands the test. For instance, the word was used of testing the purity of precious metals by examination. "The emphasis here is not on the comparative process, but on

---

[14] Fee, p. 100

their being able to discern that which God has already marked off as essential or "superlative" regarding life in Christ."[15]

Believers need to approve the things that are **excellent**, or as stated above "those things that are superlative regarding life in Christ." Later in thes letter Paul says in 4:8: Finally, brothers and sisters, whatever is true, whatever is noble, whatever is right, whatever is pure, whatever is lovely, whatever is admirable—if anything is *excellent* or praiseworthy—think about such things (Italics Mine, NIV). The excellent things are the courses of action that we choose in life to glorify God by being obedient to his word. Every act of obedience, every thought, every attitude, every decision that conforms to God's word is excellent and honors him. As love, knowledge, and discernment are working together in the right combination, believers will excel at making good choices in their expression of love toward others and leading a godly life. This will enable believers to "up their game for the Lord" and commit to behavior that is honoring to Christ.

Discerning what is excellent is for the purpose: **that you may be sincere and without offense to the day of Christ** (v. 10b). Paul is referring to being sincere *(eilikrinés)* with one's motives or having pure motives. The Greek word has the idea of being tested by the rays of the sun and was applied to motives (2 Cor 1:12; 2:17). Pottery that was cracked would often be filled with wax to hide the cracks, but when held up to the sunlight the cracks would become visible because the wax appeared darker. Some shops in the ancient world would stamp their pottery *sine cera* (without wax) as a guarantee of its superior quality.[16] Cracks are revealed as pottery was held in the sunlight, and believers' motives are revealed as they are examined against the light of God's word. In other words, one's motives need to stand the test of God's light. Disciples of Christ can't have mixed motives in serving God, their motives need to be pure and sincere.

To be **without offense** *(aproskopos)* is to make sure the disciple does nothing to cause someone to stumble or take offense at their behavior, hence the word is also translated blameless. Nobody should be able to identify any

---

[15] Fee, p. 101

[16] MacArthur, p. 50

moral deficiencies in their behavior, so the disciple will stand before the Lord blameless. Thus, Paul may be thinking that in the present situation at Philippi some may be entertaining mixed motives and were doing things that brought offense to others through their inappropriate behavior such as being divisive, self-centered, or overly concerned with themselves.

Paul prays that they may stand before Christ without offense (blameless) at his coming, which is referred to as the **day of Christ** (1:6). At that time believers will appear before the Lord at the Judgment Seat of Christ and their lives will be evaluated (Rom 14:10-12; 2 Cor 5:10). They will be rewarded for their service to Christ or suffer loss of reward, but not salvation (1 Cor 3:15). On the day of Christ believers receive their glorified bodies.

Being filled with the fruit of righteousness, that is through Jesus Christ, to the glory and praise of God. (1:11)

Paul is talking about righteousness already existing in believers at the return of Jesus, so this has nothing to do with imputed righteousness at one's conversion (Rom 4:3-5). The verb **being filled** is in the perfect tense, which refers to something that happened in the past but has continuing results in the present. When the Philippians became believers, they received the Holy Spirit and the process of sanctification began, but it continues for the duration of their lives. This means the Philippians are already filled **with the fruit of righteousness** and are going to continue to be filled because God is working in them. The fruit of righteousness is most likely to be taken as fruit *consisting of righteousness*, or good works.

The fruit of righteousness **is through Jesus Christ**. Independent of a relationship with Christ there will be no spiritual transformation. It is only because of the connection that believers have with Jesus that righteousness, or good works become characteristic of his life.[17] Paul is referring to divinely empowered spiritual formation in the Christian that results in moral conformity to Jesus' image. Paul desires the Philippians to appear before the Lord on the day of Christ sincere, blameless, and filled with the fruit of righteousness because they have made great progress in their sanctification.

---

[17] See: John 15:4-5; Eph 2:8-10; Col 1:5-6

They have been able to approve the things that are excellent, and superlative in their behavior so their righteousness has ascended to new heights and Christ is honored. This is what Paul is hopeful for.

This is all **to the glory and praise of God.** As believers grow into the likeness of Christ, God should be glorified and praised. The primary objective for any believer should be to do all things for the glory of God. The good work that God began in them will be completed at the day of Christ (1:6), so God should be praised for doing this great work of transformation in believers. Any progress made in one's spiritual transformation and journey with Christ should cause the disciple to give glory and praise to God.

Insights, Applications, and Life Lessons

This prayer was only three verses, but they are rich in content! God always will answer prayer that is focused on spiritual growth (John 15:7-8). Unfortunately, with the influence of the prosperity gospel praying can turn into something that dishonors God because it's focus is more on gratifying oneself, rather than being concerned with God's agenda(s). A prayer such as this one rightly focuses on one of the primary objectives of the Christian life—growing into the moral image of Jesus Christ. It honors God to pray this way for yourself, your friends, spouse, children, church, etc. It is intriguing to consider how much our prayers contribute to someone's maturity as a disciple of Christ. When examining the content of Paul's prayers, in praying for other churches, they focus on their spiritual development. When we focus our prayers on that topic, Jesus will answer those prayers to the glory of God (John 15:8; 16). All believers need to be urgently prayed for in this manner, and every believer should be praying this prayer for people in his church.

What is Love?

Paul prayed that the Philippians' love would abound, but what does Paul mean by love? In American culture love is a key word and a big deal. Many people write love letters, read romance novels, and enjoy listening to love songs. They often watch sit coms on TV about people in love with each other.

There are reality TV shows, such as the bachelor and the bachelorette, that focus on people looking for love—that perfect mate. Couples express their love for each other on Valentine's Day, anniversaries, birthdays, and other special occasions. People fall in love and get married, have children and start a family. Love is a big deal in our culture.

There is great disparity between the world's view of love and the Biblical meaning of love. The world will tell you that love is a great feeling—if it feels good do it. Love occurs in the bedroom because it's all about sex. Love is never having to say you're sorry. Love means being tolerant of other people's views and ways of living. The idea of Biblical love is the giving of oneself for the benefit of others. This is how God loves mankind. He is benevolent and good to the objects of his affection. This is how believers should love other people; in the same way that God loves them. However, this requires some thought to determine what is the best way to display God's love to the people in one's life. In this brief prayer Paul gives an enormous insight into love that should be reflected on, because it will help determine the best way(s) to express love to people. Note the diagram below.

TRIAD OF LOVE

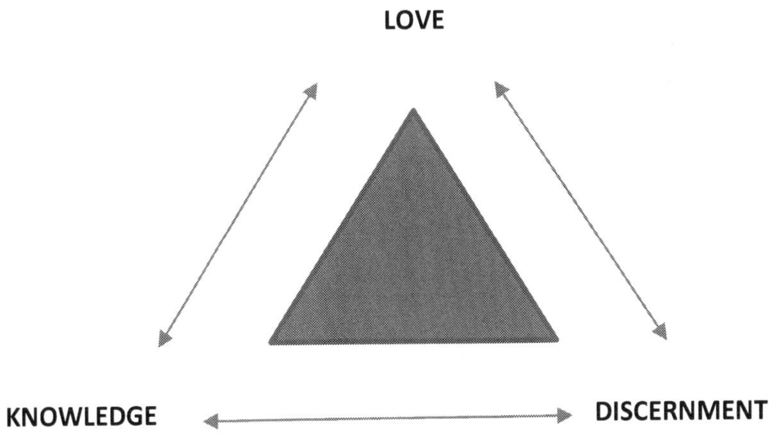

LOVE

KNOWLEDGE ⟷ **DISCERNMENT**

The above diagram depicts the relationship between love, knowledge, and discernment. Knowledge refers to knowledge of God's word, so the love that we express to others has to be governed by truth, thus establishing a link between love and knowledge. One informs the other, and together they are complementary. Discernment refers to the ability to wisely apply our knowledge of God's word in a way that is loving and serves the best interests of those toward whom our love is directed. In this regard discernment and knowledge are complementary, informing each other, so love, knowledge, and discernment placed in a triad gives people the best possibility of applying their love wisely and effectively for the other person's benefit. Love is to be displayed in a carefully thought through manner. The following illustrations will show how important it is to have the right mixture of love, knowledge, and discernment / wisdom.

#1. Love without knowledge or discernment

A Christian man and woman met at church and hit it off really well—there was an instant attraction. They developed strong feelings for each other so shortly thereafter they decided to live together. They concluded that they were in love and didn't see anything wrong with living together without being married, so he moved in with her. They disregarded the counsel of their elders to either get married or live separately, because their living situation wasn't honoring to God. They ended up leaving their church feeling they were being incorrectly judged by people and started looking for another house of worship.

This is an example of two people whose love for each other wasn't guided by *knowledge* of Scripture, nor did they have the *discernment* to understand what the consequences of their actions would be in terms of how it would affect their relationships with other people in the church, their parents, friends, their children, and so forth. They had plenty of love, but little or no knowledge and discernment to guide their expression of love to each other. The result of their actions was that they dishonored God through their disobedience, damaged their testimony, and strained many of their relationships.

#2. Knowledge Without Love and Discernment

I had a math teacher in high school who believed the best way to motivate students was through humiliation. He would randomly call on people in the class to give their answers for their homework assignment. If they couldn't correctly do a problem, he would have them come to the chalk-board and do the equation in front of the class. He was verbally abusive to his students, he would raise his voice at them, even belittle them in front of their classmates if they couldn't get it right. The students couldn't stand him, in fact, they outright hated his guts. He was totally lacking any degree of *love* for his students that he was entrusted with, and he had no *discernment* in how to teach and nurture his students. All he had was *knowledge* of mathematics. The consequences of his teaching methods were traumatized students, and most of them were left with a bad taste in their mouths for math.

#3. Discernment Without Love and Knowledge

George was in sales and learned how to play the game of negotiation. He made a good living and was very skilled at relating to people. However, in his career as a salesman he had learned how to manipulate people and situations. George had become a control freak. When having a conversation with someone he would dominate the talk to the point where it was almost impossible to get a word in a conversation with him. He evolved into the type of guy who would say anything in the moment to persuade someone to his view. He became a schmoozer! George had acquired a lot of wisdom (discernment) in relating to people, but it turned evil. He learned how to negotiate deals in a business setting, but in his everyday personal relationships his relational IQ (wisdom) was lacking love and knowledge. He would do things to manipulate people that caused them pain and he enjoyed doing this. George's problem was that his wisdom in relating to people turned evil because it wasn't guided by love and knowledge of God's word.

The above illustrations demonstrate the importance of having the right balance of love, knowledge, and discernment. The next time you have a serious conversation with someone, reflect on the right mixture of the three that you will need to have the optimal effect in showing caring concern for the other person's benefit. Doing this will go a long way in letting your love abound, as Paul has prayed, and make your relationships much more meaningful. There are many more examples of this that could be given, but the main point of this is: love must be applied intelligently, and thoughtfully always for the benefit of the other person.

Summary

Paul offered up a prayer for the Philippians' spiritual development, which is tightly woven, very compact, yet is theologically rich. The focus of his prayer is that the Philippians' love would keep growing in abundance, yet the expression of their love must be guided by knowledge of God's word, and discernment so that love is expressed wisely. When love is guided by knowledge and discernment it will be expressed intelligently, thoughtfully, wisely, and have the greatest impact in edifying people. Love that is informed by knowledge and discernment will enable the believer to make good choices in her conduct that honors God, so that she is sincere and blameless until the day the Lord Jesus returns. Growth in love will contribute to being filled with the fruit of righteousness, which can only be done through our relationship with Jesus. Church is a place where divine love should be overflowing and shared generously among the members. As believers mature spiritually God is glorified and is to be praised for the transformative work he does in their lives. This section concludes Paul's *exordium* (1:3-11).

In the next section, Paul will let the Philippians know how he is doing. They haven't seen him for a while and were no doubt concerned about him, so he will fill them in on the details.

CHAPTER FOUR

* * *

"Rejoicing in The Sovereignty of God" Philippians 1:12-18

Without a doubt, the Philippians were worried about Paul, so they sent Epaphroditus to deliver the money they raised for him and attend to his needs. They may have expected the worst to happen to Paul, so he wants to arrest any fears they have by informing them that even though he is in chains great things are happening with the gospel. The Good News is not in retreat, or just holding a defensive position, it is moving forward despite Paul's circumstances. Paul wants to assure the Philippians that God is sovereign, such that even during his imprisonment his will can be accomplished with the Good News moving forward.

In ancient letter writing this section is known as the *narratio* (1:12-26). This is where the writer gives a narrative account of what has happened to him by providing background information. Paul will relate the content that follows in his letter to events that he has reported on. Paul is employing a strategy where he is not just providing the Philippians with an update on his situation, he is giving them the example from his own life on how to conduct oneself when persecuted by the world, confronted by divisive Christians who opposed you, undermine you, and demonstrates how to display attitudes that foster unity. "Here, then, in Phil 1:12-26 we have a moving, emotional recounting of Paul's situation and a demonstration of how he continued to show grace under pressure, thus providing the audience with a positive example to follow. He exhibits the behavior that both promotes unity in Christ (not even allowing rivalry to divert him from being thankful Christ is being proclaimed) and encourages the audience to take the high road in their own situation, continuing to live lives worthy of the gospel."[18]

Philippians contains much theology by way of examples, so here Paul is showing through his own example how to live a life that is worthy of the gospel, which he will encourage them to do in 1:27. Therefore, he is preparing them for this exhortation in his *narratio* by showing them how he has done this. He puts his Christian character on display for the Philippians to see, which hopefully will provide incentive for them to take note of and emulate.

Clearly, Paul is revealing an ethos here for the Philippians to follow under dire circumstances. He is writing from a rhetorical (not an epistolary) perspective to motivate them to action. He is paving the way for the *propositio* (the main thesis) that appears in 1:27-30. He reports on his situation, so the Philippians get it straight, clearing up any false reports, or misinformation that may have come their way. Additionally, Paul is informing them about how he's doing, but he really doesn't say that much about himself. It would be remiss to read this section and miss the emphasis on the advancement of the Good News. "In this *narratio* Christ appears nine times and gospel is also prominent, making clear that the real focus should not be on Paul but on Christ and his proclamation."[19] Paul thoughtfully put this section together by mentioning the *progress* of the gospel (v. 12), then finishing it off with another mention of the Philippians' *progress* in the faith (v. 25), which is a literary device known as an inclusio. Thus, v. 12 and v. 25 are like bookends with the progress of the gospel in between.

At no point does Paul appear to be desperate and filled with anxiety over the possibility of being executed. In fact, there is a calmness with which he writes about those who are undermining him, trying to make his life miserable, but their efforts aren't succeeding. In Paul's way of thinking it's all good, because

---

[18] Witherington, Loc. 1226

[19] Fee, p. 107

Christ is being proclaimed, people are getting saved, and the gospel is moving forward. God's purposes are being accomplished.

Now I desire to have you know, brothers (and sisters), that the things which happened to me have turned out rather to the progress of the Good News;
13so that it became evident to the whole praetorian guard, and to all the rest, that my chains are in Christ; 14and that most of the brothers in the Lord,
being confident through my chains, are more abundantly bold to speak the word of God without fear. 15Some indeed preach Christ even out of envy
and strife, and some also out of good will. 16The former insincerely preach
Christ from selfish ambition, thinking that they add affliction to my chains;
17but the latter out of love, knowing that I am appointed for the defense of
the Good News. 18What does it matter? Only that in every way, whether in pretense or in truth, Christ is proclaimed. I rejoice in this, yes, and will rejoice. (Author's Translation, 1:12-18)

In telling the Philippians about his circumstances his report is more about the progress the Good News is making, rather than how he's doing. He doesn't say much about himself personally, because he probably figures Epaphroditus will fill them in on the details when he returns to Philippi. One might expect him to start by saying something like: "I'm OK, thanks for your concern, I'm still waiting for the trial, but I'm doing well." He completely bypasses himself and points to what was most important to him, which is the gospel. Paul's life and well-being were inextricably tied to the Good News of Jesus Christ, such that if the gospel was advancing he had reason to rejoice regardless of his circumstances.

The Philippians were partners with Paul in the gospel (v. 5), in praying for him, supporting him financially, and sending Epaphroditus to care for him. Naturally the Philippians wanted to see the apostle Paul have a vibrant ministry, plant churches, and lead many people to Christ. However, Paul has been off the grid for over four years. After two years in Caesarea, a shipwreck, and now two years under house arrest in Rome one would think that Paul was at the end of his rope. It wouldn't be unlikely for most people to experience some self-pity or feel that this isn't what they signed up for, or that God isn't treating them fairly, but none of that exists with Paul.

He is amazingly positive with the reason being stated in v. 12: **Now I desire to have you know, brothers (and sisters), that the things which happened to me have turned out rather to the progress of the Good News.** If the Philippians were thinking that Paul's ministry was ineffective because of his imprisonment and nothing was happening through him, he sets the record straight. He wants to make sure they understand the way God was working through his situation, which probably surprised the Philippians. This is Paul's way of saying, "It's all good." He calls them brothers, a translation of *adelphoi* (a masculine plural noun), which is the common designation for a fellow believer. However, obviously, this includes the women as well, which is why many translations of the Bible say "brothers and sisters." This is a family matter, in that Paul and the Philippians are the family of God, and he speaks to them as his spiritual brothers and sisters, not over them as an apostle infused with authority.

Because of God's sovereignty the Good News has made **progress** which is a translation of the Greek word *prokopē*. This is a compound word consisting of *pro* (in front of) and *kopto* (cut or chop down). Thus, *prokopē* is advancement by chopping down whatever impedes you. This word was used of pioneers and armies chopping down trees or other obstacles in their way, so they could make progress toward their destination.

The Good News was advancing, cutting through obstacles and making inroads, which is probably the exact opposite of what the Philippians may have been thinking. When the Good News is progressing, Paul feels good about that, so he wants the Philippians to feel the same way. Paul was an evangelist who loved to preach the gospel and lead people to Christ, but being under house arrest where were the opportunities to do this?

So that it became evident to the whole praetorian guard, and to all the rest, that my chains are in Christ; (1:13)

Any evangelist needs to be around nonbelievers to share the Good News about Christ. Paul had a captive audience—the entire Praetorian Guard. This was an elite group of soldiers numbering about 9,000 whose sole mission was to protect the Emperor. The Praetorian Guard may be the equivalent of the modern-day Secret Service whose duty is to guard the president. These were highly trained elite soldiers stationed in Rome where the Emperor resided. The Praetorian was established by Caesar Augustus, who was the Emperor at the time of Jesus' birth. Later Emperors increased the number of the soldiers in the Praetorian Guard and Tiberius built them a fortified camp in Rome. They had an intimidating presence in Rome as they were strategically deployed throughout the city to ensure that there was order. The soldiers served for a period of twelve years, but later it was increased to sixteen. At the conclusion of their term of service they were given the highest honor and a severance package. Over time they grew in power and became known as "king-makers" meaning that not only did they protect the Emperor, but also were influential in choosing the Emperor.

They guarded Paul around the clock, 24 / 7, in four-hour shifts, so many of the Praetorians would have been with Paul on a rotating basis. Paul lived in private quarters that were rented, was allowed to have people visit him (Acts 28:30-31), he could write letters, but he had to pay rent and buy food which is why the Philippians sent him money.

Paul would always be chained to the soldier that was guarding him, so he had many opportunities to share the gospel. The chain was about 18 inches long attached to his wrist and the wrist of the soldier guarding him. Over a period of two years many in the Praetorian Guard would have become familiar with the reason behind Paul's imprisonment. Paul would tell the soldiers the Jesus story and the reason for his detainment, and soldiers would talk to each other about the prisoners they were guarding, so it wouldn't be unlikely that Paul was a topic of discussion among the Praetorians. As people visited Paul the soldiers would listen in on Paul's conversations about Jesus, and if Paul was dictating this letter to Timothy they would have listened in on this inspired Scripture as it was written. There were more people that became aware of Paul's circumstances and the Good News, because he adds **and to all the rest.** These people may have been support staff and other high-ranking officials outside of the Praetorian Guard, that were members of Caesar's household.

What became evident to all was **that my chains are in Christ**, so it became known to all that Paul was a prisoner of the Emperor because of his stand for Jesus Christ, and his efforts to spread this insipient Christian faith. To the Romans Caesar is Lord, but to Christians Jesus is Lord! The Philippians were filled with civic pride about their relationship with Rome as a colony, so the fact that they continued to support Paul, as a prisoner of Rome, is a telling statement about them. Their loyalty to Paul and Christ was far greater than to Rome. They placed themselves at risk because in identifying with a prisoner who had appealed to Caesar, this could be viewed as disloyalty to Rome. It was considered shameful for Paul to be a prisoner of Rome and could easily be construed as shameful for the Philippians to support Paul.

There may be a subtle nuance here in that Paul says **my chains are In Christ.** He was a prisoner of the Emperor, but Paul understood that his circumstances were because of his service to Christ (Eph 4:1). The Lord had Paul right where he needed him to be for the sake of the Good News. Paul seems to be walking in the footsteps of Christ's suffering. Later in his letter Paul will make mention of the fact that Jesus calls his disciples to be in fellowship with his sufferings: that I may know him, and the power of his resurrection, and the fellowship of his sufferings (Phil 3:10a). Jesus once said to his disciples: if they persecuted me they will persecute you also (John 15:20). Paul experienced the reality of this throughout his entire ministry, as did the other apostles, hence he says my chains are in Christ.

and that most of the brothers (and sisters) in the Lord, being confident through my chains, are more abundantly bold to speak the word of God without fear. (1:14)

There was another positive result which came from Paul's imprisonment that caused the Good News to advance even more. The Christians at Rome were, no doubt, aware of Paul's circumstances. They knew he appealed to Caesar, that he would stand trial, that he could be executed if he is found guilty, but they were inspired by his bold stand for Christ. He put his life on the line by appealing to Caesar, and he is telling the Jesus story to the soldiers, so **most of the brothers and sisters in the Lord** became bold and aggressive in sharing the Good News. Seeing Paul's example and deep commitment to Christ ignited a holy fire in their hearts, and they became highly motivated preaching the word of God.

They became **confident** which is a translation of the Greek word *peíthō* formed from the root *pístis*, which is the word we translate faith. Therefore, the meaning of this word is to be fully persuaded, convinced, or confident. They are fully convinced, in the Lord, that they must tell the Jesus story and they were able to do so in a fashion that is **more abundantly bold to speak the word of God without fear.** A new confidence appeared in the Roman Christians through Paul's example.

Bold translates *tolmaó* which carries the meaning of being daring, and courageous **to speak the word of God without fear.** The verb "to speak" and "bold" are both written as present infinitives, which means that this was a continuous practice of those telling the Good News about Jesus. They were stirred up and aggressively telling people about Jesus without taking a break. They became fearless in their presentation of the Good News, such that Paul's example has rubbed off on the fellow believers at Rome causing their witness for Jesus to soar to new heights. It appears that God's people in Rome are stirred up, and the Holy Spirit is doing something in them, such that the gospel is moving forward in ways that are even surprising to Paul. However, all was not as it should be regarding the motives of some of the believers who were preaching Jesus.

Some indeed preach Christ even out of envy and strife, and some also out of good will. 16The former insincerely preach Christ from selfish ambition, thinking that they add affliction to my chains; 17but the latter out of love, knowing that I am appointed for the defense of the Good News. (1:15-17)

Some of the people in Rome **preach Christ even out of envy and strife and** were preaching Christ **insincerely from selfish ambition.** There is no indication in the text that these were false teachers who were presenting a corrupted gospel. These were Christians in the church at Rome who were boldly sharing the Good News about Jesus. The gospel they preached was pure, but their motives weren't. They appear to be opportunistic, thinking that with Paul out of commission in prison, this could be their chance to step under the spotlight.

Paul mentions four vices regarding their motives, the first of which is **envy** *(phthonos).* This word describes ill-will toward another person, or displeasure at someone's good or wellbeing. It is being glad when someone experiences misfortune or pain, as if someone takes "a kind of unsavory delight that enjoys kicking an opponent who is down."[20] These preachers may have been envious of Paul's calling, his vision of the risen Christ, his intellectual capabilities, his teaching skills, and more because Paul was a multi-talented individual. Envy appears in the list of the works of the flesh in Galatians 5:21, and in Romans 1:29 envy is listed as a characteristic of the ungodly. Envy and jealously can be powerful factors in guiding human behavior for evil purposes, which appears to be the case here.

The second improper motive Paul mentions is **strife**, which translates the Greek word *éris.* This word denotes a contentious spirit, a spirit of rivalry, or a readiness to argue. Some people love to argue and will go to any length to defeat their opponent. Envy and strife are a sinful combination that seem to complement each other, because when someone is envious of another person he takes more pleasure proving his adversary wrong.

The third improper motive Paul brings to the surface is that they **insincerely preach Christ,** which are the Greek words *ouch hagnōs.* The word *hagns* describes one's motives as being pure, sincere, and honest, but *ouch* negates this. Therefore, these preachers of Jesus were lacking sincerity so their motives in preaching were highly suspect. Their preaching didn't appear to be driven by a need to see people come to know Christ and bring glory to God, rather they were highly motivated to bring attention to themselves, and spite Paul.

The fourth and final improper motive Paul mentions is **selfish ambition**, which translates *eritheía.* This word refers to people who want to get ahead regardless of how their behavior affects other people. The word was used to refer to politicians who were promoting their own agendas and professionals who would ruthlessly try climbing to the top of the ladder without regard for how their actions affected others. Paul mentions that selfish ambition is unfitting for Christians (2:3).

Preaching Christ driven by **envy, strife, insincerity,** and **selfish ambition** sounds terrible. These opportunistic preachers of Christ were certainly trying to bring attention to themselves but were thinking **that they add affliction to**

[20] Fee, p. 120

my chains. With Paul in prison this may have led to many sinful thoughts such as: "Paul's usefulness in spreading the gospel is a thing of the past." "If Paul is executed the church needs new leadership." "It's time for new blood to lead the church." They wanted to rub it in Paul's face and make him miserable. It appears that Paul is being persecuted by these opportunistic preachers. **Affliction** translates *thlípsis,* a word commonly referring to the *tribulation* a believer experiences because of his relationship with Christ, which includes persecution. How ironic it is that Paul is being persecuted by Christians at Rome who are preaching the Good News of Christ. This seems really warped and twisted.

The behavior of the minority must have left Paul with some emotional scars, but he takes the high road. One would think that Paul would have been irritated by them because their actions only made his life more difficult than it already was, but of primary concern to Paul was the gospel. Their hypocrisy and personal attacks on Paul would have stung, but he has a great perspective on their actions. The gospel was advancing through these preachers despite their impure motives. Apparently, people were coming to know Jesus through their preaching, which delighted Paul, so he could deal with having his feelings hurt and being undermined. It doesn't appear that he is taking it personally. He chooses to focus on the positive aspect of this situation and find reason to rejoice in what God is doing.

Most of the preachers appear to have preached the Good News with proper motivation and concern for Paul. These are the ones who preach Christ **out of good will** (v. 15), **out of love, knowing that I am appointed for the defense of the Good News** (v. 17). The ones preaching Christ out of good will were doing so out of the desire to see people come to know Jesus. Their behavior is motived by doing something that will benefit others by hearing the Good News. They also preach out of **love**, which seems to be referring to how they felt about Christ, and the lost souls they were preaching to, but also about Paul. Unlike those who were causing trouble for Paul by inflicting more wounds on him, these preachers appear to love Paul and are deeply concerned for his well-being. They understood why Paul was imprisoned and that he was right where he was supposed to be in God's plan for his life and the Good News.

They understood Paul was appointed by Christ to **defend** the gospel. His time in Rome wasn't a coincidence, an act of fate, bad karma, random chance, or the Roman government, it was by divine appointment that Paul would defend the gospel in Rome. Most of the Roman preachers had an insight as to what God was doing through the apostle Paul and stuck with him in his imprisonment. The majority appear to be supporting Paul while only a small minority were giving him a hard time, but through all this the gospel was moving forward. Talk about an opportunity: Paul would share the Good News with some of the highest-ranking officials in the Roman Empire. God brought him to this place, and who better to defend the gospel than Paul.

What does it matter? Only that in every way, whether in pretense or in truth, Christ is proclaimed. I rejoice in this, yes, and will rejoice. (1:18)

This shows a great deal about Paul's character, the example he is providing to the Philippians, and how he feels about the gospel making progress. **What does it matter?** Despite personal attacks, being undermined by some of his fellow believers in Rome, which only added to his troublesome circumstances, he doesn't appear to be letting them get under his skin. What he chooses to focus on is how the Good News of Jesus is being proclaimed, regardless of the motives of those who are declaring the gospel. **Only that in every way, whether in pretense or in truth, Christ is proclaimed.** The gospel is advancing, even though some of those who are telling the Jesus story have highly questionable motives and are wishing Paul ill-will, the gospel is on the offensive and gaining ground. Thus, Paul can deal with the personal attacks, and keep his focus on the more important issue of the proclamation of Christ.

Those who were preaching **in pretense**, are preaching the gospel as a way of bringing attention to themselves and causing Paul trouble. The gospel they preached wasn't in error, just their motives were corrupt. Christ was being proclaimed accurately, souls were being saved, but we have no way of knowing how many were converted to Christianity through their preaching. The gospel has authority in and of itself. If the Good News is proclaimed accurately, but the preacher is sinful, has a bad attitude, is self-centered and wanting to bring attention to himself, that doesn't negate the authority of the gospel presentation. What these preachers were lacking was honesty, transparency, and the ability to renounce any type of deceptive tactics, secret and shameful ways in setting forth the Good News (2 Cor 4:2; 1 Thess 2:5).

Amazingly, Paul's conclusion is: **I rejoice in this, yes, and will rejoice.** Paul is taking the high road here by choosing not to pitch-a-fit over those who are undermining him. He has given this some thought, processed the situation in his thinking and has arrived at the conclusion that rejoicing in is order. The Good News is being proclaimed and he will continue to rejoice over this in the future. Paul is making an emphatic statement here about choosing to rejoice rather than complain. His mission in life was to see the Good News advance, by whatever means, even by those who gave him a hard time. This is a great example in taking the high road when under fire from people that undermine and disrespect you, but unfortunately are Christians. Paul is not letting these opportunistic preachers destroy his emotional well-being. Hopefully, the Philippians will follow Paul's example in working through some of their issues in their church.

Insights, Applications, and Life Lessons

So much of life is about the attitudes people choose to adopt when adversity strikes. Nobody can control the things that happen to them, but people can choose how they react to the troubling circumstances that come into their lives. Many years ago, Norman Vincent Peal wrote a book titled "The Power of Positive Thinking." It was a best seller and made a significant impression on me. It isn't uncommon to hear people throw around the phrase "positive mental attitude." Coaches use the phrase on their players, teachers use it on their students, CEOs use it on their employees, and so forth. In just about every sector of our society people affirm that it's good to have a "positive mental attitude."

Normal Vincent Peal wasn't the first person to come up with the idea of the power of positive thinking, because Paul was way ahead of him. He epitomized a positive mental attitude, but his positive outlook was centered in the Lord. Many people who don't know Jesus can approach life with positive thinking and display a great attitude, even in adversity. But unlike Christians their positive thinking isn't rooted in Christ, it's rooted in themselves, their own abilities, luck, fate, Karma, and so on. Having the understanding that God's purposes are being worked out, even in dire circumstances enabled Paul to have a positive attitude during his imprisonment. There are times when the best therapy for coping with difficult circumstances is taking our eyes off ourselves, begin looking for what God is doing in the situation, focus on that, and even rejoice in what God is doing. Paul seems to have mastered that, because he doesn't seem to be obsessing on himself, he seems to be focused on what God is doing with laser precision, which enables him to find joy during his adversity, thus providing us with a great example to follow in our own hardships.

Having people around you that have a positive mental attitude can do wonders for you. Their outlook on life can be infectious and influence you to be a positive person. Paul's example rubbed off on some of the Roman Christians such that they started preaching up a storm. On the other hand, being around people who are negative, always seeing things through the lens of doom and gloom can exert a harmful influence on you and drag you down.

Imagine what the Philippians would have thought if Paul began this section of his letter by saying:

> I desire to have you know brothers and sisters, that the things that have happened to me have been devastating to the cause of the Good News. I haven't planted any churches or visited the ones I founded in over four years. I'm sick of being cooped up in this tiny apartment, I'm getting scars on my wrists from the shackles, and some of the Christians are undermining me by saying all kinds of bad things about me. Plus, I might not make it out of here alive. It's not a pretty picture. This isn't how I thought things would turn out for me.

If Paul had said these negative things to the Philippians it could have had a devastating impact on them. Their spiritual father is complaining to them about his situation, he is disappointed in God, he is filled with self-pity and disillusioned with the Christian life. This wouldn't provide the Philippians with very much incentive to keep on making progress in their walk with the Lord Jesus. The fact that Paul is so positive in his difficulties speaks volumes to the Philippians and incentivizes them to do the same. Paul's attitude is infectious and provides the believers with hope and a good example to follow.

Imagine what Timothy and Epaphroditus would have thought if Paul started venting on them. That they were there with Paul was a great source of comfort to him, but what if Paul started saying things like this to them:

> Guys, things haven't turned out the way I thought they would. The mission to the Gentile world is in serious trouble. I haven't planted a church in over four years. It's difficult for me to keep my sanity being cooped up in this tiny place. Some of the Christians are heaping verbal abuse on me and slandering my name. I might not make it out of here alive. This isn't what I signed up for, but I'm glad that you're here with me.

If Paul had spoken to them like that it could have seriously damaged their relationship. Their spiritual leader is disappointed with what God is doing in his life and is filling them with doom and gloom by venting on them, which could have a damaging effect on their walk with Christ. If they had to listen to Paul talk like that every day it could have dragged them down spiritually. How could they stay motivated to fulfill the mission to the Gentiles, when their leader is filled with self-pity and negativity?

Imagine what the Praetorians that were guarding Paul would have thought if he was venting and complaining to them. Paul had a great opportunity to share the gospel with them, but if he cast doom and gloom on them it would have been a big turn off. Imagine Paul saying things like this to the guards:

> I hope my trial comes soon because I'm at the end of my rope. I gave up everything to follow Jesus and I've spent over four years in jail. I miss my freedom and I might be executed. Maybe I shouldn't have appealed to Caesar. Sometimes life isn't fair, and Jesus may require you to make some great sacrifices that will cost you everything. If you become a follower of Christ it will take a big toll on you. Things were much better for me before I become a follower of Christ.

The guards would get sick of listening to this every day. They would probably tell him to shut up and stop whining and complaining. Paul wouldn't make the Christian life sound very appealing to them if he had a constant pity-party. This would have made him a very bad evangelist and a negative example to his colleagues.

Handling Difficult People in Difficult Situations

What were the preachers that were giving Paul a hard time saying to him? Perhaps, some showed up for a visit at his rented quarters and told him to his face that he was finished. Imagine some of the snide, crass remarks the people may have made: "You're washed up Paul, it's time for new leadership." "If God was with you, you wouldn't be under arrest." "Paul, you're a one-night wonder, a flash in the pan, a has-been, it's time for a change." Imagine being on the receiving end of that—how hurtful that would be, and these were Christians from the church at Rome.

There was nothing that Paul could do about what his detractors said, or did, but he could choose how he would respond to them. He could have been fuming with anger, and let them get under his skin, but he didn't go there. He didn't take it personally, and, more amazingly, found cause to rejoice that the gospel was being preached by the same people that were giving him a hard time. He didn't let them get the best of him and steal his joy. This is a great lesson for us to learn from Paul's life. There will be people who give us a hard time, oppose us, say hurtful things to us, and there may be nothing that we can do about it. However, we do have options regarding the way we process those events and respond to the people. Don't let people steal your joy! Paul chose to think about the good things, rather than obsess on the bad.

The fact that Paul displayed a positive mental attitude during his adversity provided a great example to everybody. He was showing all parties concerned that one can rise above their troubling circumstances through faith in Christ. He was a living example to everyone about how to have joy, peace, and contentment despite his troubles. I believe people stood in awe of Paul's joyous outlook on life.

Additionally, if Paul had entertained negative thoughts and went down the path of self-pity and pessimism he would have been a basket case. He would probably have been depressed and begin to question his self-worth and usefulness as a human being. Paul could have greatly deteriorated, and his mental health could have gone down the drain, but that never happened. In fact, Paul was just the opposite, which is what you wouldn't expect from a man who has gone through the degree of hardships that he's been through. It seems Paul is making all the right choices in his thinking by processing things correctly, and drawing the right conclusions, which enables him to stay emotionally and spiritually healthy with the Lord's help.

God's Sovereignty in Suffering

The sovereignty of God must be appreciated in reading through Philippians. It seems like things aren't going very well for the spread of the gospel. The church was in its infancy, small in numbers, persecuted, it needed more leaders, and its master church-planter and leader, the apostle Paul, is incarcerated for over four years facing the possibility of execution. It's a grim picture, in fact, it looks like Satan is going to win this round. However, nothing could be further from the truth.

An important lesson for everyone to learn from this is: don't let dire circumstances minimize your view of what God can do! God is greater than any set of circumstances that people may face. Despite the dismal scenario Paul faced, the gospel is penetrating the heart of the Roman Empire, the Praetorian Guard is hearing the gospel as well as the rest of the support staff and other officials in Caesar's household, and these people are very close to Caesar. The other Christians in Rome were inspired by Paul's example and were boldly preaching Jesus, so there were many good things that God was doing.

If you are presently in an emotional prison and your circumstances seem overwhelming dismal, know this: God can turn things around for you in a heartbeat. He can do the impossible because he isn't limited by your troubling circumstances, so keep trusting him and keep praying.

Being under house arrest Paul had plenty of time on his hands to write his letters that have been cherished by believers for over two millennia. This was a time for Paul to reflect on his theology and further develop his thinking about the church, leadership, and other theological matters. God was using this time in Paul's life to draw him nearer to Christ and deepen his relationship with his Lord (3:10). During his long imprisonment, Paul would have had intense times of prayer, reflection, and learned a deeper level of dependence on God. Therefore, the Lord used this time in the apostle's life to create a deeper level of holiness, a more Christlike character, and brought Paul's sanctification to new heights. It is often during times of adversity that believers grow in their walk with the Lord, even though it may be painful.

The irony of this situation is overwhelming: Paul is under house arrest chained to a Praetorian around the clock, but the Good News is free as a bird. Paul is unable to travel to different cities and plant new churches, but because of the sovereignty of God Paul can witness to the Praetorians, and other high-ranking officials who are very close to the Emperor. They are hearing the Good News about Jesus Christ. The gospel is making progress right into the heart and soul of the Roman Empire. What were the Philippians thinking as they heard this read to them and became aware of how close to Caesar the gospel is advancing? Perhaps they are praising God and praying that the Emperor—Nero would come to know Christ. This was all part of God's plan for Paul's life, and Paul was right where he was supposed to be. It seems as though Paul viewed his two-years in Rome as an opportunity, not a bad situation. That is a positive mental attitude at its best!

Summary

Paul has informed the Philippians about his circumstances regarding how things are going with him. There is no trace of negativity, self-pity, or complaining from Paul, on the contrary, he is amazingly positive in reporting about how things are going. Surprisingly, the gospel is making progress! No churches have been planted by Paul for years, but members of the Praetorian Guard and Caesar's household are hearing the gospel, and it is knocking on the Emperor's door. Because of Paul's imprisonment many believers are inspired by Paul's example, are on fire for Jesus, and are preaching up a storm spreading the gospel. However, some are doing so with motives that are suspect and sinful, even to the point of wishing Paul ill-will, and giving him a hard time.

Others are preaching Christ with pure motives in support of Paul, understanding that God has him right where he's supposed to be to defend the gospel. As long as the gospel is being preached correctly Paul can handle those who oppose him, even the personal attacks and back biting. Because Christ is being proclaimed Paul chooses to rejoice, rather than take it personally. He therefore, demonstrates a great attitude for the Philippians to emulate as they work through difficulties in their congregation, and endure hardship.

In the next section, Paul lets the Philippians know how he is viewing the prospect of life or death. Much can be learned about people when they face grim situations in life, which Paul was surely facing, but death was nothing Paul feared.

CHAPTER FIVE

* * *

"Life or Death"
Philippians 1:19-26

Paul is continuing his *narratio* (1:12-26), where he is giving a brief narrative account of what has happened to him, so he is paving the way for the next section of his letter where he will present his main thesis to the Philippians. Paul is rejoicing over the fact that the Good News of Jesus Christ is spreading throughout the Praetorian Guard. There are now Christians in Caesar's household that Paul may have become friends with. These people might be able to speak on his behalf and influence his release and vindication. For a long time, Paul has lived with the threat of execution hovering over him, but he seems to be coping very well. Life or death, whatever the outcome may be, Paul is OK with either one. This passage of Scripture testifies to the fact that, for the Christian, facing death is something that doesn't need to be feared. Believers go immediately into the presence of Christ upon exiting this world, finding themselves in a far better place from which they came.

Paul looks at both possible outcomes, life or death, and doesn't seem to stress about the possibility of death. If he is executed he wants to make sure that he will do so with boldness, courage, and without shame so that Christ can be magnified. In other words, if Paul is executed he wants it to be a good death that can bring glory to Christ. If he lives, he wants his life to be for the glory of Christ, so either way, life or death, Paul's objective is to glorify the Lord Jesus Christ.

For him personally, if he dies his troubles come to a screeching halt because he will be in joyful heavenly bliss in the presence of Christ. Who wouldn't want that? However, if he is released from prison he can continue his ministry, visit the Philippians, plant more churches and strengthen those already existing, which benefits all his converts. Therefore, it's a win-win situation for Paul. Life means Paul can set forth more fruitful labor to see the gospel advance, and his converts grow in the faith. Death means his hardships are over and he finds himself in the bliss of heaven. Either way Paul wins. Either way God is glorified. Attention is now focused on how the apostle contemplates these two outcomes.

For I know that this will turn out to my deliverance, through your prayers and the supply of the Spirit of Jesus Christ, 20according to my earnest expectation and hope, that I will in no way be disappointed, but with all boldness, as always, now also Christ will be magnified in my body, whether by life, or by death. 21For to me to live is Christ, and to die is gain. 22But if I live on in the flesh, this will bring fruit from my work; yet I don't know what I will choose. 23But I am in a dilemma between the two, having the desire to depart and be with Christ, which is far better. 24Yet, to remain in the flesh is more needful for your sake. 25Having this confidence, I know that I will remain, yes, and remain with you all, for your progress and joy in the faith, 26that your rejoicing may abound in Christ Jesus in me through my presence with you again. (Author's Translation, 1:19-26)

For I know refers to the previous section where Paul stated he chooses to rejoice over the spreading of the gospel (v. 18). He is now going to cite his reasons why he will continue to rejoice. **For I know that this will turn out to my deliverance** begs the question what does Paul mean by **this**? Most likely Paul is referring to his present state of affairs, which includes everything that has happened to him: being unjustly incarcerated, his suffering, and being undermined by some of the Roman preachers, etc. He seems convinced that he will be delivered from his present circumstances, vindicated, and set free at his trial. Paul appears to be quoting Job 13:16 from the Septuagint (the Greek translation of the Hebrew Bible): "This also will be my salvation." Job is conversing with his friend Zophar when he says this. He understood that the enormity of his suffering wasn't due to God's punishment on him for some horrendous sin in his life, as his friends were asserting. Job believed he would be delivered from his suffering as well as the false accusations from his believing friends. Paul saw a similarity between his circumstances and Job's, and like Job, he felt he would be delivered and continue with his life.

Several years ago, in AD 57, Paul wrote to the Romans informing them of a glorious truth: We know that all things work together for good for those who love God, to those who are called according to his purpose (Rom 8:28). Paul's life seems to be a commentary on this verse. His conscience is clear because he knew God wasn't punishing him for gross disobedience. He knew that his current suffering would "work together for good," because the Good News would continue to advance, and he would be delivered from prison. It appears Paul is convinced that he will be released and continue serving Christ.

The Greek word translated **deliverance** is *sótéria*, which can also be translated: salvation, preservation, safety, or welfare. Was Paul just thinking that he would be delivered from his present circumstances, or was he also thinking about his final vindication (salvation) when he stands before Christ at the end of the age? The context would indicate that Paul was thinking about being delivered from his present circumstances and set free to continue his ministry. The Philippians sent Epaphroditus with money for Paul, with the hope that he would be released and continue his apostolic work. This seems to be the emphasis of their prayers, not for Paul to endure in the faith until death.

Gordon Fee sees both ideas in Paul's thought and paraphrases his idea in the following way: "This whole affair will turn out to my ultimate salvation and present vindication, when, through your prayers and the supply of the Spirit of Christ my earnest expectation and hope are realized at my trial and not only am I not brought to shame but in a very open (or bold) way Christ is magnified in every way—whether I am given life or sentenced to death."[21]

The Philippians have been praying for Paul's vindication at his trial so he can be released, not for his final vindication before God at the end of the age. At least, it would seem unlikely that they would be praying in this way, which

---

[21] Fee, p. 132

leads me to believe that Paul is thinking about his deliverance from prison, not about his vindication at the end of the age before God. The context of the passage isn't about Paul's personal salvation, it's about the advancement of the gospel and his impending trial.

One way in which the Philippians are partners with Paul in the Good News is that they were actively praying for the apostle, which he would have taken great comfort in. Paul connects the Philippians' prayers with **the supply of the Spirit of Jesus Christ.** The word **supply** is a translation of the Greek *epichorégia,* which includes the meanings: provision, support, or bountiful supply. Therefore, Paul views the Spirit as an endless power source for the Christian life. The believer receives the Spirit at the moment of his conversion, which isn't what Paul is talking about here. Rather, Paul is talking about the constant power the Spirit provides the believer in life to glorify God. Believers have unlimited resources that the Holy Spirit can supply them with in any set of circumstances. If he is released or executed, the Holy Spirit will be there for Paul and supply him with whatever he needs to glorify Christ. If he is released the Holy Spirit will empower him for more fruitful ministry. If he is executed the Holy Spirit will empower him to be courageous as he upholds his bold testimony about his faith in Jesus, such that his death glorifies the Lord.

There are two options, according to the Greek, that need to be sorted through in gaining a proper understanding of this verse. The first option is: Christ supplies the Spirit in Paul's time of need to help him. The second option is: The Spirit supplies Paul with resources when he needs assistance? This translation means that the Spirit is available to help Paul with whatever he needs to glorify God. It is very difficult to separate both ideas as Osborne says: "There is a question as to whether the emphasis is on the Spirit being supplied by Christ to Paul or on the Spirit supplying help to Paul. I prefer to see both aspects here. The prayers of the saints led to Christ supplying the Spirit to aid Paul and produced God's will in the situation. Notice the Trinitarian thrust: The Father's will is produced by Christ sending the Spirit in answer to the petitions of God's people. The title "Spirit of Jesus Christ" means that the Spirit mediates the presence of Christ to us. The Spirit's intercession in our needs constitutes Christ's living presence." [22]

It is hard to separate the two options, which is why Osborne's assessment has merit. The Spirit and the Lord Jesus are so closely linked together that they are working in cooperation with each other. The Spirit is identified as the **Spirit of Jesus Christ.** The Holy Spirit is the agent that manifests Christ in the life of a believer. Paul identifies the Spirit with Jesus in 2 Corinthians 3:17: "Now the Lord is the Spirit and where the Spirit of the Lord is, there is liberty." He also identifies the Holy Spirit as the Spirit of Christ (Rom 8:9-10; 1 Pet 1:11). The Spirit and Jesus are two persons; however, they are closely linked together in the work of the Trinity, along with the Father.

Why would Paul add the qualifier Spirit **of Jesus Christ** and not just say Holy Spirit? The emphasis on this passage is Christ and the advancement of the gospel. It is Christ, living in Paul by the Spirit, who will be magnified in his life—whether by life or death. It is Christ who will be glorified through the advancement of the gospel. It is Christ who will be magnified by Paul not being brought to shame (v. 20). Hence, Paul chooses this terminology. Paul links together the Philippians' prayers to the Spirit's presence in his confinement, which testifies to the power of prayer. As the Philippians prayed for Paul the Spirit's presence in his life seems to be amplified.

It is amazing to consider that Paul didn't regard his spiritual wellbeing as independent of other believers. "His perseverance does not take place automatically but rather through (1) the prayers of the Philippians and (2) the support provided by Jesus' Spirit. The point to note here, however, is that even Paul's personal growth—his sanctification—does not take place in isolation from the support of the church. It is indeed a sobering thought that our spiritual relationship with God is not a purely individualistic concern; we are dependent on the Spirit's power in answer to the intercessory prayers of God's people. And we may add that the Spirit's help itself is normally manifested through the koinonia of fellow-believers."[23]

---

[22] Osborne, Loc. 877

[23] Silva, p. 72

One can see why Paul considered the Philippians partners with him in the Good News. He understood that their prayers were crucial to his spiritual life, wellbeing, and the forward movement of the gospel. Believers should cherish the prayers of God's people in difficult times, because they are powerful and effective.

according to my earnest expectation and hope, that I will in no way be disappointed, but with all boldness, as always, now also Christ will be magnified in my body, whether by life, or by death. [21]For to me to live is Christ, and to die is gain. (1:20-21)

Paul is continuing to state his optimistic view of his future deliverance. Not only does he have the Philippians praying for him and the supply of the Holy Spirit to aid him in his time of need, but Paul is optimistic about his release from prison: **according to my earnest expectation and hope.** The Greek word translated **earnest expectation** is *apokaradokía*, which is only found here and Romans 8:19. It is a compound word consisting of three Greek words: *apó* (away from), *kara* (the head), and *dokéō* (to think). Literally it means: forward thinking, out-stretched head, or an eager intense expectation. In Romans 8:19 the word refers to believer's "earnest expectation" to receive their glorified body at Christ's return. This is a colorful and intense word that denotes a determined focus and firm conviction such that one "stretches his head forward" in anticipation. He couples his **earnest expectation and hope** together, thus making the words virtually synonymous.

Hope *(elpís)* is not wishful thinking that something might happen, it is a firm conviction that all of God's promises will come to pass, which enables the believer to face the future with certainty that everything will work out just as God says it will in his word. This is the basis for the Christian's positive outlook on life, for there is a glorious future in store for the people of God. What Paul is expecting and hoping for is **that I will in no way be disappointed.** He is thinking about the moment of truth when he stands before the Roman Tribunal and defends the gospel stating his loyalty to Christ. It is a life or death situation and Paul wants to set forth his testimony for the Lord Jesus **with all boldness**—speaking openly, frankly, and honestly for all to hear, but free of shame.

At his hearing, he will tell the authorities how he met Jesus on the road to Damascus, that he saw the risen glorified Christ, and was appointed by him to spread the Good News to Gentiles. Those who hear his story may think he is crazy and berate him. The world may laugh and mock believers, which can bring them shame and embarrassment, but Paul is hopeful that he will testify for Christ with boldness and bravery, while enduring the shame just as Jesus did. In fact, Paul would see bearing public humiliation and shame on Christ's behalf as a badge of honor. Most importantly Paul wants to represent Jesus well!

Paul stated that he isn't ashamed of the gospel (Rom 1:16), and he encouraged Timothy not to be ashamed to testify for Christ or be ashamed of his imprisonment (2 Tim 1:8). The point is when one identifies with the cross there will be a social stigma that appears. The world is hostile to those who identify with Christ, and may heap abuse on them, mock them, assault them, and even kill them. Under this kind of pressure, the temptation may be to shy away from a brave testimony on Christ's behalf and cave in, denying the faith. When someone identifies with Christ it goes with the territory, insults from the world will come, and humiliation from the world must be accepted, just as Christ accepted the shame and humiliation of the facing the cross (Phil 2:8; Heb 12:2).

Paul's thoughts about the moment of truth at the Tribunal are: **as always, now also Christ will be magnified in my body, whether by life, or by death. [21]For to me to live is Christ, and to die is gain.**

Paul's whole purpose in life was for the glory of Christ. Whether Christ is magnified by Paul's release from prison (life) or through his execution, as long as Christ is magnified through Paul the goal is accomplished. He is confident that he will be released, but there are times when Paul seems to be conflicted about the outcome (1:25; 2:24).

For Paul **to live is Christ.** This means that if he is released from prison he will go on serving Christ as the apostle to the Gentiles, furthering the spread of the Good News, and planting more churches. He will continue to sow into people's lives, such as the Philippians and others. For Paul, life is all about being surrendered to the will of God and serving Jesus, but what is his view of being executed? There can be no greater expression of courage that a believer can make in facing death than that which Paul writes here: **to die is gain.** If he is executed he will experience Jesus in a fuller, unrestricted way than he does in the body. In other words, if he dies he will experience the eternality of eternal life.[24]

It's a win-win situation for Paul, for if he continues in the body he will have a close relationship with Christ as he serves him, but if he dies, he will have a closer relationship with Christ in heaven. Additionally, if Paul is executed his suffering is terminated, no more hardships, beatings, attacks from Satan, or other things to worry about because he will be basking in heaven with Jesus in total peace. Therefore, to Paul death is gain, which is an accounting term also used in 3:7. Following the accounting metaphor, this is Paul's way of saying: death is the ultimate way to be in the black, not the red.

Paul's concern is that in the worst-case scenario, if he is executed he will have the courage to glorify Christ. "His comments are part of a personal reflection in which he expresses the wish that he not do anything to disgrace his Lord or shame his Christian faith if things go badly for him at his trial. He is well aware of human frailty in general, not least his own, and he wants Christ glorified whether he lives or dies. He does not want human weakness to cause him to shrink back from making the good confession."[25]

But if I live on in the flesh, this will bring fruit from my work; yet I don't know what I will choose. [23]But I am in a dilemma between the two, having the desire to depart and be with Christ, which is far better. (1:22-23)

Reading this may cause one to conclude Paul is thinking out loud and letting his readers hear him do so. He appears to be having an internal dialogue or debate with himself about his situation. He's contemplating life or death and concludes: **But if I live on in the flesh, this will bring fruit from my work; yet I don't know what I will choose.** If he is released and continues with his ministry, it will mean that his efforts will bear fruit in the lives of those with whom he interacts. He will continue to encourage people in the faith through

---

[24] Comfort, p. 163

[25] Witherington, Loc. 1425

teaching and writing, building up leaders so the gospel can continue to spread from one generation to another, as well as planting more churches, and of course, visiting the Philippians.

Paul is not in a position to choose between life and death for this is God's choice not Paul's, but he's seems to be thinking out loud: **yet I don't know what I will choose. [23]But I am in a dilemma between the two, having the desire to depart and be with Christ, which is far better.** God's will is going to be done in Paul's life, but if he has a choice in the matter and can choose the outcome, he would rather depart and be with Christ. He considers this the better option for him personally. In fact, he seems to be in a conundrum over his circumstances, it is a dilemma in which he is torn between the two possible outcomes.

Depart is a form of the word *analuó* which means to unloose or untie. The usage of the word was applied to untying a boat from its moorings, of a prisoner being freed from his chains, or an army breaking camp. It became a euphemism for death, so that for the Christian death is like being untied or breaking their earthly temporary camp, so they can journey to their heavenly permanent camp. Near the end of Paul's life, he knew death was just around the corner for him and wrote of his departure (*analusis*) to Timothy in his last letter (2 Tim 4:6).

At death Paul knew he would **be with Christ, which is far better.** For the apostle this was a no-brainer! Paul wasn't trying to write a detailed analysis of life after death for his readers, all he's pointing out is that at death the Christian goes immediately into the presence of the Lord Jesus. Exactly what that is like is somewhat of a mystery. The most commonly held understanding is that at death the believer is in the disembodied state in Jesus' presence (2 Cor 5:1-5), for he hasn't yet received his resurrection body, which occurs at the return of Christ (1 Thess 4:13f). Precisely what the disembodied or immaterial state is like is beyond human knowledge, but it really doesn't matter because Paul is simply pointing out that death is his preferable option, because that will usher him into the presence of Jesus, which is much better than continuing in the flesh. This knowledge enables believers to face death without fear and view it as better than physical life, because death is the termination of all pain and suffering that opens the door to unrivaled elation.

Yet, to remain in the flesh is more needful for your sake. [25]Having this confidence, I know that I will remain, yes, and remain with you all, for your progress and joy in the faith, [26]that your rejoicing may abound in Christ Jesus in me through my presence with you again. (1:24-26)

Paul's dilemma seems to be giving way to a sense of confidence that he will continue in the flesh. The reason is that he knows his release benefits the Philippians. It wasn't all about Paul's personal convenience, it was about what was in the best interest of the advancement of the gospel and those to whom Paul was already ministering too. The Philippians needed Paul, as their teacher and one who could greatly assist them in their spiritual development, which is why Paul says: **Yet, to remain in the flesh is more needful for your sake.** For this reason, Paul could put up with the suffering, the persecution, the offenses, and all the abuse that Satan and the world could hurl at him. The Philippians would benefit from Paul continuing in this life, but there would be a personal cost to Paul, which he is willing to pay.

It must be understood that Paul is employing a deliberative rhetoric here for the Philippians. He's persuading them to consider his train of thought and will develop his rhetoric further in 2:4 where he says: Each of you should look not only to your own interests, but also to the interests of others. This is what Paul is doing with the Philippians: his death is personal gain, but his living in the body is for the benefit of the Philippians, thus Paul is considering them more important than himself.

He is no longer ambivalent or seemingly conflicted for he says in v. 25: **Having this confidence, I know that I will remain, yes, and remain with you all, for your progress and joy in the faith.** He is now filled with confidence that he will be released and continue with his ministry. He is confident that God's calling on his life to advance the Good News is not about to end, because he will remain on the earth. In vv. 24-25 the word *ménō*, translated **remain**, appears three times in various forms. In v. 24 it is *epiménō*, written as a present infinitive which denotes on going action without end. The preposition *epi* means *on or upon* which intensifies *ménō.* Therefore, the word means to "remain with persistence." This is followed in v. 25 by *ménō,* (remain) then *paraménō,* which means: remain alongside or remain close beside. This is written in the future tense, which means vv. 24-25 paint a picture of Paul being fully persuaded that he will continue to live in the body (remain) and one day in the *future* will be alongside the Philippians again. The analysis of the above Greek words reveal that Paul has no doubt in his mind that he will be released. He states with crystal clarity and deep conviction that he believes he will remain and visit with the Philippians again, which seems to have happened (1 Tim 1:3).

Paul is unselfish and is willing to continue to put up with the suffering he became so familiar with as the apostle to the Gentiles: **for your progress and joy in the faith.** The word **progress** is *prokopé,* which is the same word used in v. 12 where Paul said that his circumstances have contributed to the **progress** of the gospel. Thus v. 12 and v. 25 are an inclusio, like bookends with the content in the middle. Paul knows if he is released from prison the Philippians will advance in the gospel by growing in **joy**, which is a major theme in this letter. That Paul mentions joy shouldn't surprise us because he sees them walking in his footsteps, in that they are going through the same sufferings that he is (1:30), so why shouldn't they experience the same level of joy that he is. This letter establishes a link between suffering and the experience of joy in the believer's life. In this context **faith** means the content of what is believed; namely the gospel and all it entails.

Paul sees his work as being incomplete because the Philippians need him to continue their growth in the Christian faith. There is a touch of irony here in that Christ demonstrated the ultimate self-sacrifice by dying on the cross, while Paul shows his self-sacrificial attitude by continuing to live and assist the Philippians in their spiritual development. This is an indirect allusion to Paul's close identification with Christ in the fellowship of his sufferings (3:10). Paul emphatically states that he will remain, which makes his confidence clear and unequivocal—there is no ambiguity in Paul's thinking.

that your rejoicing may abound in Christ Jesus in me through my presence with you again. (1:26)

Paul is thinking about the Philippians' celebration when he returns to see them. They will praise the Lord Jesus for Paul's release and bringing him back to them. Their praise will be over what Christ has done through Paul. The New Living Translation brings this point out clearly: "And when I come to you again, you will have even more reason to take pride in Christ Jesus because of what he is doing through me."

No doubt, the Philippians would be proud of Paul for staying the course, demonstrating his unshakable faith, and impeccable integrity throughout his ordeal, but their primary area of boasting is in Jesus Christ for working through Paul the way he did. There is nothing wrong with a church taking pride in their pastor / apostle and holding him in high regard, but ultimately the boasting must be directed at Christ for working in the pastor the way he has. Paul doesn't want to receive praise from the Philippians at the expense of them not boasting in Christ. This is Paul's way of being humble.

As word of Paul's release spreads to the other churches and they become fully aware of everything he's gone through, he would have celebrity status. As people contemplate what he's endured for the cause of Christ they would be amazed at him. That he was delivered from the Lion's mouth (Rome) would cause people to want to hear his story. If this occurred in the modern world Paul could write a book, go on a lecture tour, would appear on numerous talk shows, and more. He didn't need those kinds of accolades because his concern was for the spread of the Good News, the glory of Christ, and having everybody boast in Christ for what he accomplished in his life.

Insights, Applications, and Life Lessons

Paul was convinced that the prayers of the Philippians, and others, were having a deep impact on his life. In his thinking he was connecting their prayers to the powerful presence of the Holy Spirit in his life, such that he felt their prayers would influence the outcome of his trial favorably for him. With the Spirit's help he would be empowered to courageously represent Christ and be released. The power of prayer goes beyond our wildest imagination, which is why believers should be praying for each other regularly. One of the basic elements of church-life is that church is a house of prayer (Mat 21:13). Paul felt their prayers were boosting the Spirit's presence in his life.

Years ago, I had a missionary couple that served in Beirut, Lebanon, visit our church when they were home on furlough. I don't remember his name, but he taught at the university in Beirut during a time of upheaval and political unrest in Lebanon and war broke out. He shared that on one occasion things got dicey and artillery shells were exploding all around them. Buildings close by were being hit and he was yelling at his family to take cover. His wife was sitting calmly on the floor saying, "I just know people back home are praying for us." "I just know we're being prayed for." She had a sense of calm that defied description, which was attributed to the powerful presence of the Holy Spirit. She took great comfort in knowing that she and her family were being prayed for. They survived the artillery bombardment without injury.

The Christian community is by Biblical design an interconnected body where all the members are dependent on each other. One of the basic elementary functions of the church is to be a praying community, where we pray for each other's spiritual development and whatever pressing needs may arise in people's lives. Prayer is not powerless! We all need to have people praying for us, as we pray for others because God's power is potentiated in our life through prayer.

Life and Death

Paul has given believers a glimpse into life on the other side—heaven. His words have provided encouragement that enables God's people to face the inevitability of death with courage. Our culture seems to be in denial of death, but Paul welcomed it. Face lifts, tummy tucks, liposuction, paleo diets, and those 25-minute workouts that will burn fat, help prolong life and people live in a quasi-denial about aging and the inevitability of death. In the First Century death was more visible and in-your-face than today. Life expectancy was much lower, and it wasn't uncommon for a child in your family to die in the home. Today people die in hospitals, or senior care facilities, then go to the funeral home to be prepped for the memorial service. Even in warfare through modern technology warriors man their computer, take their joy-stick then launch a hellfire missile from a drone taking out the enemy somewhere in the Middle East. Then at the completion of their shift they go to their suburban home, have a nice dinner and enjoy a relaxing evening with their family. Death has become impersonal—like playing a video game. In the First

Century Roman world death was highly visible, it was common to see people crucified, which wasn't a pleasant sight to see.

Paul wasn't in denial of death, nor did he fear it. He approached life with gusto because he loved to serve Christ and plant churches, but he approached death with even more enthusiasm because through death he would experience a closer relationship with Christ. Death is an inevitable fact of life but the Christian can face death with courage because that means the end of all suffering and toil as he goes directly into the presence of Jesus.

A Prayer Request I Struggled With

I got a phone call from Jane, who attended my church, and she was emotional and very distraught. She told me about her sick mother who was hospitalized and informed me of her many complications—it was a long list and the prognosis wasn't very good. Jane asked if I would pray for God to heal her and raise her up. She had called the prayer chain, so people were already praying for her mother. I asked her how old her mom was to which she replied, "92 years old." I paused for a moment, thinking that this could be the time that God is bringing her home. She was a Christian who had lived a long fruitful life, so this could be the end of her sorrows.

I told Jane I would be happy to pray for her mother's recovery, but I gently asked her if she had considered that at age 92, with all her complications, that this might just be her moment to meet Jesus face-to-face. That would be a great moment for her.

When people are faced with losing a loved one, they often don't want to let go. Because of their love for the person they don't want to lose them, but what is in the best interest of the one who is knocking at death's door? She has lived to a ripe old age, had a full life, and walked with the Lord for decades. Death is inevitable for all people barring none. If God grants one of his people a long life and they are dying of natural causes, it's hard to let them go, but they are going to a better place. The sick person is ready to meet her Maker, but those who love her must understand that God has control over life and death, and if he calls her home, it is a great moment for her. Her survivors live on, knowing that she is in heaven, so they can be comforted with that fact as they mourn. We do not grieve as those who have no hope (1 Thess 4:13).

Paul Wasn't an Escapist

Paul had the threat of execution hanging over his head for two years and had plenty of time to think it over. He clearly understood that death was the better option for him personally as opposed to continuing in the body and doing more ministry. However, Paul wasn't an *escapist*. Paul wasn't letting go of his responsibilities and saying, "I've had enough take me home Jesus." "I don't care about the work that needs to be done in spreading the gospel—I've had enough, I'm history."

We've all had those seasons in life where things were dark and dreary, and we were in a very bad place emotionally. A traumatic event such as a divorce, a failed business, depression, death of a loved one, loss of a job, etc. may have put us in a place where we start praying or hoping for our death because we are emotionally spent. We begin to reason that death will bring us to a better place. That would be an escapist approach to the trials we face, which Paul did not maintain. Although Paul knew the better option for him personally was death, for the sake of the other people in Paul's life he needed to continue living. He knew there would be a significant cost of pain and suffering by continuing in the flesh. One only needs to read 2 Corinthians 11:23-33 to understand how much Paul suffered in his ministry for Jesus, but he was willing to do so for the sake of Christ, the Good News, and all the people in his life. He was totally unselfish in this regard as he tells the Philippians that for their sake he will continue living. He was willing to consider the ministry and the Philippians more important than himself, so he provides a great example for them to follow.

One woman I knew, that was married and had two small children, told me she suffered from severe depression. She shared with me that she had contemplated suicide more than once because her depression was extreme, and she desired to be in a place where there was no more pain and sorrow. She said that would never happen because her kids and husband give her incentive to press on with life. She was fully aware of how devastating to her family, friends, and others it would be if she suddenly departed from this world, so she endures. She realized escapism isn't the answer to her struggles. Her strength to endure was thinking about the important people in her life that are depending on her and drawing strength from the Lord to press on.

The Trial of the Century

Can you put yourself in Paul's shoes and imagine how he felt? For two years he's in Rome waiting for his trial, the outcome of which is life or death. I remember watching the trial of the century featuring OJ Simpson and his dream team of lawyers on TV every night. The case went on-and-on and was plastered on the TV, papers, radio, etc. The country was obsessed with the trial. It was like a reality TV show, no, it was better than reality TV. I remember exactly where I was when I heard the verdict over the radio. The people I was with were on the edge of their seats when the verdict was stated, and afterwards the discussion went on-and-on. What a nail-biter!

Perhaps, the Philippians were on the edge of their seats waiting to hear some news about Paul's trial. There were some big legal proceedings in the early church. The trial of Jesus would have made for great drama on all the major networks, because it was filled with more illegalities than it was legal. Imagine the commentators on CNN, and FOX NEWS having a field day on that one. However, Jesus' trial was quick, it didn't take long for him to go down. Paul's, on the other hand, took two years. His coworkers, the Philippians, and others who knew about his situation must have been constantly wondering what was going on. They were hoping to run into somebody who had some news about him and his trial. In the Gentile world, the trial of the First Century for Christianity was Paul verses the Roman Empire. Paul didn't have a dream team of lawyers like OJ Simpson did, he just had his faith in Christ, and things did turn out favorably for him because he was released. If his trial took place in today's world it would have made for great theater and would have been covered on every major network.

In thinking about the freedom Americans enjoy worshipping free of interference from the government, Christian should be grateful. A debt of gratitude should be extended to Paul, and others like him who have suffered to advance the gospel throughout the millennia. However, Paul wanted the

Philippians to praise the Lord Jesus for what he did through him. He didn't want the praise to be directed at him, but at Jesus. This is another example of Paul's humility and impeccable character. Modern-day believers owe Paul a debt of gratitude.

Summary

Missionaries have an obligation to stay in touch with the churches and people that support their ministry through prayer and financial backing. People want to know how their missionaries are doing, and how God is working through them. Most missionaries today send out monthly newsletters through email to keep their backers informed about the progress of their ministry. This is what Paul has done is vv. 12-26. He has reported to the Philippians about the status of his ministry. The bleak circumstances that Paul found himself in opened a door for a tremendous opportunity to defend the gospel before the Roman Tribunal. The Good News is spreading throughout the Praetorian Guard, so the Philippians can be assured that God is working through Paul in a mighty way, despite his imprisonment. His ministry is still alive and well, although it looks much different than they and he expected.

Most likely they realized the great opportunity that is presented to Paul and they are ramping up their prayers for the apostle. He knew that their prayers were connected to the powerful presence of the Holy Spirit in his life, enabling him to endure his difficult circumstances. Paul has given them a glimpse into his dynamic faith and attentional focus on Christ by informing them that whether he lives or dies it's all good, because either way he experiences Jesus. In life, he will be close to him, but in death he will be even closer to Jesus, so it's a win-win situation for Paul. He feels that he will be delivered from his imprisonment, continue with his ministry and visit the Philippians, which will mean more fruitful labor for him, but he is willing to do this for the sake of Christ and the people he died for. This is a demonstration of his unselfishness and how he puts others before himself.

In the next section, Paul will focus his attention entirely on the Philippians and encourage them to live in a God-honoring way during their trials and persecution.

CHAPTER SIX

* * *

"Living the Worthy Life" Philippians 1:27-30

Paul has completed reporting on his situation, so now he diverts his attention to the Philippians circumstances. The primary exhortation Paul gives the Philippians is to *live as citizens of heaven, conducting yourselves in a manner that is worthy of the Good News of Christ* (1:27). This is the key to much of the letter regarding things on their end. Paul will tell them how they can live in a way that is worthy of the Good News in what follows. In ancient letter writing this section is known as the *propositio*, where the author presents his thesis statement, or the main proposition that will be supported by the arguments which follow. No doubt Epaphroditus gave Paul a status report on the Philippian church which informed his writing.

He is calling for them to tighten things up in their walk with the Lord Jesus because they are facing adversity from their culture, which may be ramping up. Additionally, he appeals to their internal struggles calling for solidarity and unity in the fellowship. He also addresses the fact that believers are called to suffer for Christ, which is not just unique to Paul, it involves the Philippians as well because it is a normative part of the Christian life. This may be a hard pill to swallow, but it is what it is. Their challenges aren't that much different than Paul's (v. 30). They don't have their act together, so Paul exhorts them in this paragraph to consider their lifestyle, addressing their circumstances head on. He will follow this section of his letter by providing numerous examples of how they can put the *propositio* into practice including: the example of Christ (2:1-11), instructions on sanctification (2:12-16), the examples of Paul (2:17-18), Timothy (2:19-23), and lastly Epaphroditus (2:25-30).

Only live as citizens of heaven, conducting yourselves in a manner that is worthy of the Good News of Christ, that, whether I come and see you or am absent, I may hear that you stand firm in one Spirit, with one soul contending together for the faith of the Good News; [28]and in nothing being frightened by your adversaries, which is for them a proof of their destruction, but to you of salvation, and that from God. [29]Because it has been granted to you on behalf of Christ, not only to believe in him, but also to suffer for him, [30]having the same struggle which you saw in me, and now hear is in me. (Author's Translation, 1:27-30)

Paul is calling for the Philippians to live a wholesome life as disciples of Christ: **Only live as citizens of heaven**. Verse 27 presents a challenge in translating the Greek word *politeuomai,* which is literally "to live as a citizen." It is the word from which we get our English word politics and political. A form of the same word is used in 3:20 where Paul says: "our *citizenship* is in heaven." Some of the best-known translations of the Bible such as the New International Version, and the English Standard Version omit the concept of citizenship in their translations of *politeuomai*:

NIV: Whatever happens, conduct yourselves in a manner worthy of the gospel of Christ...

ESV: Only let your manner of life be worthy of the gospel of Christ...

This is unfortunate because the above translations miss a critical nuance of the word, and a key concept in the entire Philippian letter. Usually when Paul exhorts people in their conduct he uses the common Jewish metaphor of walking.[26] Believers today will talk about their "walk with the Lord" so it is common even in today's theological lingo. However, that isn't what Paul says here. It is critical to understand that Paul is making a deliberate contrast

[26] See: Gal 5:16; 1 Thess 2:12; 4:12; Rom 13:13; Phil 3:17

between their dual citizenship in the Roman Empire and Christ's Heavenly Empire, which is also true of 3:20. To miss this in the translation seems to obscure Paul's intended meaning. For these reasons, the New Living Translation and the Christian Standard Bible are the preferred translations:

NLT: Above all, you must live as citizens of heaven, conducting yourselves in a manner worthy of the Good News about Christ.

CSB: Just one thing: As citizens of heaven, live your life worthy of the gospel of Christ.

Although the word *heaven* isn't in the original Greek, it is obvious that Paul is referring to their conduct as citizens of heaven. The word *politeuomai* is written as a command in Greek and everything that follows it is descriptive of what it means to live the worthy life as a citizen of heaven. This is the key concept in the *propositio*—the thesis statement of Paul's exhortation to the Philippians.

The concept of citizenship for the Philippians was of extreme importance. They were a Roman colony in Macedonia, so many of them enjoyed the status of citizenship which afforded them special privileges such as: being exempt from certain taxes, protection under Roman law, property rights, and more. What were the characteristics of a good citizen of Rome? In the First Century Roman Empire a citizen never did anything to dishonor the state or the Emperor. They were very community conscience and were willingly subordinate to the state to serve its interests. It was understood that a person's gifts, talents, and skills were used for the benefit of society at large.

A good citizen of Rome would never do anything to bring shame and disrepute on the state, rather his actions would always be in support of Rome. It was considered shameful to disrespect the state or the Emperor. In a shame and honor-based society one always conducted himself as an honorable citizen of Rome by giving their unqualified allegiance to the Empire. They were proud of their citizenship which was reflected in their sense of civic pride, responsibility, and loyalty. Rome was the dominant power of the day—they were lightyears ahead of everyone else militarily and technologically. Roman citizens had a great sense of pride in their citizenship. Philippi, as a Roman colony, was a "little Rome."

The Philippian believers in Christ, would transfer the values of Roman citizenship, to their heavenly citizenship. Therefore, they had the same sense of honor, civic duty, and pride in their heavenly citizenship as they did with their Roman citizenship. They wouldn't do anything to dishonor their heavenly Emperor and bring shame upon themselves or their church. They would be fiercely loyal to Christ, just as they were extremely loyal to Caesar.

The Philippians' dual citizenship may have brought them in conflict with Emperor worship, which was beginning to spread throughout the Empire, but wasn't fully developed until Domitian's reign (AD 81-96). Romans are to give their allegiance to Caesar, while Christians are to give their loyalty to Jesus. This creates a problem for the Philippians. The fact that they supported Paul as a prisoner of the state, could have very easily been considered a shameful thing to do and called into question their loyalty to Rome. That Paul was detained as a prisoner of Rome was shameful, such that citizens of Rome would want to distance themselves from him, so they wouldn't bring shame upon themselves. Their loyalties to Jesus had to be greater than their loyalties to Rome and the Emperor, so the Philippians lived with a degree of tension as dual citizens.

They do need to obey the laws of the land so long as they don't conflict with obedience to the gospel (Rom 13). Their dual citizenship should instill in them a missionary mindset because their identity with Rome is only temporal, while their identity with Christ as citizens of heaven is eternal. God's people are referred to as *strangers* and *aliens* in the world, which means they are just passing through in route to their eternal home.[27] The world in which they live is passing away and coming to its finality (1 Cor 7:31; 1 John 2:17). "Paul's vision is world-transforming rather than world-negating. Only the present form of this world is passing away. He insists that resurrection and a new life on earth are coming, so even in the earthly sphere it makes best sense to focus on one's Christian citizenship."[28]

---

[27] See: Eph 2:19; Heb 11:13; 1 Pet 1:17; 2:11

[28] Witherington, Loc. 1637

Christians are of a different realm, so their primary loyalty should be to the Lord Jesus Christ not Lord Caesar. For instance, Paul says obey the governing authorities by paying taxes, respecting those in authority, and being law-abiding citizens (Rom 13). Jesus said, "Give to Caesar what is Caesar's, and to God what is God's" (Mat 22:21). He was affirming the need to recognize the governing authorities and be law abiding people. However, when citizenship of Rome pressured one to compromise their allegiance to Christ and the gospel, they must dig in and hold their ground, as they take their stand for Christ. Compromise isn't an option.

Paul never viewed Roman citizenship in a bad way, he just wants the Philippians to understand their focus should be on their heavenly citizenship because it is eternal, while their Roman Citizenship is temporary. He asserted his rights as a citizenship of Rome when he was unlawfully beaten during his trip to Philippi (Acts 16:37), and in Jerusalem when he was about to be flogged he pointed out to the Roman centurion that it's unlawful to flog a Roman citizen who hasn't even been found guilty (Acts 22:25).

Christians, in all eras of history, must live as good citizens of their state, but not compromise their stand for Christ—it's better to obey God then men (Acts 5:29). The spiritual landscape of the Roman Empire was polytheistic, meaning there were many gods and lords that were worshiped in Greco-Roman culture. The entire pantheon of the gods was commonly worshiped by the populous, which is what any good Roman citizen would do. It wasn't a problem for Christians to proclaim Jesus is Lord, because he would have been one of many lords to be worshiped. The problem was that Christians believed in only one God, which cut against the grain of their culture's belief. Disciples of Christ wouldn't worship the gods of Rome, including the Emperor. Just because Christians proclaimed Jesus is Lord, secular culture didn't regard that as a denial of the pantheon of their gods or interpret that as a refusal to worship Caesar. The problem the Romans had with Christians was their refusal to acknowledge any other god but Jesus Christ and honor the gods of Rome. That's where the collision occurred.

Christians must place their primary loyalty to Christ, secondarily they must be loyal to their governing authorities only insofar as it doesn't cause them to compromise their stand for Christ. This creates a problem for Christians in all eras of history when the values of the state conflict with the values of Scripture that Christians must live by.

Just as the Philippians have civic responsibilities as citizens of Rome, they have civic responsibilities in their new identity as citizens of heaven. What are they? Paul will describe these as the passage and the rest of the letter unfolds. He tells the Philippians: **conduct yourselves in a manner that is worthy of the Good News of Christ** (v. 27). As citizens of heaven believers must live their lives in a way that is worthy of being a subject of Christ's Kingdom. Later in 2:6-11, Paul will set forth Jesus as the example for disciples to follow in an amazing theological masterpiece, not so much to provide in depth theological instruction, but to provide an example in ethical behavior. Christians are to emulate his life and try to walk in his footsteps. He also instructs them to take note of how Timothy and Epaphroditus live, which will give them further insights about how to live a worthy life for the sake of the gospel (2:19-30). Additionally, Paul looks ahead to his possible visit with the Philippians: **that, whether I come and see you or am absent, I may hear that you stand firm in one Spirit, with one soul striving together for the faith of the Good News.**

Whether Paul can visit them in person, or only hears a report about them it is essential that they be a unified group of Jesus' worshipers. There must be solidarity and unity in the Philippian church. He is providing accountability for the Philippians, not just exhorting them. He wants them to know that he will be monitoring their behavior, whether he sees them in person or receives an oral report about them. His concern is: **That you stand firm in one Spirit. Stand firm** has military connotations, which would strike a nerve in the retired soldiers in the fellowship. It is a translation of the Greek *stékó*, written in the present tense which means Paul wants them to continually stand firm. The imagery is that of soldiers in formation locking shields together and holding their ground against attacking forces. They hold the line when under attack, not breaking ranks and retreating. One of the most successful battle formations the Romans practiced was the famous Roman wedge, where the soldiers would advance in a V shaped formation and envelop their enemy.

This battle tactic only worked if the soldiers were disciplined enough to hold the formation and stand firm in their position. It wasn't about the skill of the individual that made the formation successful, it was everyone working together in unity that made the formation lethal. Whether in an offensive or defensive formation the soldiers needed to stand firm and hold their positions.

Paul paints this word picture for the Philippians, so they can achieve more unity in their church. They had issues that threatened their solidarity, so Paul essentially says you need to do church with the same precise unity as soldiers on the battle field. They all need to march together to the beat of the drum in Philippi. Paul adds the qualifier stand firm **in one Spirit.** Notice the Spirit (capital S), refers to the Holy Spirit. If it is with a small "s" it would be a reference to the human spirit. Translators had to determine if Paul was talking about the Holy Spirit or the human spirit. Translations of the Bible differ on this, for instance:

The New International Version: stand firm in the one Spirit (the Holy Spirit)

The English Standard Version: standing firm in one spirit (the human spirit)

The New Living Translation: standing together with one spirit (the human spirit)

Capable arguments can be made to support both options. If **one spirit** is understood to be parallel and complementary to **one soul**, Paul may be referring to man's spirit. This amounts to Paul calling for a "common mind" or a "team spirit" displayed by the Philippians.

Gordon Fee see it differently: "Paul is referring to the Holy Spirit as the source of all Christian unity: That he should qualify the Spirit as "the *one* Spirit" emphasizes the *source* of their unity. Only by standing firm in the *one and only* Spirit can they hope to contend as "one person" for the gospel against their opposition. We should therefore not be surprised that this is the first thing said in the long appeal for unity (1:27-2:18) that begins with this sentence. The reason they need to "stand firm in the one Spirit" is so that they might "contend together as one person for the faith of the gospel."[29]

It is true that Paul views the Spirit as the one who bonds believers together in unity, fellowship, and community (Phil 2:1; Eph 4:3). It is also true that Paul uses the same expression *in one Spirit* to refer to the Holy Spirit elsewhere (1 Cor 12:13; Eph 2:18), so Fee's view has much merit. It would be difficult to see how Paul is appealing to unity in the Philippian church independent of any work of the Holy Spirit.

There are those who understand the phrase *in one spirit* as a reference to both the human spirit and the Holy Spirit, in the sense that the "Holy Spirit strengthens the human spirit under trial."[30] The key to unity is the Holy Spirit, who unites a group of Christians into one body, which enables them to overcome differences among individuals and work toward a common goal. Therefore, to summarize Paul is saying: the Philippians should be united in their human spirits, because they all have the Holy Spirit within them and are experiencing his ongoing work.

It seems most likely that Paul is referring to the Holy Spirit as the catalyst who enables the Philippians to display a unified team spirit as they stand against the opposition they are facing and set forth a vital witness to their culture. Unity is a must among Christians, it isn't an option, and the Holy Spirit is available to help believers live in camaraderie with one another.

Additionally, Paul exhorts them to further ratchet up their unity: **with one soul contending together for the faith of the Good News. Soul** is a translation of the Greek word *psuché*, which has a range of meaning including: life, self, person, and mind. Paul's idea is the Philippians should with *one mind*, or as *one man* be unified as they strive for the faith. He introduces another colorful word picture to encourage the Philippians to a more robust unity: **contending together for the faith of the Good News. Contending together** is a translation of *sunathleó,* which is a compound word

---

[29] Fee, p. 166

[30] Martin, p. 70

in Greek consisting of *sun* meaning together or with, and *athleó*, which means: to contend, struggle or strive. This word is the origin of the English words athlete and athletics. In the ancient world, the games featured hand-to-hand wrestling and boxing matches that were fiercely brutal. The word is also used in military contexts.

Like soldiers standing firm in formation the Philippians must contend side-by-side for the Good News. This is written as a present participle, which means this must be an ongoing practice. As the Philippians stand firm they must never stop contending side-by-side as they resist the forces that stand against the gospel. The Philippians must relentlessly keep on striving together for the faith of the Good News without stopping. Unity must be a permanent characteristic of their fellowship.

The opposition that the Philippians were experiencing must be regarded as spiritual warfare between the Kingdom of light and Kingdom of darkness. For this reason, the military metaphor fits well here. He is painting a picture for the Philippians to be unified as they strive together, against the forces of darkness, for the **faith of the Good News**, which refers to all that the Good News entails in belief and practice. The unity of the church should be rooted in the Good News that Jesus died for sinners and offers them eternal life. This is the belief that should bind all Christians together. Unity is centered on the person of Jesus Christ and his work to secure man's salvation on the cross, which is then demonstrated by each believer living a worthy life for the sake of the gospel.

As believers of every generation strive together for the faith of the Good News, they will also be setting up roadblocks to everything that opposes the gospel. It isn't just advancement of the Good News that believers strive for, it is the dissolution of everything that stands in the way of the faith of the Good News, whether it be Emperor worship, belief in fate, Karma, astrology, the occult, post-modernism, or whatever. Therefore, advancing the gospel of Christ goes hand-in-hand with resisting and refuting all other ideologies or spiritual experiences outside of Christ.

The reason the Philippians must contend side-by-side for the gospel is because there will always be opposition to the true gospel of Jesus Christ, whether it is open persecution and violent hostility, or a more peaceful distortion of the truth. The battle for truth has been raging for millennia, so the church must stand together as it contends for the faith that was delivered to the saints (Jude 3). Truth will always be challenged by Satan who uses deception, falsehood, and lies to oppose the Gospel of Christ (1 Tim 4:1). The Philippians need to exercise their discernment and recognize the errors that oppose the Good News. It doesn't appear that at the writing of this letter there were any major doctrinal issues that Paul needed to correct in the Philippian church.

This passage points out the fundamental premise that the struggles Christians face must be done within the fellowship of the believing community. Whether it is advancing the gospel or resisting other teachings that oppose the gospel believers do this side-by-side in community. The sanctification of individual believers at Philippi is not an individualistic exercise, rather it is a corporate endeavor. Christian citizenship requires involvement in the community of believers in Christ that are unified together in the Holy Spirit, hence Christians strive side-by-side as they live the worthy life trying to advance the gospel.

and in nothing being frightened by your adversaries, which is for them proof of their destruction, but to you of salvation, and that from God. (1:28)

Paul tells them not to be afraid of their adversaries, but who are they? Who is opposing the Philippians? When Paul and Silas visited Philippi, they were mistreated by being stripped, beaten severely in public, and detained in prison with their feet chained in stocks (Acts 16:22-24). This was illegal because Paul was a Roman citizen. It appears things settled down when Paul left Philippi, and when Epaphroditus arrived in Rome he would have informed Paul about whatever persecution was taking place. Certainly, that would have been one of the questions that Paul and Timothy would have asked him.

There is no mention of an all-out persecution against believers by the Roman authorities, for Paul doesn't make any references to the Philippians being beaten, imprisoned or executed. Nor does Paul say anything that suggests they are being publicly shamed or going through economic persecution in the patronage system because of their beliefs. Epaphroditus seemingly had no news of increasing hostilities so it seems most likely that Paul is referring to a generalized "bad attitude" that secular culture directs at followers of Christ. There may have been sporadic aggressive attacks against the Philippian Christians, but not one that was full-scale and sanctioned by the ruling elite. Even in countries like America, where religious freedom is granted, there is a type of opposition that Christians meet from secular culture. This isn't a violent persecution, but one that occurs on a secondary level, where the culture brands Christians as narrow-minded intolerant hypocrites.

In addition to the pagan culture, the other opponent the Philippians needed to stand firm against were the Judaizers who regularly made trouble for Paul (3:2). They do not appear to be in Philippi when Paul wrote this letter, but Paul anticipated that they would show up and do their dirty work of teaching a false gospel. He issues a warning in 3:1-9, but this appears to be nothing more than a word of caution, not a word of correction to the Philippians.

Paul tells them not to be **afraid** of their opponents, which is a translation of *pturó,* a word that is found only here in the New Testament, written as a present participle signifying ongoing action. It refers to someone who is intimidated or panicked. In Classical Greek, it was also used of a horse being startled and bolting on the battlefield, so the military metaphor may continue in these verses. Paul is concerned that the Philippians aren't intimidated by their opponents, since they are a small minority in their city. He is preparing them for a normative aspect of life for believers, in that they all face opposition of some sort because they identify with Christ and his people. In the face of mounting opposition believers must not be intimidated, rather they should band together and continue to demonstrate a worthy lifestyle to honor Christ. Christian living requires courage in the face of hostility. Paul is calling for the Philippians to continuously live free of fear as they set forth a positive witness to their culture amid persecution.

When someone takes a stand against Christ and his people he places himself in the worst possible position regarding eternity, because Paul says: **which is for them proof of their destruction, but to you of salvation, and that from God.** It is obvious who the enemies of Christ's people are because they persecute believers, which is no different than persecuting Christ (Acts 8:5). **Destruction** translates the Greek word *apóleia*, which refers to eternal punishment away from the presence of Christ. This is conscience punishment in hell, not an annihilation or cessation of consciousness. This is what awaits those who are presenting a false gospel (3:19), and this is the result of walking on the broad path that Jesus said leads to destruction (Mat 7:13). What we believe in this life truly matters and paves the way for how we live in eternity. It is a false belief that only Christians have eternal life, for all people live eternally, it is a question of where you will spend eternity—heaven or hell.

When people oppose Christians, it is proof that their destruction will occur, but for Christians Paul says: **but to you of salvation, and that from God.** The Philippians may be in the fire of persecution but can live without intimidation and fear because God will see them to the end, making their salvation and vindication complete (1:6). This verse indicates that there are only two camps that people can be in: one is believing in Jesus while the other is rejecting him in unbelief, the result being heaven or hell. This should be an encouragement to the Philippians because they will ultimately be saved, but this fact shouldn't cause them to rejoice over their opponents impending destruction. Paul isn't calling for them to wish for the worst regarding those who don't believe, for part of the worthy life Christ calls disciples to live is to advance the gospel, which means withstanding opposition while introducing nonbelievers to Christ (1 Pet 3:15-16). Later in his letter he instructs them to shine like stars as they hold forth the word of life, so Paul has an emphasis on evangelizing the unbelieving culture in which they live (2:15-16). Paul has offered reassurance to the Philippians that God is in control of their eternal destiny. This verse prepares the way for v. 29, which is a difficult truth for Christians to comprehend.

Because it has been granted to you on behalf of Christ, not only to believe in him, but also to suffer for him (v. 29).

Salvation is a gift from God, having nothing to do with a person's good deeds or attempts to live a life that is saturated with moral goodness. Faith is granted to the Philippians, and other believers, to not only believe in Christ, but to suffer for him. The word translated **granted** is *echaristhē*, which is from *charis* the word commonly translated grace in our English Bibles. Our salvation is totally God's grace, which means it is freely given as a gift (Eph 2:8-9). It is God's favor given to unworthy sinners, which should cause believers to be radically grateful to God because there is nothing that sinners can do to earn God's favor or save themselves. That it has **been granted** to people to believe in Christ points to the gracious nature of God, and the salvation that he provided by sending his Son to die for our sins and bear our punishment. It is his gift to mankind (John 3:16).

But that is only half of the equation. Our salvation experience is a gift of faith from God that includes **to suffer for him**, which is also to be considered a grace gift from God. Paul wants the Philippians to know that the suffering they are experiencing is a normative part of living the worthy life for the sake of Christ and the gospel. Most people want to avoid suffering, and would not view unpleasant circumstances, or any type of opposition to their faith as a gift, but that is what Paul challenges them to do. In fact, to many, it may seem unnatural to view suffering for Christ's sake as a gift, but it is as much a gift, as being granted to believe in Jesus is a gift. Both faith in Christ and suffering for Christ comprise the salvation experience. One doesn't exist without the other, for they go hand-in-hand.

Christ came into the world and suffered for mankind's salvation, now believers are called to walk in his footsteps and suffer so the gospel can advance, and more people can come to know Jesus. Later in Paul's letter he tells the Philippians in 3:10: I want to know Christ and the power of his resurrection and the *fellowship of his sufferings* (Italics Mine). Paul clearly understood that suffering was a part of the mission of the church, which every believer should experience. He did suffer immensely throughout his career as the apostle to the Gentiles, just as the Lord told him he would (Acts 9:16). Reading through 2 Corinthians 11:23-33 reveals in graphic detail how much Paul suffered physically and emotionally for Christ's sake. The Philippians must embrace the reality of suffering in a hostile environment for the advancement of the Good News, just as believers today need to do the same.

having the same struggle which you saw in me, and now hear is in me. (1:30)

What the Philippians are experiencing is the same thing that they saw Paul go through, and now hear about what he's going through. When Paul came into

Philippi he was harassed by a slave girl with a spirit of divination, which caused him to be troubled, so he cast the evil spirit out of the girl, resulting in an uproar in the city. The owners of the slave girl, realizing that their profit margins just dropped to zero, were outraged by Paul and stirred up the crowd. The magistrates ordered Paul and Silas to be stripped and beaten, then thrown into prison. It was there that the jailer and his family became Christians, then Paul and Silas were released (Acts 16:16-40). Paul wrote to the Thessalonian Church informing them about how he was shamefully mistreated in Philippi (1 Thess 2:2).

The Philippians that witnessed Paul and Silas publicly beaten saw for themselves the reality of suffering for the gospel's sake. Did the Philippian converts think they might someday be beaten and abused as Paul and Silas were because of their faith in Christ? Paul displayed incredible resilience and toughness to be beaten and continue preaching Jesus. In telling them not to be afraid, Paul's telling them to follow his example and show the type of courage that he had when under fire. The retired soldiers probably thought Paul and Silas were "tough guys" and respected them for taking a beating and pressing on with their mission.

Earlier in his letter Paul said the Philippians are partners with him in the gospel (1:5), which includes not only the glorious experience of knowing Jesus and receiving eternal life, but the suffering that is required to see the gospel make headway in the world. They are realizing the fellowship of sharing in Christ's suffering (Phil 3:10). They need to embrace that reality, for it is normative for Christians and is a hard pill to swallow.

The Philippians were **having the same struggle** which Paul had. **Struggle** is the Greek *agón*, from which the English words agony and agonize are derived. The word referred to athletic contests like hand-to-hand combat, wrestling or boxing matches that were part of the games. The spiritual struggle Paul is describing is no laughing matter for he views this conflict much like a grueling fight one would witness in the arena. Often competitors would fight to the point of complete exhaustion—even death. Suffering for Christ's sake is no nonsense suffering that is not to be taken lightly. Paul appears to be a fan of the games, which were very popular, so he uses many metaphors from the arena to make spiritual applications.

Paul is not talking about a specific struggle he had, he is speaking in general terms about living the worthy life in a hostile environment. Whether the source of opposition the Christian community faces is secular culture, the government, other religions, or the Judaizers who disagreed with Paul's gospel, the Philippians must live a worthy life for the sake of the Good News. I would be remiss if I didn't identify Satan, the archenemy of God's people, as the primary catalyst of all the hostility and persecution that is directed at Christians. When enduring persecution believers must always be reminded that their battle is not against flesh and blood, but against the forces of darkness (Eph 6:12). In whatever arena Christians may be in Satan and his cohorts always try to stir up trouble for God's people. Whether it is a personal struggle, issues within a church, or the external movement of God's salvation to the unsaved, Christians should expect Satan to resist their efforts. Paul's battle was before the Imperial Court of Rome, in Philippi the believer's struggle took place in their workplaces, social interactions, and homes. The gospel advances through the suffering of God's people, which Paul views as normative and as a gift from God. This is a hard-theological truth that God's people have grappled with throughout the millennia.

Insights, Applications, and Life Lessons

The thesis statement for the Philippians is to live as citizens of heaven in a manner that is worthy of the Good News. This statement challenges the reader to consider his lifestyle and ask himself whether he is living in a way that is worthy of being a citizen of heaven. Does my life honor Christ? Am I a growing Christian maturing in the faith? Am I serving in my church? Does my relationship with other Christians promote unity? Am I telling people about the Jesus story and experiencing any opposition? These questions are apropos for disciples of Christ to ask themselves.

The Importance of Unity

The Philippian believers were a tiny island amid a vast ocean of paganism, which at times was hostile toward them. In an environment like that they needed to stick together. The Philippians needed to strengthen their unity, which is why Paul exhorts them to stand firm in one Spirit and strive together for the faith of the gospel. Where there is a struggle people tend to band together. Soldiers fight for their buddies beside them in combat. In sports, teams that win championships play as unselfish cohesive units. The team is more important than the individual. The same mindset needs to exist in the church (2:1-5).

During a recent trip to Nicaragua, I was with several missionaries that were introducing me to people and showing me their ministries. They were of different theological backgrounds and different nationalities, but the vibe I got from them was refreshing, and very different than what I usually experience when being around pastors in America. They all had an entrepreneurial spirit because they're always short on resources, so they have to be creative and think outside of the box to stretch every dollar. Even though they were of different theological persuasions it didn't matter, because they all worked together to advance the gospel. They didn't let trivial matters of theology stand as roadblocks to fellowship. It was refreshing to be with these servants of Christ and see the unity they had in advancing the gospel. This was the closest thing I've ever seen to what I believe the apostle Paul is calling for.

In America denominations can inhibit unity and collaboration among believers. In fact, some pastors will tell their congregations to avoid people who are members of a church that is affiliated with a different denomination than theirs. It shouldn't be this way. Paul would strenuously object to that type of divisive mentality, for it stands at odds with what he has taught in this passage. Denominational barriers, along with trivial theological barriers that prevent believers from *standing firm in one Spirit, with one soul, striving together for the faith of the gospel,* should be removed.

The Reality of Suffering for Jesus' Sake

This brings us to a truth that is difficult to grapple with, especially here in America where we don't face the outright persecution that the Philippians and other Christians have endured. Two questions rise to the surface as we consider this passage: 1) What does Paul mean by suffering? 2) How can suffering be considered a gift?

To the first question, suffering is related to what Christians experience for the advancement of the gospel. In Western democracies, where religious freedom exists, believers have a shallow view of what it means to suffer for the gospel. I remember during the crash of 2008 when many people were going through hard economic times, some Christians I knew felt they were suffering for Jesus because their 401K took a hit, and other investments went into the tank. Foreclosures where happening in record numbers, people were losing their jobs, and companies were folding left-and-right. Many Christians had their standard of living negatively affected and understood this scenario as though it was part of bearing their cross for Jesus and the gospel. This is not what Paul would consider suffering for the gospel to mean.

My friend at the gym where I work out, has two jobs and puts in just short of eighty hours per week: one as a janitor at the gym, the other as a cook. He sends money back to Mexico where his family lives, and views this as bearing his cross and suffering for Jesus. When someone contracts a serious life-threatening disease such as cancer, or diabetes, etc. they may view this as suffering for Jesus, but this is a far cry from what Paul is talking about in Philippians. Suffering for Christ is measured by the sacrifices disciples make to advance the gospel. They will experience hostility from nonbelievers and the culture at large in their attempt to introduce people to the Good News. It is a fact of life for Christians, that as they tell people the Jesus story they will experience opposition on different levels: rejection, humiliation, economic discrimination, imprisonment, beatings, even martyrdom. This is what Paul means by suffering for the gospel.

Suffering is a Gift

To the second question: how can suffering be considered a gift? When we suffer to advance the gospel, we are proving that we are one with Christ in his mission, that we are in the battle to save souls, that we are participants in the Great Commission, and that we are involved in the drama of divine redemption of humankind. Additionally, God can transform the suffering that Christians endure to produce greater levels of holiness and conform them to Christ's image (3:10). In this regard, suffering for the sake of the Good News has a transformative effect on believers and is intricately tied to their sanctification. For instance, when Paul and Silas were publicly beaten, they suffered shame, humiliation, and, of course, the pain. Was God indifferent to their plight such that he disconnected from them and abandoned them as they were being flogged? The answer to that is NO! He was with them, revealing himself to them in a very special way, which Paul describes in 2 Corinthians 1:3-5:

> Blessed be the God and Father of our Lord Jesus Christ, the Father of mercies and God of all comfort; [4]who comforts us in all our affliction, that we may be able to comfort those who are in any affliction, through the comfort with which we ourselves are comforted by God. [5]For as the sufferings of Christ abound to us, even so our comfort also abounds through Christ.

As Paul and Silas got the tar beat out of them, and walked around grimacing in pain afterwards, they received God's comfort. God revealed the depth of his compassion, mercy, and comfort to them as they took a beating for Jesus and endured the pain. This is a deep theological truth: as believers suffer for Christ and the gospel, by bearing their cross daily (Luke 9:23), they receive a greater presence of God in their lives. If you want to know the depth of God's love, his comfort, and mercy pick up your cross and align yourself with Jesus and suffer to extend the gospel. Yes, Paul and Silas got the tar beat out of them, but they experienced more of God's comfort in their life because of it. This causes one to think of Job, who was tested by God through extreme suffering. What he endured was beyond painful, but the comfort he received from God was greater than the pain he endured. In this sense, Job had a greater revelation of God's love, comfort, and compassion than those who didn't suffer as he did. As Paul and Silas felt the sting of the rods on their backs, they also felt the presence of Christ comforting them in their affliction.

Suffering for Christ has a transformative effect in that people who receive God's comfort during their afflictions, are better equipped to extend God's comfort to those who are hurting. As Paul and Silas endured the pain of the beating they received, they also received a deep level of Christ's comfort which made them more empathetic, compassionate, and sensitive to the needs of others. In other words, they became better servants of Christ and more capable of giving God's love to others who were in dire straits.

So the formula is: Paul and Silas suffered for Christ and received his comfort, thus making them more useful to comfort God's people who suffer for Christ. As Paul endured much agony for Christ, it softened him, and made him a more lovable person, and enabled him to better extend God's love to others. He became more Christlike through his suffering. As Paul and Silas were beaten with rods one has to think of how the soldiers beat Jesus with a staff (Mark 15:19). The Lord knows what it's like to feel pain, and he can sympathize with his people as they suffer (Heb 4:15-16). This is a hard truth to grasp, but as disciples suffer for Christ and the Good News, his comfort is extended without reservation, which makes them more useful to serve Jesus and his people.

There's something else that goes along with suffering for the sake of the gospel. As believers are in the heat of persecution there is an accompanying level of supernatural joy that they experience, which defies description. As the persecution increases so does the level of divinely imparted joy (1 Pet 1:5-9). When the fires of persecution burn fiercely, Jesus is with believers in an intimate way, which Peter describes:

> Dear friends, do not be surprised at the fiery ordeal that has come on you to test you, as though something strange were happening to you. [13]But rejoice inasmuch as you participate in the *sufferings of Christ*, so that you may be overjoyed when his glory is revealed. [14]If you are insulted because of the name of Christ, you are blessed, for the Spirit of glory and of God rests on you. (1 Peter 4:12-14, Italics Mine)

The Spirit of glory and of God is the Holy Spirit, who mediates the presence of Jesus himself. In the above passage, it is important to note that when suffering for the sake of Christ, there is Trinitarian fellowship. All three members of the Godhead are mentioned. When under fire, the Christian has a special impartation of the Spirit and the realization of divine joy. Christians that don't live in persecution will have a difficult time grasping this truth about joy in suffering. Nonbelievers throughout the ages have seen the way many believers have responded when treated harshly and it made a lasting impression on them. Joy in persecution goes hand-in-hand, which can only be understood by being in the line of fire for Jesus and experiencing it for yourself.[31]

On one occasion, the apostles were in the Temple court preaching up a storm telling people the Good News about Jesus. They were brought before the Sanhedrin and ordered to stop preaching Jesus. Gamaliel was a top-notch scholar, held in high esteem by the Sanhedrin, advised them to let the men go because if their message is of human origin it will amount to nothing, but if it is of God and you oppose them, you may be found positioning yourselves against the Almighty.

Luke records what happened next in Acts 5:40-42:

> They agreed with him. Summoning the apostles, they *beat them* and commanded them not to speak in the name of Jesus, and let them go. [41]They therefore departed from the presence of the council, *rejoicing* that they were counted worthy to *suffer* dishonor for Jesus' name. [42]Every day, in the temple and at home, they never stopped teaching and preaching Jesus, the Christ. (Italics Mine)

Before they let the apostles go on their way they beat the heck out of them, which no doubt was to teach them a lesson and intimidate them from doing any more preaching. They figured taking a beating like that would shut them up, but that wasn't the case. The response of the apostles gives us a glimpse into how the early church viewed suffering for Christ. They considered it an honor to be counted worthy to suffer for Jesus' name and take a beating. They didn't complain, they didn't show any signs of intimidation, because they went right back to the Temple and kept on preaching Jesus. This is an amazing response from the apostles, who appear to be emboldened to speak even more aggressively about Jesus after being beaten. Certainly, the Holy Spirit was involved in empowering them to preach up a storm for Jesus without being intimidated. They rejoiced at the honor of taking it on the chin for Jesus.

---

[31] See: Acts 5:41, 1 Pet 1:6-8, 4:12-16, 5:10, 2 Tim 3:12, Gal 6:17, Col 1:24, 1 Thess 3:3

Don't be Afraid of Your Opponents

One would think that when living in a hostile environment believers would be filled with fear and intimidation. Paul told the Philippians not to be afraid of their opponents. When Paul initially went to Philippi he stirred up the hornets' nest when he cast the spirit of divination out of the slave girl, which infuriated her owners because they lost their source of income. Paul and Silas ended up being beaten with rods and thrown in prison (Acts 16:18-24).

This isn't exactly what you would call a warm reception by the magistrates who imposed the beating on them. Many of Paul's converts may have witnessed Paul and Silas get flogged then thrown into prison. That Paul tells them not to be afraid after he got flogged tells us something about his metal. He seems to be unstoppable and fully courageous. It is nothing short of amazing that Paul tells them not to be afraid of those who are opposing you, after they saw him and Silas beaten with rods. They felt the sting of the rods on their backs, yet they are fearless! Paul and Silas were probably walking around very carefully as they grimaced in pain because the sores on their back were still fresh. Maybe some of the Philippians tended to Paul and Silas by cleaning their wounds and putting salve on them when they met at Lydia's house. I've never been flogged, but let's face it, getting flogged hurts—it's outright painful and this happened to Paul more than once throughout his career (2 Cor 11:23b-29).

After everything Paul went through in Philippi and before, he says don't be afraid of your adversaries. You've got to be kidding! Either the Philippians thought Paul was crazy, or his courageous commitment to Christ was so impressive that they concluded there was something supernatural going on in him. When they met at Lydia's house, after being released, they may have asked Paul, "Did this ever happen to you before?" "Why do you keep preaching if you get beaten up?" "How much of this can you take before you quit?" I wonder how much Paul told them about his sufferings. Did he tell them when he and Barnabas went to Lystra that they stoned him and left him outside the city for dead (Acts 14:19)? Some of the stories of Paul's persecution and suffering may have been overly intimidating to them, but I do believe Paul's courage and resiliency made a lasting impression on them, because they saw the supernatural in him. The retired combat vets in the

Philippian church must have looked at Paul and concluded he was a battle-hardened preacher. Many of the soldiers were probably wounded in battle and felt the point of an arrow, the slash of a sword, or the tip of a spear so they could respect Paul for his tough resolve.

Summary

In this section, Paul has presented the *propositio* (his thesis statement) to the Philippians: "live as citizens of heaven, conducting yourselves in a manner worthy of the Good News about Christ." What follows will describe how they can live a Christ-honoring life. He anticipates being able to visit them in the future, but if he just hears a report about them, either way, he wants them to make progress in tightening up their unity, because there were issues in their church with leaders not in agreement with each other (4:2-3). If their lack of unity continued it could severely weaken the church and damage its witness to their city. Paul uses military metaphors to challenge the Philippians to a greater level of unity, such as *standing firm*, and *contending together* for the faith, which would resonate with the retired soldiers.

He said some hard things about living in the reality of persecution such as not being afraid of opposition, because those who oppose Christ, and his church, are heading for destruction, but for the Philippians it is proof that they will be saved. Living the Christian life in Philippi requires courage and fortitude. Additionally, Paul says salvation is a gift from God, but so is suffering for Christ's sake and the gospel. They go together, one can't be separated from the other. Paul reminds them of his visit to Philippi when he was beaten publicly and thrown in prison, which many in the church personally saw. If they didn't see Paul get abused they certainly heard about it, just as they heard Paul was currently imprisoned in Rome. Paul is reminding them that as believers in Christ they have the same struggle that he has.

In the next section, Paul will point out some of the spiritual benefits that accrue to believers because of their relationship with Christ, and the corresponding attitudes that believers should display because of that.

CHAPTER SEVEN

* * *

"A Call for Unity"
Philippians 2:1-4

Paul has made an appeal to the Philippians to be unified as part of his clarion call to live the worthy life for the gospel of Christ, which was Paul's thesis in this letter (1:27). He now provides them some ways in which they can get over their petty differences and do a better job at conducting themselves as citizens of heaven. They need to go through an attitude adjustment and learn to demonstrate humility, which would enable them to resolve any ongoing conflicts that are harming their fellowship and witness to their community. Since they have experienced the divine presence of Christ including his love, compassion, and forgiveness, they are to extend these virtues to each other. This should be the norm as Christians relate to one another, because there should be no room for vanity, selfish ambition, pride, and any other vice that is harmful to the unity of the body.

Paul is appealing to their experience with Christ to motivate them to ratchet up their unity and live the worthy life. He is using emotional language to persuade them to consider the example of Christ. Being a wise rhetorician Paul begins with positive appeals, which is known in ancient letter writing as the *probatio*, which supports his thesis regarding living the worthy life of the Good News. He will offer several appeals (2:1-4:3) tying together theology and ethics by citing the example of people's lives: including Christ, Timothy, himself, and Epaphroditus. These examples are worthy of imitation, and Paul will explain why as the passage unfolds. He also cites examples that are to be avoided (3:2-19). A capable rhetorician will cite his strongest argument first which Paul does here.

Therefore, if there is any encouragement in Christ, if any comfort of love, if any fellowship of the Spirit, if any tender mercies and compassion, [2]make my joy full, by being like-minded, having the same love, being of one accord, of one mind; [3]doing nothing through rivalry or through conceit, but in humility, each counting others better than himself; [4]each of you not just looking to his own things, but each of you also to the things of others. (Author's Translation, 2:1-4)

The word **therefore** points back to what Paul said in vv. 27-30 in his appeal for unity and the struggle they share with Paul in suffering for the gospel. To paraphrase what Paul means by **therefore,** he is saying: Considering what I've just said let me explain a little bit further...if there is any encouragement in Christ...

Paul introduces four conditional clauses with "if" to point out spiritual realities that are assumed in the Philippians' experience. The word "if" carries with it the idea of "since." "If" doesn't suggest doubt, Paul is certain the Philippians have, in fact, received these divine gifts because they are **in Christ**, which points to their spiritual union with him that occurred when they received him by faith. These divine gifts should be viewed in contrast to the suffering they are experiencing on Christ's behalf. As the Philippians and Paul suffer to advance the Good News, the presence of Christ in their lives serves as an oasis of comfort (2 Cor 1:3-5).

The first spiritual benefit Paul mentions is: **if there is any encouragement in Christ.** Encouragement translates the Greek word *parákl̄esis,* which is a compound word consisting of *para* meaning "beside" and *kl̄esis* meaning "to call." Thus, the word literally means "called alongside." It can be translated: exhortation, warning, encouragement, comfort, etc. so the context must determine the best option. In this case, the meaning seems to be that the Philippians are the recipients of Christ's encouragement or comfort. This thought runs parallel to what Paul said in 2 Corinthians 1:3-5:

> Blessed be the God and Father of our Lord Jesus Christ, the Father of mercies and God of all comfort; [4]who *comforts* us in all our affliction, that we may be able to *comfort* those who are in any affliction, through the *comfort* with which we ourselves are *comforted* by God. [5]For as the sufferings of Christ abound to us, even so our *comfort* also abounds through Christ. (Italics Mine)

In whatever difficult circumstances the Philippians face, in virtue of their union with Christ, he will provide them with spiritual encouragement and comfort to press on and rise above their difficulties. In the above passage *comfort* is the translation of *paráklēsis.*

The second spiritual benefit of being in Christ is: **if any comfort of love.** The word *paramuthion* has the meaning of: comfort, consolation, exhortation, persuasion, and encouragement. It is very close in meaning to *paráklēsis* mentioned above. The nuance Paul is bringing out is that of comfort. It could be that one term builds on the other. "The first spiritual reality centers on encouraging, and the second details the result—comforting. Christ's presence encourages, and love comforts."[32]

The question to be answered is whose love provides the comfort? Is it Christ's, God the Father's, Paul's, or the church's love? A strong case can be made for it being God's love because this clause is sandwiched in between the mention of Christ's encouragement, and the fellowship of the Spirit. Thus, the comfort believers realize in their suffering is Trinitarian in that the entire Godhead embraces believers as they suffer for the gospel (1 Pet 4:12-14). Paul, no doubt, includes himself in this solace of comfort. Perhaps, the reason Paul didn't specifically mention whose love is providing the comfort was to keep it open ended. Where divine love is present it is shared on the human level. The outpouring of Trinitarian love was being threatened by the personal conflicts the Philippians were having.

The third spiritual benefit Paul mentions is: **if any fellowship of the Spirit.** This points back to v. 27 where Paul instructed them to stand firm in one Spirit. In the Holy Spirit they are united in striving side-by-side for the gospel.

---

[32] Osborne, Loc. 1155

By the Spirit they are united to Christ and to one another, so they fellowship in the Spirit, who will provide them with the ability to be unified. This is another occurrence of the Greek word *koinonia*. The Philippians fellowship in the Holy Spirit is the solution to the problem of infighting and conflict that was weakening their church.[33]

What seems to be a Trinitarian appeal for unity is rounded off by two more spiritual realities that the Philippians and Paul have experienced: **if any tender mercies and compassion.** This is difficult to translate into English because *splagchnon* refers to the internal organs such as the intestines, which were considered the seat of one's emotions in Greek thought (see 1:8). For this reason, the King James Version translates the word bowels. **Tender mercies** obviously gives a better picture of the word's meaning. The word translated **compassion** is *oiktirmos* which connotes God's deep feelings he has for us such as pity, compassion, and mercy.

Paul omits the source of the tender mercies and compassion and leaves it open ended. He is surely thinking of the divine attributes shared by believers. Paul has these feelings for the Philippians, and the Philippians have these feelings for Paul, all which flow from the Godhead. This spiritual reality is like a prescription that can be taken to cure the dissension existing at Philippi. How can ongoing conflicts derail a church from its mission, and poison the fellowship of the body when the members are expressing divine tender mercies and compassion to one another? The Philippian church seems like a contradiction in terms. How can they be a divided congregation with leaders submerged in disagreements when they are recipients of divine expressions of love? The spiritual benefits Paul has cited carry some overlap in meaning, but all essentially point to the solace one finds in a relationship with Christ. It is a solace that the entire Godhead provides, thus the believer's suffering has a Trinitarian outpouring of spiritual benefits in his troubles.

Paul introduced four conditional clauses beginning with "if" now he will introduce the "then" clause, which is his appeal to the Philippians: **make my joy full** (2:2a). He is making a strong emotional appeal based on the deep

---

[33] The phrase "fellowship of the Spirit" is also found in the Trinitarian benediction in 2 Corinthians 13:13

feelings he has for the Philippians, which they also have for Paul. We get a glimpse into Paul's pastoral heart as he makes this command. It isn't a selfish command to inflate his ego, it is given amid Paul and the Philippians sharing divine love with each other. It seems as though Paul's well-being is tied to the well-being of his flock. So intricate and deep was the connection that Paul felt with this church that Paul's own joy will be complete, only if the Philippians get their act together and ramp up their unity. Nothing could bring Paul more joy than to see the Philippians excel at living the worthy life of the Good News.

That Paul mentions joy is important because they were a constant source of joy to him as he remembers them and prays for them (1:4). He had a stellar relationship with this church because they stayed in contact with him and supported him financially (4:10-18). Paul mentions the joy he felt over the gospel going forward even though his rivals were giving him a hard time by undermining him (1:15-16). The gospel was penetrating lives, people were being saved, which gave Paul a reason to rejoice (1:18). He mentioned how his return to them could result in more joy in their experience by rejoicing in the Lord Jesus for bringing Paul back to them (1:25-26). Paul seems to be flooding the page with joy as he writes, but there is one more thing that needs to happen for Paul's joy to be complete: they need to tighten up their unity by getting over their petty differences. This would push Paul's joy over the top.

To paraphrase what Paul is saying: if you have experienced the amazing spiritual benefits I've just mentioned, which I know you have, and since we share them together, then make by joy full by being like-minded. In essence, Paul is saying "do this for me," which is something that he couldn't say if his relationship with them wasn't so strong and unbreakable. This also points to Paul's understanding of how much he felt they loved him, so the relationship was strong on both ends. He didn't say, "Then make *Christ's* joy complete and be like-minded." Paul's persuasive appeal is anchored in an emotional and experiential reality, stemming from the bond that divine love creates when it is shared among believers. Had Paul's relationship with them been on the rocks this appeal probably wouldn't have worked, and he would have used another strategy to motivate them to action.

Additionally, the teacher-pupil relationship was much different than it is in our modern era. The teacher invests himself in his students by living closely with them, placing his life on display for them to see as he is totally transparent. He teaches not just through words but through the example of his life. The disciple can put his life under a microscope from morning until he retires for the night. This was the learning methodology of the day. Jesus demonstrated this with the twelve disciples. It was of utmost importance for the disciples to please their teacher, and for the teacher not just to lecture, but teach by example. Thus, it was important for the Philippians to want to please their teacher. This would be the concern of any student in that culture—to make his teacher happy.

Paul will now explain how they can make his joy full. The first directive is: **by being like-minded.** Basically, Paul is saying you guys need to be reading the same sheet of music. "Like-minded" or "think the same thing" translates the Greek words *auto phronēte.* This word is used ten times in Philippians and presents a problem in translation because there is no English equivalent for this word. It's meaning goes beyond the English word "to think." It refers to the way one is inclined to think—his disposition, attitude, or a mind-set one develops. In v. 5, Paul uses the same word to tell them: your *attitude* (mind-set) should be the same as Christ's.

Paul wants the Philippians to be inclined to think, then act in ways that promote unity in their church. This in no way implies that Paul expects everybody to be the same, as if they are clones of each other. He's wanting them to adopt a thought process that enables them to put aside petty differences and focus their attention on what's important in building their church. They must focus on the essentials of the Christian faith, and not get side-tracked on things that tend to deplete the spiritual energy of the people by tearing down the work of the Holy Spirit.

The second directive Paul gives them to develop unity is: **having the same love.** Paul has already prayed that their love would abound more and more (1:9), and just mentioned that they are partakers of divine love (v. 2), so love should be a natural byproduct of believers who are growing and filled with the Spirit. Having the same mind-set is linked to having the same love because all Christians should be focused on displaying this virtue, which is one of the primary characteristics of the church (Rom 12:10; 13). This love is *agápē,* which usually refers to God's love directed to man, however it also refers to man's love given to his fellow man. This is love that goes way beyond that of emotions and warm and fuzzy feelings, for it is an active volitional love. We are commanded to love one another, even our enemies (Mat 5:44; John 13:34). Where love abounds, one would think that petty differences could be eliminated, and conflict could be resolved for the greater good of the community of faith. Love becomes operative when people see the needs of others before their own. The verb **having** is written as a present participle which signifies continuous action, thus sharing love with one another should be a never ceasing practice in the body of Christ—it is a way of life.

The third directive to promote unity is: **being of one accord**, which translates *sympsychoi,* literally meaning "one-souled" and is found only here in the New Testament. This refers to sharing a common life in Christ, like *soul-brothers* living in harmony. This should enable them to be in spiritual oneness and promote unity, much like Paul and Timothy were of a kindred spirit (2:20-22).

The fourth directive is to be: **of one mind**, or more literally "thinking the same thing." This is the same word used earlier that was translated "like-minded," so he is repeating himself. His appeal is for unity of purpose, so they can get on with living as good citizens of heaven. When there is a coming together of minds and everybody focuses their attention on the essentials of the gospel, peace and harmony can result internally, and the external witness to the community will be enhanced.

These four directives overlap in meaning and are complementary to one another. They all say the same thing with a slightly different emphasis. There are some things that can detract from achieving unity in a church, which Paul will now mention in v. 3a: **doing nothing through rivalry or through conceit.** It appears Paul comes to the heart of the problem by identifying two vices, that if go unchecked can cripple a church. **Rivalry** (*eritheia*) has a range of meaning that includes: selfish ambition, self-seeking, self-interest, a feud, and factionalism. It is the same word Paul used of the preachers that were giving him a hard time by undermining him (1:17). In politics, it refers to a party spirit that tries at all costs to get its way at the expense of his opponents. One thinks of a politician who will do anything to see his agenda promoted regardless of how other people are affected. This vice describes the fallen capacity of humanity where the focus is on personal interests at the expense of others. One who displays this vice isn't displaying the love Paul is calling for and it is antithetical to the unity of the body.

The second vice mentioned is **conceit** (*kenodoksía*), which is a compound word consisting of *kenos* (empty, or vain) and *doxa* (glory or honor). When the two words are combined they have the following range of meaning: vainglory, empty pride, or vain conceit. This word was commonly used throughout the Greco-Roman world to describe people who think more highly of themselves than is warranted. They have inflated egos, and their opinion of themselves isn't founded in reality. If rivalry and conceit flourish in the Philippian church they are headed for a disaster, and their future is tentative. These two vices are antithetical to the mindset that Christ displayed (2:6-11).

After mentioning two harmful vices Paul brings into focus humility, an essential Christian virtue that will be helpful in turning things around in Philippi: **but in humility, each counting others better than himself** (v. 3b). **Humility** (lit. lowliness of mind) wasn't considered to be a virtue in the Greco-Roman world, in fact, it was considered something to be shameful. The Roman world was a culture of power, so the idea of a Messiah who humbled himself and died on a cross wasn't considered to be an admirable act. Jesus' death was considered an act of weakness and shame lacking any virtue whatsoever. At least, that's how the Romans viewed Jesus' death. It was the Christians who regarded humility as a virtue to be cultivated and displayed in relating to other people. This exposes the clash of cultural values between the Greco-Roman world and Christianity.

"Today Christians, and many others, praise humility as a virtue. This was not the case in the Roman world; there was virtually no difference between humility and humiliation—both ended with the reality of low status. Paul's call for humility is unprecedented in the ethics of his day; no self-respecting Gentile would concede that humility is a virtue. Deeds were to be done where people could see them and thus praise the one doing those actions.

Personal self-worth and value were determined in the public sphere, not in the private reflection of the individual."[34]

Humility is rooted in a person having a correct assessment of himself before God. The humble person realizes God is his Creator who has given him skills, talents, abilities, and so on, thus his only boasting should be in the Lord. He realizes he is totally dependent on God, must always be trusting God for his daily needs, and exists to serve him. Being humble doesn't mean belittling yourself or having low self-esteem where you think less of yourself than you should. Since people are made in God's image everyone should realize that they have intrinsic worth and value before God.

Paul provides his readers with his definition of humility: **but in humility, each counting others better than himself.** Paul isn't calling for believers to follow a course of self-debasing behavior, he is calling for the Philippians to develop a servant's mindset that looks outward for opportunities to help others, not use others for selfish reasons. This is what Jesus did, as Paul will point out in the Christ hymn that follows in vv. 6-11. He focused on the needs of other people and placed them over himself. "To value others above yourself does not mean to look down on yourself but rather means to look up to those around you, not to hate yourself but to love and serve others even more. You do not reject yourself but place your brothers and sisters on a pedestal above yourself."[35]

The verbs Paul uses in vv. 3-4 are present participles, which means that the Philippians are to continuously count others as being better than themselves. In other words, this is to be a way of life and a mindset that Christians develop and maintain for the duration of their lives.

The second part to Paul's definition of humility is found in v. 4: **each of you not just looking to his own things, but each of you also to the things of others.** It isn't wrong to concern yourself with your own needs, so Paul isn't speaking in absolute terms here, for one must take care of his family and tend to himself. His emphasis is on looking at those around us with a willingness

---

[34] Cohick, Loc. 2179

[35] Osborne, Loc. 1248

to help them. It isn't uncommon for people to adopt an "I've got to look out for myself" attitude, which is what Paul is speaking against here.

Paul tells his readers they should focus **to the things of others**, which means they are to consider the needs of people in a variety of situations that life may present to them. If someone needs food, clothing, money, a helping hand, encouragement, and so on, there should have an awareness of how they can help make the needy person's life a little better. One detects a tension between the individual and the community. Paul emphasizes the community of believers over the individual, however it is only as each one adopts the values Paul has set forth that the community of believers can thrive and be what God intended them to be. Therefore, there is always tension in Paul's writing where he emphasizes the family of God, but without the individual's obedience the family suffers. "The verse aims to de-center the self, not to set up guidelines that establish when enough is enough and when you can focus on yourself. The point is that just as people work to feed themselves and their families, Paul asks that they think now of their family as much larger than those who reside in their home."[36]

That the church is the family of God indicates the sense of community that should exist in any church, however, the individualism our modern American culture often cuts against the grain of the community identify that Paul calls for. In an individualistic culture, like America, Paul's teaching on the community of believers is often underemphasized and glossed over.

Insights, Applications, and Life Lessons

Wouldn't it be wonderful if in all gatherings of people unity would be instantly achieved? The fact of the matter is that unity is elusive. When it exists with a group of people it is truly joyful to see and be part of. Whether it is unity in the family, workplace, church, or team it is difficult to attain, but it is beautiful when it happens.

[36] Cohick, Loc. 2217

Who wants to go to work when the tension in the office is so thick you can cut the air with a knife. Plus, your boss picks on you and makes sarcastic remarks to you. Who wants to come home from a hard day's work when the kids are constantly fighting and are at each other's throat? Who wants to play on a team where nobody can get along and there's no comradery? Who wants to go to church that is filled with strife and the leaders are locking horns? Who needs that?

Since Christians have the Holy Spirit, who is the source of unity (1:27; 2:1), and with the Trinitarian love that exists in any gathering of Christians, one would think that unity would come naturally, but it doesn't always work that way. With divine love being shared with others in your church why are there so many divisions, church splits, and disagreements (Euodia and Syntyche, [4:2])?

The answer to that question is simple: Christians are fallen sinful people. Pride, selfishness, control issues, backbiting, nitpicking and so on, still exist in God's people. There lies the problem. It isn't that God doesn't provide the resources to build a unified church, it's that God's people are still sinners and don't always utilize his resources to live the worthy life of the gospel as Paul instructs.

Paul seems to be saying that humility is the pathway to unity: but in humility consider others better than yourselves. Each of you not just looking to his own things, but each of you also to the things of others (2:3b-4). If everybody could put this passage into practice the world would be a kinder gentler place. *Humility starts with the recognition that it's not all about me!* If everybody had the understanding that they exist to serve other people that would be a game changer. They would be walking in Jesus' footsteps and following his example he set forth in Mark 10:45: For even the Son of Man came not to be served but to serve, and to give his life as a ransom for many.

Believers need to do an *ego reduction* exercise and start thinking about how they can serve other people. Asking the following simple questions can help believers focus their attention away from themselves toward other people, so that in humility they can serve them:

- Am I aware of the needs people have in my life that I may be able to them help with? (Gal 5:13)
- What skills do I have that I can use to help other people? (Ro 12:3-8)
- How can I edify the people in my life? (1 Thess 5:11)
- How can I influence people in their walk with the Lord? (Heb 10:25)
- How can I honor those around me? (Ro 12:10)
- How can I hurt with those who are hurting? (Ro 12:10)
- How can I rejoice with those who are rejoicing? (Ro 12:10)

The way of Jesus and the apostles is to live a life of serving one another and directing our attentional focus away from ourselves toward others. As we answer the above questions, hopefully we will all go through an *ego reduction*, which will help us mature in the Christian life.

Changing a Flat Tire Changed a Person's Outlook

A group of guys I hung out with had just finished playing football on a Saturday afternoon, then we went to an ice cream stand. We were sitting outside enjoying our snack when we noticed that a BMW in the parking lot had a flat tire. Moments later a woman came out with an ice cream cone in her hand, walked over to her BMW and noticed the flat tire, then a look of despair came on her face. My friend Dave nudged me with his elbow and said, "Let's go help her out."

We walked over to her and asked if we could change the tire for her. She seemed surprised at our generous offer to help her and said, "If you don't mind that would be wonderful." So we grabbed the jack out of her trunk and in about 15 minutes or so the job was completed. She was overwhelmed with gratitude, pulled out her checkbook and offered to give us money, but we refused. Dave said, "We're Christians and we like to help people out, so there's no need to pay us." Then she said, "Let me make a donation to your church," and again Dave told her that wasn't necessary because we were just happy to help her out. She looked at us with tears in her eyes and expressed her gratitude to us, "You guys just made my day, I wish there were more people like you in the world." Both Dave and I felt really good about helping her out, it only took 15 minutes and she was blessed, but so were we. We served her by considering her needs as important. Having awareness of the people around you and keeping your eyes open for opportunities to serve others is the way of humility.

Summary

In this section, Paul places a high premium on unity, which is something that the Philippians desperately needed. Their bickering and grumbling mitigated against them being able to struggle side-by-side for the gospel and have an effective witness, so Paul shows them the attitude that can bring resolution to their issues.

Since they have realized Christ's comfort in their own experience to help them cope with the challenges they were enduring, they need to treat one another as Christ has treated them. Paul is calling for a complete attitude make over that is governed by humility, which will cause one to view the needs of others as being more important than his own. He is calling for them to develop an inclination to think and act in a way that goes against the values of their culture. Through the gospel a new set of values emerge which Christ demonstrated through his life.

The rivalry and conceit, stemming from man's fallen nature, breeds discord and divisiveness, which needs to be replaced by humility and love, so the Philippians can turn the tide and live more effectively as God's people. Paul has encouraged them to consider all they have in their relationship with the Trinity and make the orientation of their lives treating one another as Christ has treated them. The divine love available to each believer must be shared in the body of Christ, and reshape each person's thinking as well as their relationships, which will enable church-life to be a more edifying experience.

In the next chapter, Paul will point out the ultimate display of humility and selflessness through the example of Jesus, which every believer is to emulate.

CHAPTER EIGHT

* * *

"The Humility of Christ"
Philippians 2:5-8

Paul has been challenging the Philippians to go through a total *attitude makeover,* which would enable them to reorient their lives to follow the example of Jesus that Paul will set forth in this section. Adopting the mindset of Christ would be a transformative experience that would revolutionize their relationships in the church, bring unity, and increase their effectiveness in reaching out to their community. In this section, which is often referred to as the Christ Hymn, Paul offers rich theology combined with a pragmatic application. The theology is profound, covering such topics as Jesus' eternal existence, the incarnation, the subordination of Christ to the Father, the Substitutionary Atonement, Christ's exaltation, and eschatology. Covering these topics in a few verses is an amazing literary feat, but even more amazing is its practicality.

Paul offers this teaching as an example for the Philippians to follow, so this is *theology to be lived out by the Philippians.* In the ancient world, it was felt that learning by way of example was an effective way to impart knowledge to students. Hence, stories of people's lives that are worthy of imitating would be told so that the students could mimic them. This is the strategy Paul employs in writing about the mindset of Christ. It's as if Paul is saying: "let me explain what the mindset of Christ is by pointing to his life. Now let me show you some people who have adopted that mindset and are living accordingly like Timothy, Epaphroditus, and myself." If the Philippians follow their examples the petty differences that exist in their fellowship will disappear. Therefore, following the example of Christ is Paul's antibiotic for the disease of rivalry and conceit that was weakening the church.

In the Greco-Roman world, the importance of status can't be underestimated. There's was a culture of shame and honor, where appearance was vital, in that one would present a picture of himself so that he would be praised and honored. It was a culture where the quest for power, social status, and public recognition was the norm. To miss this is to read the passage with a Western understanding that is far removed from Paul's world. The city of Philippi was a "little Rome" which valued social status. One must see that for the Philippians, that may have been in the upper echelon of society, to worship with others that were on the lower rungs of the social ladder, would be unheard of in that culture.

For instance, following Christ's example of humility is contrary to the social codes of the patricians and plebeians, citizens and non-citizens, slaves and non-slaves, the honestiores and the humiliores. The patricians were the upper class that were the wealthy land owners. The plebeians were the lower class that included everyone who was not a patrician. They were sometimes just called plebs. Plebeians and Patricians rarely mixed socially, although occasionally a pleb might marry a patrician. It was unusual though, and prior to the Republic, it was against the law for a pleb to marry a patrician. During the Empire, the populace was divided broadly into two classes: 1) the honestiores were persons of status and property owners, 2) the humiliores were persons of low social status. Only the latter were subject to certain kinds of punishment: crucifixion, torture, and corporal punishment. It is crucial to understand the social categories that existed in that day to appreciate how difficult it would be for the Philippians, and other Christians in the Roman Empire, to overcome these categories and worship as a unified church.

Can the Philippians demonstrate Christ's humility and break with their social customs? Paul is calling for them to become self-forgetful, and other-focused. To think that a rich Philippian citizen of Rome, who occupies a place in the upper ranks of society, would consider the needs of a lowly slave more important than his own is a shocking, even an appalling thought for them to consider. Therefore, in order for the Philippians to apply Paul's teaching about Christ's humility they would have to break with normal social conventions and protocols.

Now that the social categories of the day have been revealed we can move on to a discussion of the passage, which is commonly referred to as the Christ hymn (2:5-11). This passage has been debated by scholars regarding whether it was sung as a hymn in worship or just recited. It probably was sung much like other passages of Scripture that may have been offered up in worship.[37] In an oral culture where not many people could read, singing a creedal hymn would be a great way to impart doctrinal information to people. Early Christian worship was related to synagogue practices where it was common to chant and sing hymns, so this was probably sung.

It is also debated whether Paul borrowed this hymn from another source and adopted it for his letter to the Philippians or wrote it himself. Most likely Paul is the author of this passage. He presents a high Christology, which reflects the view of Christ in the early church. His purpose was to use this creedal hymn as a practical teaching on the humility of Jesus for the Philippians to follow.

To proclaim that "Jesus is Lord" was like swimming in shark infested waters because a good Roman made the confession "Caesar is Lord." A Philippian church member who proclaimed that Jesus is Lord above all, could be viewed as being disloyal to Rome, and disrespectful to the Emperor. The entire imperial family was worshiped at Philippi, and it was thought that at their death they were transformed into a god—known as an *apotheosis*. Christ's journey to the earth was quite different for he was said to empty himself (2:7). Jesus' earthly trek was one of humiliation, degradation, and a painful death. The imperial family would often act generously, which was expected by the people, but they did so for self-serving reasons, such as gaining accolades from the crowds, and keeping their social status elevated in the eyes of the people.

---

[37] See: 1 Cor 14:26; Col 3:16-17; Eph 5:18-20

Jesus, on the other hand, did not exercise his power for self-serving purposes, rather, he was obedient and humbled himself to the point of death on the cross. He didn't defend himself against his accusers, didn't cry out in pain, didn't call down the angels to rescue him, he didn't assert his rights, but died to atone for the sins of mankind. Many people struggle understanding what it means to be humble. "If we define humble as that which is beneath us, and as long as we continue to see ourselves as better than our 'humble' actions, we are not modeling Christ. Only when we embrace the reality that our status as believers removes any claims to define our deeds as humble can we know the slave-humiliation of Christ. This is far from the emperor's self-understanding, and certainly of our world's today."[38]

Jesus' example of humility and the suspension his rights are all the more amazing when we consider that he occupied the highest position in the universe as the Son of God, then against all logic emptied himself and added humanity to his deity. This is called downward mobility, which was so contrary to the path of life in the Greco-Roman world, just as it is today. We now turn to our analysis of Philippians 2:5-11. This chapter will focus on vv. 5-8, which is the first half of the Christ Hymn. The next chapter will focus on the second half of the hymn.

Have this mindset in you, which was also in Christ Jesus, [6]who, existing in the form of God, didn't consider equality with God a thing to be grasped, [7]but emptied himself, taking the form of a slave, being made in the likeness of men. [8]And being found in human form, he humbled himself, becoming obedient to death, yes, the death of the cross. (Author's Translation, 2:5-8)

Verse five presents a translation issue because there is no verb in the original text. Literally it reads: Have this in your mind, which ____________ also in Christ Jesus. A verb needs to be supplied in order for it to make sense in English. Usually the word ***was*** is inserted in most translations of the Bible. This aligns with the context because Paul is calling for the believers to imitate Christ's humility and be like-minded. Where Paul says **Have this mindset in you,** it is written in the plural, so he is addressing the entire church. The NIV's translation: **In your relationships with one another, have the same mindset**

---

[38] Cholik, Loc. 2507

as Christ Jesus is appropriate because Paul is commanding the Philippians to have the mindset of Christ govern their interactions with one another. **Mindset** is another occurrence of the Greek *phronéō*, which, as mentioned earlier, is difficult to translate because it doesn't have an exact English equivalent. It means something like: to think, to direct the mind toward, or thinking that corresponds to outward action. It is one of the key words in Philippians Paul uses to challenge them to reflect on what he's teaching them. Only as believers begin to *think* like Jesus, will their *actions* follow his example. Then, and only then, can true humility and unity can be attained, because Jesus is the prototype for the kind of mindset that produces oneness and fruitful relationships. The above view calls for the mindset of Christ to be the paradigm through which believers relate to one another, hence this is referred to as the *paradigmatic view*. Disciples of Christ are called to adopt his mindset and relate to people accordingly.[39]

Verse five serves as a bridge between vv. 1-4 and 6-11, providing a smooth transition to the example of Christ. In other words, vv. 6-11 are a commentary about the mindset of Christ. The original Greek text is written in a three-line pattern of six strophes, which is reflected in the following division:

Strophe 1
Who existing in the form of God
Did not consider a thing to be grasped
Equality with God

---

[39] There are other ways scholars understand this passage: (1) The mystical view—The mystical union between Christ and the believer is the key to relationships, so: "Let your attitude toward one another arise out of your life in Christ." (2) The ecclesiological view—The phrase "in Christ" is a creedal formula stressing membership in his body as the basis for church relationships, so: "Let this mind be what is proper to have as those who are "in Christ." (3) The "drama of salvation" view—This soteriological approach stresses conversion as the moment when believers were inserted "in Christ," so: "Let this mind be in you which was made possible when you were made to be in Christ." All views contain an element of imitating Christ. (Osborne, Loc. 1298)

Strophe 2
But emptied himself
Taking on the form of a slave
Being made in the likeness of men

Strophe 3
And being found in human form
He humbled himself
Becoming obedient to death, yes, the death of the cross

Strophe 4
Therefore God also highly exalted him
And gave him the name
Which is above every name

Strophe 5
That at the name of Jesus
Every knee should bow
Of those in heaven, those on earth, and those under the earth

Strophe 6
And that every tongue confess
That Jesus Christ is Lord
To the glory of God the Father

The analysis of the passage begins with the first strophe.

who, existing in the form of God, didn't consider equality with God a thing to be grasped. (2:6)

This verse speaks to Jesus' eternality, or his pre-incarnate state. Before Jesus came to the earth, he always existed, in other words, one can go back in time and he would never find an occasion when Jesus didn't exist. He is the eternally generated Son of God—the second person of the Trinity. The word **existing** is written as a present participle, which implies continuous action, meaning that Jesus always exists as God the Son and will continue to exist forever as the Son of God.

The word **form** *(morphḗ)* is defined as the outward form that corresponds to the inner essence. Jesus didn't just appear to be divine, he is in every way deity—of the same essence or substance of God the Father and is coequal. This is an important passage about the deity of Christ because Jesus wasn't a created being, rather he is the Creator[40] and he eternally existed (John 8:58; Heb 7:3).

Jesus **existing in the form of God** refers to his essence, but he "**didn't consider equality" with God a thing to be grasped**, points to his relationship with God the Father. At no point did Jesus ever stop being God, but in his earthly state Jesus lived in a different mode of existence. He demonstrated his subordination to the will of the Father, even though he is fully God, and didn't try to grasp (or exploit) for selfish reasons his equality with God. The word **grasped** is a translation of the Greek *harpagmós*, which has a range of meaning including: to seize, exploit, grasp, take hold of, and robbery.

This means that Jesus, in his heavenly state, didn't exploit his coequal status with God to his own advantage. In other words, rather than exploiting his divine status and privileges he did the unexpected—he gave up his rights in obedience to God the Father and provided mankind with the greatest act of humility ever. When he came to earth, he didn't arrive with a display of pomp and splendor, demanding that the entire world worship him as God, which was one of the temptations that Satan presented to him (Mat 4; Luke 4). Jesus didn't seek instant glorification, no, he came as the suffering servant (Isa 53) to fulfill his destiny of dying on the cross and left the subsequent glorification up to God.

Jesus took this course of action because he didn't **consider** equality with God a thing to be grasped. The Greek word *hégeomai* is translated **consider**, which has a range of meaning that includes: the leading thought in one's mind, to esteem, regard highly, or to think. This reveals that Jesus went through a deliberate thought process and concluded that he wouldn't press his rights and exploit his divine status. Instead, he chose to suspend his rights, giving up what was already his as God the Son. **Consider** is written in the

---

[40] See: John 1:3–5; Col 1:16; Heb 1:2

aorist tense, which means there was a decisive point in the past where Jesus decided to lay aside his rights and empty himself (v. 7).

But emptied himself, taking the form of a slave, being made in the likeness of men. (2:7)

This brings us to the second strophe, which establishes a contrast with v. 6. Rather than deciding to exploit his divine status as the Son of God he did this: **but emptied himself**. The meaning of this has been the subject of much debate among scholars centering on the meaning of **emptied**, which is a form of the word *kenoō.* Taken to an extreme, some have set forth the view that Jesus emptied himself of his deity and was just a human being. This has been known as the *kenotic heresy* and is to be rejected because it doesn't square up with the rest of the teaching in Philippians and the New Testament about Jesus' divine status. The question to be answered is what did Jesus empty himself of(?), because the passage doesn't tell us. There have been several views set forth on this difficult issue, one of which is the view that he emptied himself of the *prerogatives of deity*, such as the use of his powers, his omnipresence, his face-to-face relationship with the Father, leaving the realm of glory, and so on. Another way this is understood is that Jesus emptied himself of whatever prevented him from becoming a human being. There is a bit of mystery in grasping exactly what Paul means here, so the precise meaning may elude the reader.

Even though there are some self-imposed limitations Jesus willingly assumed, the best way to read and understand the passage is in a social way considering the societal peaking order existing in Philippi.[41] In a society like Philippi, and other Roman cities, that are driven by status and rank, Jesus did what no ordinary Roman citizen would do—give up his high and lofty status. Christ decided to empty himself of his rank, standing, privileges, and status, to move downward by assuming humanity and experiencing all the limitations that accompany that state of being. He went from the highest place to the lowest place taking on the form of a slave, to self-sacrificially obey God the Father and serve mankind. The word slave (*doulos*) is the same word Paul used to identify himself and Timothy as slaves of Jesus Christ (1:1).

---

[41] Witherington, Loc. 2216

Jesus taking the "form of a slave" is parallel to "form of God" (v. 6). In both cases the word **form** is *morphē*: The outward form that corresponds to the inner essence.

Jesus never stopped being God, he demonstrated humility by becoming a human being, and Paul wants the Philippians to be humble like Jesus. He wants them to adopt the attitude of Jesus, which would lead them to rethink their understanding of social status and privileges. This should lead to behavior that is opposed to **rivalry and conceit** (2:3) as each of the Philippians would: **in humility, each counting others better than himself; [4]each of you not just looking to his own things, but each of you also to the things of others (vv. 3b-4).** This is what Jesus modeled for mankind, and all his disciples should seek to do the same.

In taking on the limitations of humanity he occupied the position of a slave, which was the lowest place in Greco-Roman society. Slaves were property that were sold in the marketplace, they had no rights, they were under the orders of their master, and could even be put to death if their master chose to do so. Their life wasn't their own for they were bought and sold as commodities. Jesus' mission in coming to earth as a man was to serve humanity by dying on the cross and leaving mankind an example of how to live a life of humility.

In Jesus' emptying himself he became a fully human being: **being made in the likeness of men.** The word **likeness** is a translation of *homoióma*, which means: something that is similar, bearing a resemblance or likeness, but not an exact copy. Because of the ambiguity of this word it suggests that Jesus was like us in some ways, but not in others. One of the bedrocks of Christian belief is the full humanity of Jesus, which is affirmed in this passage and by this author. However, Jesus' humanity isn't exactly like our humanity, in that it isn't an exact copy or duplicate of ours. Jesus' humanity is similar to our humanity in some respects and dissimilar in others. What is similar is that he is fully human, just as we are (Heb 2:17). In the incarnation Jesus became "like us" in the sense of "the same as we are." What is dissimilar is that he didn't bear the corruption of sin (Heb 4:15), and that he is fully God. Therefore, Paul says that Jesus appeared in the likeness of sinful flesh in Romans 8:3, meaning that Jesus was "like us" but "not exactly the same as" regarding our sinfulness. Thus, the usage of *homoióma* makes sense in this way. Jesus is fully human and fully God, two natures coexisting in one person, which makes Jesus the most unique person to ever live.

Quite often scholars get bogged down in the theological discussion of what Jesus emptied himself of, and the social / ethical emphases of the passage are thrown under the bus and left out of the conversation. This is unfortunate because it misses Paul's challenge to the Philippians to rethink their social conventions regarding status, privilege, shame and honor, and realign them according to the example of Christ's humility.

"In Christ Jesus God has thus shown his true nature; this is what it means for Christ to be "equal with God"—to pour himself out for the sake of others and to do so by taking the role of a slave. Hereby he not only reveals the character of God, but from the perspective of the present context also reveals what it means for us to be created in God's image, to bear his likeness and have his "mindset." It means taking the role of the slave for the sake of others."[42]

The Philippians need to adopt this attitude which would cause their definition of honor and shame to be altered, as well as the cross to be seen not through the lens of shame, but as the ultimate example of selfless love. It is this to which Paul is calling on the Philippians to consider.

This brings us to the third strophe:

And being found in human form, he humbled himself, becoming obedient to death, yes, the death of the cross. (2:8)

The descent of Jesus from heavenly glory to earthly existence continues: **And being found in human form.** The word **form** is a translation of the Greek word *schéma,* from which the English word scheme, or schematic is derived. It refers to the outward shape or appearance of something, not the inner essence. When people saw Jesus, they recognized him as a male human being. When Jesus was hanging on the cross the people saw a human being.

---

[42] Fee, p. 214

This phrase parallels **being made in the likeness of men** (v. 7), so the two phrases taken together highlight Jesus' full humanity.

Jesus **being found** indicates that there was a time when Jesus was not a human being. He always existed as the eternally begotten Son of God, but in the incarnation, when he was conceived by the Holy Spirit and born of a virgin he became something that he had not been previously—a human being. How the human mind can fathom this requires the element of faith. This is a divine mystery that can't be fully comprehended or explained, but it is totally truthful. Jesus is now the God man—fully divine, fully human, with two natures in one person.

As a man **he humbled himself, becoming obedient to death, yes, the death of the cross.** When Jesus was in the form of God he "emptied himself" (vv. 6-7), when he was found in human form he "humbled himself" (v. 8). He lowered himself to a place that is at the bottom of the barrel, for one can't go any lower than dying on the cross. His humility was shown in his obedience to the Father, by assuming humanity and dying on the cross to atone for the sins of mankind.

This is where the reader must step out of his world and make sure he places himself squarely into the First Century context. The cross was a symbol of death and shame. A Roman citizen couldn't be crucified, it was for non-citizens, criminals, insurrectionists, and for those who were considered the scum of the earth. Crucifixion was perfected by the Romans almost to the point of being an art form, where pain was maximized, shame and humiliation were brought to the foreground as the victims were hanging on the cross naked. Scourging, which accompanied crucifixion, was brutal and enhanced the pain of the whole event. It was common for people to die of the scourging, done with the "cat of nine tails" before they were nailed to the cross.

One thinks of dying a good death, one with honor, but crucifixion wasn't a good death—it was the worst kind of death with no honor attached to it whatsoever. It was completely degrading, involving horrific pain, suffering, torture and total shame. One also must consider the abuse Jesus suffered along with his crucifixion. He was rejected by his own people, his siblings,

Judas betrayed him, his disciples deserted him, people hurled verbal abuse at him, the Jewish religious leaders rejected him as the Messiah, and handed him over to the Romans who mocked him, beat him, plucked out his beard, scourged him, then crucified him. Jesus cried out "My God why have you forsaken me?" It can't get any worse than that. To have God the Father pour out his wrath on his Son to punish him for all the sin of humankind is something that no other human being will ever experience. Jesus bore the unmitigated, unrestricted, unreserved wrath of God as the punishment for man's sin, so that we wouldn't have to be punished.

It is difficult to imagine how many more ways he could have suffered. It is equally difficult to imagine how much more obedient to the divine will someone can be than Christ was. Literally, Jesus has descended from the highest place in the universe, to the lowest place on earth dying a criminal's death. His descent is complete, he has suffered and died. In the normal social conventions of Paul's day Jesus' shame and humiliation couldn't be greater. He is left without honor, social status, only having total shame and degradation accompanying him.

Scholars have debated the degree to which this Philippian hymn echoes the Suffering Servant of Isaiah. Paul may have borrowed from the Isaiah 53 passage and used it as a source to write the hymn. It wasn't considered a Messianic passage by the Jews, it was figuratively applied to the nation of Israel. In reading the following passage (Isa 53:4-7) it is difficult not to see this as pointing to Jesus' death on the cross:

> Surely he has borne our sickness, and carried our suffering; yet we considered him plagued, struck by God, and afflicted. 5But he was pierced for our transgressions. He was crushed for our iniquities. The punishment that brought our peace was on him; and by his wounds we are healed. 6We all like sheep have gone astray. Everyone has turned to his own way; and Yahweh has laid on him the iniquity of us all. 7He was oppressed, yet when he was afflicted he didn't open his mouth. As a lamb that is led to the slaughter, and as a sheep that before its shearers is silent, so he didn't open his mouth.

Surely this passage must be an allusion to Jesus' death on the cross. Paul isn't presenting a theology of atonement in the Philippian passage as he does, for example, in Romans chapter three. He is showing his Philippian audience that Jesus was willing to go to extreme lengths to demonstrate what Paul said in vv. 3b-4: **but in humility, each counting others better than himself; [4]each of you not just looking to his own things, but each of you also to the things of others.** Paul presents a "shock effect" on his audience to stimulate them to follow Christ's example of selflessness, humility, and self-sacrifice, because this is the remedy to the backbiting, selfishness, and self-centeredness that was causing tension in the community of faith. It was normal in that culture to climb higher up the ladder of societal honor and seek greater levels of social status. However, after the Philippians consider Christ's example the quest for public recognition and elevated status should come to a screeching halt, especially in their church relationships.

The cross was a five-letter word that people avoided speaking in respectable company. Speaking about the cross was obscene and inappropriate in Roman culture. It was a dirty, foul word to speak. Jews would view the cross as a sign of being cursed by God (Deu 21:23; Gal 3:13). For them to think of the Lord's anointed Messiah being cursed by God and dying on a cross willingly was unthinkable. For Gentiles, dying on a cross lacked any type of nobility, or power—it was totally shameful. The Jews stumbled over the cross, and the Gentiles thought it was foolishness, but it was the power and wisdom of God (1 Cor 1:18-26).

In the eyes of Greco-Roman culture, when Jesus was crucified he was stripped of all special status, honor and brought to a place of total shame. The Philippians are challenged to turn their cultural norms upside-down and see Jesus' death on the cross as something to celebrate, something that is honorable, noble, even as an example of selfless love to follow. This is no easy task for them to accomplish given their cultural values.[43]

---

[43] To help the Philippians realign their cultural values regarding Jesus' death, they must consider that when God raised Jesus from the dead, he was totally vindicated and proven to be God. It is difficult to see how the Christian faith would have survived, with the absence of the resurrection.

The first half of the hymn comes to an end with the unspeakable word in Roman society being mentioned last—CROSS.

Insights, Applications, and Life Lessons

I've traveled many times in the last two and a half years to various places in Latin America. At the end of every trip I'm always looking forward to coming home so I can see my wife and get back to my normal life, riding my bike, lifting weights, etc. As we approach Sacramento, where I live, the pilot addresses the passengers and says, "We are beginning our descent into Sacramento." It's music to my ears! Then I start thinking about a normal safe descent to the runway. From 36,000 feet to touchdown on the runway, I'm home—finally!

The Descent of Jesus

The descent of Jesus wasn't normal; in fact, it was the most abnormal, unexpected descent in world history. That a god descended to earth wouldn't have been surprising to the Romans, for on one occasion when Paul and Barnabas were in Lystra Paul healed a man, which resulted in the crowd thinking that the gods have descended to earth in human form. They thought Paul was Hermes, and Barnabas was Zeus (Acts 14:8-13). What would be outright shocking to the Romans is that Jesus, who is fully God, descended to earth as a man, taking the role of a slave and dying the most shameful death possible on a cross. This wouldn't compute in their way of thinking because there was nothing honorable, or worthy about being crucified. The thought of the Son of God being crucified was abhorrent to them.

From today's perspective, as Twenty First Century Christians, it is understood that Jesus' death was noble, honorable, self-sacrificial, and a demonstration of humility for all to follow. However, those in the First Century Greco-Roman world struggled to see Jesus' death in that light. The Philippians needed to go through a thought re-evaluation, so they could view the cross in an entirely new light. No longer is it a picture of shame, disgrace, and humiliation, because it is redefined by Christ as the greatest act of humility, love, and self-sacrificial service ever. It is important to appreciate how difficult this would be for Romans to comprehend because it cut against the grain of their culture.

It is essential to grasp Paul's rhetorical strategy in this passage. He is challenging the Philippians to follow Jesus' example of humility, so they put a stop to the infighting and rivalry that was weakening their church. Where people adopt the mindset of Christ, and walk in his footsteps, petty differences that divide Christians should quickly dissipate. If we could follow Jesus' example of humility in all our relationships the result would be more fruitful marriages, parenting relationships, friendships, church relationships, etc.

The Cross in Today's World

We see images of the cross are all over the place. The next time you go for a drive keep your eyes open for churches. When you see a church, you will most likely see a cross somewhere on the building. Go into a church and you will see a cross. It will be on printed materials, included in the church logo, on the walls, bulletin boards, etc. Christians today identify with the cross, and will do it proudly, after all, the cross is the logo of the Christian faith—it's Jesus' trademark. The cross in our day doesn't have the stigma it had in the First Century Roman culture of Philippi.

Being 2,000 years after Jesus' death on the cross it is difficult for the modern reader to understand the social stigma that the cross had in Jesus' day. It was a dirty word that wasn't spoken in good company. Today we go into jewelry stores and buy necklaces with a gold cross, or people get a tattoo of a cross, we wear T-shirts that have embedded crosses, we buy coffee mugs with crosses and we think it is stylish to do this. Christians will openly identify with the cross, but in First Century Philippi that wasn't the case. By comparison it would be like someone today wearing a piece of jewelry fashioned into an electric chair worn around their neck. There wouldn't be anything considered noble about that and I've never seen anybody with a piece of jewelry fashioned into an electric chair. Things have changed significantly from Paul's day to our own.

Summary

In this section, which is the first half of the Christ Hymn, Paul presents a literary and theological masterpiece. He has been hammering away at the need for a more unified congregation, so he directs the Philippians' attention to the example of humility provided by Jesus. The preexistent Christ took on humanity while retaining his divine status, thus he emptied himself of whatever prevented him from becoming human. Theologians have extensively debated exactly what Jesus emptied himself of, but it is clear that his deity was somewhat veiled in his earthly trek.

It is important to read this from the Philippians' cultural perspective of shame and honor. In their world status, prestige, and power were everything, so nobody would do what Jesus did by descending from the highest to the lowest place and die on a cross. Nothing could be considered more shameful than what Jesus did, especially since he is the eternally begotten Son of God. This thought wouldn't compute to the Philippians, which caused them to rethink their social conventions of shame and honor. Jesus did something completely honorable, noble, and significant for all humanity by descending and dying on the cross. The Philippians would have to go through a complete attitude makeover to understand this. Humility wasn't a virtue in the ancient world, in fact, it was something loathsome in Greco-Roman culture. It was Jesus and the Christians that presented humility as a virtue to be ascribed to in governing human behavior.

In the next section, God the Father appears and swings into action by exalting Jesus to the highest place and conferring on him the divine name which is above every other name.

CHAPTER NINE

* * *

"The Exaltation of Christ" Philippians 2:9-11

In the first half of the Christ Hymn Jesus descended to earth by emptying himself and taking the form of a slave dying on the cross. Jesus' death is presented to the Philippians to demonstrate his humility. In the second half of the Christ Hymn God the Father is the focus of attention as he exalts Jesus to the place from which he came and gives us a forward glimpse into the end of the age. All creation will bow the knee to Jesus in submission and pay him homage. Jesus fulfilled his mission in obedience to his Father, now the Father exalts the Son to the highest place in the universe.

Therefore God also highly exalted him, and gave to him the name which is above every name; [10]that at the name of Jesus every knee should bow, of those in heaven, those on earth, and those under the earth, [11]and that every tongue should confess that Jesus Christ is Lord, to the glory of God the Father. (2:9-11)

The fourth strophe begins:

Therefore God also highly exalted him, and gave to him the name which is above every name; (2:9)

Therefore, connects us to the previous section by introducing God's response to Jesus' death, who has been the subject of vv. 6-8, now God the Father is the subject of vv. 9-11. Jesus couldn't have lowered himself any more than he did, **therefore God also highly exalted him.** It was the work of God the Father to **highly exalt** Jesus, which is a translation of the Greek word *huperupsoó.* This is a compound word consisting of *hypér*, meaning "beyond or above" and *hypsóō*, meaning "elevate." Thus, the word literally means to "elevate above." To paraphrase, Paul is saying: "Therefore God also *super-exalted* him." This is the only occurrence of the word in the New Testament.

God the Father highly exalted Jesus to the uppermost place in the universe. The Son of God descended from the highest to the lowest place possible by assuming humanity and being obedient to death on the cross. Now God highly exalts Jesus by bringing him to the most glorious, lofty place in the universe. There is no higher place that Jesus could have been exalted to. The reversal is complete in that Jesus descended from the realm of glory to the earth, now God highly exalts the Son and he ascends back into the realm of glory from which he came. Although the resurrection and ascension aren't specifically mentioned they are assumed in this passage. The resurrection points to the fact that Jesus lives forever and has defeated death thereby paving the way for our resurrection (1 Cor 15:54). The exaltation of Jesus points us toward Jesus' sovereign reign over the universe, which will be realized in its fullness at his return (1 Cor 15:27-28). "To use a limited analogy, in God's 'new math,' Incarnation + Humiliation = Exaltation."[44]

God is returning to Jesus the glory he always had but was veiled in his earthly state. On one occasion, during the transfiguration, Jesus' glory shined through his earthly body, exposing his pre-existent radiance.[45] God the Father is now restoring Jesus back to the place of glory he occupied before the incarnation. There is now a bestowal of glory to Jesus which wasn't recognizable while he was in his earthly state.

This would be shocking to Paul's readers in that Jesus, who died a shameful death on a cross as a common criminal, would be highly exalted by God. This

---

[44] Cohick, Loc. 2816

[45] See: Mat 17:2; Mark 9:2-3; Luke 9:29

would be totally unexpected and incomprehensible to the Philippians. It would appear to everyone that the cross was a place of shame and a crushing defeat for Jesus. However, in God's plan the cross was the place where total victory occurred over all the forces of darkness.

"Let us rehearse these final events from a heavenly perspective. Satan had entered Judas and acted powerfully to send Jesus to the cross, as Jesus says in John 14:30, but in actuality Satan's action was to become his own great defeat (John 12:31; 16:11). The moment Jesus died, he proclaimed to the demonic realm its collapse (1 Pet 3:19); then he disarmed the cosmic powers and led them in his victory procession through the heavens as he ascended to his Father (Col 2:15). At that moment God affirmed Christ's eternal victory and 'exalted him to the highest place.' In Ephesians 1:20 Paul describes this as God raising him from the dead and seating 'him at his right hand in the heavenly realms,' fulfilling Psalm 110:1."[46]

To see the cross as a place of cosmic victory would not compute to those living in Greco-Roman culture. In fact, people would see it as the polar opposite of victory—it would be a crushing defeat. However, it was through Jesus' work on the cross that sin was atoned for, thus making that event one of the most pivotal moments in world history, along with the resurrection. To describe the extent of God's exaltation of Jesus to the highest place he **gave to him the name which is above every name.**

The name given to Jesus is *Lord* (v. 11). One can't help seeing a connection between Isaiah 45:23-24 and the passage under consideration. In the Septuagint, which is the Greek translation of the Hebrew Bible, the word "Lord" (*kurios*) is used as a synonym of *Yahweh*, the very name of God. That *Yahweh* is called Lord (*kurios*), and Jesus is called Lord (*kurios*) points to the deity of Christ. Scripture assigns the work of Yahweh to the work of Jesus (Joel 2:32 fulfilled in Acts 2:21). This is the name given to Jesus which is above every other name in the universe, meaning that Jesus occupies a place that is unrivaled. There is no higher place that Jesus could be elevated to, and there is no other name that is higher than the very name of *Yahweh*.

---

[46] Osborne, Loc. 1470

"Yahweh had conferred on Jesus his own covenant name, as recognized in the "I AM" sayings of John 8:24, 28, 58; 13:19, echoing the "I AM" of Isaiah 43:10; 47:8, 10. This is both a name and a title, indicating that Jesus is a member of the Triune Godhead named "Yahweh," as well as Lord of all creation. The Suffering Servant is now proclaimed to be the sovereign Lord."[47]

One of the earliest Christian confessions was "Jesus is Lord" (Rom 10:9; 1 Cor 12:3). The Philippians, who had previously worshiped many lords, and were accustomed to proclaiming "Caesar is Lord" would find themselves walking on thin ice by declaring "Jesus is Lord." Jesus' name is far greater than Caesar's name. Paul, himself, was a prisoner of the Emperor as he wrote his letter to the Philippians, so he is fully aware of the danger involved in making such a bold statement in a Roman colony.

The fifth strophe:

that at the name of Jesus every knee should bow, of those in heaven, those on earth, and those under the earth, (2:10)

The **name of Jesus** is Lord (*kurios)* the name used for *Yahweh*—God's covenantal name, which is above every other name. Because of the high place that God has elevated Jesus, all of creation will worship him. Bowing the knee is an expression of paying homage and submission, acknowledging his exalted reign over the universe. The worship of Jesus is exhaustive in that **"every" knee will bow.** None will be able to withhold worship from the exalted Lord Jesus Christ in all locations: **of those in heaven, those on earth, and those under the earth.**

Jesus Christ is the Creator of the entire universe, so nothing exists that Jesus did not bring into existence. Those in heaven would include the spirit beings—angels and demons. Those on the earth would include the people living on the planet when Jesus returns, and those under the earth could include the dead, who would be raised at his coming, and the demonic realm.

---

[47] Osborne, Loc. 1490

The name of Jesus focuses our attention on his earthly trek, where he has atoned for the sin of the world and been vindicated through the resurrection and ascension. In being given the name above every name God directs the worship of the creation to his Son—the exalted Lord of all. It doesn't appear that only believers will be worshiping Jesus, it seems that all beings, even those who rejected Jesus will bow the knee in submission to him. Believers will do so out of reverent adoration, others may do so out of spite, but all will bow the knee to Jesus. An important passage in James 2:19 sheds some light on this, "for the demons believe in God and they shudder in fear and trepidation" but are certainly not redeemed creatures. They recognize God's existence and will one day in the future bow the knee to Jesus. The focus that Paul presents here is the inevitability and undisputed fact that all creatures will acknowledge that Jesus is Lord. His concern isn't with the attitude of the heart of each creature, rather it is that each creature will acknowledge the Lordship of Christ.

Verse 11 brings us to the sixth and final strophe:

and that every tongue should confess that Jesus Christ is Lord, to the glory of God the Father. (2:11)

In addition to bowing the knee in submission every created being **should confess that Jesus Christ is Lord.** The word **confess** is a translation of the Greek *exomologeó,* which doesn't necessarily mean a confession with an attitude of praise, it can mean just to admit or acknowledge something openly. Bowing the knee in submission and confessing the Lordship of Christ is something all created beings will do, whether out of love or spite. It is an irrefutable fact that Jesus is Lord, and no one will be able to deny it, rather all will proclaim it.

The confession "Jesus is Lord" was the dividing line between believer and nonbeliever. Paul has said that no one can confess "Jesus is Lord" except by the Spirit (1 Cor 12:3), which ties the work of the Spirit to regeneration. In Romans 10:9 the confession "Jesus is Lord" is tied to the belief in the resurrection, which is alluded to here. In the end, all created beings will declare that Jesus is Lord *(Yahweh)* but the confession will not be for conversion, but of final acknowledgement that God has made this Jesus, whom you crucified, both Lord and Christ (Acts 2:36).

The confession "Jesus is Lord" arose in the early Jewish Christian communities, which is supported by the use of the Aramaic word *maranatha* in 1 Corinthians 16:22: "Come O Lord!" Now the early Christians are assigning words to Jesus that belonged solely to God. The early believers have transferred the name "Lord" to the risen Jesus, thus seeing Jesus as God (*Yahweh*).

One can't help seeing that Paul was drawing from Isaiah 45:18-25 in writing the Philippian passage. It's importance in God assigning to Jesus the divine name must not be overlooked:

> *For Yahweh who created the heavens, the God who formed the earth and made it, who established it and didn't create it a waste, who formed it to be inhabited says: "I am Yahweh; and there is no other.* [19]I have not spoken in secret, in a place of the land of darkness. I didn't say to the offspring of Jacob, 'Seek me in vain.' I, *Yahweh*, speak righteousness. I declare things that are right. [20]"Assemble yourselves and come. Draw near together, you who have escaped from the nations. Those have no knowledge who carry the wood of their engraved image, and pray to a god that can't save. [21]Declare and present it. Yes, let them take counsel together. Who has shown this from ancient time? Who has declared it of old? *Haven't I, Yahweh? There is no other God besides me, a just God and a Savior; There is no one besides me.* [22]*"Look to me, and be saved, all the ends of the earth; for I am God, and there is no other.* [23]I have sworn by myself. The word has gone out of my mouth in righteousness, and will not be revoked, *that to me every knee shall bow, every tongue shall take an oath.* [24]They will say of me, 'There is righteousness and strength only in *Yahweh*.'" Even to him shall men come; and all those who raged against him shall be disappointed. [25]All the offspring of Israel will be justified in *Yahweh*, and will rejoice! (Italics Mine)

In this passage, the victory of *Yahweh* is celebrated over the nations. That the name *Yahweh* is the name given to Jesus (2:11) identifies him as the

Creator, the only God, and the one to whom all worship is due. That Jesus has the divine name conferred on him points to his exaltation by God the Father, but also speaks to the high view of Jesus maintained by the early church.

The exaltation of the Son, by God, is done to his glory, for the hymn ends with: **to the glory of God the Father.** There is no competition between the Father and the Son, for one acts to promote the glory of the other. Jesus brought glory to God the Father while he walked his earthly trek, and God the Father glorified Jesus as he obeyed him.[48]

All the work that Jesus has done to secure our salvation has been done to the glory of the Father, so the Father has returned glory to Jesus by exalting him to the highest place. This points to the perfect harmony that exists within the Godhead, but more importantly it points to the Father and the Son being of the same essence. This protects Paul's concept of monotheism (1 Cor 8:6).

An amazing use of the Isaiah 45:23 passage is Paul applying it to God the Father in Romans 14:10-12:

> You, then, why do you judge your brother or sister? Or why do you treat them with contempt? For we will all stand before God's judgment seat. [11]It is written: "'As surely as I live,' says the Lord, *'every knee will bow before me; every tongue will acknowledge God.'"* [12]So then, each of us will give an account of ourselves to God. (NIV, italics mine)

In Romans 14 Paul alternates between Christ and God. "In 2 Corinthians 5:10 believers stand before the 'Judgment seat of Christ,' in the Romans 14 passage it is the 'judgment seat of God.' This isn't to signal confusion on Paul's part, instead, it demonstrates the very close relationship between them. Christ functions as God's representative in the judgment, so judgment for Paul can be ascribed either to Christ (2 Cor 5:10) or to God (Rom 14:10)."[49]

---

[48] See: John 8:54; 12:28; 13:32; 17:1; 5

[49] Schreiner, p. 722

There is something more that must be brought into the picture. In the Christ Hymn, at the end of the age all worship is directed toward Jesus, but this doesn't detract from the glory of the Father it only adds to his glory. As the Father exalts Christ and confers on him the divine name, the Father doesn't suffer any reduction in rank or status. "Even the Father, by doing this exalting and giving of a divine name to the Son, is in one sense modeling the role of a servant. Even more stunning is that in this same Isaianic material in Isa. 48.11 God says he will never give his glory to another! One can only conclude that Paul believed that the Son was not "another" in the sense that Isaiah had in mind, another order of being, someone less than God the Father."[50]

The conclusion to be drawn is that Jesus is fully God—*Yahweh*—the Triune God. The nature of God has been revealed in Christ who showed humanity that deity isn't about self-exaltation, asserting one's rights, gaining prestige, status, and recognition. The true nature of God is to give and serve for the welfare of others, which is clearly stated in 1 John 4:10: "In this is love, not that we loved God, but that he loved us, and sent his Son as the atoning sacrifice for our sins." Jesus came as the servant, not the one to be served (Mark 10:45). This is the nature of the Triune God.

Insights, Applications, and Life Lessons

In American culture we have been conditioned by the American Dream, which says your movement should always be upward—that is upward mobility. People should climb the corporate ladder, make more money, get promotions, earn another degree, upgrade the size of their house, buy a nicer car, gain more prestige, and position yourself for a comfortable retirement. To attain this, some people may use questionable means to achieve that end. They may deliberately try to dominate others, jockey for positions of power, play office politics, and so forth. Such is the conventional wisdom of life in America, but this goes against Jesus' example of humility.

In coming to earth Jesus did what nobody would have expected in that his mobility was downward. A stark contrast exists between the upward mobility

---

[50] Witherington, Loc. 2386

that the world advocates, and the downward mobility which Jesus demonstrated. Jesus' descent to the earth was countercultural, for it cuts against the grain of today's cultural norms as well as those of the First Century Roman world. Jesus did the opposite of what many people do in seeking to realize the American dream.

In God's Kingdom humility, suffering, and taking up your cross daily following Jesus is the pathway to glory and exaltation. When Jesus was tempted by Satan at the beginning of his ministry, he took Jesus to a high mountain and showed him all the kingdoms of the world and offered them to him if he would bow down and worship him (Mat 4:8-9). Jesus would have nothing to do with that, because he recognized God's path for him was serving mankind, and dying on the cross, but he also knew that exaltation would follow his humiliation. This is the way of things in God's Kingdom. Serving in humility precedes God exalting believers at the end of the age. Everyone needs to be humble before God and man, and let God do the exalting. Usually when people try to exalt themselves they end up being humbled. Pride goes before a fall (Pro 16:18), but if people walk with God in obedience and humility he will do the exalting.

Can Jesus' Teaching Help Unify America?

The church at Philippi was divided, which is the same place America is today. There is a consensus that our country is fractured by socio-economic distinctions, a myriad of political issues, race, values, and so on. How can Paul's teaching on humility and the example of Jesus help Americans come together as a nation, rather than continuing down the road of animosity and division?

The USA gives people freedom of speech, so they are entitled to freely assert their views and stand up for their rights. This results in people speaking out for such things as: civil rights, women's rights, immigration rights, personal rights, gay rights, political rights, constitutional rights, minority rights, right to bear arms, and so forth. A problem occurs when people express their views and marginalize those who disagree with them. Watching the news on TV night-after-night reveals the depth of animosity, even hatred that existed toward people who maintain views that are different than their own. Political parties seem to be warring factions, rather than working together for the good of the country. This is a problem! How can America be unified when people are constantly vilifying and demonizing those who don't see things their way? This behavior kills the opportunity to have an intelligent dialogue on issues and stands in stark contrast to the humility Jesus demonstrated.

It is perfectly acceptable for people to assert their convictions and opinions to those who may disagree and see things differently. However, the way of Jesus is to consider the views of those who differ with our own in a respectful, dignified manner without slinging mud at them. People need to stick to the issues under discussion and not launch personal attacks when someone disagrees with them. Everyone can take a lesson on humility from Jesus, which will make America a much better place.

The End Times

Talk to people about Jesus and you will discover that many opinions exist about who he is. Some people believe he was merely an enlightened man, a prophet, a moralist, an ethicist, a great teacher, but not the divine Son of God. In fact, some people don't believe Jesus ever existed. Throughout world history many people have rejected Jesus and died in unbelief. On the other hand, there are many that have placed their faith in Jesus and are reconciled to God. At the end of the age every created being that ever existed will bow their knee and confess with one voice "Jesus Christ is Lord."

Everyone will know this with absolute certainty. Christ's Lordship will be an undeniable fact which nobody will be able to refute. The entire created order will pay homage to Jesus, both the saved and unsaved. There will be no question about Jesus' identity because all will know the glorious truth that Jesus is Lord and reigns supreme over the universe. In the eternal state there will be no more varying opinions about Jesus, confusion about who he is and what he did, because all that will be cleared up. With crystal clarity all will know that Jesus Christ is Lord. Unbelief in Jesus Christ will be a thing of the past, it will not exist.

Summary

Jesus' earthly descent to the lowest place is now reversed and God exalts his Son to the highest place where there are no rivals. The entire created order will worship him and confess his Lordship. God has conferred his own covenant name on his Son—Yahweh. All the creation will worship him which gives us a glimpse into the culmination of world history. Jesus reigns supreme over the universe to the glory of God the Father. Paul presented the Christ Hymn to challenge the Philippians to imitate the humility of Jesus and adopt the mind of Christ which will heighten unity, strengthen fellowship, foster teamwork, and make relationships more harmonious. An important takeaway from this is that humility and suffering for the sake of Christ and the gospel precedes exaltation. It is God who will do the exalting.

In the next section, Paul will instruct the Philippians to apply this teaching to their own lives and church.

CHAPTER TEN

* * *

"A Spiritual Workout"
Philippians 2:12-18

Paul has just presented his readers with the greatest display of humility in world history—a display of humility that will never be matched or exceeded. The house lights were dimmed, the curtains opened, and the stage lights came on illuminating the incarnation of Christ and his amazing attitude of servanthood and humility. Now the curtain closes, the house lights come on and believers in Philippi are challenged to follow his example of humility, so that their church relationships can be fruitful and harmonious. It's time to go to work and follow Jesus' example, but how do the Philippians apply this passage to their lives? How can they walk in Jesus' footsteps and demonstrate his humility?

Paul offers instruction to the Philippians as to how they can do this. The believer is to "work out his salvation" because it is God who "works in you." This passage sheds a great deal of light on the journey of spiritual development that all believers are traveling. Sanctification is the theological term that refers to the believer's separation from sin and growth in Christlike character. This is a process that goes on for the duration of the believer's life making sanctification a progressive experience. In this process believers play a part which is referred to as "working out your salvation" while God plays the dominant part cited as "for God is at work in you." Because God is at work in the individual he can work out his salvation. Thus, God and man are working together to bring life transformation. The Philippians must take this to heart, as should today's believer, if they are to develop spiritually and be a unified church.

When thinking of sanctification it is often done in individual terms. This is a tragic mistake, for Paul desires to see the Philippian church moving to maturity, which should enable them to resolve their internal squabbles and be a healthy church. Therefore, sanctification is an individual experience worked out in fellowship with other believers.

The Christ hymn has profound implications for the way the Philippians must order their personal lives and corporate experience as a worshiping community. Jesus' life regarding his attitudes, behavior, habits, and relationships must be imitated, which is what Paul is trying to drive home to his readers. The application of the Christ hymn (vv. 12-18) should be seen in relation to the main thesis (the *propositio* [1:27-30]). Paul is offering commentary in this section on how one can live his life in a way that is worthy of the Good News (1:27). In terms of ancient rhetoric, he is continuing his *probatio*, which are arguments that support his main thesis.

So then, my beloved, even as you have always obeyed, not only in my presence, but now much more in my absence, work out your own salvation with fear and trembling. 13For it is God who works in you both to will and to work, for his good pleasure. 14Do all things without murmurings and disputes, 15that you may become blameless and harmless, children of God without defect in the middle of a crooked and perverse generation, among whom you are seen as lights in the world, 16holding up the word of life; that I may have something to boast in the day of Christ, that I didn't run in vain nor labor in vain. 17Yes, and if I am poured out on the sacrifice and service of your faith, I rejoice, and rejoice with you all. 18In the same way, you also rejoice, and rejoice with me. (2:12-18)

So then indicates Paul is drawing a conclusion from the previous section, which was the Christ Hymn (2:5-11). Paul loves the Philippians and gives them a pat on the back by calling them **my beloved**, which translates the Greek word *agapétos* a form of *agape*—a word used to describe divine love. It is a very strong word reflecting Paul's deep feelings for them. In persuading them to reform their behavior it is always good to do so in a positive way and acknowledge what the Philippians have done well. Thus, Paul points to their history of obedience: **even as you have always obeyed, not only in my presence, but now much more in my absence.** A foundation has been laid in Philippi such that Paul isn't calling the believers from a state of disobedience and rebellion to obedience. He's trying to strengthen what already exists by establishing unity in their church and encouraging them to live the worthy life of the gospel. They face many challenges from a hostile world, and the internal conflicts need to be resolved so they must continue in their obedience.

That Paul is calling on them to be obedient establishes a link between Christ's obedience to death on the cross (Phil 2:8) and their future obedience. The Greek word translated obey is *hupakouó*, which is a compound word consisting of *hupo* (meaning under) and *akouó* (meaning listen) from which our English word acoustics is derived. The word *hupo* intensifies the idea of listening or hearing. Therefore, the idea of the word is to *place oneself under what is heard,* so the word is translated into English as "obey." Their obedience has a long history, because they demonstrated obedience when Paul was with them founding the church, and they will continue much more in their obedience in Paul's absence. Their obedience to Christ should be a constant whether Paul is with them or away from them (1:27). He was hundreds of miles away from Philippi when he wrote this letter from Rome, but they must continue with obedience to the Lord. No group of believers should become overly dependent upon their pastor, teacher, or apostle. They must establish a pattern of obedience in their life whether their leaders are with them or not.

Paul issues a command for them to obey: **work out your own salvation with fear and trembling.** The main verb of the sentence is *katergazomai*, (translated "work out") which is a compound word consisting of *kata* meaning "down" or "according to," and *ergazomai* meaning "to work" or "accomplish." Putting the two words together presents the idea: *to work out to a precise end* or *work out to completion*. It is written as a command in the present tense, so this is something the Philippians are to continuously do. It is a lifelong objective to be relentlessly pursued.

In the context of this passage **salvation** *(sōtēria)* certainly doesn't refer to one's conversion experience, when they invited Jesus into their hearts and experienced the new birth. Paul is referring to salvation in the sense of their sanctification, which is their growth in godliness and maturing in the faith. Salvation is a spacious word that includes conversion to Christ, the life-long journey of sanctification, and final salvation at the end of the age. In the passage under consideration Paul is speaking of their sanctification, and he is doing so in the plural—speaking to the entire community. Thus, every believer must *work to a precise end* their salvation (sanctification) in cooperation with the other members in their church to bring about peaceful relationships and end the bickering and conflict that was threatening the church. Sanctification is both an individual and a corporate experience, which brings to the surface the interaction between the individual and community. Paul desires to see the entire Philippian church mature as a community of faith, but that can only happen as each member does his part. This is essentially what Paul had in mind when he was speaking about the maturity of the body in Ephesians 4:11-16:

> So Christ himself gave the apostles, the prophets, the evangelists, the pastors and teachers, **12**to equip his people for works of service, so that the body of Christ may be built up **13**until we all reach unity in the faith and in the knowledge of the Son of God and become mature, attaining to the whole measure of the fullness of Christ. **14**Then we will no longer be infants, tossed back and forth by the waves, and blown here and there by every wind of teaching and by the cunning and craftiness of people in their deceitful scheming. **15**Instead, speaking the truth in love, we will grow to become in every respect the mature body of him who is the head, that is, Christ. **16**From him the whole body, joined and held together by every supporting ligament, grows and builds itself up in love, as each part does its work. (NIV)

In the above passage, Paul is speaking about the maturity of the entire church at Ephesus. What is true of the individual must be true of the church. In other words, each believer must mature along with the other believers he worships with, so the entire body of Christ is in the process of growing spiritually. Paul is speaking in the plural to the Ephesians (and Philippians) and sees sanctification as something each believer works out in the context of his church relationships.

In working out their sanctification, the Philippians must do this with the attitude of **fear and trembling.** The Christian life is to be taken seriously for it isn't a laughing matter. **Fear** is often associated with holding God in a place of reverential awe and wonder. A holy fear of the Lord exists where people have a deep love and adoration for God, which certainly Paul has in mind here. However, with the combination of **trembling** there is more to it than just a reverential awe that Paul is thinking about. **Trembling** is a translation of *trómos*, which means: to quake, shake, or tremble with fear. Consider what Moses told the Israelites in Exodus 20:20: "Do not be afraid. God has come to test you, so that the fear of God will be with you to keep you from sinning." This involves more than holding God in reverence, it also involves a having a healthy respect for God's disciplinary activity in the believer's life, much like children have a healthy respect for their parent's discipline when they are misbehaving.

If one takes seriously 2:9-11 of the Christ hymn, realizing that one day the entire created order will bow down to Jesus and confess his Lordship, he can't help but stand in awe of God and have a sense of holy trembling. One doesn't live with the fear that if he is disobedient God will crush him, because perfect love overcomes fear of God's judgment (1 John 4:17-18). With God's Spirit present in the believer new desires emerge that give him the willingness to affect the changes in behavior that please him (Rom 12:1-2). When God's love is poured into the sinner's heart by the Holy Spirit (Rom 5:5) a new disposition exists toward God that propels the believer to obedience not in a begrudging way, but out of love and gratitude toward God for his gracious gift of salvation.

For it is God who works in you both to will and to work, for his good pleasure. (2:13)

The reason believers can work out their salvation is because **it is God who works in you**. God, the Holy Spirit, lives in the believer which should foster the sense of holy fear and trembling that Paul is calling for. It is necessary to see the connection between vv. 12 and 13. If God wasn't residing in the believer how could she work out her salvation? It is precisely because God is in you (plural) that believers can work out their salvation—as a community. This indicates that God and man both play an important part in their spiritual development. God's role is dominant in the sense that he does the work of spiritual transformation, bearing the fruit of the Spirit, and producing greater levels of holiness. Man can't do this independently of God. If God were absent from a person any changes made would be based solely on his human will-power, for there could be no spiritual fruit in the person who doesn't have the Spirit (Rom 8:9b).

The word **works** is *energeó*, which is found twice in this verse. It means to work, be operative, or accomplish something. The English words "energy" and "energize" are derived from this Greek word. Both times the word is written in a form that indicates that God is continuously at work in the community of faith assisting believers in their sanctification. Paul understands God working to their final salvation at the end of the age (2:16) for he has already expressed with certainty that God will bring their salvation to completion on the Day of Christ (1:6; 9-11; 28). Therefore, it seems best to understand Paul meaning that sanctification leads to final glorification. He believes that Christians' behavior really matters in their sanctification and is tied to their final salvation at the end of the age.

One's conversion, where he is justified by faith, his sanctification, and final glorification can't be compartmentalized and separated into neat categories, because they are integrated. Paul saw his sanctification in process (3:12-14) since he had not yet attained perfection and understood it would be realized when Jesus returns (3:20-21). Therefore, we are reminded that salvation is depicted as something that the believer already has, but he is growing in his salvation, so it's not yet completed. The "already" but "not yet" tension is apparent in Philippians.

God is at work **in you both to will and to work, for his good pleasure.** God's **will** influences the human will to greater levels of obedience, so the Philippians can resolve the petty differences they were having. That God is in the Philippians **to will and to work**, describes his enablement that makes believers able to voluntarily obey his commands so one's free will is intact. In other words, as God wills and works (energizes), he enables his people to bring their will into harmony with his, so they can affect the changes necessary to grow in the Christian life. There is a degree of tension between the sovereignty of God and human free will, but Scripture affirms both.

Believers don't have to worry about not having sufficient strength to do what God requires, because he **wills and works** in the community of faith so that his resources provide the fuel for positive transformation. God is constantly at work in the community for both verbs (will and work) are written as present infinitives, which means never ceasing action. God doesn't rest in the fellowship of believers, for he is always available to provide the resources required to mend broken relationships that weaken the church, while providing the strength to stand firm against a hostile world and have an effective witness.

God's willing and working is **for his good pleasure,** which involves believers doing the things that please the Lord. Where God is at work in a community of believers, they will be fulfilling his purposes which will bring glory to God and please him. As the Philippians get their act together by unifying their congregation, and enduring hostile treatment from the world, God will be pleased because his people are obedient, and his purposes are being fulfilled. All God's purposes and his good pleasure is entirely benevolent toward his worshipers, for there is nothing capricious about him. "God's pleasure is pure love, so what he does 'for the sake of his good pleasure' is by that very fact also on behalf of those he loves. After all, it delights God to delight his people."[51]

Paul has just told the Philippians to work out their salvation / sanctification. Now he's going to get specific and point to the areas that need improvement in their fellowship.

Do all things without murmurings and disputes, [15]that you may become blameless and harmless, children of God without defect in the middle of a crooked and perverse generation, among whom you are seen as lights in the world, [16]holding up the word of life; (2:14-16)

---

[51] Fee, p. 240

There were evidently some complainers in the church that were causing problems and throwing logs on the fire, only causing the flames of conflict and disunity to continue burning. He begins by issuing a command to **do all things without murmurings and disputes.** Doing **all things** involves the totality of a person's life—both inside and outside the church. The Philippians must stop complaining and bickering because that goes against living the worthy life of the gospel (1:27), the example of Christ (2:5-11), and God's good pleasure (2:13). Paul is calling for them to walk in humility and adopt a servant's mentality rather than whining and grumbling about everything.

Most likely Paul is alluding to the wilderness wanderings of the Israelites after they left Egypt. They were miraculously delivered from the Egyptians but failed to express their gratitude to God. Instead, they constantly grumbled against God, which brought his anger to bear on them.[52] The people also complained against Moses, which the Lord considered no different than complaining against him (Exo 16:2; Num 14:2). Elsewhere, Paul pointed to the grumbling Israelites as instruction of how not to behave (1 Cor 10:10-12; Heb 3:7-19). It appears that the Philippians are walking down the same path that the Israelites did by complaining and grumbling. They could have been complaining about leaders such as Euodia and Syntyche because of their inability to resolve their differences and more (4:2). Paul doesn't want the Philippians to suffer the same fate the Israelites met in the wilderness.

This type of complaining weakens the church and does harm to the churches' witness to their community. After all, what do nonbelievers think when they see Christians fighting and displaying a bad attitude as they complain about everything. Who would want to become part of a community like that? Jesus said that the most effective aspect of the Christian witness is the love and unity believers display toward one another (John 13:34-35; 17:22-23). The murmurings and disputes that the Philippians were having are light years away from the conduct Jesus calls for. The purpose for which Paul is calling for a stop to the complaining is stated next.

---

[52] See: Exo 16:6-12; Num 14:27-30; 21:4-5; Deu 32:5

that you may become blameless and harmless, children of God without defect in the middle of a crooked and perverse generation, among whom you are seen as lights in the world, [16]holding up the word of life. (2:15-16a)

How can God's people be **blameless and harmless** if they are governed by constant complaining? Paul has already prayed that they would be blameless, because as God's children that should be normal behavior, and that is how they should be progressing for the day of Christ (1:10). **Blameless**, which is a translation of *amemptos*, refers to being without moral defect or blemish. The word was used of Zechariah and Elizabeth to describe their spirituality (Luke 1:6), and of Paul being blameless as far as keeping the law was concerned (Phil 3:6). Thus, the word calls for moral purity. **Harmless**, is a translation of *akeraios*, which has the meaning of being unmixed and was a term used to describe wine that was pure in that it wasn't watered down. The word was also used to describe pure metal that wasn't mixed with alloys, therefore the believers conduct is to be pure—not mixed with sinful behavior such as grumbling and complaining.

The Philippians need to be reminded that they are **children of God.** As family members, brothers and sisters in the Lord, they share a common identity as the family of God with the same heavenly Father. God's children are to be distinct from the world by acting **without defect.** The Greek word *ámōmos* is translated **defect** and is used numerous times in the Septuagint regarding sacrificial animals being without defect (Num 6:14; 19:2). In fact, all three of the Greek terms in v. 15 were used in the Septuagint to describe the perfect animal sacrifices that were to be presented to God. When people brought animals to their priest to be sacrificed, the priest was to inspect the animal and make sure it matched the criteria found in Scripture. If the animal was blind, crippled, diseased, or old and sickly the priest wasn't to accept this animal for sacrifice.[53] Paul applies this to the believer in the sense that he should be innocent and beyond reproach in his conduct. His lifestyle should be pure, moral, and wholesome such that he is free from public censure, as if his life is an acceptable sacrifice to God (Rom 12:1-2).

---

[53] See: Malachi 1:6-14 where God rebuked the priests for offering less than perfect sacrifices

By using these terms, Paul is calling for the Philippians to be on their best behavior because they live **in the middle of a crooked and perverse generation.** This is an allusion to Deuteronomy 32:5, which was a description of the Israelites under-performance as the children of God. Because of their lack of faith and constant grumbling they are given a harsh rebuke by Moses: "They have dealt corruptly with him. They are not his children, because of their defect. They are a perverse and crooked generation."

Paul doesn't apply this passage to the Philippians because he sees better things in store them. They are working out their salvation (2:12) and are on the path to becoming blameless and harmless (2:15). Paul wants to disassociate the Philippians from the sinful Israelites, so he applies the Deuteronomy 32:5 passage to the pagan culture of Philippi. That culture, in which the Philippian believers find themselves, is a **crooked and perverse generation.**

The term **crooked** is a translation of the Greek *skolios,* which refers to something that is twisted, curved, or bent. The medical condition scoliosis is an abnormal curvature of the spine. Spiritually speaking the word refers to behavior that deviates or bends away from God's word,[54] so the pagan culture of Philippi is morally deviant—it's twisted. The word **perverse** is a translation of *diastrephó,* a compound word consisting of *dia* (through) and *strephó* (turning). The meaning of the word is something that is thoroughly turned, twisted, or distorted, hence the translation **perverse**. The prefix *dia* intensifies *strephó,* therefore this word is similar in meaning to **crooked** (*skolios*) but stronger.[55]

Crooked and perverse describes the pagan culture of Philippi: immoral, polytheistic in that they worshiped many gods, and they proclaimed Caesar is Lord. Paul already alluded to the opposition the Philippians were enduring from their culture, so it isn't a pretty picture (1:28). However, this description can probably be applied to every pagan culture throughout history—including our American culture. When believers live in a culture like Philippi they must distinguish themselves by standing out from the crowd. As the

---

[54] See: Proverbs 2:13-15; 21:8; 28:18

[55] See: Mat 17:17; Acts 13:10

Philippians interact with their culture Paul says: **among whom you are seen as lights in the world.** The church must be the polar opposite of the world, for the church's sense of morality, its worldview, ethics, and values all clash with the world's. The world system is that which rejects God, is humanistic and is energized by Satan. God's people are to be the light that shines in darkness (John 1:5; Mat 5:14). The word **lights** (*phóstér*) can also refer to heavenly bodies such as the stars (a possible allusion to Daniel 12:3), so the NIV says "shine like stars." Either translation refers to God's people living in purity to present an illuminated witness to their crooked and perverse generation.

Paul said something similar to the Ephesian believers:

> For you were once darkness, but now you are light in the Lord. Live as children of light [9](for the fruit of the light consists in all goodness, righteousness and truth) [10]and find out what pleases the Lord. [11]Have nothing to do with the fruitless deeds of darkness, but rather expose them. [12]It is shameful even to mention what the disobedient do in secret. [13]But everything exposed by the light becomes visible—and everything that is illuminated becomes a light. (Eph 5:8-13)

The above passage, and the Philippian passage, demonstrate the importance of God's people living in the light and showing the light of God's love to the world. This is a crucial theme for Paul. They need to set forth a good witness to the community in which they live. God's people live in a world that is marred by sin and depravity, which is why the Bible describes the world as a place of darkness. The Philippians must be the opposite of their culture and shine the light of Jesus to the sin-darkened world in which they live. As light-bearers the Philippians will not be able to shine brightly to their culture if they don't stop the petty bickering that is going on in their church.

Another aspect of being a light-bearer is **holding up the word of life** (v. 16a), which is the Scripture, but more specifically the Good News. **Holding up** translates *epechó*, written as a present participle, so Paul is telling the Philippians to keep on holding up (or holding forth) the gospel to the sin-darkened culture they live in. This is one way in which they shine like stars and are the light of the world. Offering the redeeming gospel—**the word of**

life—to a wicked paganized culture is the task of the church throughout history. People live in a state of spiritual death, which Paul describes elsewhere as being dead in our sins and trespasses, but the gospel imparts life, such that when it is believed the sinner becomes alive in Christ (Eph 2:1-6). When people receive the Good News of Jesus they go from death to life. Therefore, the animated witness Paul is calling for the Philippians to set forth to their culture involves shining like stars, in that they demonstrate attitudes and behavior that is clearly distinct from the world, while they are God's messengers extending the gospel to a sin-saturated culture (2 Cor 5:18-20).

Some translations, such as the ESV and NASB, say "holding fast" the word of life, rather than "holding up" the word of life. According to this translation Paul isn't speaking about evangelism, he's telling them to be faithful to the word of life by enduring and staying the course. In all their troubles and challenges they face from their culture they must be faithful to God's word and not cave into the pressure from their culture and compromise their Christian values. This is a possible interpretation, but the context better supports the previous option. There seems to be an evangelistic thrust by Paul's use of **word of life**, which is the only place he uses this expression in his writings, and the concept of shining like stars seems to allude to the Israelites being a light to a darkened world (Isa 49:6). For these reasons the translation "holding up the word of life" seems to better fit the evangelistic emphasis.

Paul abruptly shifts gears from speaking about the Philippians to when he stands before the Lord on judgment day.

that I may have something to boast in the day of Christ, that I didn't run in vain nor labor in vain. 17Yes, and if I am poured out on the sacrifice and service of your faith, I rejoice, and rejoice with you all. 18In the same way, you also rejoice, and rejoice with me. (2:16-18)

Doesn't this seem to be a bit egotistical and self-centered for Paul to be thinking of boasting about his ministry when he stands before the Lord? A cursory understanding of Paul's statement may lend itself to this conclusion, however personal boasting about his accomplishments is totally out of character for Paul. He has made it clear that the only grounds for boasting is in the Lord (1 Cor 1:31; 2 Cor 10:17). In other words, Paul is proud or boasting about the work God is doing in his ministry. He is delighted to see the transforming work of God in the Philippian congregation, and looks forward to boasting about how God has assisted them in working out their salvation. God gets all the glory—not Paul.

He has already expressed his confidence that God's work will be completed in 1:6: "being confident of this very thing, that he who began a good work in you will complete it until the *day of Christ Jesus* (Italics Mine)." Paul acknowledges that it is God's work that is being accomplished. He also prayed for their spiritual development culminating on the Day of Christ in 1:9-11: "This I pray, that your love may abound yet more and more in knowledge and all discernment; [10]so that you may approve the things that are excellent; that you may be sincere and without offense to the *day of Christ*; [11]being filled with the fruits of righteousness, which are through Jesus Christ, to the glory and praise of God." (Italics Mine)

Paul concludes this brief prayer giving all the glory to God for the anticipated progress the Philippians will make. He knew that God was working through him in his ministry to touch people's lives, but he always gave the glory to God for the results of spiritual transformation of those to whom he ministered.

Paul anticipated the Philippian congregation boasting in Christ when he returns to them (1:26). Thus, the boasting is always in the work that God is doing. Both the apostle and the congregation boast in the Lord about what he is doing: the Philippians boast about how Christ is working in Paul, and Paul boasts about how the Lord is working in the Philippians.

Paul desires to see the Philippians succeed in accomplishing everything he mentioned in vv. 14-16a for the purpose: **that I may have something to boast in the day of Christ, that I didn't run in vain nor labor in vain.** The **day of Christ** is the same as the Day of the Lord (Phil 1:6; 10) mentioned numerous times in the Old Testament (Zech 14:1; Mal 4:5). It is the day that the Lord Jesus will return and bring this age of history to its conclusion. It is the time that believers will receive their glorified bodies, which is the basis of the believer's hope and longing for the Lord Jesus' return. Additionally, believers will have their lives evaluated by the Lord at the Judgment Seat, so they may receive rewards for their faithful service to Christ (2 Cor 5:10; Rom 14:11-12).

Paul knew one of the things that the Lord would evaluate him on was the quality of his ministry (1 Cor 3:11-15). He wanted to have a positive outcome on judgment day, which is what he is anticipating. He sees himself before the Lord boasting about God's work in the lives of the Philippians and being proud of them. He specifically is boasting **that I didn't run in vain nor labor in vain.**

Ministry is hard work, for Paul uses an athletic metaphor to describe his ministry as running a race. The other depiction of his ministry is **labor**, which is a translation of *kopiáō,* a word meaning manual labor, or physically exhausting labor. Perhaps Paul was thinking of how hard he worked as a tent-maker and saw doing ministry as physically and emotionally exhausting work as well. Since Paul has already expressed his confidence that God will complete the work he started (1:6) in what sense could Paul entertain the possibility that his ministry to the Philippians could be in vain? Is he thinking that the possibility exists that his beloved Philippians will not work out their salvation and the church will go south, self-destructing with conflict and tension? Paul doesn't want to stand before the Lord under that scenario and face that disappointment.

It could be that this is Paul's way of saying to the Philippians: "Make me proud of you on judgment day." "Show me my hard work has paid off and wasn't for nothing." When he came to Philippi he was grossly mistreated, physically beaten, which no doubt some of the converts witnessed, plus they knew of his long ordeal being imprisoned. He has done all this for the sake of the gospel and the people he is serving. Paul has invested his whole life into building the body of Christ at great personal cost to himself, for he made many sacrifices so that people could mature in the faith. The payoff for Paul was seeing his Philippian converts, and others, standing with him before the Lord rejoicing on judgment day (Phil 4:1; 1 Thess 2:19-20). All the hard work has paid off, and he boasts in the Lord's work.

By mentioning the day of Christ, he is getting them to think about judgment day as well. They need to understand that if they fail to work out their salvation as Paul has instructed there will be consequences they face as they stand before the Lord. It matters how you live in the present! As he is anticipating a positive result on judgment day he wants the Philippians to embrace this thought as well, to provide incentive for them to get busy and work out their issues and get their act together. Paul comes to the end of his argument with a celebratory symphony of praise.

Yes, and if I am poured out on the sacrifice and service of your faith, I rejoice, and rejoice with you all. [18]In the same way, you also rejoice, and rejoice with me. (2:17-18)

Paul's allusion to being **poured out** is a metaphorical statement that is difficult to decipher and assign a precise meaning to, as are many metaphors in Scripture. He directs the reader's attention back into the Old Testament sacrificial system by alluding to the drink offering. The priest would sacrifice an animal, which was accompanied by a grain offering, and a drink offering consisting of wine that would be poured out before the Lord in the sanctuary.[56] It would be poured out on the sacrifice or around the altar. This imagery was also common to the Gentiles because in their religious practices they would often pour wine on the ground as an offering to their gods, so in both the Jewish and Gentile context they would connect with this practice.

What is Paul saying to his readers through this imagery? Most scholars understand Paul being **poured out** to be a reference to his possible martyrdom. Even though Paul has expressed his expectation that he will be released and return to visit the Philippians (1:25-27; 2:24), he seems to waver back-and-forth on this issue recognizing the possibility that things could go south for him. In 2 Timothy 4:6, Paul uses the same language to describe his imminent death: "For I am already being *poured out* like a drink offering, and the time for my departure is near" (NIV, Italics Mine). This is an obvious reference to his martyrdom, thus his reference to being **poured out** in the Philippian passage most likely points to his possible martyrdom as well. In both the Philippian and 2 Timothy passage Paul uses the word *spéndō*, which is translated **poured out** referring to a libation.

---

[56] See: Num 15:4-5; 27:7; 28:7

Paul's life was **poured out on the sacrifice and service of your faith.** Paul viewed the Philippians' faith as an acceptable sacrifice and service to God. Their **faith** was expressed in all that they did for God including their financial support of Paul (4:10-18), their partnership in the gospel with him (1:5), and the hostility they endured in being Christ's witnesses (1:27-30). The term **sacrifice**, refers to animals that were killed to atone for sin in the Old Covenant, so Paul is speaking metaphorically in that the Philippians faith is an acceptable sacrifice to God (Rom 12:1). The term **service** is the Greek *leitourgía,* which refers to priestly service. The English word "liturgy" is derived from this Greek word, which Paul uses in 2:30.[57] The Philippians have presented themselves as an acceptable sacrifice to God (Rom 12:1-2) and are offering priestly service to him by partnering with Paul in the gospel.

Both the Philippians and Paul were serving the Lord together and Paul wants to acknowledge their sacrifice and service to God. In the same way that the drink offering completed the sacrifice, Paul's death would then complete the sacrifice the Philippians were making to God. The implication is that the Philippians have made the greater sacrifice and Paul's life being poured out is the libation poured on top of them. The Philippians are pouring themselves out to God, and Paul is pouring himself on the Philippians. This is a beautiful picture of Paul unselfishly spending himself for the sake of Christ, the gospel, the Philippians, and all those under his care.[58]

Given the context of the passage, and Paul's circumstances, it is difficult to see how the thought of Paul's possible execution is totally absent from his thinking. For a long time, over four years, Paul has been imprisoned, and for the last two years in Rome he has been waiting for the verdict. "Paul viewed the Philippians' service to the Lord as a sacrifice of faith upon which he would pour out his life as a drink offering. Since they had displayed sacrificial faith and loving service, what would be more fitting than for Paul to crown that consecration with the drink offering of his life? Thus, Paul considered his

---

[57] The word is also used in 2 Cor 8:2 and 9:12 to describe a monetary gift

[58] MacArthur sees it differently. Paul was not here speaking of his eventual martyrdom. The present tense (of being poured out) clearly indicates that he was speaking of his current experience as a prisoner in Rome. He saw his life, not his death, as his ultimate act of sacrifice to the Lord. He was a living sacrifice, not a dead one (Rom 12:1). MacArthur, p. 192

suffering a libation (see 2 Tim 4:6) poured out to consummate the Philippians' faithful service (Rom 12:1; 15:16). Paul's offering could refer to his present suffering or to the blood of his death, if he were to die as a martyr."[59]

This seems to be the best way to understand Paul "being poured out." The model for Paul's sacrifice is Christ, who died a horrendous death on the cross in obedience to God (2:8). Paul is walking in Jesus' footsteps and providing the Philippians with an example from his own life about how one can emulate the humility and sacrificial service that Christ offered. As Jesus gave himself up in death, so Paul is willing to give himself up in death to complete the sacrifice the Philippians are making to God. Jesus emptied himself (2:7), while Paul poured himself out (2:17). If he should be executed Paul would be OK with that because to live is Christ, to die is gain (1:21-23).

The Philippians are also suffering for the sake of Christ because they are enduring opposition from their opponents and are enduring the same suffering that Paul faced (1:27-30). Therefore, Paul and the church at Philippi were partners in suffering for the sake of Christ. This isn't done in a begrudging way for Paul says: **I rejoice, and rejoice with you all. [18]In the same way, you also rejoice, and rejoice with me** (2:17b-18). Paul's service to Christ came at a great personal cost to him,[60] but never does Paul seem to be resentful, or regretting that his life has been filled with so much anguish. Paul's service to the Philippians is a source of joy to him. As he contemplates his outcome in prison he is filled with joy and rejoices with the Philippians. They are commanded to be glad and filled with joy as they are making their sacrifice to God in partnership with Paul (1:5). In other words, this is mutually shared joy, an outright celebration, a festive occasion that Paul is inviting them into. Sixteen times in this letter Paul uses *chairó* (I rejoice) and its cognates. There is no room for bitterness or thinking that in his service to Christ he was given a raw deal—for that thought doesn't even exist in Paul's thinking. It's been a tough road for Paul in his imprisonment, but he has only room for rejoicing in what God is accomplishing through him and his beloved Philippians. This is a demonstration of Paul's self-sacrificial attitude in line with Jesus' mindset (2:5).

---

[59] Comfort, p. 185

[60] See: Acts 9:15-16; 2 Cor 11:23-28

This presents a mystery of the faith: that in times of suffering for the sake of the gospel, God's people can be overwhelmed with joy. It doesn't seem to make sense, but that is the reality of those who walk with Christ amid a hostile culture even to the point of threatening their lives. Thoughts of self-pity, regret, and disappointment are overcome with spiritually imparted joy for serving Christ. Considering all the abuse and torture Jesus suffered, the author of Hebrews says something amazing: who for the *joy* set before him endured the cross, scorning its shame (Heb 12:2, Italics Mine). Joy is realized in serving regardless of the personal cost.

Joy seems to be somewhat elusive for many people who search for it, but don't find it—including many Christians. The joy Paul is talking about is the joy that comes from one's relationship with Christ and his disciples, added to the certainty of God's promises that in the future he will bring to finality this age and transform our mortal bodies into glorified bodies, at which time there will be no more suffering. Additionally, believers must be reminded that there is joy in being involved in God's mission to bring people into the joy of knowing and serving Christ. "The suffering must be the direct result of trying to bring others in on the joy, or it deflects from Christ's suffering. Only so can we also rejoice in one another's suffering—as evidence that the proper 'sacrifices' are being offered up to God."[61]

It almost sounds like a contradiction, that in the joy we have, we suffer to bring people in on that joy, then in their joy, they suffer to bring others into the joy of knowing Christ. It's a long road of suffering, but it is accompanied by indescribable joy (1 Pet 1:8).

Insights, Applications, and Life Lessons

This topic is of great importance to every Christian because they are all going through the process of sanctification, so it behooves them to do some serious thinking about it. Christians are on a life-long journey with the Lord as they mature in the faith and become more Christlike. This journey is a cooperative effort between the Christian and God, with God's part being dominant. Only

[61] Fee, p. 258

God can transform the believer and produce spiritual fruit in her life, but what is the believer's role in the journey of sanctification, or as Paul said: "work out your salvation with fear and trembling."

When someone becomes a believer in Christ there is much work to be done in this journey. Good habits need to be developed in believers' lives that will promote spiritual growth, which is often referred to as *spiritual formation*. What are some of the basic disciplines that every Christian should practice that will contribute to their sanctification?

- Studying God's word (2 Tim 3:16-17)
- Praying regularly (1 Thess 5:17)
- Serving in your church (1 Pet 4:10)
- Using your spiritual gifts (Rom 12:6-8)
- Developing relationships with believers (Rom 12:10)
- Working through conflicts (Phil 4:2-3)
- Sharing your faith (1 Pet 3:15)
- Practicing good stewardship (1 Cor 16:2)

The above things are crucial and should be regarded as disciplines that should be instilled in one's life. In other words, these disciplines should become a way of life for disciples of Christ, which is why this is referred to as *spiritual formation*. It takes time, effort, and commitment to establish these habits in your life, but the payoff is great. God works through the spiritual disciplines you practice by transforming you into Christ's likeness.

The New Testament does not suggest any short-cuts by which we can grow in sanctification, but simply encourages us repeatedly to give ourselves to the old-fashioned, time-honored means of Bible reading and meditation (Ps 1:2; Matt 4:4; John 17:17), prayer (Eph 6:18; Phil 4:6), worship (Eph 5:18-20), witnessing (Matt 28:19-20), Christian fellowship (Heb 10:24-25), and self-discipline or self-control (Gal 5:23; Titus 1:8)."[62]

Growing in the Christian life has no short-cuts, quick fixes, or overnight success stories. Maturing as a Christian is a process that goes on for the

---

[62] Grudem, p. 755

duration of the believer's life and requires consistently giving oneself to the above mentioned spiritual disciplines.

Paul has commanded the Philippians, the entire church, to work on their sanctification in the context of their relationships with each other. This is accomplished in small group Bible studies, worshiping with other believers, serving together, praying together, and so on. But one part of corporate sanctification is resolving conflict situations that may appear in one's church. Conflict is a normal part of life, so it will occur, but it needs to be resolved. This part of sanctification can be messy such that many people may want to avoid it. If things get dicey and people start feeling uneasy with conflict that exists, they might just leave and go to another church. In First Century Philippi that wasn't an option because there was only one church in the city.

When believers are in conflict with each other they need to sit down and talk things over. Paul will bring up two leading ladies in the church that needed to sit down and work through their differences (4:2-3). When people are humble and display the mindset of Christ (2:5), they will take responsibility for their actions, confess where they made mistakes and ask for forgiveness. They will extend forgiveness when necessary and reconciliation can occur. In fact, it's a beautiful thing to see two believers forgive each other and reconcile. I've seen this happen many times, but there are occasions where people met to talk things over and the outcome was quite different. People weren't humble and willing to confess their part of a conflict and it went south. The people didn't display the mindset of Christ because they were more concerned with their own interests, rather than the overall good of the church. Cases like this can be ugly and they take a toll on the pastor. People may leave the church, spread gossip and cause collateral damage which is dishonoring to Christ.

Summary

Paul acknowledges their history of obedience, encouraging them to continue down that path, even more so in his absence. He wants them to ratchet up their sanctification, resolve the lack of the unity that exists, and stop their whining and complaining. They can be assured that their efforts will not be in vain because God is working in their fellowship to transform the Philippians into the image of Christ. Their witness to the community will be improved through behavior that is blameless and harmless as they live like the family of God in their perverse culture. They must shine like stars as they hold forth the word of life to their depraved culture.

Paul anticipates the day of Christ, when he returns, and looks forward to being able to boast in what the Lord did in the Philippians, such that his work wasn't for nothing. Using a metaphor from the sacrificial system, Paul sees himself as being poured out as a drink offering on the Philippians sacrifice and service of their faith, which is a picturesque way of demonstrating his humility by being spent for the Philippians, in the same way Jesus spent himself on the cross. As Paul contemplates this he is filled with joy, and wishes to rejoice with the Philippians, as they mutually rejoice with Paul, all to the glory of God.

In the next section, Paul presents Timothy as one who has the mindset of Christ and serves as an example for the Philippians to follow.

CHAPTER ELEVEN

* * *

"The Example of Timothy" Philippians 2:19-24

Paul is presenting the Philippians with a travelogue of sorts, in that he is alerting them to an impending visit from Timothy. Why the visit? When Epaphroditus showed up in Rome and presented the monetary gift to Paul, he no doubt, informed him of some of the troubling circumstances that existed in the church that were causing the disunity, and hurting their witness to the community. Paul felt the situation required immediate action, but due to his imprisonment he couldn't go himself, so he would send his representative Timothy to Philippi to help them work through their issues. Timothy would report back to Paul and inform him about how the church is doing, so this section serves as a letter of commendation regarding Timothy. Paul wanted them to know that Timothy has his full support, and delegated authority to help them work things out.

Before Timothy was dispatched, Paul would send Epaphroditus back home to Philippi to hand deliver this letter to them, which would lay the ground work for Timothy's visit. The letter also explained why Paul decided to send Epaphroditus home earlier than expected, because of his near fatal illness. Paul thought that the best thing for all parties concerned would be to have Epaphroditus return to Philippi. To read this section and conclude these are just mundane travel plans, with no theological implications, would be to miss a vital part of Paul's rhetorical strategy in writing this letter. This section continues the *probatio*, which in ancient rhetoric is offering proofs to support the author's thesis (1:27-30).

Paul has given the Philippians the example of Christ's humility, the greatest example of all, to encourage them to mend their relationships so that they can have a unified church, and a healthy presence in their city. Now Paul will give them examples that are more down to earth and touchable to motivate them to action. He will present the example of Timothy, which will be the discussion of this chapter, then Epaphroditus in the next. These are real people that the Philippians know and can learn much from watching and interacting with. These people are living proof of how believers can live out what Paul previously taught. They are living examples, not theoretical models, of the worthy life that Paul is calling for the Philippians to live. Timothy's lifestyle promotes unity and exudes selflessness, like Jesus, and his relationship with Paul is a model of how the relationships of the Philippians should be with one another.

Timothy occupies a special place in Paul's heart. He was a key person in Paul's leadership team who served as his protégé and was most likely the closest thing that Paul had to a son. He was much younger than Paul and started traveling with him on his second missionary journey as a teenager (Acts 16:1-3). Paul's feelings for Timothy ran deep because he refers to his relationship with him as a father with his son (2:22). There were several occasions when Paul sent Timothy to churches to represent him, so Timothy proved to be a valuable asset to Paul in furthering the gospel and to him personally.[63] Paul mentored Timothy, so he had great training in many areas including evangelism, theology, conflict resolution, leadership, and more. Paul would have coached Timothy on how to help the Philippians work through their issues before he was dispatched.

But I hope in the Lord Jesus to send Timothy to you soon, that I also may be cheered up when I know how you are doing. [20]For I have no one else like-minded, who will truly care about you. [21]For they all seek their own, not the things of Jesus Christ. [22]But you know the proof of him, that, as a child serves a father, so he served with me in furtherance of the Good News. [23]Therefore

[63] See: Acts 17:14; 1 Thess 3:2-3; 1 Cor 4:17

I hope to send him at once, as soon as I see how it will go with me. [24]But I trust in the Lord that I myself also will come shortly. (2:19-24)

All plans that people make are subject to the Lord's sovereignty for Paul says: **But I hope in the Lord Jesus to send Timothy to you soon.** This is Paul's way of saying: "Lord willing I want to send Timothy to you in the near future." He is simply acknowledging that all of man's plans are subject to the Lord who has control over all the events that take place. There were many times in Paul's ministry where his plans changed due to circumstances beyond his control. Paul wanted to go to Asia, but somehow the Holy Spirit prevented him from going there. He tried to enter Bithynia, and again the Spirit of Jesus closed that door, then in response to a vision from God Paul ended up going to Philippi under the Lord's direction (Acts 16:6-12). He had promised to visit Corinth twice, but the Lord led him not to return after the church gave him bad vibes on his previous visit (2 Cor 1:12-2:1; 1 Cor 16:7). Paul had to defend himself for changing his itinerary, and explain that he wasn't being flippant, and all over the map with them. Changes in plans are often beyond one's control, so it must be recognized that God is sovereign in directing people's steps.

Being in prison Paul couldn't go to render assistance to the Philippian church, so he had to send someone in his place to represent him. Anybody who selects someone to represent them must be very careful who they pick, because their representative is a reflection on them. If Paul sent someone to represent him and he made a mess of things, that would make Paul look very bad. Paul sent Timothy as his representative with his full authority delegated to him, because Paul trusted him and knew his character. He worked closely with Timothy, taught him the basics of ministry, and had Paul's full confidence in his ability to help the church work through their issues. It was a sensitive mission for the young Timothy to go on and help them restore unity to their fellowship. Paul would have given Timothy extensive coaching on how to go about handling some of the issues that were plaguing the Philippians, so it wasn't as if Timothy didn't have some specialized training. His mentor was one of the best people in the history of Christendom.

Paul is overwhelmingly optimistic in that when Timothy returns from visiting them the outcome will be positive because he says: **that I also may be**

cheered up when I know how you are doing. He believes Timothy will bring back a good report to him about how well things are going in Philippi, because they are working out their problems, and taking a step closer to adopting the mindset of Christ and living as good citizens of heaven. Paul could have been very negative and said: "I hope Timothy doesn't bring back bad news that things aren't going well in Philippi."

Persuasion always works best through positive encouragement. He is expressing his faith in the Philippians' ability to unify their congregation, which would cause him to feel **cheered up**, which translates the Greek word *eupsucheó*: a compound word consisting of *eu* (good or well) and *psuché* (soul), so literally the word means "to be good-souled." Things would be well with Paul's soul if he hears a good report from Timothy about the Philippians. This gives you an indication of how important the Philippians were to Paul and how deeply embedded in his heart they were. His soul was troubled, but with a good report from Timothy his soul would be comforted, and he would be of good cheer, so Paul has a sense of urgency to send Timothy.

Paul is providing the Philippians with reasons why they should embrace Timothy when he arrives. He wants to make sure that Timothy is given every courtesy and respected despite his younger age. One reason they should give Timothy every consideration is: **For I have no one else like-minded.** Timothy and Paul were of a kindred spirit. Paul is encouraging the Philippians to ramp up their unity, in doing so they should consider the unity that exists between Paul and Timothy. Their thinking is in line with the mindset of Christ (2:5), they share the same values, they work together in harmony to accomplish God's purposes, both trying to further the gospel and live as good citizens of heaven. If you want to get an insight into Paul's thinking and heart for doing ministry take a good look at Timothy. That is quit a complimentary statement for Paul to make about the younger Timothy.

He understands and lives out what Paul has taught about having the right attitudes that line up with those of Christ's. In other words, Timothy gets it! Paul is persuading them to examine Timothy's life and make the necessary reforms in their behavior, so they can adopt the mindset of Christ. There is much to be learned from people who are walking the walk and talking the talk. Essentially, Paul is saying: "now that I've taught you about Jesus and his remarkable humility, self-sacrificial life, and willingness to place others before himself, take a good look at Timothy, because he can demonstrate this for you in real time. Note his example and try to emulate him to the degree that he emulates Jesus."

Paul loved the Philippians, and Timothy shared that love for them with Paul, for he says Timothy is one **who will truly care about you.** He had a genuine concern for the Philippians welfare just as Paul did. There was nothing fake about Timothy, for his heart was fully engaged for the Philippians' improvement just as Paul's was. He was confident that Timothy would show the same concern to the Philippians that he would, if he could go and visit them.

Now Paul contrasts Timothy with others: **For they all seek their own, not the things of Jesus Christ** (v. 21). Reading this verse should be done by reflecting back on 2:3-4. Timothy is an example of one who considers others better than himself and looks to the interests of others before his own, thus demonstrating the mindset of Christ (2:5). Who is Paul referring to when he says: For **they all** seek their own, not the things of Jesus Christ? It seems unbelievable that the "they all" refers to Paul's other colleagues in ministry. Paul had some very dedicated coworkers that traveled with him and were, no doubt, on fire for the Lord and the advancement of the gospel. That Paul would say his colleagues only seek their own interests, not those of the Lord Jesus would make no sense and be an offensive thing to say about them, so let's rule that option out.

Paul is probably referring to those in Rome who preach Christ with motives that are suspect (1:15; 17), thus proving that their preaching had a self-seeking motivation to cause trouble for Paul and bring recognition to themselves. Certainly, Paul has come across many people who served Christ during his career that did so with motives that were less than pure. Timothy is not one of those people. Therefore, Paul is emphasizing his fine character, and underscoring that Timothy is much like he is: being like-minded and sharing his deep concern for the Philippians. In other words, Timothy is the real deal! He is a man whose motivation is seeking the things of Christ, thus Paul presents Timothy to the Philippians as a living example of all he's said in

2:1-5. Timothy gets it! By commending Timothy in this way, Paul is laying a red carpet for his arrival and ministry to the people.

Additionally, there were people in the Philippian church that were focused on their own interests, which is why they were lacking unity, and he is probably alluding to them as well. When the Philippians hear this letter read out loud in their gathering, there may be some ambiguity as to whom Paul is referring to when he says **they all**, just as there is some ambiguity to the modern-day reader as well. Hopefully, as the Philippians hear this they would all do some soul-searching and reflect on their own motives.

Now Paul will give us a glimpse into his heart regarding how special Timothy was to him: **But you know the proof of him, that, as a child serves a father, so he served with me in furtherance of the Good News** (2:22). Paul didn't speak with such high regard for Timothy just because he liked him, rather he spoke highly of him because he has proven himself worthy of such commendation. In other words, Timothy had a track record. He traveled with Paul beginning on his second missionary journey and was with Paul when he planted the church in Philippi (Acts 16:16-40), so they would have known Timothy and had an insight into his competency as a minister of the gospel.

Timothy has been around the block, so to speak, and was a young experienced minister of the gospel. Paul also used similar language in his letter to the Corinthians when referring to Timothy: "Because of this I have sent Timothy to you, who is my beloved and faithful child in the Lord, who will remind you of my ways which are in Christ, even as I teach everywhere in every assembly" (1 Cor 4:17). This verse demonstrates Paul's trust in Timothy and testifies to the quality of his walk with the Lord. In the Philippian passage under consideration, Paul identifies Timothy as a child serving his father. "In the Greco-Roman world, a son works side-by-side with his father in learning the family trade."[64] Paul was Timothy's spiritual father teaching him the trade of being a minister of the gospel. Paul viewed Timothy as his child in the Lord, and was his protégé, so family allusions are in this text. Perhaps, Paul viewed Timothy as the son he never had, which speaks to the special quality of their relationship.

---

[64] Caird, p. 129

Timothy has served side-by-side with Paul in that: **he served with me in furtherance of the Good News.** This is Paul's mission in life, the very reason for which Christ called him as the apostle to the Gentiles. Timothy shared this mission with Paul by traveling with him and helping him plant new churches. Paul has already stated to the Philippians how his circumstances have helped to further the gospel (1:12), and how the gospel has advanced with the Philippians' maturing in the faith (1:25). Paul's key objective in life was spreading the gospel and Timothy worked side-by-side with Paul in that endeavor. In the original Greek the word furtherance is not in text, but it is implied. Literally it says: as a father with a child he has served with me in the gospel. The gospel ministry is hard word and involves planting churches, teaching God's people, enduring hardship, persecution, training leaders, and more. Timothy experienced this firsthand with Paul.

Therefore I hope to send him at once, as soon as I see how it will go with me. 24But I trust in the Lord that I myself also will come shortly. (2:23-24)

Therefore, is Paul's conclusion about Timothy's itinerary. He has stated he wants to send Timothy to Philippi, so he can assess the situation there, then return to Paul, and hopefully, offer him a good report about the Philippians' progress (2:19). It makes sense that Paul would not dispatch Timothy until the verdict is handed down so that he can report to the Philippians about how things have gone for him. Therefore, his mission is threefold: 1) report to the Philippians about how Paul is doing, 2) help them work through their issues, 3) report back to Paul about how the Philippians are doing. Epaphroditus will hand deliver the letter to them, before Timothy's visit, then Timothy can report back to Paul about how the letter has been received by them. Timothy can also clarify things that Paul said in his letter to them, for it wouldn't be unlikely that they may have some questions about things Paul wrote, and who better to clarify Paul's letter than Timothy. After all, he was with Paul when he wrote it, and the two of them may have discussed some of the content of the letter as he was writing it.

Paul is overwhelming optimistic about his circumstances for he says: **But I trust in the Lord that I myself also will come shortly.** He is confident that he will be set free and visit the Philippians soon after he receives the verdict. He feels it's God's will for him to be released and continue his ministry. It appears throughout the letter that there is wavering and ambiguity in Paul's thinking about the verdict—life or death. It seems that **in the Lord** Paul is confident of his release (1:19-25), but in the human side of Paul doubt seems to be lingering in his thinking, for he has been acknowledging that things could go south, and he would face martyrdom (1:23). This is the human dilemma: there are times when we are strong in our faith in the Lord's will, and there are times when in our weak humanity we may struggle with our faith. I believe this was the struggle Paul had as he awaited the verdict, which would be the same for anybody in his situation.[65]

There is an obvious tension in Paul's thinking about his circumstances, where faith is strong, and he is confident in his release, while other times he seems to recognize that it may not go well for him and he might be executed. In v. 23 he says, "as soon as I see how things go with me" then in v. 24 he says, "but I trust in the Lord that I may come shortly." Faith and uncertainty about his circumstances exist side-by-side. If he was absolutely certain he would be released why didn't he say in v. 23: **Therefore I hope to send him at once, *as soon as I am released.*** Rather than: **Therefore I hope to send him at once, as soon as I see how it will go with me.** This is the human dilemma that is faced when considering what might happen in the future. It would be difficult to believe that Paul never entertained doubts about whether he would make it out of there alive.

Insights, Applications, and Life Lessons

Leadership has become a big area of study in Christian colleges and seminaries. In fact, many of them offer degree programs in Christian leadership. If you go into any bookstore you will find a multitude of books on leadership, both secular and Christian, because it's a trending topic in today's world. Paul's leadership skills where at a very high level, so much can be learned from studying his strategies.

---

[65] Fee doesn't see it that way: "It is hard to make it plainer, given the outcome is still in the future, that he fully expects to be released, and therefore that the talk about "death" in 1:21-23 was a yearning, not an anticipation of the near future. Which in turn also indicates that the metaphor in v. 17 above is unlikely to be a reflection on martyrdom, but a reference to his present suffering." (Fee, p. 270)

Paul was a hands-on person, but he had to delegate this work to others, for he had no other choice. While in prison he could have visitors, who may have hand delivered letters to him, and he may have written other letters (not inspired) that he had people hand deliver, so he directed the entire operation from his rented quarters in Rome (Acts 28:28-30). We have no way of knowing how many people visited Paul, or how many letters he wrote and received while in Rome, but of the many people that paid him a visit he would have discussed matters of theology, church issues, and gave some of them specialized training for assignments he delegated to them. It would have been interesting to listen in on some the conversations Paul had with his visitors.

He ran the entire operation from the joint (prison), which is truly an amazing feat to consider. I wonder if Paul had a spreadsheet that detailed all his workers, and home churches in every city that he had hanging on a wall in his quarters. Perhaps, he had a special chart with all the home churches in Rome and was monitoring everything that was going on.

Timothy and Epaphroditus were two spokes in the wheel of Paul's complex network of coworkers and associates that he utilized in spreading the gospel and strengthening the churches. In Paul's travels he took people with him, so he could train them, develop relationships with them, and through these people his efforts could be multiplied. Training capable leaders expands Paul's ability to influence people and spread the gospel. Leaders are an extension of those who train them.

Developing leaders was crucial to Paul so that the Christian faith could survive and multiply in the next generation, so Paul wasn't a one man show. He dispatched Timothy to go to Thessalonica on a care mission, then he reported back to him (1 Thess 2:2-5), and to Corinth to remind them of his way of life (1 Cor 4:17). Titus and Tychicus seem to be other spokes in Paul's leadership wheel that he utilized in much the same way.[66] Reading through Romans 16 reveals the many colleagues that Paul had in his network in Rome and were very important to him for they were invaluable assets in building the church. Don't forget about Barnabas, Silas, Luke, Mark, and others, who were key

---

[66] See: 2 Cor 8:16; 24; 12:18; Eph 6:21-22; Col 4:7; 2 Tim 4:12; Titus 1:5; 3:12

people in Paul's leadership network and left their imprint on the Christian movement.

Had Paul not raised up leaders, during the four years and several months that he was imprisoned, the Christian movement would have been crippled. The fact that Paul worked hard at training leaders, mentoring people, and delegating assignments to them enabled the church to survive his imprisonment. Paul was the key man, the apostle to the Gentiles, but he was locked up and unable to travel, so he depended on the leaders that he trained to do his bidding, and they did it well. This is testimony to Paul's leadership development strategy and his delegation skills.

In Philippi Lydia, Euodia, Syntyche, Clement, the loyal yokefellow (whoever he was), and Epaphroditus were the key leaders of the church, who were special to Paul, and may have been numbered with the overseers and deacons (1:1). The situation Paul was in required utilizing his colleagues, which offered them the benefit of gaining vital experience. Paul may have concluded that one of the byproducts of his imprisonment was the maturing of some of his key leaders. He was always thinking about identifying and training leaders, because the future of the Jesus movement depended on it. It should be the same in today's church.

Timothy – a First Century Millennial

Timothy represented the next generation because of his youth. As I think about Paul's relationship with Timothy I think of today's Millennials—those who are in their 20s. Those who are older experienced pastors and theologians must use their influence to raise up the Timothy's of the next generation. When Paul had died, Timothy was still on line doing the work of furthering the gospel. Consider what Paul told Timothy: And the things you have heard me say in the presence of many witnesses entrust to reliable people who will also be qualified to teach others (2 Timothy 2:2, NIV). Paul had taught Timothy, now Timothy must in turn teach other people to continue the gospel ministry from his generation to the next. Failure to do this would be the nail in the coffin for the Christian faith. The church was in its infancy, weak, and small in numbers, so without well-trained leaders it might not have a future.

It is in vogue these days to have a mentor or a life coach. To have Paul as a mentor as Timothy did would be special. Many people would kill to have Paul as their mentor, so Timothy was truly blessed. Paul could mold him into the kind of leader, preacher, and man of God that would be a good example to others, but also to take the mantle of leadership into the next generation. Every Paul needs a Timothy to mentor, and every Timothy needs a Paul to mentor him.

What Can You Pass on to the Next Generation?

Who do you know that can benefit from your years of acquired wisdom, life experiences, and your specialized skills? Parents can do a great service to their children by mentoring them and passing on their skills. Quite often when I ask people how they got into their line of work they say something like: "My dad worked on cars every weekend, so I grew up learning how to fix cars and I became a mechanic." "My mother was a piano teacher and she started giving me lessons when I was just a kid, now I'm giving piano lessons." We all have skills that we can pass on to other people, especially our kids, however, it's tragic when we don't let younger people benefit from our years of experience and specialized talents. Paul passed on to Timothy his knowledge of Scripture and taught him the craft of doing ministry.

Summary

Paul feels action must be taken so the situation in Philippi doesn't deteriorate. He is confident that they will make the necessary reforms to ratchet up their unity, which would be comforting for Paul's soul. The time for action is now, so he's going to send Timothy to them as soon as he gets the verdict. Therefore, this section serves as a letter of commendation for Timothy, so they know Paul is sending Timothy to represent him with his full delegated authority and wants the Philippians to extend every courtesy imaginable to him. They already know Timothy because he was with Paul during the founding of the church, so he has a track record with them.

Timothy is of a kindred spirit with Paul and is someone who lives out the values of Christ. The Philippians can see a living example of what Paul taught in 2:1-5, by examining Timothy's way of life. Much can be learned by living in proximity to a mature believer and seeing firsthand their walk with Christ. Paul has built up Timothy in the eyes of the Philippians by presenting him as a trusted colleague with impeccable character who is genuinely concerned about their welfare. Timothy will inform them of the verdict handed down to Paul, help them work through their issues, then report back to Paul, that is if he isn't executed.

In the next section, Paul has another example for the Philippians to follow, Epaphroditus, who is one of their own. Like Timothy, Epaphroditus gets it! He lives according to the mindset of Christ.

CHAPTER TWELVE

* * *

"The Example of Epaphroditus"
Philippians 2:25-30

This is where things get dicey for Paul and the Philippians. They had sent Epaphroditus, who was a faithful member of their church to hand deliver the monetary gift they raised for Paul and to be a friend to him (4:18). He was to serve as an aid to Paul by looking after his needs and making his uncomfortable situation a little more manageable. His mission was to make life easier for Paul, but he got sick and nearly died. News of his illness reached the home church in Philippi, which caused them deep concern for his wellbeing and Epaphroditus was distressed at their concern for him, so he longed to see them again.

Most likely, on the road to Rome he took sick. It is unlikely that he was traveling alone because he had a considerable sum of money to give Paul. It can be speculated that when he took sick, one or more of his traveling companions returned to Philippi to inform them that he became seriously ill. Epaphroditus and possibly others pressed on to Rome. Shortly after arriving in Rome he fell deathly ill.

When he had recovered from his illness Paul dispatched him with the letter we call "Philippians" to hand deliver to the church, but how would they receive him? He was sent to Paul to relieve his burdens and bring comfort to him, but because of his illness he ended up becoming a burden to Paul—a source of anxiety and stress. Would the Philippians be upset with Epaphroditus and view his ministry to Paul as a failure? Would they think that he blew it? And how did Epaphroditus feel about himself? Did he feel like he was a failure and was plagued by feelings of guilt? Would he go back to Philippi with his head hanging low, filled with shame, feeling like he let his church down and was a burden to Paul? Before Paul dispatched Epaphroditus back to Philippi, he would have counseled him and dissuaded him from all feelings of failure, shame, and guilt. This type of thinking was unnecessary for Epaphroditus to entertain.

Paul wanted to make sure that the Philippians didn't think Epaphroditus failed in his mission either, so he commends him in his letter, in a manner like he commended Timothy. He wants to elevate Epaphroditus' worth in the eyes of the Philippians so that they would hold him in high regard just as Paul does—not thinking anything less of him because he got sick, became a burden to Paul, and was sent home earlier than expected. Paul cites reasons why they should maintain their high view of him by offering a brief commendation of Epaphroditus.

Another thought to consider in this dicey situation is: did the Philippians think Paul was offended that they sent him someone who become a burden to him? After all, Paul could have been a jerk and thought something like: "next time don't send me a guy who gets sick, I've got enough to worry about without having to take care of a guy who nearly dies on me." In this commendation of Epaphroditus he wants to set the record straight for all parties concerned, making sure nobody starts jumping to inappropriate conclusions about the situation. Paul is surely not offended by the Philippians because Epaphroditus got sick.

It is important to see how this commendation of Epaphroditus fits into the whole of the letter. Paul has offered the example of Timothy as one who is worthy of imitation because he follows the example of Christ. Now he points to Epaphroditus as one who also is worthy of imitation because he, like Timothy, also demonstrates the characteristics of the mindset of the Lord Jesus (2:5). One thing about Paul is that he built people up and gave them credit where it was due. He isn't one to heap guilt, condemnation, and judgment on people when things don't go as planned. Epaphroditus has fulfilled the mission the church sent him on and Paul wants to make sure they know that. It's all good! Paul will navigate through the stormy waters with great skill and smooth things over, so everybody is happy, and eliminate any cause for people jumping to reckless conclusions.

But I counted it necessary to send to you Epaphroditus, my brother, fellow worker, fellow soldier, and your apostle and servant of my need; [26]since he longed for you all, and was very troubled, because you had heard that he was sick. [27]For indeed he was sick, nearly to death, but God had mercy on him; and not on him only, but on me also, that I might not have sorrow on sorrow. [28]I have sent him therefore the more diligently, that, when you see him again, you may rejoice, and that I may be the less sorrowful. [29]Receive him therefore in the Lord with all joy, and hold such in honor, [30]because for the work of Christ he came near to death, risking his life to supply that which was lacking in your service toward me. (2:25-30)

Paul is going to state the reasons why he felt it was necessary to send Epaphroditus back to the Philippians: **But I counted it necessary to send to you Epaphroditus.** This was no quick impulsive decision Paul made, because he **counted it** necessary to send him back. **Counted** it is a translation of *hégeomai,* which means: to think, consider, suppose, or have a leading thought. Before Paul made his decision to send Epaphroditus home, he had thought through the matter very carefully and determined it was necessary to do this for the benefit of all parties concerned. He probably discussed the matter with Timothy, prayed about it then decided to release him.

In Paul's description of Epaphroditus it is evident that he held a special place in his heart for him by calling him **my brother.** That is the common designation for fellow believers living in the community of faith. To call someone a brother or sister in the Lord is to identify them as being in the family of God. Thus, Epaphroditus is a brother to Paul just as the rest of the Philippians are. However, because Paul calls him **my brother** it goes beyond a simple designation of the two being in the family of God. They were friends that were close to each other and had developed a bond as they served together in the work of the gospel. Paul held him affectionately in his heart.

The second description of Epaphroditus is that he is Paul's **fellow worker**, which is a translation of the Greek word *synergon*: a compound word consisting of *syn* (with, or fellow) and *ergon* (work). Of the thirteen instances this word is used in the New Testament they are all from Paul, with the exception of 3 John 8. In every case the word indicates a close working relationship with a sense of comradery. Paul viewed him as a teammate, a close associate, a colleague, so this isn't a term used to describe someone placed in a position and given a title with no relationship. Paul also used this term to describe his relationship with Euodia and Syntyche who were at odds with each other (4:2-3).

In Paul's third description of Epaphroditus he calls him my **fellow soldier**. Like brothers in arms they fought side-by-side for the cause of the gospel. The Greek word translated soldier is *stratiōtēs*, which is the most commonly used word for soldiers in the New Testament. Used in a metaphorical sense, being a fellow soldier of Paul's indicates that the work of advancing the gospel is like warfare against the forces of darkness. Paul encouraged Timothy to suffer hardship as a good soldier of Christ (2 Tim 2:3), so being a minister of the gospel is nothing to be taken lightly, for there are many hardships that soldiers on the battle field endure, just as there are many hardships that Christ's servants endure. Paul doesn't describe Epaphroditus as a soldier under Paul's command, rather, he describes him as a **fellow soldier**, like an equal to Paul—a combatant for Jesus.

Paul is going to shift gears and describe Epaphroditus' relationship to the Philippians by stating he is **your apostle**. The term *apostolos*, means someone who is sent, a messenger, envoy, or delegate. There are primary apostles, like the 12 and the apostle Paul, but there are also secondary apostles who served as messengers of local churches. Epaphroditus is an apostle in the secondary sense of being a messenger, for the Philippians sent him as their representative to deliver the money they raised for Paul and take care of his needs (cf. 2 Corinthians 8:23). He is reminding the Philippians that they held him in high esteem such that they found him worthy of being sent on this mission, and they should continue to hold him in high regard when he returns to them. No demotions are in order. He is to continue his ministry among the Philippians and Paul.

In addition to the title of apostle he is described as a **servant of my need.** The term *leitourgos* is translated servant, but more often it is translated "minister." It is the Greek word from which the English word "liturgy" is derived and was used of priestly service to the Lord (2:17; Rom 15:16). Therefore, the Philippians have offered priestly service to God through Epaphroditus' traveling to Rome and attending to Paul's needs. On behalf of the Philippians, Epaphroditus was fulfilling for them what they couldn't personally do for Paul. He was sent to attend to Paul's personal needs and offer whatever help he could in his ministry.

Paul will now speak from Epaphroditus' perspective regarding why he feels it is necessary to send him home as soon as he recovers from his illness and has the strength to travel: **since he longed for you all, and was very troubled, because you had heard that he was sick.** It appears that Epaphroditus was overcome with emotion because he **longed** to be with the Philippians, which is the same word used in 1:8 where Paul said: For God is my witness, how I *long after* all of you in the tender mercies of Christ Jesus. It is a word expressing a deep emotional longing to be with someone.

There was more that Epaphroditus was feeling: **and was very troubled**. The Greek word *adémoneó*, means to be deeply distressed, full of heaviness, or deeply troubled. This same word was used to describe Jesus' anguish in the Garden of Gethsemane (Matt 26:37; Mark 14:33). Both words: **longed for** and **very troubled** are written as present participles, which means Epaphroditus was continuously deeply distressed, so it must have been an emotionally draining time for him. Epaphroditus was a hurting unit because of his circumstances. He was physically sick and emotionally he appears to be at the end of his rope.

Some conclude Epaphroditus' homesickness reflected his immaturity, which seems to be out of character for a grown man. Others suggest that he suffered from some type of nervous disorder or may have been depressed even to the point of being suicidal, thus rendering him unfit to continue with his ministry to Paul.[67] However, these conclusions aren't warranted. It's better to see Epaphroditus as wanting to return home because he had an

---

[67] Martin, Hawthorne, p. 165

intense longing to see them and was very troubled knowing the Philippians **had heard that he was sick**, but they didn't know the outcome. His illness was almost to the point of death, so the Philippians knowing that, were no doubt deeply concerned about him. In our modern era we can pick up the phone, text, skype, email, or face book somebody and we have the news in an instant, but back then those options didn't exist. Paul felt the best thing to do was send him back to Philippi.

What was the illness that Epaphroditus contracted? Nobody knows, but it was serious for Paul emphasizes that his sickness was much more than the common cold: **For indeed he was sick, nearly to death.** This sickness took Epaphroditus right to the threshold of the grave, **but God had mercy on him; and not on him only, but on me also, that I might not have sorrow on sorrow.** God intervened and Epaphroditus recovered from his illness. What dreaded disease had he contracted is left to the imagination for the text gives us no clues. Suffice it to say that it was serious, and it almost killed him, had God not intervened. The fact that Paul mentions again how serious the illness was in v. 30, underscores how lethal the illness was. In our modern era where medicine is readily available, serious illnesses can be cured by having your doctor write a prescription and picking it up at the drug store, but that scenario didn't exist in the First Century. In those days when someone became seriously ill they usually died—end of story. Epaphroditus' recovery is attributed to God's healing intervention—his mercy.

God's mercy is spacious, for not only did it extend to Epaphroditus in healing him, but it also extended to Paul, because he views himself as having received God's mercy as well through his healing intervention. Paul indicates that God had mercy **on me also, that I might not have sorrow on sorrow.** Paul would no doubt have experienced sorrow if Epaphroditus died, which shouldn't be surprising considering how fond of him he was. Anybody would feel sorrow over the loss of a close friend and colleague, but what is the second layer of sorrow that Paul is referring to when he says **sorrow on sorrow**? Most likely he is referring to his life in general. He's had a rough go of things being imprisoned for so long, suffering for the gospel, and being poured out for the gospel (2:17). It's interesting to consider that even though Paul is going through tough times he is experiencing a high level of joy as this letter indicates. "Joy does not mean the absence of sorrow, but the capacity to rejoice in the midst of it."[68] Paul's life is a demonstration of this truth. As God's people suffer for the gospel and bear their cross daily, there is a God-given joy that accompanies the suffering.

I have sent him therefore the more diligently, that, when you see him again, you may rejoice, and that I may be the less sorrowful. (2:28)

Paul wants to make it crystal clear to the Philippians that it was *his decision* to send Epaphroditus home not because of any shortcomings on his part, but because Paul felt it was in the best interest of all parties concerned. He felt a sense of urgency to have Epaphroditus reunited with his friends in Philippi, so he says: **I have sent him therefore the more diligently,** so when he was strong enough to make the journey Paul would send him home.

When someone has a serious illness that is life-threatening we want to hear updates on their progress—even daily updates. In our modern-day that is possible by utilizing all the technology that exists, but back then it didn't work that way. People would have to wait for weeks, even months to hear the news about a sick friend. Paul felt the best thing to do was to send him home, so the Philippians could see for themselves that he was alive and well. The result of this for the Philippians would be: **when you see him again, you may rejoice.** The Philippians were probably biting their nails worrying about Epaphroditus. They loved him and were deeply concerned about his welfare. Paul knew that when he is reunited with his church family they will rejoice over his return **and that I may be the less sorrowful.** Paul would have a huge burden lifted from his shoulders when Epaphroditus returns home to the Philippians and everybody will rejoice that he is alive and well. He knew how much Epaphroditus loved the Philippians and saw nothing but a good outcome by sending him home.

Earlier in his letter Paul expressed his desire for the mercy of death (1:21; 23). Mercy is granted in two forms: one is death, which takes us immediately into the presence of Christ and ends our suffering. The other is the mercy of healing, which reunites us with our friends, prolongs our ministry for the benefit of others and relieves grief.

---

[68] Fee, p. 280

Receive him therefore in the Lord with all joy, and hold such in honor (2:29a)

As a conclusion to what Paul has said he commands them to: **Receive him therefore in the Lord with all joy.** Paul wants to make sure that they understand the situation by seeing nothing deficient in Epaphroditus. It was Paul's decision to send him home, so it's time for rejoicing in the Lord. They should receive him **in the Lord** and make this a celebration. Receiving him in the Lord is to recognize God's sovereignty in this matter, that Epaphroditus' recovery from his illness, and his return to Philippi wasn't happenstance, or random chance, but the hand of Almighty God. Thus, they should give him a warm reception as if they understood the Lord brought him home to their doorstep.

In addition to the celebration of rejoicing they should do one more thing: **and hold such in honor.** This is written as a command, instructing the Philippians to hold him in high esteem because he has served the Lord with distinction. The mission that the Philippians sent him on has been accomplished, he has not failed them. When Paul says hold **such** in honor he is indicating there is a class of God's servants that should be held in high regard in the body of Christ for their work in furthering the gospel. It is, of course, holding them in honor because of the work God is doing in the person, thus it is not withdrawing glory from God, it is enhancing his glory by recognizing his work in people like Epaphroditus.

Perhaps, the Philippians would have a banquet for Epaphroditus or a special service to honor him for what he had done on behalf of the church and for Paul. Such celebrations should be a normal part of church life. God's people should recognize those whom the Lord raised up to do ministry in the church. Every church should recognize that God gives servants to congregations as his gifts to build up the church and be a blessing to them (Eph 4:11-12). It is entirely appropriate to celebrate this by giving thanks to God for the gift of pastors, leaders, workers, etc. and holding them in high regard through expressions of love, gifts, and giving them honor through public recognition.

because for the work of Christ he came near to death, risking his life to supply that which was lacking in your service toward me. (2:30)

Paul restates one of his reasons for giving Epaphroditus honor: **because for the work of Christ he came near to death.** Paul has mentioned the severity of his illness several times, which makes one wonder what it was, but it is left to the imagination. It was serious enough that without God's direct intervention Epaphroditus' life would have been over. He almost gave up his life in service to Christ, not the church at Philippi, or for Paul, but ultimately speaking in service to Christ he came close to death's door. He should receive his Purple Heart for his service to Christ.

The fact that Epaphroditus came near to death's door establishes a link between him and Christ's obedience on to death (2:8), as well as Paul pouring himself out for the gospel (2:17). However, Paul was willing to continue in this life to conduct his ministry for the benefit of the churches under his care. Both Paul and Epaphroditus pursued their course of action in service to Christ and brought glory to God.

It is difficult to know what Paul means by Epaphroditus: **risking his life to supply that which was lacking in your service toward me.** In what way did he risk his life? Since the risking of his life is connected to delivering the financial gift to Paul, it seems to support the view that he took sick on the road to Rome, but rather than turning back he courageously pressed on, thus risking his life. He arrived in Rome and handed the gift to Paul then became ill to the point of death, but he accomplished the mission the church had sent him on.

Another way of understanding **risking his life** is that the name Epaphroditus means "favored of Aphrodite." She was the goddess of gambling, among other things, and men would say "Epaphroditus" as they cast the dice, hoping to gain favor from Aphrodite and win some money. The word **risking** is a translation of *parabouleuomai*, which means: gambled, risked, or voluntarily exposing oneself to danger. Those who favor the translation "gambled with his life" say in a figurative sense that Epaphroditus rolled the dice and gambled with his own life to complete the mission the church sent him on.

Of interest is after New Testament times an association of Christians was formed that identified themselves as the *Parabolani*, which means "The Gamblers." They took Epaphroditus as their model and visited prisoners and ministered to the sick, especially those with dangerous communicable diseases whom no one else would help. They also boldly proclaimed the gospel wherever they went.[69]

Epaphroditus risked his life **to supply that which was lacking in your service toward me.** As an apostle (messenger) of the church at Philippi Epaphroditus was able to do what they couldn't. His ministry is therefore on their behalf, for they would have liked to be there with Paul, but that wasn't possible. **Service** refers to duties of a priest, or priestly service.[70] The church sent Epaphroditus to fulfill their priestly duty to Paul by ministering to him financially and attending to his needs.

Traveling would often put one at risk because there was danger from robbers and bandits, plus people mostly walked, or if they were fortunate enough they could ride a horse or ride in a carriage. To walk from Philippi to Rome was no easy task and carrying a large sum of money made it even riskier.

Insights, Applications, and Life Lessons

A cursory reading of this passage might leave the reader a little bored or puzzled as to why Paul wrote this. After all, who cares about when Timothy and Epaphroditus are going to Philippi. There doesn't seem to be much deep theology in this section such as the atonement, the deity of Christ, the end times, or other profound teaching that Paul offered his readers elsewhere. To draw that conclusion would be unfortunate, because Paul wasn't just an intellectual robot, he was a human being with a deep loving concern for the Philippians.

Paul had a big heart, which was expressed by the high regard he had for Timothy and Epaphroditus—two people he truly loved. Paul's heart ached as he longed to see his converts. To miss this is to gloss over a big part of who Paul is and what makes him tick. Reading this section of Philippians brings this aspect of Paul to center-stage. He was a no nonsense guy who didn't do

---

[69] Barclay, p. 50

[70] "Service" translates the Greek word *leitourgos* also used in 2:17; 25

anything half-heartedly. He gave everything his total effort including writing, traveling, planting churches, sharing the gospel, and loving his converts. As Paul spent much time under house arrest in Rome we can't underestimate how longing to see his converts must have affected him. He could write letters to churches and send other coworkers in his place, but that isn't the same as being able to see people in person. With the possibility of execution hanging over his head he also faced the real possibility that he would never see the Philippians, and other friends he loved ever again, that is, on this side of heaven. This must have been excruciating for Paul and gut-wrenching.

Being away from those you love is difficult, but he had Timothy and Epaphroditus with him, so they could be a solace and comfort to him. Paul would release Epaphroditus, which meant that he might never see him again. This must have been excruciatingly painful for Paul, but the gospel work must go on.

Imagine You Are There

It's about noon and Paul is sitting on the floor talking with Timothy as the Praetorian is listening on the conversation. Someone appears at the door, "Paul are you here?" "It's Epaphroditus from Philippi." Paul stands up as Timothy rushes to the door and gives him a big hug. Then Paul comes to him and embraces him. He comes in and sits down, but Paul recognizes that he doesn't look good. "Are you alright?" "You don't look well," says Paul. Timothy gives him some water to drink and Epaphroditus says, "I'm not feeling well, I feel like I'm coming down with something and I need to rest." But first he gives Paul the money they raised for him. He tells Paul: "The church at Philippi loves you and we raised this money for you as an expression of our concern for your welfare. We are praying for you every day and hope you will be released soon. I'm going to stay with you and help you in any way I can." Paul is overwhelmed with gratitude for the gift, which enables him to pay the rent and eat. Epaphroditus lays down and quickly falls asleep.

Paul and Timothy recognize the next morning that Epaphroditus is very sick, and they're burdened with his welfare. Paul has faced every trial imaginable over the past four years and couldn't bear to see Epaphroditus die. They pray for him and trust God to raise him up. It doesn't look very good for

Epaphroditus, so Paul and Timothy are deeply concerned for him. He lays there day-after-day and isn't doing well. He's burning up with fever, he's in a cold sweat, barely conscience, and his breathing is erratic. They try talking to him, but he can't make sense of their words because he's not totally coherent. Paul and Timothy are thinking he might not make it.

The home church is aware of Epaphroditus' condition and are deeply concerned for his welfare. As Epaphroditus gains consciousness they inform him that his friends at Philippi are worried about him, which makes him feel even worse. He starts thinking he's causing trouble for everyone: Paul and Timothy, and now the home church is worried about him. He apologizes to Paul for letting him down, but Paul will have none of that, because it isn't his fault that he got sick. Paul talks the situation over with Timothy, and after much deliberation he decides to send him back home when he is strong enough to make the journey. He can hand deliver the letter to them that we call Philippians.

The above narrative is my interpretation of how it may have played out. There are times when the best made plans don't work out because of unforeseen causes. It happens all the time. The Philippians planned to send Epaphroditus to deliver their financial gift to Paul and care for his needs, but who would have ever thought that he would have gotten sick to the point of death. Usually when things don't work out as planned somebody needs to be responsible and take the blame—there needs to be a scapegoat.

In the military, after every mission they have an "after action review," where they assess their mission and evaluate how they could have done it better, where the mistakes were made, what was done well, and so forth. When the Philippians had their "after action review" I hope they concluded that Epaphroditus' mission wasn't a failure and understood that his sickness was nobody's fault. It wouldn't be justifiable for the Philippians to be upset with Epaphroditus because he got sick. There are some things that can't be controlled, for human beings have no control over who gets sick, who dies, when the stock market crashes, when a war starts, when the car breaks down, etc. We can't control all the variables of life.

Why did Epaphroditus get sick? Only God can answer that question. All we can say is that it happened under the sovereignty of God, for reasons known only to him. We make our plans and subject them to God, hoping for the best. Paul knew that and wanted to make sure that the Philippians weren't upset with him, as if he was a failure. He was also very sensitive and aware of how Epaphroditus felt. Perhaps, while bed-ridden he told Paul that he felt guilty for being a burden to him, and he felt like he let his church down because he couldn't attend to his needs as originally intended. He may have apologized to Paul for being a source of stress to him. Paul made sure he relieved Epaphroditus of any feelings of guilt, failure, and shame. He wanted him to return home with his head held high, not in shame and disgrace. He wanted the Philippians to know that he has no hard feelings toward Epaphroditus because he got sick—everything is good.

Additionally, Paul wanted the Philippians to hold Epaphroditus in high regard and give him honor for the work he completed. Being over 2,000 years removed from that culture it is difficult for the modern reader to understand the cultural ethos of shame and honor that governed that society, and because of that, how people may have looked at Epaphroditus as a failure.

Another aspect to this delicate situation is that the Philippians may have thought Paul is offended. They sent him their best man, but he got sick and became another burden for Paul to carry, only making his situation worse. This line of thought would be totally out of character for Paul, but the Philippians may have thought Paul was upset that they sent him someone who got sick and became a source of anxiety to him.

Paul had great sensitivity in how he handled the situation with Epaphroditus and the Philippians. I wonder if Epaphroditus read the letter, or if Paul read the letter to him—I suspect he did. When he got to this section of the letter what emotions did Epaphroditus feel? Did he cry? Did he feel relieved? Did he give Paul a big hug? I wonder what emotions the Philippians felt when the letter was read out loud to them. Did they give Epaphroditus a big round of applause? Did they give him hugs, and thank him for his work? It must have been a sensitive moment, but Paul wanted it to end in rejoicing in the Lord? We can only guess how everyone responded, but clearly, Paul had great sensitivity in how he handled this fragile situation.

Summary

Epaphroditus was dispatched by the Philippians to deliver money they raised for Paul and to be a personal aid to him. However, he became gravely ill, almost to the point of death, so Paul thought it over and decided to send him back home and hand deliver the letter we call "Philippians" to the church. He includes this commendation of Epaphroditus in his letter because like Timothy, he displays the mindset of Christ and his lifestyle is worthy of imitating. He expresses his deep feelings for him and encourages the Philippians to welcome him home with great joy and honor him. He is to be commended because he risked his life for the gospel as the Philippians' representative. Paul released Epaphroditus knowing that he may never see him again if he is executed, which made it all the more difficult for him.

In the next section, Paul offers a warning to the Philippians to watch out for false teachers that may appear and try to sway them away from the only true gospel.

CHAPTER THIRTEEN

* * *

"Beware, These Dogs Have a Nasty Bite!" Philippians 3:1-4a

After presenting his travel-log for Timothy and Epaphroditus Paul transitions to focusing on the Philippians (3:1-4:3). Chapter three of Paul's letter presents some challenges to interpreters. There is an abrupt change in the direction Paul is going, such that it seems strange, maybe even illogical for him to plot, what seems to be, an entirely new course. Because of this, some have concluded that this section is a fragment from another letter that Paul inserted into Philippians. If we read 3:1a: "Furthermore, my brothers and sisters, rejoice in the Lord." Then skip to 4:1: "Therefore, my brothers and sisters, beloved and longed for, my joy and crown, so stand firm in the Lord, my beloved," the letter reads somewhat smoothly.

Paul begins the third chapter with *to loipon*, which is most often translated **finally**, so it sounds like Paul is beginning to wrap things up and conclude his letter. This is where the confusion lies because *to loipon* can also be translated: furthermore, beyond that, in addition to, or now then. Thus, *to loipon* doesn't have to be taken as a word implying conclusion, as if Paul is coming to the end of his letter. It can be taken as a word designating transition to a new topic, which appears to be the case here. For these reasons, I've chosen the translation **furthermore.**

Therefore, it isn't necessary to view this section as a fragment of another letter that Paul inserted into Philippians, he's just transitioning to a new topic. This is a warning passage that Paul offers the Philippians, regarding false teachers that were perverting the gospel. They followed Paul around and gave him a hard time as they infiltrated some of his churches presenting a different gospel than his. They posed a threat to Paul's congregations such that he had to correct the errors that they spread. We see this in Galatians, Romans, Colossians, etc. While Paul was in Philippi it is safe to assume that he warned them about the false teachers, exposing their error, because he thought it was very possible that they would show up in their city. He wanted the Philippians to be prepared if the false teachers did show up. Therefore, it appears Paul is reinforcing to the Philippians what he previously told them about the false teachers—BEWARE! If they show up in Philippi, Paul wants them to remember what he previously told them, so they don't embrace their teaching.

Osborne sees it differently in that he thinks as Paul was writing his letter it came to his attention that the false teachers just arrived in Philippi and were starting to make inroads in the church, which happened just as Paul came to the end of 3:1a. Therefore, he immediately stopped writing his conclusion and started writing a diatribe against his enemies of the recent past.[71] This position does account for the abrupt change from 3:1 to 3:2, but there is nothing in the text that warrants that conclusion. Nothing in the text suggests that false teachers were in Philippi making inroads into their church. It is better to see this section as Paul simply transitioning to a new topic where he is exhorting the Philippians to be on guard if the false teachers show up and present their corrupt gospel.

In going through this passage three questions must be answered: 1) who are the false teachers? 2) what were they teaching? 3) why the sever warning?

Furthermore, my brothers (and sisters), rejoice in the Lord. To write the same things to you, to me indeed is not tiresome, but for you it is a safeguard. [2]Beware of the dogs, beware of the evil workers, beware of the false circumcision. [3]For we are the circumcision, who worship God in the

---

[71] Osborne, Loc. 1981

Spirit, and rejoice in Christ Jesus, and have no confidence in the flesh; 4though I myself might have confidence even in the flesh. (Author's Translation, 3:1-4a)

Paul begins by returning to the theme of Joy, which is one of the most amazing features of his letter. **Furthermore, my brothers (and sisters), rejoice in the Lord.** Paul has spoken about joy earlier, in all cases related to the joy he feels over the advancement of the gospel in Rome and back at Philippi.[72] Paul writes this as a command in Greek in the present tense, so they are to keep on rejoicing in the Lord. When believers find themselves in dire circumstances, like Paul, rejoicing is to be done in consideration of God's grace, the fullness of the Spirit, and the hope they have in their future relationship with Christ.[73] Rejoicing is to be a continuous practice of disciples of Christ. Quite often the experience of supernatural joy is most pervasive when believers are suffering for the gospel. When disciples of Christ focus on the joy of the Lord, the petty issues the Philippians had should dissipate, enabling them to serve the Lord in harmony and unity with one another.

After stating the positive examples of Timothy and Epaphroditus, rejoicing **in the Lord** seems like a fitting thing to say at this half-way point in the letter. Especially regarding Epaphroditus, one of the Philippian's own, who received God's mercy through a divine intervention of healing. Paul also considered this God's mercy on him, in that he was sparred much grief had Epaphroditus died. Now that he can return home to Philippi and be reunited with his church, it's cause for celebration and time to rejoice in the Lord. God has raised up Epaphroditus and sparred him from the grave, so celebrating is in order. Since Paul refers to them as **my brothers (and sisters)** he again points out the family nature of the body of Christ, so with Epaphroditus returning home it is like a family reunion. It's time for them to celebrate because their brother has returned home.

Paul reflects on what he told the Philippians when he was with them earlier: **To write the same things to you, to me indeed is not tiresome, but for you it is a safeguard.** Another possible link with rejoicing in the Lord that Paul

---

[72] See: Phil 1:18; 26; 2:17-18

[73] See: Phil 1:6; 10; 21; 23; 2:16

just spoke of, is to not be swayed by anybody teaching a different gospel than his. No matter how attractive or persuasive another teaching might be, to deviate from the one true gospel can have grave consequences, one of which is a loss of joyfulness. For the Philippians to lose their joy by being duped into believing a false gospel would be most catastrophic. Therefore, Paul's command to rejoice serves as a smooth transition from Epaphroditus' return and the warning that Paul is now giving them.

To write the same things to you, must refer to previous teaching Paul had imparted to the Philippians while he was there. Perhaps he left them with some documents about the false teaching, or he is just referring to the oral teaching he had already given them. Paul feels a sense of urgency about this matter for he says: **to me indeed is not tiresome, but for you it is a safeguard.** Writing this warning isn't a repetitive annoyance to Paul, it is a **safeguard** to them, which translates the Greek word *asphalés*, a compound word consisting of *a* (meaning "not") and *sphallō* (meaning "to totter" or "cast down"). Therefore, the word means "to be secure on solid footing," or "built on what does not totter." When someone embraces the true gospel, they are standing on a solid footing, but when false teaching is received it can bring instability into a church, such that their spiritual foundation begins to totter.

Paul wants to make sure this doesn't happen to the Philippians, so he is reminding them of his previous teaching to keep things stable, in the event the false teachers show up in Philippi. Reinforcing this teaching to them can avert a spiritually traumatic situation of the type the Galatian churches went through. For these reasons, it is a safeguard for them to hear this teaching again.

Beware of the dogs, beware of the evil workers, beware of the false circumcision. (3:2)

Paul gets to the heart of the warning now by repeating **beware** three times, written as a command in Greek. The first of which is **beware of the dogs**, which begs the question: who is Paul referring to? There is much agreement among scholars that these were the Judaizers, who were a group of Jewish people that believed in Jesus but advocated that all disciples of Christ needed to convert to Judaism. They wanted Gentile believers in Jesus to Judaize: get circumcised, keep the Sabbath, eat kosher, and keep the Mosaic Law along with all 613 commandments in the Hebrew Bible. In this sense, they were Jewish nationalists upholding the Law of Moses and the ancestral traditions.

He calls the false teachers **dogs**. In those days, most dogs were wild scavengers that roamed around in packs looking for food and were often diseased and sickly. These dogs weren't man's best friend, because they were often mean and ferocious. Paul is referring to the false teachers as this type of dog. Witherington suggests Paul is referring to the false teachers as "guard dogs" that see themselves as guardians of Jewish orthopraxy.[74] They were the guardians of the oral traditions that were passed along from one generation to another, so they thought it was necessary to impose them on Paul's Gentile converts.

Although this is an interesting observation it's better to see the reference to dogs as a pejorative term used by Jews to refer to Gentiles, because dogs were considered unclean like the Gentiles. Perhaps, the Jewish false teachers were trying to make the unclean Gentile dogs clean through circumcision, but Paul, using a twist of irony, says the Jewish false teachers are the unclean dogs to be avoided, not the Gentiles.[75]

After Peter visited Cornelius and the Spirit of God was poured out on the Gentiles (Acts 10), he went to Jerusalem and met with the apostles. He recapped the story about the Gentiles receiving the Spirit and seems to have successfully won over those who objected to the Gentiles being included in the church *without being* circumcised (Acts 11:2-3; 17-18). However, opposition arose within the community of Jewish believers to Gentiles being accepted by God without becoming Jewish. In other words, their position was that salvation was incomplete until they were circumcised and became converts to Judaism, then, and only then, would they be saved.

These same people went to Antioch and opposed Paul and Barnabas, so they decided to travel to Jerusalem and discuss this issue with the apostles, in what came to be known as the Jerusalem Council (Acts 15:1-2). They

---

[74] Witherington, Loc. 2906

[75] Guckelberg, Loc. 6647

presented their view that Gentiles needed to be circumcised, but their view didn't gain traction in the council and they were defeated. However, they continued to visit the churches Paul planted and tried to persuade the Gentile believers that they needed to convert to Judaism in order to be saved. These are the people who cast their influence in the Galatian churches, and seem to have made significant inroads. Paul considered their teaching to be another gospel, which was to be avoided like the plague. At the time of writing Philippians, Paul had been doing battle with these "dogs" for a decade.

Paul issues his second warning: **beware of the evil workers.** The Jews felt that Gentiles were evil because they rejected the Torah (law) and God.[76] Paul does another reversal and considers the false teachers to be **evil workers** because they are undermining the true gospel of Jesus Christ, as they are advocating their "works" gospel. Paul made it clear that by the works of the law no one will be justified.[77] They were advocating a system that was completely powerless to save someone from their sins and place a sinner in a right standing with God. For this reason, Paul strenuously objected to their teaching and identified it as a false gospel—a toxic brew. They positioned themselves in direct opposition to Paul's mission and the teaching of Jesus, so Paul labels them evil workers.

The third warning Paul presents against the Judaizers is: **beware of the false circumcision.** The sign of membership in the covenant community was circumcision, which goes all the way back to Abraham (Gen 17:9-14). Every male child was circumcised on the eighth day. It was one of the primary boundary-markers of one's Jewishness. Circumcision, in the New Covenant era, is nothing more than an empty ritual, no different than some of the rituals that the Gentiles practiced in their pagan religions. So, we have another reversal here in that Paul is saying anyone who presents circumcision as the pathway to the covenant community, is himself not part of God's covenant community. The reversal is complete for this means that the Judaizers are the new Gentiles, while the Christians, whether of Jewish or Gentile descent, are the true Jews (Rom 2:28-29).

---

[76] See: Psalm 6:8; 14:4; 36:12; 94:4

[77] See: Rom 3:20; 27-28; Gal 2:16; 3:2; 10

The Greek word for circumcision is *peritomē*, which literally means "cutting around." The term Paul uses here for circumcision is *katatomé* which literally means "mutilation," or "cutting to pieces." Paul felt the Judaizers should go all the way and not just circumcise themselves but castrate themselves (Gal 5:12). This is the most derogatory statement that Paul will make against those who advocate circumcision. It's almost as if Paul is saying: "since you have replaced the cross and the gospel of Christ with circumcision, performing this ritual is "cutting off" yourself from God's covenant community, so go ahead and castrate yourselves." To practice circumcision as a means of entrance into the New Covenant community is to place oneself entirely outside of the New Covenant, ending up with nothing. These false teachers (dogs) weren't true Christians, and Paul wants to make sure that if they show up in Philippi his Gentile converts don't get conned into following their ways.

This shows us how far Paul has moved away from his Pharisaic roots, for one couldn't imagine Paul saying something this radical before he became a Christian (Gal 5:6; 6:15). Paul isn't anti-Jewish, for he is a firm believer in the Hebrew Scriptures and believes the New Covenant has supplanted the Old Covenant. He does see continuity between the Old and New covenants because he says Gentiles are heirs of Abraham through faith in Christ, not by circumcision, being a disciple of Moses, or worshiping in a synagogue, but by faith in Christ—the seed of Abraham (Gal 3:16).

Paul has mentioned three things that the Philippians should beware of, the last of which was those who advocate circumcision. He is going to add a commentary on this where he sets up a comparison between himself and those who have confidence in the flesh (human effort / works), which will be discussed in the next section (Phil 3:4-12): **For we are the circumcision, who worship God in the Spirit, and rejoice in Christ Jesus, and have no confidence in the flesh (3:3).**

The boundary markers that the Jews pointed to for establishing their Jewishness, and incorporation into the covenant community are now obsolete. Paul says: **For we are the circumcision**, that is all true Christians, both of Jewish and Gentile descent. He wants to include the Philippians and himself in this statement for he says **we** are the circumcision. Paul must be alluding to Deuteronomy 10:16 and 30:6:

> Circumcise therefore the foreskin of your heart, and be no more stiff-necked. (Deu 10:16)
>
> Yahweh your God will circumcise your heart, and the heart of your offspring, to love Yahweh your God with all your heart, and with all your soul, that you may live. (Deu 30:6)

The Hebrew Scriptures foretold a time when God would circumcise the hearts of the people, and circumcision would be of the Spirit (Rom 2:28-29), done by Christ (Col 2:10). The prophesy of Jeremiah predicts the arrival of the New Covenant, which was to be written on the hearts of the people (Jer 31:33). Thus, in the New Testament circumcision is of a spiritual nature, indicating a spiritual transformation occurs when one receives Christ into their heart. External appearance doesn't identify the true people of God, it is the inner transformation that makes one a member of the New Covenant gathering.

One of the characteristics of the true circumcision (Christians) is they are those: **who worship God in the Spirit, and rejoice in Christ Jesus.** The only way to receive the Holy Spirit is by placing your trust in Jesus at which time the Spirit lives in the heart of the believer and seals him, which indicates a mark of ownership.[78] The Judaizers claimed they were worshiping and serving God through Torah observance, but they were doing this without the Spirit, so their obedience to the Torah was rooted in their human effort—which is the epitome of the works of flesh.

Secondly, Paul says true Christians **rejoice in Christ Jesus.** A more literal rendering of *kauchaomai*, is "boasting" rather than "rejoicing." Christians don't boast in themselves and their personal accomplishments, but in Christ and what he has provided for them.[79] The Judaizers boasted in their flesh, that is their personal ability to keep the Torah. They prided themselves in ritual purity, the rite of circumcision, and Torah observance, but none of

---

[78] See: Rom 8:14-17; 1 Cor 6:19; Eph 1:13-14; 4:30

[79] See: Jer 9:24; 1 Cor 1:31; 2 Cor 10:17

those things can make someone right with God. It is only through Christ's work on the cross, and faith in him that can bring a sinner into a right relationship with God, which is precisely why Paul says that Christians: **have no confidence in the flesh.** Christians don't rely on their own efforts to impress God. It is important to understand the theological implications of the term **flesh**, which is a translation of the Greek word *sarx*. This is the same word that is translated *sinful nature*, in many translations of the Bible (Gal 5:16-21). It refers to man's inclination toward evil, and propensity to move away from God in rebellion and sinful behavior. All people are said to be born with a sinful nature which we inherited from Adam (Rom 3:23; 5:12).

There are two spiritual realms of existence that one can be part of. One is being "in the Spirit" which is the realm of existence that all Christians live. The other is "in the flesh" which is the spiritual realm that all nonbelievers exist—including the Judaizers. These two realms are mutually exclusive, for one can't live in both places at the same time because they are totally incompatible. Those who live in the Spirit glory in Christ Jesus, while those who live in the flesh do not glory in Christ—they glory in their human efforts. The Judaizers are boasting in their human achievements and self-righteousness, which is repulsive to God.

The sinful nature is still a powerful force in the life of believers, as Paul made clear in his own experience. He has the desire to do what is right before God but doesn't always follow through on his good intentions because of sin (Rom 7:14-25). He depicts sin as a tyrant that will try to dominate a believer and rule over him, which is why Paul tells the Romans not to let sin rule over them, and to offer their bodies to God as instruments of righteousness (Rom 6:12-14; 12:1-2).

Paul knows all about boasting in his ability to keep the law from his life before he met Jesus: **though I myself might have confidence even in the flesh** (v. 4a). He lived as a strict Pharisaic Jew, so he's been there done that, but now he lives by the grace of God in the Spirit. He no longer puts confidence in the flesh meaning his personal righteousness, and all his painstaking efforts at Torah-observance. He's been liberated from all that and found a better way of life in the Spirit through Christ. Now Paul boasts about his life in Christ, and all the provisions of grace extended to him. For Christians to put confidence in the flesh doesn't make sense because it gives them no spiritual advantage whatsoever. "The circumcision of the flesh, as preached by the Judaizers, became for Paul the symbol of a total mindset that is opposed to the Spirit and leads to death (Rom 8:5-8; Gal 5:16-21)."[80]

Jewish and Gentile believers united in Christ is the circumcision! The literal rite of circumcision means nothing (Gal 5:6; 6:15). This is striking because Jews referred to the "circumcision" or "the circumcised" as one of the boundary markers between Jews and Gentiles, or the people of God and those outside the community of faith. The boundary marker in the New Covenant era that identifies the people of God from those outside the covenant community is the presence of the Spirit. The proof that the Philippians are members of God's New Covenant community is that they have the Spirit within them, which is not the case with the Judaizers.

That the Judaizers were pressuring the Gentile Christians to practice circumcision, basically becoming Jewish, indicates that they were headed in the wrong spiritual direction. They were going backwards not forwards into life in the Spirit. They failed to see the historical significance of what Jesus had done in fulfilling the law (Mat 5:17) and ushering in the New Covenant era. It wasn't that the Judaizers were trying to convert the Gentile Christians to Christ, for they already believed in him. It was that they wanted them to adhere to the Torah, displaying the evidence that they were obeying God by being circumcised, which was the sign of incorporation into the Old Covenant people of God. But this is going backwards in the spiritual timeline to a bygone era. The only thing necessary for salvation is faith in Christ, for his work on the cross paid the penalty for our sins—end of story. Paul wants the Philippians to have nothing to do with these false teachers if they should show up in their city.

Insights, Applications, and Life Lessons

Warnings are necessary because there is a lot of competition for the hearts and minds of people as they consider which spiritual path they want to walk.

---

[80] Silva, p. 149

There is Buddha, Gandhi, Muhammad, Confucius, the Dali Lama, Joseph Smith and a host of others that offer a way of satisfying one's spiritual appetite. Christians believe there is only one path to God, which is faith in Jesus Christ—end of story! The biggest lie of Satan is that there are many roads that lead to heaven, so each person can choose the one that sounds the most appealing to him. Every Christian should know this and steer clear of any other spiritual teaching outside of Jesus Christ.

Within the Christian community there is much false teaching that occurs that is subtle and more difficult to discern; that is, if you don't know your Bible. Just because someone says, "I believe in Jesus" that doesn't mean they are entertaining a pure gospel. Many people believe that Jesus was a great teacher, an enlightened man, a prophet, a moralist, but not the divine son of God. There is every kind of teaching imaginable for people to choose from, much like going to a spiritual shopping mall. You can check out all the different teachings and choose the one that sounds the most enlightening and attractive to you. In a sense, examining the spiritual landscape of Christianity in America is like going into a shopping mall and looking for your brand. The fact of the matter is there are many different brands of Christianity to choose from such as:

- The live your best life now gospel
- The prosperity gospel
- The name it claim it gospel
- The everybody goes to heaven gospel
- The love of God but no wrath gospel
- The Jesus can make your dreams come true gospel
- The self-help gospel, Jesus only helps those who help themselves
- The gospel without judgment day
- The social activism gospel minus the cross
- The gospel of works—legalism minus grace
- The gospel with no call to discipleship
- The mystical gospel of emotion
- The gospel of perfect health this side of heaven

If additional time was spent thinking about it I could probably come up with more, but these are commonly found in the spiritual landscape of American Christianity. The problem with each of the above "brands" is that they contain errors—some greater than others. The only way to discern these errors is by knowing what the Bible says and being grounded in the primary doctrines of the faith. The bottom line is "BEWARE!"

The error the dogs presented was that Jesus' death on the cross wasn't enough for one's salvation, such that something had to be added to it, in this case circumcision. This is a grave error because adding some type of good work(s) to the cross for salvation is the ultimate slap in the face to Jesus. Was his death only 90% effective to save a sinner, such that he needs to add 10% of good works to complete his salvation? Or is it a 60 / 40 split, or a 70 / 30 split? If man did have to add something to Christ's sacrifice for his salvation, what good work could possibly be added that God would find so noble that he would then be saved? To say Christ's death on the cross wasn't enough to atone for man's sins is false teaching to be avoided like the plague.

Another Gospel

Paul's warning is to beware of those who teach another gospel—that is, a false gospel. Paul warns his churches that there is another Jesus, another Spirit, and another gospel (2 Cor 11:4). Plus, Satan is a great imitator, who loves to twist the truth just enough to make another gospel sound attractive, but it is deadly to those who embrace it (2 Cor 11:14). With all the different brands of Christianity that are being presented today, it is necessary for every believer to know their Bible and the core doctrines of the faith, which is the best defense against those who teach a false gospel.

Summary

When Paul founded the church in Philippi, he warned them about the possibility of false teachers showing up and trying to convince them that they needed to be circumcised to complete their salvation—as if faith in Christ wasn't enough. They were known as Judaizers, because they wanted people to become converts to Judaism. Make no mistake about it, Paul considered their teaching to be dangerous—to be avoided like a dreaded disease. The Philippians were already Christians because they had the Spirit, which is the marker of the New Covenant community of believers. The Old Covenant marker for God's people was circumcision, which is what the false teachers wanted Paul's converts to practice. If the Philippians would practice circumcision they would be going backwards in their spiritual timeline to a bygone era, which would be of no benefit to them. The Philippians need to stand fast in the gospel that Paul taught them and not be influenced by any teaching that deviated from his.

In the next section, Paul will give us a glimpse into his own personal journey out of Pharisaic Judaism into his relationship with Christ.

CHAPTER FOURTEEN

* * *

"Boasting as Saul the Pharisee" Philippians 3:4b-6

Paul has issued a warning to be taken seriously by the Philippians, because the false teachers posed a clear and present danger if they show up in their city. These false teaching dogs (3:2), viewed Paul as a heretic who was trying to subvert the Law of Moses and lead people down the wrong path. What they were advocating was nothing new to Paul. These false teachers were strict Pharisees, like Paul used to be, but they failed to connect the dots regarding Jesus ushering in the New Covenant and fulfilling the law (Mat 5:17). If the false teachers (the Judaizers) persuaded the Philippians to embrace their teaching, they would be escorting them to a departed era on the spiritual timeline. They would be taking the Philippians back to life under the Old Covenant. Paul had lived in that former era until the time that he met Jesus on the road to Damascus, which led to his radical transformation. Unlike the Judaizers, Paul was able to connect the dots and understand the historical significance of Jesus' coming as the Messiah and fulfilling the predictions in the Hebrew Bible. He understood the New Covenant was inaugurated by Christ, which was vastly superior to the Old Covenant and rendered it obsolete.

He was liberated from Torah observance, and the traditions of the elders that had been handed down from generation-to-generation, which made keeping the Torah a painstaking endeavor. Paul understood, unlike the Judaizers, that the boundary markers between those who are in the covenant community are no longer circumcision, eating kosher, keeping the Sabbath, and worshiping in the synagogue. The new boundary marker for those who are in the covenant community is the presence of the Holy Spirit, those without the Spirit are outside the covenant gathering.

Paul knows what the Judaizers are all about. If they show up and start boasting about their spiritual credentials (boasting in the flesh), trying to persuade the Philippians to buy into their teaching, Paul can show them that before he met Christ he was just like the Judaizers, but in greater degree. Everything that the Judaizers may try to impose on the Philippians, Paul gave up because he saw that it gave him no spiritual advantage with God, in fact, it was spiritually harmful. Paul will establish a contrast between his spiritual accomplishments and those of his opponents—the Judaizers, and Paul will blow them away. The strategy employed by the apostle is to convince the Philippians how ridiculous it would be to go down the path the Judaizers want to take them, especially since he once walked that path, but changed directions to plot a new course with Jesus. The path the Philippians are on with Christ is the one they need to stay on, no course correction is necessary.

Paul is telling the Philippians from his own personal experience: "don't listen to the false teachers because I've done what they're doing, and I walked away from that theology. It will give you no advantage before God." Paul will list a catalogue of his spiritual accomplishments, which are impressive to say the least, then renounce every one of them to show that knowing Christ is far better than his achievements as a Pharisaic Jew.

There are some social factors that need to be considered, which could make the Judaizers teaching sound like a fantastic deal to the Philippians. When they became Christians they were persecuted, they saw Paul grossly mistreated, they were no longer able to worship in the temples of their pagan religions, and no longer participate in Emperor worship. Given that many were Roman citizens and retired military they might feel a bit estranged on the religious scene. Judaism was a recognized legitimate religion by the Roman Empire, which gave its adherents the liberty not to offer sacrifices to the Emperor or pay local temple taxes, so they could pay taxes to their

Temple in Jerusalem. Christianity did not have the status of being a legitimate religion of the Empire.

In those days religion was all about temples, priests, sacrifices, rituals, festivals, and celebrations. Judaism had all these things, which made it appear similar to their pagan religions more so than Christianity. The disciples of Christ met in homes, or outdoors, and seemed dissimilar to the normal pagan religions of the day, so they stood out like a sore thumb. Most importantly, the Judaizers weren't asking the Gentile converts to Christianity to renounce their faith in Christ, they were calling for supplementing their belief in Jesus with the rite of circumcision and conversion to Judaism.

Crucifixion was a dirty word to the Romans, but Judaism didn't require a belief that the Messiah would die on the cross and suffer the ultimate shame in Roman culture. If the Judaizers would downplay the death of Jesus on the cross, without denying it, they may be able to persuade some of the Philippians to embrace their teaching. Paul, on the other hand, was in-your-face about the cross, and gave it a central place in his teaching along with the resurrection. Being a pagan and worshiping the entire pantheon of gods could be confusing to the worshipers. Who needs to be thanked, sacrificed to, prayed to, placated, and so forth. Judaism was a monotheistic religion that swept the floor clear of all but one God to worship and simplified things for the worshipers.

For these reasons the Judaizers' teaching might gain some traction with the mostly Gentile Christian audience in Philippi. Paul must persuade them that any benefits they might seek by converting to Judaism, as the Judaizers suggest, will give them no benefits at all. He can speak from his own experience because he was a strict Pharisee who practiced all the Jewish rituals, but he walked away from that because it gave him no special favor with God. He came to see that the righteousness apart from the law, found in a relationship with Christ was the best, and only way to go (Rom 3:20-21). He will contrast himself with his Judaizing opponents and blow them away, with the hopes of being able to persuade the Philippians that the deal they are offering them is not a good deal at all. Paul considers their teaching to be a witch's brew and doesn't consider the Judaizers to be true Christians.

If any other man thinks that he has confidence in the flesh, I yet more: [5]circumcised the eighth day, of the stock of Israel, of the tribe of Benjamin, a Hebrew of Hebrews; concerning the law, a Pharisee; [6]concerning zeal, persecuting the assembly; concerning the righteousness which is in the law, found blameless. (3:4b-6)

The **any other man** refers to the false teachers, who have **confidence in the flesh**. He will now speak about his life before he met Christ and explain that at one time he had confidence in the flesh, but in a far greater way than the Judaizers. Paul is talking about people who have extreme confidence in their own ability to be righteous through Torah observance. Because of his past, he can speak with greater authority on this subject than his opponents, because he used to be super-confident in his ability to be righteous by keeping the law. He now presents his spiritual resume and lists those things that he was super-confident about in gaining God's favor.

Boast #1. Circumcised the eighth day: Circumcision was a big deal to Jews. Every male child was circumcised on the eighth day in keeping with the Abrahamic Covenant (Gen 17:3-14) and was the sign of being incorporated into the covenant community. If they weren't circumcised they were to be cut off from the community of the faithful, for they broke the covenant, indicating that God considered this serious business (Gen 17:14). Paul was born into a Jewish family, which means that he was circumcised in accordance with the law, which all occurred long before the Philippians ever heard about Jesus. The Judaizers were insisting on Gentiles being circumcised, so Paul begins his list of boasting in the flesh with this item.

Boast #2. Of the stock of Israel: Paul's parents were Israelites, so by birth Paul is of Hebrew stock—he's a full-fledged Israelite. This affords him the privileges mentioned in Romans 9:4: "Israelites; whose is the adoption, the glory, the covenants, the giving of the law, the service, and the promises," etc. This distinguishes him from proselytes, which were converts to Judaism that were often regarded as second-class citizens by Jews. The Judaizers were hoping to persuade the Gentile believers to become part of the community of God's people by being circumcised. Paul was part of the covenant community from birth, and was of pure Israelite stock, unlike the Gentiles at Philippi.

Boast #3. Of the tribe of Benjamin: During the years of exile many Jews intermarried, which made it difficult to trace one's tribal descent. By the First Century most Jews didn't know what tribe they descended from, but Paul's family remained pure Benjamites. Most likely the Judaizers couldn't make the same claim as Paul and trace their ancestry back to its origin. The tribe of Benjamin has a prolific history in that they remained faithful to the Davidic covenant and sided with Judah as opposed to the ten Northern tribes who split and went their own way. Benjamin was Jacob's favorite son (Gen 42:38), Saul was Israel's first King who was from the tribe of Benjamin, and Moses blessed the tribe as the "beloved of the Lord" (Deu 33:12). Its territory included the city of Jerusalem (Jud 1:21) and Paul seems to have been proud of his tribal ancestry (Rom 11:1).

The first three boasts in the flesh that Paul cites were his by way of birth, which the Judaizers most likely couldn't match. He did nothing to receive these badges of honor, but the next four highlight Paul's personal achievements. Of these, he can really boast in the flesh, for he will blow away the Judaizers in stating his spiritual accomplishments.

Boast #4. A Hebrew of Hebrews: Paul couldn't be any more Jewish than he was. He was of pure Hebrew stock and as he grew into adulthood he maintained his Jewish heritage. This may also imply that at home Paul spoke Aramaic, and he also knew Hebrew. Paul was born in Tarsus, which is a cosmopolitan city located in Asia Minor. Many of the Jews who lived outside of Israel in the Diaspora became Hellenized, which means that they became assimilated into Greco-Roman culture. This did not happen to Paul, for he remained true to his ancestral traditions, and studied under the esteemed rabbi Gamaliel. He was so deeply committed to keeping his Jewish heritage that he confidently asserted: "all Jews know my manner of life from my youth up, which from the beginning was spent among my own nation and at Jerusalem" (Acts 26:4). Few people could compete with Paul's devotion to his Jewish heritage, including the Judaizers.

Boast #5. Concerning the law, a Pharisee: This sect within Judaism prided themselves in studying the law and considered their role to be guardians of the ancestral traditions. In other words, Paul isn't just talking about the Hebrew Scriptures, he is talking about the oral traditions that accompanied them and provided a commentary on the Scriptures. Pharisees had to be devoted to strict Torah observance, which Paul prided himself in by calling himself a "Pharisee, a son of Pharisees" (Acts 23:6), and "I lived as a Pharisee according to the strictest sect of our religion" (Acts 26:5). Paul claimed to be advancing beyond his contemporaries because he was extremely zealous for the ancestral traditions (Gal 1:14). That Paul studied under the famed Gamaliel qualified to him to speak authoritatively on Jewish legal matters, more so than his opponents. Pharisees may not have been the largest sect within Judaism, but they were very influential in their culture, and were held in high regard by the people. If the Judaizers, who were most likely Pharisees, think they were devoted to keeping the law and oral traditions, they should think twice before comparing themselves to Saul the Pharisee.

Boast #6. Concerning zeal, persecuting the assembly: To describe Paul as zealous doesn't do him justice, because he was fanatically zealous. When thinking of the top ten religious fanatics throughout history Paul has to be included in the conversation. Overly zealous people often go to extremes that are dangerous. In their love for God and passion to serve him they often end up hating everything that stands in opposition to their beliefs. Such was the case with Paul, who hated Jesus, saw him as a false Messiah, and viewed the Christians as a heretical sect within Judaism that needed to be exterminated to keep Judaism pure.

Paul's zeal was intense but misguided such that he persecuted Jewish Christians to the death. He wasn't one to take prisoners, for he was a no nonsense kind of guy. He was in full agreement with the stoning of Stephen (Acts 8:1) and was the ringleader of the mass persecution that broke out in Jerusalem on the same day that Stephen was martyred (Acts 8:1-3). He wanted to weed out Jewish Christians to keep the religion pure from the infection of these heretics. The Judaizers may have been zealous, but Paul's level of zeal dwarfs there's. All they wanted to do was convert Gentile Christians to Judaism and have them circumcised, but Paul took it over the top and persecuted Jewish Christians to their death.

As a side note, think about how the Philippians felt as they heard this read to them in their worship service. Paul presents himself, in his former life before Christ, as one who persecuted Christians even to the death. Paul comes to

Philippi and got the tar beat out of him, was thrown in jail, then locked in stocks because he is a Christian. There is a twist of irony here. The Philippians saw Paul severely beaten for being a Christian, which was the same thing Paul did to Christians before he became a disciple of Christ. Now Paul is on the receiving end of persecution, prior to life in Christ he was the one dishing it out.

Boast #7. Concerning the righteousness which is in the law, found blameless: The righteousness which is in the law points to Paul's behavior. He meticulously kept the commands and the oral traditions to the point where every "i" was dotted, and every "t" was crossed. His obedience was impressive to say the least. He kept the law and knew he was good at it, in a way like Zacharias and Elizabeth (Luke 1:6). Few Jews could come even remotely close to Paul's ability to keep the law and the ancestral traditions. That he was found **blameless**, translates the Greek word *amemptos*, also translated "without blemish" or "faultless" and was used to describe the animals that were to be used for sacrifices. Therefore, this is Paul's way of saying that his record of Torah-keeping is without blemish, just like a perfect animal presented for sacrifice. He scrupulously adhered to the Sabbath regulations, dietary codes, ritual cleanness, and the oral traditions passed down from generation-to-generation.

Paul is taking a backward glance at his life and is speaking here as Saul the Pharisee. Paul the Christian knows that he wasn't without fault in God's eyes, for he rejected Jesus and persecuted his people. But as far as his efforts as Saul the Pharisee in keeping the law he stood out among his contemporary's. How could the Judaizers possibly outdo Paul in these matters? The truth of the matter is that Paul has just blown them out of the water, for they can't compete with his spiritual accomplishments—his boasting in the flesh far exceeds what they can boast about.

Insights, Applications, and Life Lessons

Prior to Paul's conversion to Christianity, when he was Saul the Pharisee, it appears that his conscience was clear before God as a law-keeper. Who could possibly accuse Saul of being a law-breaker, because he was without blemish and squeaky clean. As we read about Saul the Pharisee there is no evidence to suggest that at that time in his life he was overwhelmed with guilt, viewing himself as a sinner in need of God's grace and forgiveness. Saul the Pharisee saw himself as having received a passing grade of 100% from God regarding his spiritual performance. In Romans 7:13-25 we have a picture of Paul the Christian, who is describing his battle of wanting to do good, but not always being able to follow through with obedience because of the capacity to sin that he battles against, as we all do. In Philippians 3:6, Saul the Pharisee has a clear conscience before God and is convinced that through his meticulous Torah observance God is totally pleased with him and has given him a passing grade.

"Paul's problem was not that he couldn't make the grade; it was that he *did* make it, only to find out that it was the wrong standard of measurement."[81] Paul became aware of his misguided zeal after he met Christ on the road to Damascus, at which time he felt guilt and remorse for persecuting Jesus and his people.[82] It was after becoming a Christ-follower that Paul traded in his tape measure that he used to measure his faultless behavior in keeping the Law, for a new tape measure that defined righteousness apart from the law found only through faith in Christ, as he mentions in Romans 3:20-23:

> Therefore no one will be declared righteous in God's sight by the works of the law; rather, through the law we become conscious of our sin. [21]But now apart from the law the righteousness of God has been made known, to which the Law and the Prophets testify. [22]This righteousness is given through faith in Jesus Christ to all who believe. There is no difference between Jew and Gentile, [23]for all have sinned and fall short of the glory of God.

One must see the radical transformation that occurred in Paul to make such a statement, because it is nearly impossible to imagine Saul the Pharisee saying this. The *works of the law* is what Paul was all about and, in his view, he was righteous in God's sight as Saul the Pharisee. Reading this statement reveals Paul's new tape measure concerning righteousness being given through faith in Jesus, not meticulous adherence to the Law of Moses.

---

[81] Flemming, p. 165

[82] See: Gal 1:13; 1 Cor 15:9; 1 Tim 1:13

It was after the road to Damascus meeting with Christ that Paul's theology developed, and he became aware of his battle with sin as he described in Romans 7:13-25. This is not a description of Saul the Pharisee, this is a description of Paul the Christian fighting the battle against sin that all Christians are fighting.

The Treadmill of Human Effort

Paul isn't the only one who has confidence in his own human efforts to be righteous before God. Most nonbelievers will say that they are good people and, on that basis, when they stand before God on judgment day he will accept them because of their goodness. They are saying their own righteousness is sufficient for their salvation. Their efforts at being a good person are so impressive that God will surely accept them into heaven. There is a problem with that type of thinking because it stands at odds with Paul's teaching.

This passage reveals that when it comes to one's human effort, and energy expended to be righteous few could match Paul. He lived a blameless life before God scrupulously keeping the Torah, and the ancestral traditions, but it was his righteousness, his goodness, his moral excellence, which he discovered after becoming a follower of Christ gives him no special favor with God. People must understand that there is only one way to be considered righteous before God, which is through faith in Jesus Christ. Apart from the moment of placing one's faith in Jesus for salvation all good works, even one's best most altruistic works, and good morals aren't sufficient for God to consider him righteous, and grant him access to heaven. Trying to impress God by being a good moral person is like running on a treadmill going nowhere.

Summary

Paul has taken a backward glance at his life before he met Christ and listed the things he boasted about regarding his spiritual performance as a strict Pharisaic Jew. His opponents were also Pharisees, but they couldn't come even remotely close to matching Paul. They are Minor League players whereas Paul was a Major League All-Star in Judaism. Paul gave up his life as a Pharisaic Jew and left that all behind, so when the Judaizers try to convince the Philippian Gentiles to become converts to Judaism Paul can energetically say: "Why would you want to go there, I walked further down that path than they did, and I gave it all up because it has no spiritual benefit." That Paul can speak from his own personal experience should make his warning even more meaningful to the Philippians. This should render the Judaizers' appeal a "no brainer" to avoid. Paul has given his beloved Philippians sufficient warning to steer clear of the Judaizers, if they show up in town, and have nothing to do with them and their false gospel because it is a toxic brew.

In the next section, Paul will renounce all his past spiritual accomplishments as a Pharisaic Jew in favor of simply being in a relationship with Jesus Christ.

CHAPTER FIFTEEN

* * *

"Paul's Excel Spreadsheet"
Philippians 3:7-11

After boasting about his spiritual accomplishments, as Saul the Pharisee, by showing his readers his spiritual transcripts from Judaism, which are indeed impressive, he is going to renounce every one of them in favor of knowing Christ. Should false teachers (the dogs) show up in Philippi and try to maul the Gentile believers with their nasty bite of false teaching, Paul is showing them why they should reject their appeals. Paul shows the Philippians why he renounced the path that the false teachers want the Gentile Christians to walk down. He knows far more about Judaism and is more qualified to speak on matters of the law and oral traditions than the Judaizers. In doing this, Paul will use accounting language where he sets up a profit and loss column, like an excel spreadsheet, where he shows us that as Saul the Pharisee he was deep in the red spiritually, but after meeting Jesus and becoming Paul the Christian he is now in the black spiritually.

However, I consider those things that were gain to me as a loss for Christ.
8Yes most certainly, and I count all things to be a loss for the excellency of
the knowledge of Christ Jesus, my Lord, for whom I suffered the loss of all
things, and count them nothing but refuse, that I may gain Christ 9and be
found in him, not having a righteousness of my own, that which is of the
law, but that which is through faith in Christ, the righteousness which is

from God by faith; [10]that I may know him, and the power of his resurrection, and the fellowship of his sufferings, becoming conformed to his death; [11]if by any means I may attain to the resurrection from the dead. (3:7-11)

In v. 7 he makes a conclusion about how he views his former spiritual accomplishments that he listed in vv. 4-6. He does this through an accounting metaphor utilizing the term **gain** which translates the word *kérdos,* meaning "profit" or "gain," along with the term loss, which translates the word *zēmía,* meaning "loss," a "bad deal," or "an unsuccessful business transaction." Therefore, Paul presents a spiritual ledger to compare his life as Saul the Pharisee with his life as Paul the Christian.

At this point in Paul's life he claims: **However, I consider those things that were gain to me as a loss for Christ.** Those things that were gain to Paul were the things he mentioned in vv. 4-6, that he could so proudly boast about as a Pharisaic Jew, but he's had a complete reversal in his thinking. He previously thought his accomplishments put him in the *black* spiritually, but now he sees that they actually put him in the *red* before God. Like a good accountant, Paul is moving everything into the loss column and keeping an accurate ledger of his spiritual performance. Those accomplishments Paul was so proud of as Saul the Pharisee, now became liabilities to him, deficits, and payables as Paul the Christian.

Paul obviously gave this a great deal of thought because he said: **I consider those things.** He didn't arrive at this conclusion over night, he probably went through a great deal reflection about his life in Judaism and saw that in his relationship with Christ the things he was proud of were spiritual deficits and moved them to the loss column. When Jesus became the focal point of Paul's spiritual experience he had a new outlook on things. Whenever people make Jesus the focal point of their life they realize the things they took pride in before knowing him, such as: their spiritual achievements, spiritual heritage, education, career achievements, and whatever other accomplishments they may boast in, are all deficits or losses, because they do not put one in a right relationship with God. These achievements in life, that people may have worked very hard at do not make them acceptable to God, regardless of how moral, upright, ethical and squeaky clean they may have lived.

Yes most certainly, and I count all things to be a loss for the excellency of the knowledge of Christ Jesus, my Lord, for whom I suffered the loss of all things, and count them nothing but refuse, that I may gain Christ. (3:8)

Yes most certainly is more literally translated: **but, yes, rather, indeed, therefore,** a string of five Greek particles that are almost impossible to translate. Paul is using this language to make the statement that follows hyper-emphatic: **I count all things to be a loss for the excellency of the knowledge of Christ Jesus, my Lord. I count** is the same word Paul used in the previous verse translated "consider," which is the Greek word *hégeomai.* Paul spent some time thinking about this and concluded **all things,** which include the impressive list of his spiritual achievements (vv. 4-6) and would include his present accomplishments in serving Jesus to be **a loss**. People would look at Paul and say he was a successful theologian, leader, writer, evangelist, teacher, and church planter, but for Paul, he would place all these accomplishments secondary to knowing Jesus. The term **knowledge** (*gnosis*) refers to knowledge acquired through first-hand experience, which connects theory to application—applied knowledge. In other words, Paul is speaking about his intimate relationship with Jesus, not something he read about in a text book.

This is nothing less than an all-out renunciation of everything Paul was proud of prior to becoming a believer in Christ and would include even the successes he's had since becoming a Christian. In essence, Paul is saying everything in life is a loss compared to the greatness of being in a relationship with Christ—no matter what it is.

That Paul identifies the Lord as **Christ Jesus, *my Lord*** is important. This points out the place that Jesus occupies in his life. There is no higher place that Jesus can occupy in a person's life than where Paul places him—he is **my Lord**. Paul is completely submitted to Christ, is living his life for the glory of Christ, in obedience to Christ, spreading Christ's gospel, but all these things pale in comparison to Paul simply knowing Christ. This is intensely personal for Paul, as it should be for every Christian. To call Jesus **my Lord** is the most cherished thing that a person can claim in life.

The renunciation is complete: **for whom I suffered the loss of all things, and count them nothing but refuse, that I may gain Christ** (v. 8b). He continues the accounting metaphor with the use of **loss** and **gain** terminology, however, he now switches to the verbal form of the words, rather than using the nouns as he did previously. This means that he is no longer *considering* these things as **loss** and **gain** (v. 7), but he is *actively experiencing* them as **loss** and **gain**. The verb **I suffered** is written in the passive voice, which means he had things taken away from him when he became a Christian that were out of his control, which include: his status in Judaism, his excellent standing as a Pharisee, friends, family, his inheritance, and more. Unquestionably, becoming a believer in Christ cost Paul dearly, but he has no remorse whatsoever because to know Christ made it worthwhile.

After reflection, Paul has deliberately placed his former accomplishments in the loss column **and count them nothing but refuse, that I may gain Christ.** Paul renounces all these things and considers them nothing but **refuse**, which translates the Greek word *skubalon*, which also means: rubbish, scraps for dogs, dung, or excrement. What a reversal! It's as if Paul is saying: "all the things that I once took pride in I've thrown in the manure pile, because that's where they belong." If Paul is thinking about the scraps thrown in the street for dogs, he could be using a twist of irony in that he is referring to the false teaching dogs (3:2). Paul sees all his spiritual accomplishments that he valued as Saul the Pharisee, to be nothing but table-scraps for the false teaching dogs to feed on, now that he is Paul the Christian.

The purpose for this great renunciation Paul makes is: **that I may gain Christ.** Paul has moved everything from the gain column to the loss column and considers them so disgusting he refers to them as dung. But we now find in the gain column Paul's relationship with Christ, which puts him way in the black spiritually. That is the ultimate reversal Paul makes by throwing all his personal achievements in the manure pile, so that a relationship with Jesus can be pursued. How can a person associate with Christ if he hasn't renounced all things that stand in the way of that relationship? All worldly attachments must be renounced in order to gain Christ. Paul, like a good accountant, has redone his spiritual spreadsheet and is ready to be audited by the Lord Jesus. His books are totally in order, his spreadsheet balances, and he is in the black with Jesus.

The graphs below reflect Paul's view of himself before and after meeting Christ. He creates a profit and loss spreadsheet that depicts the things he did that he thought would place him in a favorable standing with God. These are the things Paul took pride in and refers to them as *confidence in the flesh*, or his human effort to please God.

Before Christ

PROFIT	LOSS
Confidence in the flesh Circumcised Stock of Israel Tribe of Benjamin Hebrew of Hebrews Pharisee Zealous-persecuted the church Legalistic righteousness faultless	Paul was aware of nothing he was doing spiritually that put him in the loss column with God

Paul considered the things he took pride in before he became a Christian a loss once he met Jesus. He's in the black with Jesus, but he renounced all his spiritual accomplishments when he became a believer and put them in the loss column. He came to see that all his confidence in his human ability to impress God only put him in the red, so he redid his spiritual spreadsheet below.

After Christ

PROFIT	LOSS
To Know Christ Paul is in a right standing with God only through faith in Jesus. Paul is righteous only because he placed his faith in Christ	Confidence in the flesh Circumcised Stock of Israel Tribe of Benjamin Hebrew of Hebrews Pharisee Zealous-persecuted the church Legalistic righteousness faultless Paul considers this *skubalon* (dung)

and be found in him, not having a righteousness of my own, that which is of the law, but that which is through faith in Christ, the righteousness which is from God by faith; (3:9)

What does Paul mean when he says: **and be found in him (Christ)?** Found by whom? Found when? That Paul is already "in Christ" is clear, for all Christians are said to be "in Christ," which describes their union with him occurring when they place their faith in him. So being found "in him" is a present reality for Paul, and all Christians, but there is a future aspect to this as well. At Christ's return Christians will be found in him and receive their inheritance. Therefore, the present aspect of being found "in him," will match up with the future of life "with Christ" for all believers. This is another example of the "already" but "not yet" tension in Philippians.

What Paul says next is a watershed statement for him: **not having a righteousness of my own, that which is of the law.** In Christ, Paul's personal righteousness through Torah keeping has been thrown on the manure pile because it is meaningless. Coming to Christ by faith redefines Paul's view of righteousness: **but that which is through faith in Christ, the righteousness which is from God by faith.** When the sinner is justified by faith in Christ he is placed in a right relationship with God and has Christ's righteousness imputed to him, as a gift from God."[83] God declares the sinner not guilty, he is acquitted, totally forgiven of all sins, and is reconciled to God.

According to the Greek text another way of translating **faith in Christ**, is **Christ's faithfulness**, which has gained traction among some scholars.[84] Understood this way Paul would be referring to Jesus' faithfulness in dying on the cross in obedience to the will of God the Father, so the verse would read like this:

and be found in him, not having a righteousness of my own, that which is of the law, but that which is through *Christ's faithfulness*, the righteousness which is from God by faith; (3:9)

If this translation is correct "the contrast is between Paul's obedience/faithfulness that draws its sense of righteousness from following the law, and Christ's obedience/faithfulness that overcame the power of sin and fulfilled the law. The contrast is between Paul and Christ, not two activities of Paul — blameless law-keeping and faith."[85]

Although, this translation is grammatically and theologically correct, it better fits the context to keep it as **faith in Christ**, as Paul uses the phrase elsewhere.[86]

The righteousness that comes through faith in Christ, stands in stark contrast to self-righteousness, which was so typical of Saul the Pharisaic Jew. This isn't **righteousness of my own** in that it isn't worked for, earned, labored for, or strived for through Torah keeping, because it is given only when one places his faith in Christ. This is a shocking statement for Paul to make because it shows us how far Saul the Pharisee has come in his transformation to Paul the Christian. This is new theology for Paul.

---

[83] See: Rom 3:21-4:25; 5:17
[84] Witherington, Loc. 3123
[85] Cohick, Loc. 4143
[86] See: Gal 2:16; 3:22; Rom 3:22, 26

that I may know him, and the power of his resurrection, and the fellowship of his sufferings, becoming conformed to his death; [11]if by any means I may attain to the resurrection from the dead. (3:10-11)

The most important thing in Paul's life, his focus, his goal, his purpose, his type A driven personality is consumed with: **that I may know him.** Knowing Christ was what life was all about for Paul (1:21). This is intimate knowledge (*gnosis*) that points to a deeply personal relationship with Jesus. Thinking about all the effort involved in keeping the Law brings one to the conclusion that is was exhausting. It is not necessary to keep a record of the good deeds one has done to achieve personal righteousness. Living the Christian life certainly involves a degree of effort, but the effort should be focused on the objective of knowing Christ in a more intimate way, not keeping a detailed list of good deeds one has done so he can be considered righteous as a law-keeper. Throughout a believer's life she should be growing in her intimate relationship with Christ and continuously learning more about him, just as one would in knowing another person. This should be a life-long pursuit for every believer. Paul gives us further insights into what it means to know Christ more intimately: **and the power of his resurrection**.

When converted to Christ the believer experiences the **power of his resurrection**, as he is brought from death to life in his union with him (Rom 6:3-4). He is said to be raised up with him seated in heavenly places,[87] thus the resurrection power of Christ is operative in the believer in this age (2 Cor 4:7-17). **Power** translates the word *dunamis* one of the words that is translated "miracle" thus referring to God's limitless power. That the believer can know the **power** of his resurrection means God's power is operative in the individual, which enables her to overcome temptations and live a victorious life over sin and Satan. It must be emphasized that Paul isn't using the term **power** in a triumphalistic way, as if he is suggesting that sin can be completely eradicated, and the believer can walk in sinless perfection in this life. He made it clear in his own experience that God's power becomes operative in his human weaknesses (2 Cor 12:12). In the next section, Paul makes it clear that perfection will not occur until the next age, at which time believers will be resurrected by God's power (Phil 3:12-21). However,

[87] See: Eph 1:19-20; 2:6; Col 3:1

believers are not left without resources in their sanctification in the present, in that they have the resurrection life of Christ working in them, through the presence of the Spirit (Phil 2:12-13).

Moreover, when the resurrection of the body occurs, at the time determined by God, believers will be raised to immortality and will be glorified.[88] Therefore, the resurrection is a present reality (the already), but also a future event (the not yet) that God's people hope for with great expectation (Phil 3:20-21). Acquiring knowledge of Christ involves knowing the **power of his resurrection** to live a worthy life of the gospel as citizens of heaven, through faith and dependence on him.

In addition to knowing Christ in the power of his resurrection, Paul desires to know Christ more intimately in another way: **and the fellowship of his sufferings.** Paul saw the risen Christ on the road to Damascus, so the resurrection wasn't an abstraction in Paul's thinking, it is a reality that guarantees his own resurrection and gave him a unique perspective on suffering. Gordon Fee puts it this way: "Because of Christ's resurrection Paul could throw himself into the present with a kind of holy abandon, full of rejoicing and thanksgiving; and that not because he enjoyed suffering, but because Christ's resurrection had given him a unique perspective on present suffering...as well as an empowering presence whereby the suffering was transformed into intimate fellowship with Christ himself."[89]

Suffering for suffering's sake is not what Paul is talking about. He says the **fellowship** of his sufferings, which is yet another occurrence of the word *koinonia*.[90] To know Christ is also to know **his sufferings**, which means to suffer for the sake of Christ and the advancement of the gospel. In other words, as believers forsake everything to follow Jesus, and truly live on mission for the Lord, the inevitable result of that commitment will be the fellowship of his sufferings. The resurrection power of Christ is most evident in a believer's life during times of suffering and persecution. The Philippians

---

[88] See: 1 Rom 8:30; 1 Cor 15:52-54; 1 Thess 4:13-17

[89] Fee, p. 331

[90] Mentioned in Phil 1:5; 2:1; 4:15

have already experienced suffering and persecution just as Paul has, so this is not a foreign concept to them (1:27-30).

It is during times of weakness and persecution that resurrection power becomes evident in the believer's life and in the church. Paul said that he prefers to boast about his weaknesses because it is through human frailty that Christ's power is displayed, so he delights in the persecution he has endured because it opens the door to Christ's power in his life (2 Cor 12:9-10). One reason why Philippians is full of joyful exhortations is because Paul has suffered intensely for the gospel, being under house arrest for two years, so Paul has not only experienced the weakness of his situation, but through that weakness he has experienced Christ's resurrection power, thus deepening his relationship with the Lord Jesus. One must consider that Paul's circumstances enabled him to grow significantly and know more about Christ, which reminds us that God works all things together for good (Rom 8:28). In the difficult circumstances Paul faced, God was doing a mighty work in him which caused his relationship with Christ to soar to new heights, bringing him to a greater level of holiness.

As mentioned earlier, it seems like a paradox in the Christian experience; that as the disciple of Christ suffers for the sake of the gospel there is a corresponding level of joy that accompanies the suffering.[91] The foundation of joy in the Lord is participation in his mission for the redemption of the world, which will lead to the fellowship of his sufferings, experiencing his resurrection power, and growing deeper in our relationship with him.

It is important to see a link between this passage and Christ emptying himself and suffering as he died on the cross (Phil 2:7-8). The believer must empty himself of all worldly attachments and deepen his commitment to the mission of introducing people to Jesus for their salvation. It should be a comfort to believers that as they suffer for Jesus' sake they don't suffer alone, they suffer with Jesus as if he is a partner with them. When Paul met Jesus on the road to Damascus, Jesus said, "Saul, Saul, why do you persecute me" (Acts 9:4)? As the church suffers Jesus joins them in the suffering. Not only does Jesus fellowship with us in suffering, the Spirit, and God the Father are

---

[91] See: Col 1:24; 1 Thess 1:6; 1 Pet 1:6

deeply involved in the lives of the suffering church. Therefore, suffering for the sake of the gospel is a Trinitarian experience, in that the entire Godhead is present with believers to provide strength, comfort, and encouragement as the church struggles to advance the Good News.[92]

Additionally, Paul brings to the surface another aspect of knowing Christ: **becoming conformed to his death.** This phrase modifies "to know him," so Paul is still talking about how one gains greater intimacy in their walk with Christ. **Becoming conformed** is a translation of the Greek *symmorphóō*, consisting of *sýn* ("with" or "together") and *morphe*, ("same form" or "inner essence"). This word was also used to describe Christ who existed in the form (*morphe*) of God (Phil 2:6), taking the form (*morphe*) of a slave (Phil 2:7), and humbling himself to the point of death on a cross (Phil 2:8). Paul seems to be establishing a verbal link between his own narrative and Christ's story (Phil 2:6-11). **Becoming conformed** is a present participle which indicates continuous action, but it is written in the passive voice, which means it is God who is doing the conforming. Throughout the believer's life she is continuously being conformed to Christ's image, in this case his death. Thus, it is an ongoing experience in the believer's life that is attributed to God (2:13).

But what does it mean to be conformed to Jesus' death? Paul views his own life as following the pattern of Jesus' death and resurrection. Every time Paul speaks of his trek with Jesus in his death it is in the context of the suffering he endured in the totality of his ministry. For example, when Paul was called as the apostle to the Gentiles he was told he would suffer greatly for the name of Jesus (Acts 9:16). Paul had to deal with false teachers that followed him around and threatened the health of the churches he planted, he had to correct the childish behavior of immature Christians that was emotionally draining to him, and his travels brought him into deadly peril over-and-over (2 Cor 11:23-27). On one occasion, he was stoned (Acts 14:19), he faced the emotional pressure of being burdened with all the churches under his care (2 Cor 11:28), he was imprisoned more than once, he was mistreated in Philippi (which some of the converts probably witnessed [Acts 16:22-24]), he was run

[92] See: Phil 1:19; 2:1; 2 Cor 1:3-5; 1 Pet 4:13-14

out of town by false teachers on several occasions (Acts 14:5-6), and finally was martyred for Christ.

Make no mistake about it, Paul had a rough go of it, but there is a positive side to this. "Just as Christ's death was the means through which God worked the miracle of the resurrection, so Paul's own suffering in faithfulness to his calling is the means through which God is bringing spiritual life to the congregations of believers he has been establishing (2 Cor 4:7-11; cf. Col 1:24). As a result, Paul tells the Corinthians, "death is at work in us, but life is at work in you" (2 Cor 4:12)."[93]

This is what Paul means when he tells the Philippians that he is **being conformed to his death**, for this is part of knowing Christ intimately. Another paradox exists in that when someone becomes a believer they are said to have died with Christ, meaning there is a spiritual death to sin that the new convert experiences.[94] This is a one-time event that takes place at the moment of conversion, but in this passage, Paul is talking about a continuous process of being conformed to Christ's death throughout the believer's life.

The same is true of the resurrection. When a sinner receives Jesus into his heart he experiences his resurrection power (Rom 6:3-4), however, in the future he will participate in the physical resurrection of the body at which time we will be glorified—living in the immortal state. In the Philippian passage under consideration, Paul doesn't leave it at being conformed to Jesus' death, for he continues: **if by any means I may attain to the resurrection from the dead** (v. 11). Death precedes resurrection. That was the case with Jesus (Phil 2:8-11) and that will be the case with Paul and other believers. The fact that Christ rose bodily from the dead is the guarantee of believers' resurrection from the dead.[95] Paul saw the risen Christ, and he wrote this under the inspiration of the Spirit, so he knows the resurrection of believers is a certainty to happen, not something that is a mere possibility or likelihood.

---

[93] Thielman, p. 173

[94] See: Rom 6:1-7; Gal 2:20; Col 2:20

[95] See: Rom 8:23; 1 Cor 15:20-23; 1 Thes 4:13-18

The phrase **if by any means** (*ei pós katantaó*) is translated in several different ways, some of which seem to imply that Paul was doubtful about his participation in the resurrection. Note the following translations:

The NIV: and so, somehow, attaining to the resurrection from the dead.

The CSB: assuming that I will somehow reach the resurrection from among the dead.

The NLT: so that one way or another I will experience the resurrection from the dead!

These translations seem to imply that Paul was doubtful as to whether he would be one of the resurrected at the end of the age, but that is not the case. Surely, Paul had no doubts about the resurrection of believers, or his participation in it. Paul is speaking to *the means by which* he will reach the moment where he will be resurrected. "The uncertainty relates instead to the path that each of us will take before we arrive at that point—specifically, the sufferings and difficulties that await us and the spiritual warfare we will endure on our way to that goal. There can be no doubt about the reality of the future promise, but each of us will nonetheless arrive with difficulty as we 'take up [our] cross' (Mark 8:34)."[96]

Believers walk different paths pertaining to the degree they suffer for the sake of Christ and the gospel. This idea seems to best fit the context of the passage (3:10). The path of suffering each person walks is unique, but all Christians will end up in the same place: resurrected in glorified bodies at the end of the age. However, there are two other ways this is understood.

A second possibility is that Paul is being humble and trying not to be presumptuous about the resurrection, such that he is saying something like: "by the grace of God I pray that he will count me worthy to participate in the resurrection." Therefore, Paul isn't doubtful in any way, he's just being humble.

---

[96] Osborne, Loc. 2325

A third possibility is that Paul is thinking about the condition the believer is in when resurrection occurs. For instance, at the moment of death the believer finds himself in the presence of Christ in the intermediate state but doesn't have his resurrection body. Whether the person lived a long life and died of natural causes, was martyred, or died early in life due to an illness, or accident, etc. he immediately goes to heaven. How one dies and arrives in heaven is unique for each person. For the believers who are alive at the time of Christ's coming, they would never experience physical death, rather they will be translated in the twinkling of an eye, and their natural bodies will be instantly glorified.[97] Therefore, Paul is thinking about each person's prelude to resurrection.

Whichever view one takes of the above three, Paul wasn't doubtful about the future resurrection of believers or his participation in it.

The resurrection from the dead is the glorious place that Jesus will take believers, which Paul will comment on in 3:20-21. It is the resurrection that gives believers hope for the future, it is their final inheritance, and what Peter calls a living hope (1 Pet 1:3). This is the point at which Christians' battle with sin is history, because in the resurrected state there will be no possibility of sinning—end of story. A triumphant celebration of God's people occurs when they meet the Lord, the evil age ends, and they find themselves living in perfection in glorified bodies—perfectly conformed to the image of Christ.

Insights, Applications, and Life Lessons

Paul is telling us his story—as if he's writing a narrative of his spiritual life. There are striking parallels between the path of his life and the path of Jesus' life that can't be dismissed as coincidental:

- Jesus emptied himself (2:7), Paul poured himself out (2:17)
- Jesus humbled himself as a slave (2:8), Paul humbled himself as a slave (Phil 1:1)
- Jesus suffered (2:8), Paul knows the fellowship of his sufferings (3:10)

[97] See: 1 Cor 15:51-52; 1 Thess 4:13-18

- Jesus was obedient to death (2:8), Paul is being conformed to his death (3:10)
- Jesus was resurrected (2:9-11), Paul wants to know the power of his resurrection (3:10)
- Jesus was exalted by God (2:9-11), Paul will be exalted through resurrection (3:21)

He is showing the Philippians how he himself, is walking in Jesus' footsteps, and encouraging them to do the same. His life narrative is running parallel to Jesus' narrative. Hopefully, the Philippians are making these connections with Paul and Jesus. Paul's rhetorical strategy is to teach by way of example, so he is presenting himself as one who follows Jesus' example and the Philippians can follow Paul's example.

Personal Mission Statements

Writing out personal mission statements is trending these days. In fact, some churches have as part of their membership class the requirement that each member write out a mission statement for her life. When Paul says: "I want to know Christ" that pretty much tells us what his heart and mind are focused on. This is what life is all about for Paul—knowing Christ. He has completely renounced his past spiritual accomplishments as a Pharisaic Jew, in favor of knowing Christ in a more profound and deeper way.

Every believer, in whatever place God has them in their life, can make this their life's passion. Whether your profession is a doctor, engineer, cook, house wife, etc., every Christian's ultimate objective in life should be to know Christ and grow in their relationship with him. Every believer needs to ask themselves whether this is the over-riding passion of their life, or if this is just a part-time pursuit done when it's convenient. Is Jesus only for the weekends? Is he a hobby, a recreational activity, or someone you call on when you're in a jamb? Where is Jesus on the list of your priorities?
If he is anywhere but on the top of the list, the believer needs to rethink that. If every Christian in America made their primary focus in life knowing Christ, like Paul, I am convinced that revival would break out, and there would be an unparalleled move of God's Spirit across our land. Growing as Jesus'

committed disciple needs to be taken seriously! We can all learn a lesson from Paul on spiritual passion.

Your Spiritual Spreadsheet

Let's do the same thing Paul did below. List the things in your profit column that you took pride in, or thought would cause God to look upon you favorably *before* you were a Christian. For instance, did you think that being a moral person, having a good work ethic, being a good student, a kind person, etc. would place you in good standing with God? List those things in the profit column below. List the things that you knew put you in the loss column with God such as immorality, dishonesty, stealing, etc.

Before Christ

PROFIT	LOSS

Now that you are a Christian, in the chart that follows, move all the things listed above to the loss column while renouncing every one of them in favor of knowing the Lord Jesus. Everything pales in comparison to knowing Christ. This exercise in spiritual accounting will give you a glimpse of your life before you met Jesus and after knowing him. It will also cause you to evaluate your priorities and make sure that Jesus really is in the place he should be in your life.

After Christ

PROFIT	LOSS
To Know Christ	

The New Perspective on Paul

I would be remiss at this point if I didn't comment on the New Perspective on Paul, because Philippians 3:9 is an important passage for those who hold to that view. In a nutshell, this view maintains that Paul has been read incorrectly from the time of the Reformation. Judaism in Paul's day wasn't a legalistic religion where one tried to earn his salvation by following the Torah and being righteous through that means. Jews were thought to already be in the family of God from birth, by way of the Abrahamic covenant, and were obeying the Torah out of gratitude for his special calling as God's people.

According to the New Perspective, Paul was keeping the Torah because of his identity as a Jew—a member of God's covenant people. Jews who didn't live by the law may be considered apostates, who were cut off from the community of Jewish worshipers. Paul is arguing against using the law as a boundary marker that would require Gentiles to convert to Judaism to join the body of Christ. Therefore, salvation / righteousness wasn't achieved by observing the Torah, it is an ethnic-oriented righteousness associated with being a Torah observant Jew. The New Perspective argues that the phrase "works of the law" does not refer to one's effort to earn God's approval and be saved. When the Gentiles converted to the one true God, the law provided guidance on how to live as faithful members of his family. This is what Paul means by "works of the law."

When Paul speaks of a "righteousness of my own that comes from the law" (3:9), he isn't saying he tried to earn his salvation through Torah observance. According to the New Perspective, Paul isn't arguing against obeying the law as a means of being righteous. Zechariah and Elizabeth were considered righteous, because they walked in his ways and followed his commandments (Luke 1:6), and Joseph is described as a righteous man (Matt 1:19). Therefore, when Paul speaks of his own righteousness based on the law as "faultless" (3:6), he's referring to keeping the covenant between God and himself as an Israelite, not about earning his salvation. When Paul says in v. 9 he has a righteousness that comes from God on the basis of faith in Christ, he is saying he is righteous before God because in placing his faith in Christ he is now in a right standing with God and had Christ's righteousness imputed to him.[98] Therefore, the components of the law that divided Jew and Gentile at the national level are now obsolete because of Jesus' work on the cross, so the Law isn't a dividing line between Jews and Gentiles.

The New Perspective on Paul is gaining traction in some circles, but caution must be taken in walking down that path. To think that since the Reformation that Paul has been read incorrectly could be presumptuous. When reading the passage under consideration in context, in my opinion, the New Perspective doesn't seem to fit. Paul has warned the Philippians to avoid the Judaizers because they advocated the position that righteousness was attained by the works of the law, which is self-righteousness.

"A righteousness attained through the law is inadequate because Christ has fulfilled the law (Matt 5:17–20; Rom 10:4), and only that which comes through Christ and the cross can be true righteousness. There can be nothing of self in true righteousness; it is never "my own" but is always and entirely the gift of God through Christ's atoning work on the cross (Gal 2:20; Eph 2:8–

[98] See: Rom 4:1-5; 20-25; 5:17

9). So the true basis of being "found in him" is "through faith in Christ—that righteousness that comes from God on the basis of faith."[99]

The righteousness inherent in the gospel is based on one's relationship with Christ. It is not granted to the sinner because of his expenditure of energy in keeping the commandments, it is entirely based on Christ's work on the cross which is appropriated by faith. Righteousness in Christ is given as a gift, it isn't awarded as a trophy or medal. Righteousness is the new status that comes to the sinner when justified by faith. God has rendered a legal verdict declaring sinners fully acquitted and in right relationship with himself, through Jesus' work on the cross. Christ's righteousness is imputed to the new believer, so God considers Christ's righteousness to be the believer's righteousness. That is the basis of being righteous before God.

Summary

Paul describes his personal experience in becoming a disciple of Christ out of Pharisaic Judaism. In doing so he reveals his deep spiritual passion and zeal to know more about Jesus. Saul's fanatical zeal as a Pharisaic Jew is retained in his walk with Christ as Paul the Christian. He has experienced a complete reversal of the things he was proud of in his life before Christ, because he now sees them as spiritual deficits that placed him in the red spiritually. Using a metaphor from accounting he moves all his accomplishments to the "loss" column and places his relationship with Christ in the "gain" column. Paul is now in the black spiritually and is turning a spiritual profit through his relationship with Christ. The watershed moment for Paul was when he discovered that his own righteousness gave him no advantage before God. He discovered a different righteousness that comes only through faith in Christ. That is an earthshattering discovery for Paul, which caused him to rethink his whole understanding of righteousness, and how one is accepted by God. Righteousness is rooted in one's relationship with Christ.

Now Paul's total passion in life is simply to know Christ! He pursues his relationship with Jesus with all out abandon, holding nothing back, demonstrating the same kind of zeal he had as Saul the Pharisee, but now his

---

[99] Osborne, Loc. 2243

passion is properly guided as Paul the Christian. Knowing Christ involves knowing his resurrection power which enables one to live the Christian life, share in Christ's suffering, and conformity to his death for the advancement of the gospel, and finally to experience bodily resurrection—entering the glorified state. This is what made Paul tick, and was the goal of his life.

In the next section, Paul will lay in the coffin the belief that spiritual perfection is attainable this side of heaven.

CHAPTER SIXTEEN

* * *

"Winning the Prize"
Philippians 3:12-14

Throughout history there have been people that taught some form of spiritual perfection was attainable in this life. Paul certainly wasn't one of them. In fact, he makes it clear in this section of his letter that attaining spiritual perfection this side of heaven isn't possible. Was there a group of people that showed up in Philippi that was introducing this teaching to the church? Is this why Paul is speaking against spiritual perfection? In addressing this issue there are several possibilities to consider.

First, Paul has already issued a warning against the Judaizers, the Jewish false teachers he called dogs, who weren't present in Philippi at the time Paul wrote this letter (3:2-3). Were they advocating a form of spiritual perfection being attainable through keeping the Law? Osborne points out that many Jews believed that a person could observe the Torah faithfully, make atonement for any transgressions, and be completely right with God—as the young ruler tells Jesus in Mark 10:20.[100] Were the dogs including this belief in their teaching that Paul is telling them to beware of, and offering a correction against this theological error? It could be, but there is no way of knowing because the text doesn't say.

---

[100] Osborne, Loc. 2361

A second possibility is that there was a group distinct from the dogs that were spreading this teaching to the Philippians, and Paul is correcting their error. Who exactly they were is difficult to ascertain. It could be a group of proto-gnostics, who were the forerunners to the gnostics, which was a Second Century heresy that taught perfection was attainable through acquiring knowledge.

A third possibility is that when Epaphroditus arrived in Rome and briefed Paul about the situation in Philippi, he informed him that there was an element of perfectionism beginning to take root in the church. Thus, Paul wants to nip-it-in-the-bud and offer a corrective to this error. He doesn't want this teaching to poison the church like it did in Corinth.

"The Hellenistic world was full of ideas pertaining to spiritual perfection, which could easily be mixed with the gospel in Philippi, just as it was at Corinth. Might the disunity at Philippi, like the disunity in Corinth be related to the germination of this error. Might there be people who were claiming to have attained a type of spiritual perfection that was above and beyond others they worshiped with that caused friction in the church. Displaying a snobbish attitude toward those who were regarded as less spiritual can only divide the oneness a congregation should display in worshiping the Lord Jesus. If this is the case it doesn't appear that it was as serious as it was in Corinth, for it seems to have made significant inroads there, and was causing problems."[101]

Paul wants to make sure he addresses this issue before things go south as they did in Corinth. Therefore, when Paul says: **If in anything you think otherwise, God will also reveal that to you** (3:15b), this is his mild corrective to the Philippians to be cautious about this teaching.

Surveying the mountain of commentaries written on Philippians reveals that many people try to find a group of opponents that were there in Philippi teaching a form of spiritual perfection. "The difficulty with doing so, however, is that it requires one to "mirror read" the text with remarkable clairvoyance, since nothing else explicit in the letter comes forward to offer

---

[101] Thielman, p. 197

help; the nature of the "opposition," therefore, lies strictly in the eyes of the beholder, not in the text of Paul."[102]

It's best to avoid finding a group of opponents that were at Philippi teaching spiritual perfection, because it isn't mentioned. It may be that part of the teaching the dogs advocated was a form of spiritual perfectionism through Torah-keeping, but it is only speculation. Since spiritual perfection was a common theme in the pagan religions of the day, it is best to see Paul being cautious and making sure this teaching doesn't take root in Philippi, as it did in Corinth. Epaphroditus may have mentioned to Paul that some were beginning to embrace this belief, so he speaks to the impossibility of attaining spiritual perfection in this life.

Paul is continuing his thoughts from the previous section where he so passionately claimed his desire to know Christ (vv. 10-11). He has not completed his knowledge acquisition of Christ—he still has more to learn about Jesus. He is showing his readers how passionate he is in his walk with Christ, and how he wants to grow as a Christian, which is something that the Philippians should take note of and want to emulate. He uses athletic metaphors to describe the effort he puts forth in his quest to deepen his relationship with Jesus. Growing as a disciple of Christ takes hard work, make no mistake about it, and Paul was one who was willing to do that heavy lifting. Growing as a committed disciple of the Lord is no walk in the park, it isn't a leisurely stroll, it is more like a runner straining with everything he's got as he approaches the finish line, or like a boxer that leaves everything on the canvas with nothing left when the bell rings and the fight is over. This is Paul's reckless abandon he mobilizes in wanting to know Jesus.

The Philippians might look at Paul and hold him in such high esteem that they think he is a super Christian. Who could possibly come even remotely close to Paul's level of commitment, maturity, intellectual prowess, and knowledge of the Scriptures. It may seem to the Philippians that Paul, their spiritual father, is so far beyond where they are spiritually that they think he is almost there, on the verge of having the Christian life mastered. Perhaps, Paul's rhetorical strategy is to show them that they should take him off the pedestal

---

[102] Fee, p. 341

they have him on and understand that he is no different than they are. Thirty years after becoming a disciple of Christ, he is still growing and learning about the Lord and making strides in his personal sanctification.

It isn't uncommon for people to hold their leaders in such high regard that they place them on a pedestal and forget that they are human—a fallen human with a sinful nature. Thus, Paul wants to teach them about growing in the Christian life, as he talks about accomplishing the "goal" and "winning the prize." Paul is presenting himself to the Philippians as an example of one who doesn't quit but keeps pressing on to seize the moment and gain more of Christ.

Not that I have already obtained this, or am already made perfect; but I press on, so that I may take hold of that for which also I was taken hold of by Christ Jesus. 13Brothers (and sisters), I don't regard myself as yet having taken hold of it, but one thing I do: Forgetting the things which are behind me, and stretching forward to the things which are ahead of me, 14I press on toward the goal for the prize of the heavenly calling of God in Christ Jesus. (Author's Translation, 3:12-14)

Paul has a no nonsense approach to growing as a disciple of Christ, which he describes in his personal walk with Christ. When he says: **Not that I have already obtained "this", or am already made perfect, "this"** refers back to what he said in vv. 10-11. He doesn't have complete knowledge of Christ. He's still growing in his walk with the Lord and learning more about him. Nor has he been made perfect, he's still going through the process of sanctification (2:12-13). Paul has been a Christian for about 30 years, and he recognizes he is a long way from being **perfect**, which translates the Greek word *teleióō*, written in the passive voice, which means that Paul hasn't *been made* perfect. Only God could make Paul perfect, whereas the verb **obtained**, is in the active voice and describes Paul's *personal effort* in knowing Christ. Therefore, Paul is on the receiving end of God transforming him to perfection, which hasn't happened yet, but Paul is actively striving to obtain more knowledge about Christ.

When will Paul have his cherished and highly sought after complete knowledge of Christ and been made perfect? It will occur at the resurrection

(Phil 3:20-21), or as Fee says: "the 'goal' is not 'perfection' but the eschatological conclusion of present life, while the 'prize' is none other than the final realization of his lifelong passion—the full 'knowing' of Christ."[103]

The eschatological conclusion of the present life is resurrection, which will occur at the second coming of Christ. Paul isn't taking a "lay back and take it easy" approach as he waits for the Lord to return. Rather he says: **but I press on, so that I may take hold of that for which also I was taken hold of by Christ Jesus.** There is no laziness in Paul's spiritual performance whatsoever. He is actively pursuing and aggressively seeking to know more about Jesus. **I press on**, translates the Greek *diókó*, written in the present tense, which is a word used to describe the following: a hunter chasing his prey, pursuing an enemy, or running a race. Paul is using an athletic metaphor where he views himself as a runner who keeps on running without ever stopping. Paul keeps on pressing on, running as if he is in a life-long marathon **so that I may take hold of that for which also I was taken hold of by Christ Jesus.** When Paul was on the road to Damascus the risen Lord Jesus appeared to him and Paul **was taken hold of by Christ Jesus**, which translates the Greek *katalambánō*, which describes an aggressive taking, seizing tight hold of, or grasping something in a forceful manner. Make no mistake about it: Jesus got hold of Paul when he appeared to him—he had his undivided attention.

His was a dramatic conversion, for how many people get to see the risen Christ and have a conversation with him when they become his disciple (Acts 9:3-8)? Paul describes his meeting Jesus on the road to Damascus as: **I was taken hold of by Christ Jesus.** If anything, that is a gross understatement. But the first part of the sentence says: ***so that I may take hold*** **of that for which also I was taken hold of by Christ Jesus.** Since Christ took hold of Paul, he responds in like fashion and takes hold of Christ, but for what purpose did Christ take hold of Paul? For what purpose did Paul take hold of Christ?

Christ took hold of Paul first and foremost to make Paul one of his own. Jesus saved Paul on the road to Damascus—he took hold of him—to accomplish the objective of taking Paul down the path of being conformed to his image (Rom 8:29). When God chooses a sinner for salvation he does so to make him

---

[103] Fee, p. 341

like Jesus, which for the believer is a journey he travels throughout his life and culminates at resurrection (3:20-21). This is what Jesus took hold of Paul for, as well as every believer. In response to Christ taking hold of him, Paul aggressively takes hold of Christ and pursues the objective of deepening his relationship with him. Paul takes hold of Christ with intense rigor, in response to Christ taking hold of Paul.

Should anybody in Philippi think that Paul is crossing the threshold of complete knowledge of Christ and attaining a level of spiritual perfection, they shouldn't draw that conclusion because Paul says: **Brothers (and sisters), I don't regard myself as yet having taken hold of it.** By calling them brothers and sisters he is gently admonishing them to take heart to what he's got to say. He's not talking down to them, but he is standing beside them as their brother in the family of God. He wants them to know that he isn't perfect, even though he's known Christ for three decades, he's still growing, learning, maturing in the Christian faith and deepening his relationship with Christ. If anybody is entertaining the idea that spiritual perfection is attainable in this life, they should consider that if Paul viewed himself as an imperfect man still moving forward in his life as a disciple, then they should adopt the same viewpoint. They should actively take hold of Christ in the same way Paul has. He describes how he is giving it his maximum effort by running after Christ with everything he's got. The rhetorical aspect of the next verses are designed to motivate his Philippian brothers and sisters to increase their passion and desire to pursue Christ as he is.

But one thing I do: Forgetting the things which are behind me, and stretching forward to the things which are ahead of me, 14I press on toward the goal for the prize of the heavenly calling of God in Christ Jesus.

What are the things that Paul wants to forget that are behind him? He left behind his accomplishments as a Pharisaic Jew, and as a Christian he doesn't live in the past thinking about all his spiritual successes such as: having planted many churches, leading many people to Christ, raising up leaders, writing Scripture, and so on. Additionally, he doesn't dwell on missed opportunities, mistakes he may have made, sins committed, and failed plans. In other words, his orientation in life is always forward moving to capture more of Christ and become a more sanctified individual. Living in the past is counterproductive to maturing as a believer in Christ. The focus for Christians should be the present and future. That **forgetting** is written as a present participle indicates that Paul keeps on forgetting the past—he is continuously doing this. He doesn't allow himself to be trapped by anger, regret, dwelling on unfortunate circumstances, or in any way get stuck living in the negative past. This also includes not dwelling on his past successes and slipping into a "celebration mode" at the expense of future objectives. Like an experienced runner, Paul keeps his focus on the finish line—always moving forward to gain more of Christ.

Paul continues the athletic metaphor as he speaks to the forward aspect of his life: **and stretching forward to the things which are ahead of me**, as if Paul is running a race, increasing his speed as he approaches the finish line, he's giving it everything he's got in his pursuit of Christ. **Stretching forward** translates the Greek participle *epekteinómenos*, from the verb *teinó* (to stretch). The word is used in a variety of contexts such as: a predatory animal pursuing its prey, an army pursuing its foe, and a runner exerting maximum effort. Paul imagines that he is running a race stretching and straining every muscle, holding nothing back in his pursuit of the finish line where he will have complete knowledge of Christ. This is what is ahead of Paul, so he keeps on running with reckless abandon. There is no quit in Paul. This is no laughing matter for him, nothing can divert his attention away from running to the finish line.

I press on toward the goal for the prize of the high calling of God in Christ Jesus. With his focus on the future Paul presses on (*diókó*: same word used in v. 12), and keeps running the race, casting aside all distractions, and is coming closer to the goal of gaining more of Christ.

The **goal** is the *skopós*, which was the marker at the finish line. This is what the runner sets his entire focus on, straining with all his might to reach. Paul is portraying himself as the runner approaching the finish line holding nothing back. At the end of the race the awards are given out, which Paul refers to as the **prize**. Anybody who watches the Olympics on TV has certainly viewed the award ceremony, where the winners stand on the platform and are awarded their metals as the national anthems are played. In the ancient world, they also had an award ceremony where the victor would stand on a platform and be awarded. What is the prize Paul is referring to? It is the final realization of completely knowing Christ—being conformed to his image at resurrection.

Moises Silva describes the **prize** in various ways: "conformity to Christ (Rom 8:29-30), fellowship with Christ (1 Cor 1:9), the peace of Christ (Col 3:15), sanctification (1 Thess 4:7), salvation through sanctification (2 Thess 2:13-14), and eternal life (1 Tim 6:12). The "prize" is clearly the culmination of the whole work of salvation—with all its implications—to which God has called us. That is the great hope that sustained Paul, even in the midst of discouragement and frustration."[104]

The prize is further explained as **the heavenly calling of God in Christ Jesus.** The heavenly calling is the source of the calling and where it ultimately leads. "We are called to join and run the race, with the goal of knowing Christ more intimately every day. And we are called 'upward' to a deeper and deeper experience of Christ, and the race will end with the final 'heavenward' prize when we stand with Christ for all eternity. This is the best option; the prize is comprehensive, and the crown of life (Jas 1:12; Rev 2:10) and everlasting joy is Christ in all his fullness."[105]

At the moment of the sinner's conversion she is called to enter the race and begins running forward to the goal of knowing more about Christ. This call is from God, who calls the sinner to himself, and is based on the historical work of Christ in his life, death, resurrection, and ascension, which places the new believer in the spiritual locus of being **in Christ**. That God issues the call implies that the call is given in grace, and his power is provided to Paul as he runs the race to gain more of Christ. The "prize" is truly comprehensive, meaning that all God's work of salvation is completed in his people when they cross the finish line. They stand before God glorified and perfect in every way. Considering this great truth fills believers with hope and provides incentive to keep running the race (Rom 8:23-25).

---

[104] Silva, p. 177

[105] Osborne, Loc. 2442

Tension exists between the heavenly sovereign call of God on the sinner, and his free will response to the call. Paul was always conscience of God's grace being operative in his life, not only in being called, but his dependence on God's grace throughout his life was very evident (Gal 1:6; 15). In Paul's thinking, everything given to him by God is given in grace, for there is no merit theology in Paul's understanding of salvation (Eph 2:8-9). Every blessing God gives is through Christ, and is all God's grace extended to the sinner (Eph 1:3-6). However, Paul is expressing his personal choice to aggressively pursue gaining more knowledge of Christ, with the grace God provides. Paul's free will response is working hand-in-hand with the powerful grace of God operative in his life.

Insights, Applications, and Life Lessons

In the beginning of 2017 I was in Cuba teaching some pastors about sanctification. We were discussing how important it is for believers to develop the right habits in their life that will facilitate their spiritual growth such as: Scripture reading, prayer, serving, and so forth. One of the pastors, who spoke pretty good English, came up to me during the break and told me he was concerned about some of the people in his church because they seemed disinterested in the Christian life. He shared that they don't read their Bible, they don't attend the mid-week activities, so he wanted me to give him suggestions about how he could get them motivated. He was deeply concerned that they weren't showing any signs of being "on fire" for Jesus.

His concern is shared by every pastor in existence including myself. How does a pastor motivate people to get going in their Christian life? What will inspire people to take God seriously? Not only is this concern held by pastors, it is a deep concern for Christian parents who don't see their children making much headway in their spiritual development. It is a deep concern someone may have for their spouse who appears to be going to church just to keep everybody happy, but really doesn't want to be there. This concern could also be for a friend who seems to be stagnant in their spiritual development and is drifting away from their church. If I could come up with a definitive answer to this dilemma and write a book on it, I think it would be a best seller in the evangelical world.

I told this Cuban pastor to keep preaching the word, praying for them, be lovingly patient with them, and hope that the Holy Spirit gets hold of them, such that they respond to God's call on their life. Studying this passage in Philippians reinforces that growing as a believer in Christ is no easy task! It takes a lot of hard work, just like any other worthwhile pursuit in life. This passage, perhaps more than any other, reveals how Paul approached his personal walk with Christ, and is one that every Christian should study and pray about. We all need to light a holy fire in our hearts at times, because the flame doesn't always burn very bright, and this passage could be one that makes the holy fire burn a little hotter and brighter for the Lord Jesus.

Be Forgetful

Paul said he is *forgetting* what was behind so that he can move forward (v. 13). When running a race, you keep your eyes forward and don't look back at the other runners. You keep your focus on the finish line. The application of this is that you can't live in the past thinking about the "good old days" such that it retards your performance in the present. It's not uncommon for me to meet people that appear to have given up on church and are totally disconnected from any fellowship. Perhaps, they had a great experience in their previous church, then a job change brought them to a new city and they haven't found a church to their liking. They have given up on their search and are dwelling in the past thinking about how good it was at First Church in Sheboygan, WI. They loved the pastor and found his sermons to be inspiring and enlightening, they were involved in the leadership of the church, and had many friends. They are living in the glory days of the past, at the expense of their present experience with Christ. In this case, they aren't running, at best they're going for a slow walk, a leisurely stroll in their spiritual experience.

Paul would have none of that, for he wouldn't live in the past thinking about all his spiritual successes, such that he took a seat in his reclining chair and reminisced about the good old days when he met Barnabas and ministered with him in Antioch. Then think about when Barnabas introduced him to the elders and apostles in Jerusalem, and when he went on his first missionary journey, and on-and-on-and-on. Paul didn't get stuck in the present because he was too busy celebrating his past accomplishments. He realized that if he was going to accomplish the goal of getting to know Christ in a more profound way he had to keep moving forward, which required him to not be stuck in the past.

The same can be said about the negative experiences Paul had. He suffered abuse, was beaten countless times, thrown in prison, stoned on one occasion and was badly mistreated throughout his career as the apostle to the Gentiles. Paul didn't live in the past thinking about those bad things either. He didn't become bitter, filled with regret, become resentful toward God, such that he was a prisoner to his past. He maintained a positive attitude, kept his eyes to the front and kept on running forward.

This principle doesn't just apply to one's walk as a Christian, it involves any worthwhile pursuit in life. It isn't possible to move forward in a new career until a break is made with the old one. It isn't possible to move forward in a new relationship until the old one is ended, and so on. The bottom line for everybody is this: don't get stuck in the present because of living in the past ruminating about the good old days or dwelling on the bad times. Live in the now!

Summary

Paul's ambition in life is knowing Christ. He utilizes a sports metaphor of a runner giving it everything he's got as he strains toward the finish line, to describe his aggressive pursuit of knowing Christ. He makes it clear that he hasn't reached perfection but keeps moving forward to know more about him. Jesus took hold of Paul on the road to Damascus when he became his disciple to mold Paul into his image and bring him into the perfected state at resurrection. Paul took hold of Christ to know more about him and continue growing as a believer.

In moving forward, he must forget the things that lie behind him, such as his past successes and failures, and keep his focus on the finish line. He anticipates crossing the finish line winning the prize for which God called him heavenward in Christ. The prize is the culmination of God's entire plan of salvation for the redemption of humanity. At that time believers will be in glorified bodies where sin is a thing of the past. At that time, Paul's knowledge of Christ will be complete. That is Paul's hope for the future and it should be the hope of every believer throughout the ages. He hopes the Philippians will be motivated to follow his example of spiritual passion.

In the next section, Paul encourages the Philippians to press on in their walk with Christ, which will culminate in resurrection at the return of Jesus.

CHAPTER SEVENTEEN

* * *

"The Mature Christian Mindset"
Philippians 3:15-19

Paul has finished describing his personal quest to grow deeper in the Christian life and learn more about Jesus. Like a runner, he keeps moving forward to the finish line to gain more of Christ, realizing that he will not reach perfection in this life. After speaking about his own walk with the Lord, he now shifts his focus to the Philippians, and offers an application of what he's just said for their situation. Additionally, Paul offers himself as an example for them to follow and provides false teachers as an example not to follow. They are not to drink of their teaching because it is a witch's brew that will leave them spiritually poisoned.

Therefore, as many as are perfect, think this way. If in anything you think otherwise, God will also reveal that to you. 16Nevertheless, to what we have already attained, let us walk by the same rule. 17Brothers (and sisters), be imitators together of me, and note those who walk this way, even as you have us for an example. 18For many walk, of whom I told you often, and now tell you even weeping, as the enemies of the cross of Christ, 19whose end is destruction, whose god is the belly, and whose glory is in their shame, who think about earthly things. (Author's Translation, 3:15-19)

Therefore, connects this to what preceded and marks Paul's conclusion to the matter. **As many as are perfect, think this way. Perfect** translates the

Greek *téleioi*, which typically is translated perfect, complete or mature. It is a form of the same word Paul used in v. 12 (*teteleiōmai*) to describe himself as not having been perfected, so he is using a play on words to make his point. Therefore, Paul is saying something like this: "Those of us who are *perfect* (mature) will realize that we are not *perfect* and adopt the viewpoint that I've been advocating." By saying **as many as are perfect, think this way**, implies there are those who don't think this way, and they should adopt the view Paul has presented.

The important verb that ties this section to 2:5 is *phronéō*, which we have seen several times and means "mindset," or "think this way." In 2:5 Paul encouraged them to have this *mindset* which was in Christ, now he's calling for the Philippians to have the same mindset that he does on this issue in 3:15. That the same word is used isn't coincidental, it ties the sections together.

Paul could have commanded them in the name of Jesus to stop thinking this way, but he didn't. He is gently encouraging them to think it over: **If in anything you think otherwise, God will also reveal that to you.** Paul displays great sensitivity here because he doesn't drop the hammer on them like he did on the Galatians (Gal 1:6-9). However, the false teaching seems to have permeated the Galatian churches, but in Philippi it doesn't seem to have made any significant inroads. He is telling them to think about what he's said, and if they aren't sure about it God will show them the truth. Pray about it, seek the Lord's wisdom on the matter and he will lead you to the correct understanding. He's giving them the courtesy of allowing them to think it over and process it. That's always a good approach to offering correction, for people need time to adjust their thinking. When Paul says **think otherwise**, he's using *phronéō* again, God will give you the right mindset.

He doesn't say how God will reveal the right mindset on this issue, nor does he say what he means by **if in anything you think otherwise**. There may have been some minor points that they weren't clear on, or had petty disagreements over, so God would reveal the truth to them probably by means of group discussion, prayer, studying Scripture, and, of course, the guidance of the Holy Spirit will be center stage in the search for clarity and truth. The church has debated points of doctrine forever, and the role of the

Holy Spirit navigating the church through the troubled waters of doctrinal error to bring them to the safe harbor of truth can't be minimized. In fact, Paul has been discussing learning more about Jesus, which indicates that one of the characteristics of a mature believer is the willingness to open oneself up to reflection on the doctrines of Scripture, being willing to change where a clearer understanding has been acquired. This should be a normal part of the Christian experience.

Nevertheless, to what we have already attained, let us walk by the same rule. (3:16)

Paul has been challenging the Philippians to consider his teaching on perfectionism and do some deep reflecting on it, which means some may have to adjust their thinking. The Christian life isn't just about right thinking, it's about right living, so whatever is learned must put into practice in one's daily experience. Whatever knowledge the Philippians **have already attained** they must live according to that standard. Paul includes himself in this because he says, "to what **we** have already attained let **us** walk by the same rule." **Walk** is a euphemism for live, and translates the Greek word *stoichéō*, which has military connotations including: marching in step, keeping the cadence, and walking in line. Like soldiers marching in step, the Philippians must march in cadence to the teaching they have acquired. They can't break the cadence and deviate in any way into the errors false teachers may present to them.

Believers must live according to the light they have, because if they don't how can they expect God to give them more? Where obedience exists along with submission to God's word the door is open for further growth in godliness. Whatever level of knowledge a believer has attained she is responsible to walk according to that rule. In other words, that is the standard by which she must keep living. There is nothing passive about being a disciple of Christ because learning more about Christ is continuous, with the challenge to constantly apply knowledge to one's life. There is no laid-back approach in being a disciple of Christ where one takes a seat in the recliner with the remote in hand, then coasts all the way to heaven where Jesus is met face-to-face. That type of thinking doesn't exist in Paul's mind, for the believer keeps running to the finish line.

Brothers (and sisters), be imitators together of me, and note those who walk this way, even as you have us for an example. (3:17)

Brothers (and sisters), be imitators together of me makes it another family matter in that he calls them his spiritual siblings—brothers and sisters in Christ—emphasizing the familial nature of the body of Christ. As their spiritual father who led them to Christ, Paul exhorts them to imitate his walk with the Lord. Learning by imitation was a common teaching methodology in the Greco-Roman world, and among the Jews. It was thought that knowledge could be better transmitted orally from the teacher to the student, and by careful examination of the teacher's life the student had the best opportunity for personal growth. This, of course, requires a close relationship between the mentor and the student, which is what Jesus did with the twelve. He lived in close proximity with them, such that they didn't just hear his electrifying teaching, they also learned by watching the way he lived. They had the best seats in the house to witness Jesus live the exemplary life that should be the standard for all Christians to measure themselves.

To effect positive change in the Philippians they need someone to imitate, and who better than Paul. He must have had a great deal of confidence in himself to make this statement, but it isn't to be taken as if Paul is an egomaniac. It might sound that way from our Western perspective, but in the ancient world imitation was a common teaching methodology, nonetheless he did have a humble, holy confidence in his walk with Christ.

The problem is that Paul was under house arrest in Rome, so he couldn't be there with them. Upon his release he can go back to Philippi and continue presenting himself as a model to them. He commands them to **note those** who follow his example, and you have **us** (including himself) for an example. Most likely he is paving the way for Timothy and Epaphroditus to come visit them. They are people whose life should be noted for they provide the type of example that Paul is speaking about. In other words, it behooves every believer to take note and carefully observe the mature believers he worships with. To the degree that they follow Christ, they can be imitated. The word **example** is a translation of the Greek *typos*, which means: a pattern, model, a stamp struck by a die, or a copy. Paul is saying observe the mature believers in your church and use their life as a blueprint for your own.

It can't be stressed enough that the church was like a fragile infant at that time. It was the first generation, with few leaders, preachers, and no New Testament. They were living in a hostile environment as a minority in a pagan culture that at times persecuted them. There was no precedent or history to fall back on for the church was new, living in the New Covenant era was brand new, so what better way could there be to teach them besides having a person serve as a model. When Paul says **brothers (and sisters), be imitators together of me** his sense of urgency comes out in challenging the Philippians to grow, for there was much at stake. Following the athletic metaphor Paul has used of the race, the Christian marathon involves passing a baton from one runner to the next, and the baton can't be dropped otherwise disqualification results. In the Christian race the baton must be passed from one generation to the next to ensure that the church survives. If the baton is dropped the church won't survive, for there will be no one to run in the next generation (2 Tim 2:2).

One of the ways the church can be poisoned for future generations is by following the examples of those who don't live like Paul, Timothy, or Epaphroditus, and don't live even remotely close to following the example of Christ. These people present the wrong kind of example that the Philippians are to avoid like the plague. Therefore, Paul is making a contrast between himself (and his colleagues) as an example to follow, and in vv. 18-19 he provides the wrong example, which should be avoided at all costs.

For many walk, of whom I told you often, and now tell you even weeping, as the enemies of the cross of Christ, [19]whose end is destruction, whose god is the belly, and whose glory is in their shame, who think about earthly things. (3:18-19)

When Paul was at Philippi he issued warnings to beware of false teachers (3:1-2). Who is Paul referring to when he says: **For many walk, of whom I told you often?** Most likely the Judaizers (dogs) would be included in this, because he already told them to avoid them at all costs. It was of great importance to warn the fragile believers at Philippi more than once about the dangers of false teachers. One would think that Paul would view these false teachers as bad people and would harbor hostile feelings toward them, but he doesn't seem to be that way at all. He says: **and now tell you even**

weeping, which translates *klaíō,* meaning: to weep aloud, expressing uncontainable audible grief, lamenting, or mourning. This isn't a word used to describe someone who is just shedding a tear, this is crying out in grief, weeping in agony, and crying out loud. It is written as a present participle, which means that Paul continuously experienced a deep sense of grief and wept over the plight of these misguided individuals. This is the only place in the New Testament where Paul describes himself as crying in the present tense, so he was a person who wore his emotions for all to see.

The reason for Paul's deep emotion is that these people present themselves **as the enemies of the cross of Christ.** This is the worst possible way people can position themselves with Jesus. His death on the cross is the only means by which someone can be saved from their sins, so if one positions himself as an enemy of the cross, spiritually speaking he has slit his own throat. The word **enemy** is a translation of *echthrós,* which has a range of meaning including: someone openly hostile or animated by deep-seated hatred. It implies irreconcilable hostility proceeding out of a personal hatred bent on inflicting harm. As can be seen this is a powerful word not to be taken lightly. Paul is referring to those who don't passively reject Jesus as the Messiah in unbelief, he is describing those who are hostile and driven by a sense of hatred toward Jesus and the gospel—the heart of which is the cross. How strange this is because Paul was once an enemy of the cross, who hated Jesus and his people, so he has firsthand experience in this.

These people caused Paul much grief because he was a man whose mission in life was to lead people to Christ, so they could be forgiven of their sins and enjoy a relationship with Jesus. He was very passionate about spreading the gospel and fully understood the consequences of rejecting Jesus—and the cross. As he contemplated the destiny of those who reject Christ, it brought Paul much personal grief. Furthermore, the problems these enemies of the cross caused the churches Paul planted was sever and caused him much misery. A great deal of Paul's ministry was tied up in doing battle against false teachers who tried to undo his teaching and lead his congregations astray.

But who are these enemies of the cross? Are they a specific group distinct from the dogs? Examining the context of the passage reveals that the only group Paul has mentioned is the dogs (3:1-2), and their teaching certainly made them enemies of the cross, for they were teaching a different gospel than his. That they were Jews, Paul's fellow countrymen, brought him much grief as he contemplated their error, which was once his own (Acts 9:4-5; Rom 9:1-3). The dogs were teaching a false gospel because their teaching advocated keeping the Torah as the means for salvation which included: circumcision, the Sabbath, the dietary laws, and so forth. This belief negates Christ's substitutionary sacrifice as being effective for salvation all by itself. They wanted to add something to the cross to make it complete—keeping the Torah. However, there could be a harmful Gentile influence Paul was concerned about making inroads in Philippi, which will unfold in the next verse. Paul gives us a further description of the enemies of the cross.

whose end is destruction, whose god is the belly, and whose glory is in their shame, who think about earthly things. (3:19)

The first description relates to their eternal destiny: **whose end is destruction.** Unlike those who believe in Jesus and embrace the cross as the only means of salvation, these enemies of the cross face **destruction**, which is a translation of *apoleia*. The range of meaning includes: being cut off, severed, perdition, or destruction. It is used in several places to describe eternal separation from God for those who reject Christ.[106] To reject the cross was to lose one's soul and forfeit eternal life.[107] This points to one reason why Paul wept over the plight of these false teachers, who rejected the efficacy of the cross. One must see the contrast Paul is establishing between himself and the enemies of the cross. They are running down the path of rejecting the cross ending in destruction when they cross the finish line, while Paul is running down the road seeking to know more about Christ and will end up in perfection when he crosses the finish line. The end of the race will be resurrection for Paul and the Philippians, but for the enemies of the cross their path leads to destruction.

The second description Paul offers regarding the enemies of the cross is **whose god is the belly.** Paul could be using a twist of irony here in that he is referring to the dietary laws that the Jews followed scrupulously. In their

---

[106] See: Mat 7:13; 2 Pet 3:7; Rev 17:8; 11

[107] See: Mat 10:38-39; Mark 8:34-37; Luke 9:23-25

traditions they had elevated their practices regarding food to a point that even superseded the law of God (Mark 7:1-16). In this sense, Paul is using irony to describe their fanatical obsession to their dietary regulations. Paul used a twist of irony in 3:2 referring to the Jewish false teachers as dogs (unclean animals), evildoers (by Torah-observance for salvation), and mutilators (regarding circumcision), and he is speaking with the same sense of irony here as well.

Additionally, **whose glory is in their shame.** Their glory is in circumcision, which they were very proud of because it reflected their adherence to the Abrahamic Covenant and was a sign of being incorporated into the community of God's people, but in Paul's twist of irony, he says it is to their shame. They were proud of circumcision and regarded the practice as necessary—feeling nothing shameful about it at all. But with Paul's sense of irony that which they boasted in, was actually to their shame because it gave them no advantage with God whatsoever.

Most scholars understand this description pointing to the dogs, the Jewish false teachers Paul has already mentioned. However, Osborne sees it differently. He considers the description of the enemies of the cross to be Gentiles, thus making them a group distinct from the Judaizers. "The data indicates a group of Gentile converts who were proto-gnostics following a libertine, sensual lifestyle (similar to the false teachers in 1 John). So I find it probable that verses 2–3 refer to Judaizers and verses 18–19 to Gentile libertines."[108] Gnosticism was a heresy that became full-grown in the Second Century, which advocated that salvation was possible through the acquisition of knowledge. They held the belief in a strict dichotomy between the material world and the spiritual world; the first being evil, the second being good. Thus, they advocated that living a sensual, hedonistic lifestyle was acceptable and wouldn't defile one spiritually. They cast aside the moral requirements set forth in the gospel and claimed it didn't matter how people lived.

These enemies of the cross "live" or "walk" (*peripateō*), a word used to describe how Christians conduct themselves. Since Paul has warned the Philippians previously and is presently weeping over their plight suggests that

[108] Osborne, Loc. 188

these are people within the Christian community, but they have fallen away. "The most likely scenario is that they were itinerant 'Christian' false teachers who had begun to make inroads into the church at Philippi (similar to the Judaizers). However, Paul does not discuss what they were teaching; his emphasis is on their lifestyle, with all four descriptions in verse 19 relating to behavior rather than doctrine."[109]

The language here seems to favor an earth-centered, libertine movement like that described in 1 John or Jude. These were people who considered themselves Christians who preferred a pagan way of life, and Paul's weeping stemmed from his deep concern both for these people and for those they were influencing in Philippi. Perhaps, Paul knew some of the people in the Philippian church that were duped into believing this teaching and fell away, which is why Paul wept as he considered their condition.

Perhaps, these were Romans who continued with their licentious way of life and syncretized it with Christianity. Their teaching may have included the belief that one could continue to live as a lude and lascivious Roman, while being a Christian at the same time. That their god was their belly indicates that they were libertines, a group who lived to gratify their passions, "belly" being a euphemism for a hedonistic lifestyle. Their glory is their shame refers to their boasting of their self-indulgent lifestyle of hedonism, when in reality it is to their shame. These were people who claimed they were right with God, but by the testimony of their lives they were anything but right with God, because their lifestyles were shameful. These people preached the cross, but their teaching didn't promote a right lifestyle, thus making them enemies of the cross. These people brought Paul to a place of grave concern for them and the Philippians.

To see a group of people teaching this doctrine and making significant inroads into the Philippian church seems to be stretching it. There is no evidence in the passage under consideration that suggests there was a specific group of people in Philippi that were making inroads into the church and leading some of the members astray.

---

[109] Osborne, Loc. 2519

"Paul is probably describing some itinerants, whose view of the faith is such that it allows them a great deal of undisciplined self-indulgence. Whether they have taken Paul's view of 'justification by faith' to a libertine conclusion, as many think, is plausible, but probably too specific in terms of what Paul actually says in the text. In any case, they have not appeared heretofore in the letter, and do not appear again. They have served their immediate purpose of standing in sharp relief to Paul's own "walk" and to his heavenly pursuit, so crucial to this letter, and toward which Paul now turns once more as he begins to draw this appeal to an end."[110] That these people were itinerant preachers who showed up periodically makes much more sense than seeing a specific group of people infecting the Philippian church. Most likely Epaphroditus informed Paul in his status report that there were itinerant preachers showing every-so-often advocating a libertine lifestyle.

These people see themselves as being within the Christian community, but Paul doesn't regard them as insiders. Their lifestyle stands as a contradiction to the teaching of Jesus, being totally inconsistent with one who is redeemed by the cross. Right belief must translate into right living, which is not happening with these people, so they are regarded as enemies of the cross by Paul.

It is certainly difficult to put a face on those Paul is describing in vv. 18-19. It could be a further description of the Judaizing dogs, and it could be a reference to Gentile hedonists. At this point one could flip a coin because both views can be defended. Regardless of who Paul is speaking against, the fourth description that he offers of the false teachers is: **who think about earthly things.** Their thought-process is completely different than Paul's, for he is constantly focusing his attention on knowing Christ, fixating on the heavenly call of Christ, running the race to cross the finish line and realize resurrection at the end of the age. In other words, Paul's thinking is heavenly focused, as opposed to the enemies of the cross whose mindset is fixated on earthly things.

Whether they are Jewish false teachers or licentious Gentiles claiming to be Christians, their mindset is earthly and worldly focused. If Paul is referring to

---

[110] Fee, p. 375

Jewish false teachers, their confidence in the flesh regarding Torah keeping, particularly circumcision, is an earthly nonspiritual way of thinking. If the Gentiles are in view here, their lude hedonistic behavior is self-centered and is earthly-based. James reminds his readers that friendship with the world is hatred toward God (Jam 4:4).

If Paul is focusing his attention on the Jewish false teachers they were the ones who were adding to the gospel, if he has in mind Gentile false teachers they were the ones who were subtracting from the gospel. In the first case, Torah-observance needs to be added to the cross as the only means of salvation. In the second case, the moral demands set forth in Scripture go out the window in favor of licentious living. Both addition and subtraction are errors, because the gospel is perfect in itself. Is Paul describing Jewish false teachers (the Judaizers), or Gentile false teachers (the hedonists)? It's hard to know, but I believe the scales tip in favor of these being Gentiles: proto-gnostics advocating a morally depraved lifestyle as perfectly acceptable. Whoever they are, the Philippians need to avoid them and not drink of their teaching for it is spiritual moonshine and will leave them with an eternal hangover.

Caution must be taken in concluding that Judaizers were already in Philippi casting their influence on the Philippians, because it doesn't appear that they are there at the time Paul wrote this. Caution must also be taken in seeing a group of Gentile libertine preachers that were there in Philippi making inroads into the church as well, because the text doesn't say that. As mentioned earlier, upon Epaphroditus' arrival he informed Paul of what was happening in Philippi, but we just don't know with certainty what he told him about false teachers.

Insights, Applications, and Life Lessons

I asked my wife how she would feel if we were attending a church where the pastor said in one of his sermons, "Be imitators of me." "I'll show you what the Christian life should look like." Carol said, "I would find a new church." I asked her how she would feel if she met a Christian who had known the Lord for a long period of time and said to Carol, "Imitate me in the Christian life." Carol said she would run in the opposite direction from that person.

When someone says, "Imitate me" it may be interpreted as prideful and arrogant. From our Western perspective I can understand how people would say, "Who do you think you are!" People may also feel that Paul is being overbearing in the use of his authority. He's feeding his ego, being pushy and domineering, which is not a good example for people to follow.

Paul qualifies what he means by telling the Corinthians: Be imitators of me, even as I also am of Christ (1 Cor 11:1). In other words, to the degree that Paul imitates Christ, people can imitate Paul. He isn't calling for a carte blanc imitation, he qualifies it. Paul is seeking the good of those who have come to know Christ, by offering himself as an example for them to follow. It isn't that Paul has delusions of grandeur and is an egomaniac, rather people need examples to follow in the Christian life, especially since 85% of the people were illiterate in that day. Since many people couldn't read they needed to imitate those who presented a good example to follow.

There is a pattern of imitation that can be seen in Paul's life. Paul imitates Christ (1 Cor 11:1), Paul's churches imitates him (1 Thess 1:5-6), and churches imitate other communities of believers (1 Thess 1:7-8; 2:14; 2 Cor 8:1-6). What might be surprising in the above examples is that in the ancient world imitation wasn't just personal, where one person imitated another, it was in the public sphere as well. Communities imitated communities.

In the modern-day church in America, having a correct understanding of doctrine is sometimes viewed as an end in itself. In other words, if you know the core doctrines of the faith you've arrived and have all the bases covered in your spiritual journey. But where is the emphasis on right living? Paul never separated right doctrine from a corresponding lifestyle that reflected those teachings. Knowledge and lifestyle were always connected in Paul's instruction to his churches. However, in our modern situation the primary emphasis is often placed on right understanding, such that in some circles there is a disconnect from living out the truths of Scripture in one's daily experience. What better way to learn how to apply the truths of Scripture to daily living, than to watch someone who has experience, has known the Lord for a long time, and does well at imitating Christ.

In the ancient world it was considered good pedagogy to teach by way of example for both Jews and Gentiles. The Stoic philosopher Seneca[111] said: "Let us choose men who teach us by their lives, men who teach us what we ought to do and then prove it by their practice, who show us what we should avoid, and then are never caught doing that which they have ordered us to avoid. Choose as a guide one whom you admire more when you see him act than when you hear him speak."[112]

This is good mentoring and typical of rhetoricians in the ancient world. The idea of being a disciple or an apprentice was a normal part of life in the First Century. Father's served as a model for their sons in teaching them their craft. When Jews studied under a rabbi or scribe, they didn't just listen to his teaching, they examined his life. That was part of the teaching methodology, which was understood by the teacher and student. This is how Jesus taught his disciples: he lived with them, traveled with them, they saw him in a variety of different settings, so they had a clear picture of how he lived his life. One can attend a college for years and study under many different professors, but not have a clue about how they live their lives, or their level of integrity.

In sports having a trainer, coach, mentor, instructor, etc. is a necessity. Can you think of a high-level athlete that doesn't have a conditioning coach, or a team that doesn't have a staff of coaches: head coach, assistants, strength coaches, nutritionists, etc.? A good coach doesn't just teach the fundamentals of the game, he takes an interest in the players and helps them develop life skills. In the Christian arena, what would be wrong with someone imitating a person who has been a Christian for a long time, and lives a dedicated life that is sincere, genuine, and authentic. Much could be learned by developing a meaningful relationship with a person like that, which could only benefit one spiritually. In today's modern church this part of discipleship has been greatly minimized.

---

[111] Seneca was a Stoic Philosopher of Rome (4 BC – 65 AD) and was a leading intellectual figure of his day

[112] (Epistle 52.8). Witherington, Loc. 3275

In today's world having a mentor or life coach has gained a lot of traction, but why not in the church? Why can't new believers look at themselves as though they are apprentices that are acquiring new skills in prayer, Bible study, serving, practicing good stewardship, and so on? They are learning a new spiritual craft, a new trade that requires developing specialized skills as an apprentice with someone to guide them.

Paul is the only New Testament author to ask his congregations to imitate him. He was confident that he knew his stuff, but also lived it out in his practice. This isn't being prideful and vain, he has a *holy sanctified sense of confidence* in his walk with the Lord.

This is the same Paul who also called himself the worst of sinners (1 Tim 1:16), and readily admitted that he doesn't always do the things he knows he should do because of his sinful tendencies (Rom 7:14-25). Paul knew he was a sinner saved by grace, and that he wasn't living in perfection, but he still confidently asserted they should imitate him. Paul didn't call for people to follow him, he called for them to imitate him. Jesus, on the other hand, called people to follow him as his disciple (Mark 2:14). There is a difference, because Paul followed Christ as every other disciple would. Paul doesn't ask churches that don't know him to imitate him (Colossae, and Rome), because imitation without personal relationship and physical presence isn't possible.

Cholick makes an insightful comment about the learning methodology of that time: "Paul's example suggests a model of apprentice and master rather than student and teacher. This model of education was commonplace around the Mediterranean world, with its emphasis on manual labor and handmade crafts and a predominantly illiterate population. Boys learned their father's trade; girls learned housekeeping and childcare from their mothers. Men and women worked in shops with their children helping them. Slaves (male and female) were apprenticed to master weavers or potters, to learn a trade that would add income to the family. People apprenticed or learned by watching and then imitating the master."[113]

---

[113] Cohick, Loc. 4468

What happened to the apprentice / master model in our churches today? Could it be that people are fearful of accepting the responsibility of being the mentor, such that they shy away from that type of thinking, or only reserve that high and lofty title for those who have been through Bible Seminary and are ordained? Conversely, it could be that people don't want to lower themselves and be considered an apprentice, because our culture is so individualistic that each person can figure it out on their own. All one has to do is order some books from amazon.com, that will arrive on your doorstep the next day, and start reading and growing in the Christian life through that means. Being a disciple means being in relationship with other people. Just reading great books on various topics of Scripture removes that critical element of discipleship.

Enemies of the Cross – Adding to or Subtracting from the Good News

We have identified the dogs as the Jewish false teachers, also known as the Judaizers (3:2). Their error was that they were *adding* something to faith in Christ for salvation; namely circumcision and conversion to Judaism. This is a grievous error of addition that rendered their gospel incapable of saving someone.

If Paul was identifying the enemies of the cross as being Gentiles who advocated faith in Christ for salvation, but claimed it was perfectly acceptable to live a libertine hedonistic lifestyle, they were *subtracting* from the true gospel. To throw out all the moral imperatives in the Bible in favor of a licentious lifestyle is a grievous error. Christ alone is all we need for our salvation. We must never embrace teaching that adds to or subtracts from the gospel of Jesus Christ.

The words of John the revelator should be taken seriously to heart:

> I testify to everyone who hears the words of the prophecy of this book, if anyone *adds to* them, may God add to him the plagues which are written in this book. [19]If anyone *takes away* from the words of the book of this prophecy, may God take away his part from the tree of life, and out of the holy city, which are written in this book. (Revelation 22:18-19, Italics Mine)

Summary

After explaining to the Philippians that he hasn't reached perfection, and he won't reach it until resurrection occurs, Paul is challenging them to think this view over. He wants the Philippians, some of whom may have thought perfection was attainable in this life, to give some consideration to his view that perfection won't occur until resurrection. Mature Christians understand that they aren't perfect yet, so Paul wants them to think about it and let God show them the truth of this teaching, but make sure they live up to the standard that they have already attained. Paul is challenging the Philippians to follow his example, and the example of others that live as he does, such as Timothy, and Epaphroditus, who demonstrate through their lifestyle that they live according to the mindset of Christ (2:5).

Paul offers the wrong kind of example which is to be avoided—the false teachers who are enemies of the cross. Whoever these people were they brought much personal grief to Paul, for he continuously weeps over their impending destruction. Whether they are Jewish false teachers or Gentile hedonists who claim to be Christians, they are to be avoided like the plague.

In the next section, Paul speaks about the glorious moment of Christ's return when our bodies will be glorified.

CHAPTER EIGHTEEN

* * *

"Crossing The Finish Line" Philippians 3:20-21

Paul has encouraged the Philippians to follow his example and that of his colleagues, Timothy and Epaphroditus, because they can demonstrate how to live as good citizens of heaven. The example the false teachers present must be shunned, because their teaching can traumatize one spiritually. The portrait Paul painted of the false teachers isn't a pretty one. Their destiny is destruction because they have positioned themselves as enemies of the cross, thereby slamming the door on eternal life in God's presence. However, for those who embrace the cross, like Paul and the Philippians, they have a glorious destiny to look forward to with great hopeful anticipation.

For our citizenship is in heaven, from where we also wait for a Savior, the Lord Jesus Christ; [21]who will change the body of our humiliation to be conformed to the body of his glory, according to the working by which he is able even to subject all things to himself. (3:20-21)

The destiny of Christians is glorious, to say the least: **For our citizenship is in heaven.** It is crucial to see the earth (3:19) – heaven (3:20) contrast between Paul and the false teachers. The word *politeuma*, is translated **citizenship**, which refers to the status one has as a member of the commonwealth, where one's name is placed on the register of citizens. This is the only occurrence of the word in the New Testament, although its related verb *politeuomai* is used in 1:27 (see comments there). Once somebody becomes a Christian they experience a radical change of address, and their relationship with the world changes. Their existence as Romans, Spaniards, Americans, and so on, is a temporary one and becomes subservient to their new identity as citizens of heaven. Many of the Philippians were retired military who had Roman citizenship, which was highly valued and hard to come by. Therefore, Paul is telling them they have dual citizenship with Jesus as their King reigning from heaven, in contrast to Caesar who rules from Rome. They have two emperors: one earthly, one heavenly. They belong to two kingdoms: one earthly, one heavenly.

Once somebody becomes a citizen of heaven, they become aliens and strangers in the world, and are not to be friendly with the world.[114] Christians are just passing through the world on their way to their permanent homeland in heaven. The Philippians now share a common identity as God's people, which should prop up their unity for they have become a tiny outpost in a pagan environment that is often hostile. As the believer goes through life her thoughts and focus must be directed heavenward. Paul has been focusing on the upward call of God (3:14), whereas the enemies of the cross focus their attention on earthly things (3:19). Heaven isn't just a future reality, it is a present experience for believers. When John the Baptist began his ministry, he announced that the Kingdom of heaven was at hand (Mat 3:2), Jesus made the same proclamation when he began his preaching ministry (Mat 4:17). He announced the Kingdom has come when he cast out demons (Luke 11:20), but Jesus also said, "My Kingdom is not of this world" (John 18:36). Therefore, the Kingdom of heaven is a veiled empire on this earth that human eyes can't see, however when Jesus returns his Kingdom will be visible for all to see.

The Kingdom of heaven is ruled by the Lord Jesus, in contrast to the Kingdom of this world which is ruled by Satan—the god of this age (2 Cor 4:4). The Kingdoms coexist side-by-side, which brings them into conflict. The Bible depicts God's people being engaged in spiritual warfare against the forces of darkness—Satan and his battalions of demons. Therefore, God's people need to put their armor on (Eph 6:10-18) and utilize their weapons of warfare to

---

[114] See: 1 Pet 1:1; 17; 2 Pet 2:11; Jam 4:3

destroy strongholds (2 Cor 10:3-5). Once a sinner becomes a believer in Christ she is the recipient of all heavenly blessing (Eph 1:3) and is seated in the heavenly realm with him (Eph 2:6-7; Col 3:1-2). Christians live in two kingdoms: the earthly one is fading away, while the heavenly one is permanent and will be realized in its fullness when Jesus returns.

The hope and anticipation of every believer throughout the ages is the coming of Christ. Paul says: **from where we also wait for a Savior, the Lord Jesus Christ.** That Jesus Christ is the **Savior** is clear because there is salvation in no other name but his (Acts 4:12). "Savior" was also the term that was used of Caesar. The Savior is the **Lord Jesus Christ**, which depicts Jesus in his lofty position at the right hand of God. That Jesus is the **Savior** points to his coming to earth and dying on the cross as depicted in the Christ Hymn (2:5-11). That Jesus is the **Lord Jesus Christ** points to God highly exalting him and giving him the name that is above every name (2:9-11). Therefore, when Paul calls Jesus **Savior, the Lord Jesus Christ**, he is alluding to his incarnation, which includes everything he did in his life to secure the salvation of mankind, including his resurrection and ascension to glory where he is seated at the right hand of God the Father.

Jesus' coming isn't a likelihood it is a certainty, but God's people must **wait**, which translates the Greek word *apekdéchomai*, which describes: an eager expectation, waiting, but waiting that decisively "puts away" all that should remain behind. Thus, there is the thought of separation in this word. The idea being that the believer *looks away* from this world as he waits for the Savior to return from heaven.

As Christians wait for the Lord to come back there is the need to be patient, but not passive (James 5:7). Paul has described in detail his aggressive posture in seeking to know more about Christ during his life, such that he spoke metaphorically as though he was running a race, seizing the moment to acquire more personal knowledge about Jesus. Paul wasn't being passive as he waited for the Lord to return, he was looking away from the world and focusing his thoughts heavenward. The Lord gave marching orders to the church known as the Great Commission (Mat 28:16-20), which is something that every believer should participate in enthusiastically as they wait for Jesus' return. Paul's life is testimony to an aggressive Christian way of living, for there is nothing passive about Paul's life and service to Christ—he is the no nonsense apostle. Therefore, waiting for the Lord to return doesn't mean passivity, it means looking away from the things of the world and shifting our attentional focus to Christ's agenda.

Nobody knows the time of Jesus' coming, so believers wait patiently with great anticipation because when Jesus returns he **will change the body of our humiliation to be conformed to the body of his glory, according to the working by which he is able even to subject all things to himself.** This is the moment believers wait eagerly for because their bodies will **change**, which is a translation of *metaschēmatízō,* which means to change the form of, or the outward appearance of. Therefore, Jesus will return and give his people a total body makeover. He changes the present status of the body, which is described as the **body of our humiliation**, because we bear the stain and corruption of sin. The human body deteriorates, is subject to sickness, aging, and degradation. Jesus' total body makeover will bring the human body **to be conformed to the body of his glory.** The word conformed is *sýmmorphos*, which means: to conform to the same inner essence. The new body will be conformed to be like Jesus' body after he was resurrected (the body of his glory). The physical properties of the body will change such that believers will be immortal (1 Cor 15:50-58). Therefore, the outward appearance and the inner essence of the body will be transformed to be like Jesus' glorified body.

Death will no longer be part of the human condition for it will be a thing of the past, nor will sin, for in the glorified state even the possibility of sinning will not exist. God's people will be in the perfected state—fully redeemed. In the glorified condition, there will be no pain or suffering for God's people, there is only constant joy in the presence of the Triune God (Rev 20:4). It is important to understand that salvation is completed with resurrection, not when the believer dies and goes to heaven.

There are many verbal links between 3:20-21 and the Christ hymn (2:6-11), which would support Pauline authorship of the Hymn, and reveals his rhetorical strategy in writing this section. By using forms of the same verbs in these two sections he's showing the Philippians that the believer's life is running parallel to Jesus' life. Most likely 3:20-21 was recited or sung as a hymn in the early church.

The verbal and thematic links between 2:6-11 and 3:20-21 are intentional not coincidental. Note the following links:

Christ existed in the form (*morphē*) of God (2:6), links with believers being conformed (*sýmmorphos*) to the body of his glory

Jesus came in the likeness (*schéma*) of a human being (2:8), links with the believer's body of humiliation being changed (*metaschēmatízō*) to the body of his glory (3:21)

Jesus being (*hupárchōn*) in the form of God (2:6a), links with our citizenship being (*hupárchei*) in heaven (3:20)

Jesus *humbling* (*etapeinōsen*) himself (2:8), links with our bodies of *humiliation* (*tapeinósis*) in 3:21

To the *glory* (*doxa*) of God the Father (2:11), links with the body of his *glory* (*doxa*) in 3:21

Jesus Christ is Lord (2:11), links with the Lord Jesus Christ (3:21)

These verbal links reveal Paul's strategy in tying these two sections together. In a sense, the believer walks in the footsteps of Jesus. This passage, 3:20-21, seems to pick up where the Christ Hymn of 2:6-11 left off. Believers know that they are citizens of heaven because they have confessed that Jesus Christ is Lord. Jesus ascended into heaven after his resurrection and exaltation, thus paving the way for his disciples. However, they have yet to enter into the reality of that citizenship, so they are waiting for the return of Christ at which time resurrection occurs and their citizenship is completed.

The verbal and thematic links with 3:20-21 and the Christ Hymn are important to note. The links reveal Paul's strategy in writing this letter. The dual citizenship Christian's have will become singular when Christ returns. Earthly citizenship will be a thing of the past. Jesus has gone into heaven and paved the way for the culmination of man's salvation through resurrection.

How will this amazing transformation take place? Paul says it is: **according to the working by which he is able even to subject all things to himself.** The Lord Jesus is all powerful, which Paul points out by using two power words in this verse. **Working** translates *enérgeia*, a word describing God's power, work, or energy, and is the origin of our English words energy and energize. The second power word is **he is able**, which is the Greek *dunamai*, a word used to describe Jesus' miracles (Mark 9:39). Therefore, both these words describe the Lord's inexhaustible, unlimited power that Jesus will utilize when he appears and transforms the believer's body to be like his glorious body. This is truly miraculous!

This power is that **which he is able even to subject all things to himself.** When the Lord returns resurrection occurs, the entire universe will be subject to him, all will confess his Lordship, then he turns the Kingdom over to God the Father (1 Cor 15:23-28). The entire created order will pay homage to Jesus (2:9-11), and all things will be brought into submission to the Lord Jesus Christ, even the greatest enemy of mankind, which is death will be obliterated. There is nothing left to subjugate, all rebellion will have ceased, for his Kingdom will be fully manifested and God's people will be living in glory—end of story.

Insights, Applications, and Life Lessons

It isn't possible to grasp how awesome life in the glorified body will be. Living in perfection will exceed our wildest imaginations. Quite often, I think about the suffering that some believers have endured and it saddens me. I've known many people that had poor health, were confined to wheel chairs, lived with chronic pain, became sick and died early in life. Additionally, I've known many people who suffered from extreme emotional trauma because of depression and anxiety. In fact, the other day I tweaked my shoulder when I was lifting weights at the gym and it's causing me some problems. I've been an athlete all my life: martials arts, weight lifting, bike riding, running, golf, etc., and have always had to deal with nagging injuries. At age 62 my knee hurts so I stopped running, my lower back hurts at times, my right shoulder hurts, I've had insomnia my whole life, my neck frequently hurts, I used to get migraine headaches, I had surgery to repair a torn rotator cuff on my left shoulder, but I still workout every day.

I can't wait to receive my glorified body and get rid of all those nagging aches and pains and lingering injuries. If there are gyms in the glorified state, my workouts will soar to new heights with a brand new perfect body. YES!

When I contrast the weakness of our fallen humanity with the glorified body we will receive at Christ's return it makes me long for that day to occur. Christians should fix their hope on the glorious moment of Christ's return (1 Pet 1:13) and draw strength from thinking about what God has in store for them in the future. Paul told the Philippians: But our citizenship is in heaven. And we *eagerly await* a Savior from there, the Lord Jesus Christ (3:20, Italics Mine), and the Thessalonians: *to wait* for his Son from heaven, whom he raised from the dead—Jesus, who delivers us from the wrath to come (1 Thess 1:10, Italics Mine). This is the hope and longing of every believer throughout the ages.

It Ends With Resurrection

This passage points out that God's plan of salvation ends with resurrection. Often people think it's all over when they die and go to heaven, for even Paul mentioned in 1:23 that when he dies he will find himself in the presence of Christ (see comments there). If Paul was executed he would go to heaven, but he wouldn't have his resurrection body.

When a believer dies their body is placed in the grave undergoing corruption, and their spirit, which is the immaterial part of their existence goes immediately to heaven in Jesus' presence, but she doesn't have her glorified body. She must wait for the Lord to return to earth, then she will receive her resurrection body along with all the other saints. For this reason, the time between death and resurrection is referred to as the *intermediate state*, in that it is in between physical death and bodily resurrection. It is also known as the *disembodied state*, because the believer doesn't have her body. It is difficult to know what that condition is like for nobody has ever been there to film it or do a documentary on it.

Paul shed some light on this state in 2 Corinthians 5:1-5. He referred to the resurrection body as being clothed with our heavenly dwelling, and the disembodied state being unclothed, or naked. Paul's desire is that he not be in the disembodied state (unclothed), but to be clothed with his resurrection body. In no way is Paul trying to indicate that being unclothed in heaven is a bad place to be, he is implying the resurrected state is better and he longs to be there. Therefore, it is essential for believers to understand God's plan of salvation is completed at resurrection, not when the believer dies and goes to heaven.

What about the false teachers, the enemies of the cross, and those who persecute Christians whose destiny is destruction (1:28; 3:19)? They spend eternity in hell away from the presence of God, but will they experience resurrection? Both believers and nonbelievers will be resurrected, the former to glory, the latter to judgment (John 5:28-29; Rev 20:11-15). Scripture doesn't say that nonbelievers will receive glorified bodies, that privilege is reserved for citizens of heaven. However, it is a myth that only believers have eternal life, nonbelievers have eternal life as well, they just spend it in a different place.

Summary

In contrast to the false teachers whose minds are focused on earthly things, Paul has an orientation that is focused upward toward heaven, where the believer's citizenship lies. Believers wait for the Lord to return at which time he will subject all things under his control and transform our bodies to be like his glorified body through resurrection. If a believer is alive at the coming of Christ he will not experience physical death, rather the physical properties of his body are instantly changed, and he will be glorified. This is the hope of all believers: to have the Lord return and end this age of history, which will also end their battle with sin and death, for they will be immortal. This is what life will be like for citizens of heaven.

In the next section, Paul exhorts the Philippians to stand firm and clean up some of their internal issues. Two high-powered women are locking horns and causing quite a disturbance. It's time to call a cease fire and negotiate a truce.

CHAPTER NINETEEN

* * *

"Stand Firm"
Philippians 4:1-3

The church is always under attack because the world has a value system that is diametrically opposed to the values set forth in Scripture. Churches must be careful not to assimilate worldly values into their thinking and practice, which would cause them to lose the distinction between themselves and the world. Whether it is political correctness, changing views of sexuality, marriage, family, etc. the church in America is fighting a clash of values with the world. Such was the case with the church at Philippi.

In addition to the clash of values, they suffered outright persecution at times. Christianity in Paul's day wasn't a recognized religion of the state. Paul was deeply concerned about the future of the Jesus movement because it was in its infancy, fragile, needing more leaders, and it was small in number. If someone became a Christian in Paul's day a very high probability existed that he would be persecuted.

Paul has already warned them about the dangers false teachers pose to their spiritual health. One can't dismiss the work of Satan behind all this, who twists the truth of Scripture to cause confusion and introduce false doctrine (1 Tim 4:1-2). Therefore, Paul warned them to keep their guard up if false teachers show up and try to impose a false gospel on them.

Between the clash of values with the world, persecution, danger from false teachers, and attacks of the Devil the Philippians must be extra cautious. In addition to the above, there was another issue that threatened to derail the fellowship. There were two leading ladies of the church that seemed to be at each other's throats. There was discord in the ranks of the leadership that needed to be resolved quickly, so they could avoid a disaster down the road. With all the pressures from their pagan culture and their internal disorder they were facing, Paul gives the order to STAND FIRM in the Lord.

Therefore, my brothers (and sisters), beloved and longed for, my joy and crown, so stand firm in the Lord, my beloved. [2]I exhort Euodia, and I exhort Syntyche, to think the same way in the Lord. [3]Yes, I beg you also, true partner, help these women, for they labored with me in the Good News, with Clement also, and the rest of my fellow workers, whose names are in the book of life. (4:1-3)

Paul connects this section to what preceded using **therefore**. Because Christians have a glorious future that will be realized at Christ's return when resurrection occurs (3:20-21), believers can't be miss led by false teachers that he has been speaking against (3:2; 3:18-19), so they need to stand firm in the Lord.

His pastor's heart rises to the surface again as he calls the Philippians **my brothers (and sisters)**, so Paul is speaking to them on the same level because they are his spiritual siblings, members of the family of God through Christ. He describes them **as beloved and longed for**, so **beloved** modifies **brothers**. **Beloved** is one of the strongest Greek words to express love (*agapētos*), and Paul uses this word twice in v. 1, which points to the special place the Philippians occupied in his heart. This word is a derivative of *agápē* a word indicating God's love expressed to man and the love of God cultivated in disciples' hearts. Additionally, Paul adds to beloved: **and longed for**, *epipothētos*, which is the only occurrence of the word in the New Testament. A form of the same word (*epipotheō*), was used in 1:8, where Paul said he "longed for them" with the affection of Christ. The word is deeply emotional and expresses Paul's feelings for his brothers and sisters in Philippi. He longed to be there with them and missed their good company.

He also considers his brothers to be: **my joy**. As Paul thought of the Philippians it brought him joy, but the fact that he considers them **my joy** makes it more personal.[115] They weren't bothersome and annoying to him, he always experienced joy as he remembered them and prayed for them. These were people that Paul led to Christ, so he had a vested interest in them. In addition to joy, he adds **and crown** (*stéphanos*), which was the laurel wreath or victor's crown awarded to the winner of athletic games. This crown will be received when Paul and the Philippians cross the finish line and receive their resurrection bodies. Why does Paul call the Philippians "my crown?" Following the athletic metaphor, the Philippians would be Paul's reward in the sense that they are proof of his apostleship (1 Cor 9:2), that Paul was their spiritual father who brought them into the Kingdom, and the proof that he had not labored in vain (1 Cor 15:58; Phil 2:16). His work paid off and the Philippians have endured to the end.

One can't help seeing the eschatological coloring of this passage. Paul is imagining that he and the Philippians are standing in the presence of the Lord at the end of the age rejoicing together (2:16-18). His confidence that the Lord would complete the good work he began in them has proven to be correct (1:6). They are his crown on the final day, which is why some consider the "crown of joy" as the soul winners crown awarded at the Judgment Seat of Christ.[116] Paul would be joyful as a modern-day Olympic athlete winning a gold metal standing on the platform as the national anthem is played. Thus, when Paul links "joy" with "crown" he is pointing us to end times imagery, where there is cause for celebrating in the presence of the Lord for all will be in the glorified state—resurrection will have been accomplished.

There is a similar thought that Paul expresses in his first letter to the church at Thessalonica (2:19-20): "For what is our hope, or joy, or crown of rejoicing? Isn't it even you, before our Lord Jesus at his coming? **20**For you are our glory and our joy." That this takes place at the end of the age when Jesus returns is clear from the passage. This moment will be a time of great celebration for Paul and all his converts, as they together rejoice in the presence of Christ.

---

[115] See: Phil 1:4; 25; 2:2; 29

[116] Wall, p. 152-154

In light of this Paul says: **so stand firm in the Lord, my beloved.** The verb *stékó* comes into English as **stand firm**, (also 1:27), written as a present imperative, which means it is a command that is to be done continuously. This is the main verb that governs everything from verses 1-9. The word has military connotations, which the retired soldiers in the congregation would connect with (see comments on 1:27). The command to **stand firm**, informs the soldiers to: "hold your ground," "hold the line," "stand fast," or "stand firm." The soldiers must be working together in unity for their battle formations to be effective. Paul wants the Philippian Christians to "hold their ground" against all the challenges that threaten their existence from false teachers, to internal conflicts and, of course, behind all this are the attacks of the Devil. Like the imagery in Ephesians where Paul pictures Christians putting on their armor for battle, they must stand firm against the forces of darkness (Eph 6:10-18). They must be unified as they "hold the line" and ward off any attacks from their culture, false teachers, clean up their internal problems, and keep fighting the battle as good soldiers of Christ (1:27-30). If they don't their ability to live as good citizens of heaven will be greatly diminished, as will their witness to their city.

Their unity must be **in the Lord**, such that if they are not sharing the mind of Christ (2:1-5) and aren't finding their source of unity in Christ and the Holy Spirit (1:27) then their efforts will be fruitless. They must stand firm in their identity as God's people, being in Christ, while presenting a glowing witness to their city. Paul calls them **my beloved** for the second time in the verse. He is giving them strong words of affirmation, as he expresses his confidence in them and love for them.

I exhort Euodia, and I exhort Syntyche, to think the same way in the Lord. (4:2)

One way the Philippians need to stand firm in the Lord, is to resolve a conflict scenario between two women, Euodia and Syntyche, who were key leaders in the church. When unity is lacking between members of a congregation it can have a harmful effect on the church, but when key leaders are at odds with each other it can cripple a church and rip it apart. Paul thought this issue was serious enough to be brought before the whole congregation.

He has brought to the attention of the Philippians one positive example after another: Christ, Timothy, Epaphroditus, and himself for the church to emulate. He presented the false teachers as an example to avoid like the plague, and these two women, even though they are leading ladies in the church, are serving as a poor example to the congregation. They need to get their act together and put into practice the teaching Paul has given thus far about being positive examples, especially 2:1-5. Their inability to work things out serves as a poor example of how to "live as citizens of heaven, conducting yourselves in a manner worthy of the Good News of Christ" (1:27). That Paul singles them out before the entire church testifies to their importance, and the volatility of their disagreement(s) with each other. Women were not usually mentioned by name in Greek and Roman oratory unless they were prominent, notable, or notorious. These two women, Euodia and Syntyche, need to check back into spiritual reality and come to grips with the harmful impact they are having on their church. They need to get over themselves.

Paul is hopeful that the entire fellowship can assist these women in getting over their differences and reconcile, thus making themselves good examples to the congregation. When two prominent leaders can overcome their differences, they serve as a positive example to their church. Much can be learned by watching leaders work through their issues and reconcile.

What the issues were that divided them isn't found in the passage, it is totally left to the imagination. It is certain that the bone of contention wasn't a matter of doctrine, for if it was Paul would simply have corrected the error as he does in all his letters. Their issues must have been of a personal nature. Perhaps, they had disagreements about approaches to ministry, how to do outreach, or it may have been over social factors, but we just don't know with exactitude what they were butting heads over.

Paul doesn't want them to step down from ministry and take a break until they get their act together, he wants to see them unified and have a mutual cease fire. These were friends of Paul that worked with him in ministry and did much to help the church at Philippi. These two women are not bad people who are labeled as immature or worldly carnal Christians. The fact that he names them testifies to the friendship that he has with them, for in those days enemies were left unnamed so they would be denigrated by anonymity. In other words, you killed your enemy with silence—by ignoring them.

It should not surprise anybody that women are in the church and occupying key roles for it was founded by Gentile women, who were God-fearers, that worshiped on the Sabbath and met by the river for prayer (Acts 16:13-15). Lydia seems to have become a patron of the small apostolic band of leaders and the church met in her home. She was automatically a leader in the church, since heads of households assumed the same role in the church that was centered in their home.

These women were most likely of Macedonian origin, because there were Macedonian families that were involved in all levels of Philippian society, so the influence of Greeks occupying positions of social status in a city like Philippi can't be underestimated.[117] When prominent women converted to Christianity they would most likely expect to play an important part in their new church. It is possible that Euodia and Syntyche were part of the overseers and deacons (1:1) and were patrons of the Philippian church. These were women that were probably of high social standing and means, who could rely on their servants to do much of the domestic work, so their time was freed up to work with Paul.

Euodia and **Syntyche** are Greek names, which roughly mean Success and Lucky respectively. With a sense of urgency, he **exhorts** them equally, which means he isn't taking sides, and he isn't trying to determine who's in the right and who's in the wrong. He isn't in any way, shape, or form trying to cast blame on either one of them, he just wants them **to think the same way in the Lord.** The Greek word *phronéō*, which we've already seen several times, is translated **to think** and is written as a present participle, which means they are to continuously have a cease fire and be of the same mindset or think the same way **in the Lord.** They must learn to agree, to disagree, agreeably, so the church can get on with its business and find unity. It could be that with the use of *phronéō* (to think) here, and in 2:2, that Paul is linking these passages together: "make my joy full, by being **like-minded** (*phronéō*), having the same love, being of one accord, of one mind." Paul could have been

[117] Witherington, Loc. 3641; Fee, p. 390-391

thinking of these two high-powered women as he wrote 2:1-5, as the leading instigators that are fueling the fires at Philippi and contributing to the disunity in the congregation. Euodia and Syntyche are not standing firm in the Lord, they have a serious rift, and need to work it out.

It could be that through all the examples that Paul has given throughout his letter, he has been building up to this point to identify the parties that are being destructive to the welfare of the church. Looking at 2:1-5 and applying it to their situation would seem to indicate that they were more concerned about themselves and their own interests, rather than the overall good of the church. They were leading ladies in the church, and probably had considerable social standing in the community as well, but their conduct wasn't conducive to being citizens of heaven (1:27).

Yes, I beg you also, true partner, help these women, for they labored with me in the Good News, with Clement also, and the rest of my fellow workers, whose names are in the book of life. (4:3)

It doesn't seem as though the two women will make any headway without some help: **Yes, I beg you also, true partner, help these women.** Paul's appeal is urgent, as he calls upon **true partner** (*suzugos*), to help the women resolve their differences. The Greek word *suzugos* refers to: a companion, colleague, partner, or comrade. The image is of two people yoked together like a team of oxen, sharing a common burden. It is translated a variety of ways including: faithful friend (NCV), loyal friend (CEB), loyal companion (NRSV), true companion (NASB, ESV, NIV), and my true teammate (NLT), but who is he referring to? It must be one of Paul's co-workers that traveled with him and was a close partner that shared the burdens of ministry with him. People have tried to identify Epaphroditus, Timothy, Silas, and Luke as this individual.[118] Witherington thinks the most plausible option is that Epaphroditus is the true partner, because by putting this in the letter it gives him authority in writing to intervene when he arrives there and serves as a peacemaker.[119] At the end of the day it's all speculation. The individual must

[118] Fee makes a good case for Dr. Luke being the true partner (Fee, p. 394-395)
[119] Witherington, Loc. 3677

have been so well known to the Philippians that Paul didn't have to mention him by his true name.

The important thing is that Paul asks the true partner to **help these women**. Help is a translation of (*syllambanō*), a word that describes active participation, to seize, or to apprehend, and is written to the true partner as a command. They need an arbitrator to sit them down and help them come to agreement in the Lord. A third party who can provide hands on help in resolving a conflict situation is a valuable asset to have in any organization. Before things go completely south and the situation can't be salvaged the true partner must be utilized to bring peace between these women.

Paul affirms both leading ladies of the congregation: **for they labored with me in the Good News. Labored** is *sunathleó*, also translated contended, or fight alongside. The word has an athletic nuance, therefore like athletes competing together in an event, Euodia and Syntyche were at Paul's side as they spread the gospel in Macedonia. These were good people, faithful workers and tough competitors in the gospel arena. They were in good company for Paul says: **with Clement also, and the rest of my fellow workers, whose names are in the book of life.** Nothing is known of Clement except that he worked with Paul and is Roman, but the fact that Paul mentions him by name indicates that he was a high value asset in his ministry. The rest of Paul's fellow workers who contributed to the spread of the gospel in Macedonia are omitted in this letter, but their names are, more importantly, written in the **book of life**, also people's names are written in heaven.[120]

The **book of life** seems to be an idea taken from lists of true citizens of ancient city-states and from the book containing the names of the righteous.[121] The book of life refers to the roster of those who belong to heaven, where their names are inscribed in the divine book. Just as the Philippians had their names written in the ledger of citizens in Philippi, their names are also written in the heavenly roster, which contains all the names of those who are citizens of heaven.

---

[120] See: Revelation 3:5; 13:8; 17:8; 20:12, 15; 21:27; Luke 10:20; Heb 12:23

[121] See: Psalm 9:5; 87:6; Isa 4:3; Ps 69:28; Dan 12:1

Paul has affirmed these women even though they are causing trouble. That they are key people to Paul, have worked well with him to advance the gospel, and their names are written in the book of life make their inability to be at peace with each other seem totally out of place for sisters in Christ! He hasn't said a negative word about them and appears to believe that they can work it out after hearing this letter read out loud. This is a public rebuke, but Paul believes these women are mature enough to get over it, take the right strides to call a cease fire, reconcile, and be positive examples to the church. Paul has high hopes for Euodia and Syntyche, having confidence that they can work it out with true partner's help and the help of the fellowship.

Insights, Applications, and Life Lessons

Churches need to stand firm against external threats as well as internal conflicts that can weaken a gathering of believers. Leaders can be high powered people, aggressive, love to have influence, and often be hard to work with. What do you do when two talented, hardworking leaders that have a good track record are locking horns with each other and are hurting the organization, whether it be a church, business, non-profit, family, football team, and so on? This presents a problem for any organization.

The Philippians need to stand firm in the Lord by everybody working out this conflict scenario because it truly threatened the church's future. He brings this to the attention of the entire church, so Euodia and Syntyche are not alone in this, they are accountable to the whole church to negotiate a truce. Churches may be better able to cope with persecution from the world, then they can with internal battles between leaders. Churches are often strengthened when persecuted, but when leaders are unable to work together and are spreading discord among the people, this can be the more destructive threat to the church's future.

How Would This Situation Be Handled in the Workplace?

Usually when two people are having a rough time with each other, the one in authority tries to identify the guilty party. Somebody has to take the blame, but Paul didn't go there. He affirmed both as high value assets to his ministry.

Usually the one in authority may tend to favor one over the other, but Paul didn't do that. He affirmed them both as valuable colleagues and seems to be completely impartial.

Usually when the boss approaches two people having a rough time with each other their normal response is to blame it on the other person. Each individual digs-in and fortifies their position. "It's not my fault." Of course, it's always the other person's fault! It's human nature to overlook one's faults but see the other person's issues with glaring clarity. Part of working through conflicts between people is getting them to own their part of it and not be in denial.

One strategy that the boss could employ is to punish them, have them resign, or step out of ministry for a time until cooler heads prevail. Paul didn't go there either. He didn't recommend attending a seminar on anger management, fire them, belittle them, issue ultimatums, dock them pay, suspend privileges, he did none of that. He must have had a high degree of trust in them to work things out between each other, with the help of the true partner.

Another problem that occurs when two high profile leaders are at odds with each other is that people tend to take sides. Paul wouldn't do that, but people in the church at Philippi may have been polarizing—some siding with Euodia others with Syntyche. This is a dangerous situation, because friends tend to stick together. This is how church splits occur. Those who were friends with Euodia would tend to side with her, while those who were friendly with Syntyche would tend to side with her. Euodia's friends may be bearing an offense against Syntyche, while her friends are bearing an offense against Euodia. It's possible that each of these women had a gathering in their home like Lydia did. This means the possibility existed for each house to be warring against the other one. It's not uncommon for people to takes sides when arguments occur. That Paul wouldn't do that serves as an example for the Philippians not to take sides either.

Even the best Christians will at times have serious disagreements with other Christians they work with. This doesn't mean they're bad people, it means they're human. They must utilize their resources in the Holy Spirit to forgive each other and focus on the greater cause of promoting the gospel, while retaining unity in their fellowship rather than focusing on their own agendas (2:1-5). It must be remembered that Paul had a serious rift with Barnabas. He initially had a great relationship with him, and Paul was indebted to him because Barnabas introduced him to the elders and apostles in Jerusalem. He gave Paul an opportunity to teach with him in Antioch and the two of them did great work in building up that church. They were a truly high-powered team—a real one-two-punch!

However, they had a serious disagreement, a real blow out and they parted company (Acts 15:36-41). The bone of contention was about whether they should take Mark on a missionary journey, after he deserted them on the previous one. Paul would not tolerate having a deserter, but Barnabas wanted to take him along and give him another chance. Over this issue the high-powered team, had a high-powered disagreement and they parted company. In the future, they appeared to have reconciled and later in Paul's life he affirmed Mark as a high value asset in ministry (2 Tim 4:11). Mark also wrote the gospel that bears his name, so his contribution to Christendom is enormous. Paul knew what it was like to have a major conflict with someone, so I believe this heightened his empathy for the two leading ladies. Who among us has never had a serious disagreement with someone?

Imagine You Are There

The people gather, maybe at Lydia's house or are meeting outside near the river. They sing a few songs and have a prayer time. Epaphroditus has returned so everybody is happy to see him recovered from his illness and wants to hear about his trip to Rome. The whole church is excited because it has been announced that he has a letter from Paul addressed to the church that will be read. Euodia and Syntyche are in attendance but are on opposite sides of the gathering from each other. The reader stands up, opens the scroll and says, "I'm going read Paul's letter to you." The place goes deafly silent with all eyes focused on the reader and ears wide open. Then he begins to read loudly, so everybody can hear him and not too fast, so everybody can follow him.

When he reads Paul's opening words and they hear his heartfelt emotions for them, smiles appear on their faces. Some of the women tear up and get emotional. As they hear about the gospel advancing through the Praetorian guard and the believers in Rome boldly preaching Christ big smiles appear on their faces. A look of awe is on their faces as they hear about the joy Paul has in the Lord. They marvel at the Christ Hymn, and nod their heads in agreement that they are citizens of heaven.

They are listening with attentive ears to every word that is spoken and then they hear the words: **I exhort Euodia, and I exhort Syntyche, to think the same way in the Lord. Yes, I beg you also, true partner, help these women, for they labored with me in the Good News, with Clement also, and the rest of my fellow workers, whose names are in the book of life.**

When the leading ladies heard their names did their pulse rise, their blood pressure increase, did they blush, did they hang their heads in shame? Perhaps, Euodia thought: "I'm not the problem it's Syntyche she's causing the trouble." Maybe Syntyche thought: "Euodia is the bane of my existence, if only she weren't here this fellowship would be better off." Did they turn and look at each other making eye contact and then walk toward each other and hug, kiss, and ask each other for forgiveness? What did the other people do as the reader mentioned their names? Did every head in the place turn to look at the women? Were people saying to themselves: "You two have to get past this." "It's time to bury the hatchet."

At the end of the reading they probably had a discussion time and talked about some of the things Paul said. I wonder if somebody said to the ladies, "We will be praying for you." "What can we do to help you come together in the Lord." Perhaps, the true partner and Clement went to Euodia and Syntyche and said, "When do you want to meet with us and talk it over?" "We want to help you resolve your differences."

Perhaps the Holy Spirit moved mightily, causing the women to feel conviction and things started to move in the right direction. We just don't know the outcome, but Paul's strategy in dealing with these two high-powered leading ladies is brilliant. After the letter was read out loud and everybody heard the admonition from Paul, they are now accountable to everybody in the church to come together in the Lord. This wasn't about who's right and wrong, but about doing what's best for all concerned, for that is the mind of Christ (2:5).

Euodia and Syntyche may not have ever become best friends, but they didn't have to. They just needed to consider the needs of others as being more important than themselves and acknowledge that they don't see things eye-to-eye, but they can exist together. They must acknowledge that they can agree, to disagree, on issues agreeably. In life we don't always get our way. In a business, family, a soccer team, in relationships, and so on, we must sometimes swallow our pride and do what's best for the entire group.

In my ministry I've had situations where leaders had disagreements that I've had to help them work through with much difficulty. I've also butted heads with other leaders I've worked with and had to resolve issues with them. Conflict is a normal part of life, so people must learn how to deal with difficult situations and resolve their issues with other people.

Summary

Paul expresses his love to the Philippians, for they are his dear brothers and sisters in the Lord, whom he longs to see. He affectionately refers to them as his joy and crown, in that they are the result of his apostleship, and the fruit of his labor in the gospel ministry. Like giving an order to soldiers in battle he commands the church to stand firm in the Lord against all the forces that threatened them, including internal conflicts between key leaders like Euodia and Syntyche. Whatever their issues were they needed to resolve their differences and be of the same mind in the Lord, so the work of ministry could move forward and the congregation could be unified.

Paul brings this to the attention of the entire congregation, for the letter would be read out loud during a gathering, so it must have been a serious rift between these two ladies. Paul is giving them a rebuke, but he doesn't take sides in the conflict. He masterfully affirms them both and the contribution they made to his ministry and the church at Philippi, while including them with the rest of his co-workers. He enlists the help of true partner to help the women sort through their issues, but we don't know who he was. That Euodia and Syntyche are sisters in the Lord and that their names are written in the book of life, along with all the other leaders, makes their conflict seem even more out of place and inappropriate. They should be working together in a state of unity—standing firm in the Lord together, but that isn't happening. Paul isn't demoting them by calling them to step down from ministry, he is hopeful that with help Euodia and Syntyche can get it together and be one in the Lord. This concludes Paul's *probatio,* which served the purpose of backing up his thesis statement (1:27-30).

In the next section, Paul gives us one of the most often quoted passages of Scripture in the Bible. He offers guidance in helping people cope with anxiety by experiencing the peace of God.

CHAPTER TWENTY

* * *

"Stop Worrying"
Philippians 4:4-7

At this point, Paul brings us to the *peroratio*, which in ancient rhetoric serves the purpose of reiterating the themes of a discourse, while evoking the emotions of the audience so they embrace the appeals made to them. The *peroratio* is the emotional climax of the discourse, then in the *denouement* which follows he addresses any final concerns. This section is a summary of some of the key elements of his letter, while vv. 8-9 is an emotional appeal to embrace the virtues necessary to live as citizens of heaven in a manner that is worthy of the Good News (1:27).

Paul makes clear in his *peroratio* that his letter was mainly about ethics and orthopraxy (right practice), following good examples, avoiding bad examples, cultivating virtues while eliminating harmful vices. Philippians isn't primarily an exercise in theology, such as Paul's letter to the Romans, although there is rich theology in the Christ Hymn (2:5-11). Philippians is more about how to live the Christian life. Even the Christ Hymn was primarily motivational rather than theological.

Paul begins a new section of his letter by returning to the theme of joy, which has occupied a great deal of his thinking throughout his writing. This passage has provided countless numbers of Christians with comfort and encouragement throughout the millennia to sustain them during difficult times. Who doesn't want the peace of God in their life? Who doesn't want to overcome the stress and anxiety that comes into the human condition so often? Paul gives his readers insights about how they can be filled with joy, tap into God's peace, and put the brakes on their worrying. The threefold expression of Jewish piety comes out in vv. 4-7: rejoicing in the Lord, prayer, and thanksgiving. This triad of spiritual practices should be instilled in every believer.

Rejoice in the Lord always! Again I will say, "Rejoice!" [5]Let your gentleness be known to all men. The Lord is at hand. [6]In nothing be anxious, but in everything, by prayer and petition with thanksgiving, let your requests be made known to God. [7]And the peace of God, which surpasses all understanding, will guard your hearts and your thoughts in Christ Jesus. (4:4-7)

Knowing Christ is an ever-present blessing and source of joy, so rejoicing should be done **in the Lord.** That a believer can have fellowship with the Lord Jesus, know him (3:10), and continuously deepen his relationship with him should be cause for rejoicing. Knowing that our names are written in the book of life (4:3), is truly something to rejoice over. Paul writes this by way of a command, and in the present continuous tense, which means it should be an ongoing practice in the believer's life. He is writing this in the plural, so it is directed to the entire congregation. Churches are communities that should practice the discipline of rejoicing, praising the Lord, and giving thanks to God. Rejoicing in the Lord is a corporate matter, but it begins with each individual mobilizing his praise to the Lord.

Rejoice in the Lord always! Why always? Life doesn't always present people with pleasant circumstances such that the first thing they would do is rejoice. In fact, many times people do the opposite in troubling moments. The point is that even in negative circumstances that may cause pain, undergirding the believer can be a sense of joy that never disappears. Even in trials believers are to consider it all joy (Jam 1:2). Having one's soul filled with joy is an exhilarating experience that can brighten up one's life. Joy isn't just an emotion, it stems from a deep-seated confidence that God is in control of all things, including one's life from beginning to end. The only constant source of joy in life is the Lord, because other people will disappoint us, hurt us, and let us down. Favorable circumstances can change overnight into catastrophes. Material possessions are fleeting and don't provide people with any deep lasting sense of joy, because the excitement of a new purchase fads quickly. It isn't circumstances that dictate the level of joy people realize, but the presence of the Lord in their lives. Therefore, believers can rejoice continually—it is a way of life, especially since their names are written in the book of life (4:3).

Rejoicing in the Lord isn't an option for believers it is an emphatic command for Paul mentions this twice in the same verse: **Again I will say, "Rejoice!"** Individual believers would do well to consider "rejoicing in the Lord" a habit to infuse in their daily practice, and churches would do well to consider themselves as communities of rejoicers—constantly praising the Lord. Church should be a celebratory experience as God's people consider that their names are written in heaven.

Let your gentleness be known to all men. The Lord is at hand. (4:5)

Paul has been exhorting the church at Philippi to be unified, stand firm, and be of the same mind, especially Euodia and Syntyche (4:2). One virtue that will greatly facilitate the unity of the body is **gentleness**, which is a translation of the Greek word *epieikēs*. Translating this word into English is virtually impossible because there is no English equivalent for this Greek word. At best, we can say in English it means something like: reasonableness, moderation, forbearing, considerate, generosity, being lenient toward other's faults, graciousness, or a sweet spirit. People who display this quality can withstand injustices, and persecution without lashing out in retaliation and seeking revenge. The person in possession of this virtue tends to go the extra mile with people in difficult circumstances and keep the relationship intact, rather than severing the ties. The word describes someone who is easy-going, and has a sweep spirit, or a pleasant way about her.

In a church like Philippi, where unity seems to be in short supply, having the virtue of gentleness could cause the people to "chill" and bring everyone together for good fellowship. People with this virtue won't be quick to press their rights, and demand that things be their way at everyone else's expense, for this isn't the mindset of Christ (2:1-5). When people focus on themselves it should not be surprising that unity will suffer, thus Paul issues this as a command: **Let your gentleness be known to all men.** It is written in the passive voice, which means the source of gentleness is the Holy Spirit, it is not the product of human effort. As the Spirit of God controls the lives of believers he will produce this fruit in their lives.

Not only is this virtue to be extended to those within the church, but also to outsiders. The face all Christians should wear in public is gentleness, which will help them to be good witnesses for Christ and give outsiders a positive impression of the Christian community. Even in the face of hostile opposition, like Jesus endured, believers are to put their best foot forward and be a good example to all (1 Pet 2:23).

The next phrase **The Lord is at hand** seems unexpected, even out of place, and is difficult to connect the dots with what precedes and follows. Is Paul saying the Lord is at hand in terms of fellowship, such as the Lord is near to the brokenhearted (Ps 34:18), or the Lord is near those who call upon him (Ps 145:18-19)? Could it be that Paul is referring to the second coming of the Lord? At this point one could almost flip a coin to ascertain which Paul has in mind. To paraphrase, if Paul is thinking about the Lord being near regarding fellowship and presence he means: "Because the Lord is here with us display your gentleness and rejoice in the Lord. He is here to help us in times of discouragement and alleviate our moments of anxiety."

On the other hand, if Paul is thinking of the second coming of the Lord he is saying: "Because Christ could return at any moment, rejoice and let your gentleness be evident to all and don't be anxious about anything because this age is about to end."

Paul has had a significant eschatological emphasis throughout Philippians, so he probably has in mind the second coming of Christ. Osborne points out: "Frequently in the New Testament, a passage of admonition segues into a reminder that the end is coming soon (for example, Rom 13:12; 1 Cor 16:22; Heb 10:25, 37; Jas 5:8; 1 Pet 4:7). This is both a promise and a warning—a promise that our future glory will be worth our present hardship and a warning that God expects us to live in light of Christ's return and will hold us accountable for how we live. God's people are to be loving; as such, we do our part to rescue the perishing and usher in God's final kingdom."[122]

The Lord's second coming is near, but the Lord is near to those who call on his name. Perhaps, as Fee suggests, it is an intentional double entendre.[123] It could be that Paul has a little bit of both ideas in mind. The term **at hand** is a translation of *eggus*, which is used both in a spatial sense to refer to the Lord's presence here and now, but also regarding the Lord's coming, so the word can support either presence, or his second coming. "The Lord who will soon return is the Lord who once came so close to humanity (Phil 2:6-8) as actually to share the human lot and who though absent now in body is still near at hand in his Spirit to guide, instruct, encourage, infuse with strength, assist, transform, and renew."[124] Thus, the Lord is near both in the sense of his imminent return and is near to offer comfort to the believer as she calls on his name—both are true.

In nothing be anxious, but in everything, by prayer and petition with thanksgiving, let your requests be made known to God. [7]And the peace of God, which surpasses all understanding, will guard your hearts and your thoughts in Christ Jesus. (4:6-7)

Uncountable numbers of Christians have found great comfort in the above two verses. It certainly is a passage that I've cherished in my own experience and given a great deal of attention to. There are some things that people read in the Bible and conclude something to the effect: "You've got to be kidding!" "Really!" "How can anybody actually do that?" This is one of the things Paul says that to me is mind boggling: **In nothing be anxious.** How can a person go through life not being anxious? Paul writes this as a command, in the present continuous tense, so he is commanding the Philippians to cease and desist from all anxiety, and not start being anxious again. This is shocking when considering the number of things that people can be anxious about. At Philippi there were things that caused them some anxiety such as Epaphroditus' illness and return, they were concerned about how things

---

[122] Osborne, Loc. 2775

[123] Fee, p. 407

[124] Martin and Hawthorne, p. 245

would turn out for Paul, at times they faced hostility from their culture, they were poor, plus they had issues to work through in their church, so their anxiety meter may have been in the red zone. Plus, look at all that Paul has been through—he must have struggled with a high degree of anxiety considering his circumstances, but he tells them not to be anxious about anything.

Anxious, is a translation of *merimnaō*, which means: to worry, to stress, be overly concerned, or be distracted. This is the same word Jesus used six times in the Sermon on the Mount (Mat 6:25-34), one of which was: "Therefore I tell you, don't be *anxious* for your life: what you will eat, or what you will drink; nor yet for your body, what you will wear."[125] Since God is the heavenly Father, he is committed to taking care of the needs of his sons and daughters. In a sense, believers are in his loving hands and he won't let them down. He will provide his people with food, clothing, shelter, and whatever else is necessary to sustain them. Since God has obligated himself to believers in this way, it is unnecessary to worry about the necessities of life. Epaphroditus showed up with a gift of money that provided for Paul's needs, which he certainly viewed as God's provision. The Philippians can be free from anxious thinking, and undistracted so they can focus on living as good citizens of heaven and being at their best for God (1:27).

In nothing be anxious, but in everything, by prayer and petition with thanksgiving, let your requests be made known to God. [7]And the peace of God, which surpasses all understanding, will guard your hearts and your thoughts in Christ Jesus. (4:6-7)

It is important to see the contrast between **nothing** and **everything.** The reason believers can be anxious for **nothing** is because in **everything**, all circumstances of life, they express their dependence on God through prayer. This is profoundly simple theology on prayer. In troubling circumstances pray, pray some more, and keep on praying. Paul uses three different Greek words for prayer, (prayer, petition, requests) not that they have different meanings or are different aspects of prayer, he is piling up synonyms to express the importance of prayer, especially in difficult circumstances that

---

[125] See: Mat 6:25; 27; 28; 31; 34 [twice]

make one anxious. Prayer must be accompanied with thanksgiving, which refers to the demeanor of the one who is praying. Disciples don't present their requests to God with a "bad attitude" where they are whining, complaining, grumbling, or are upset over their circumstances, for this could certainly stall their prayer engine and grieve the Holy Spirit. One only needs to think of how the ancient Israelites grumbled against God and Moses in their wilderness trek, and how upset God was with them because of that. Being thankful to God should be a constant in the life of a Christian, not just as he prays, but all the time.

Combining prayer with an attitude of thanksgiving can be the vaccine that cures the disease of anxiety. As Christians focus their attention away from themselves, start thinking about their heavenly Father, and present their requests to him with a thankful heart anxiety should begin to dissipate. In v. 4, Paul commanded them to rejoice in the Lord, twice in the same verse, so when prayer is offered it should retain that joyful mindset, including expressions of gratitude. Therefore, the mind that is filled with thankfulness and the joy of the Lord should be present as disciples pray.

Paul commanded the Philippians to stop worrying, now he commands them to **let your requests be made known to God. Made known** is a translation of *gnórizó* written as a command, in the present tense, so the Philippians are to make prayer a continuous practice. It must be a habit that is instilled in every believer's life. Prayer isn't something that believers do when the ship is about to go down, or all other options have been exhausted. No, prayer is a habit, a way of life, a way of off-loading stress, and keeping the connection with the Almighty strong.

As prayer requests are presented to God there is an exchange that takes place: **And the peace of God, which surpasses all understanding, will guard your hearts and your thoughts in Christ Jesus.** Believers offload their anxieties to God through prayer, then he replaces the anxiety with his peace. Peter said: casting all your *worries* (anxiety) on him, because he cares for you (1 Pet 5:7, Italics Mine). There is a spiritual transaction that takes place as believers give God, through prayer, all the things that distract them, trouble them, and stress them out. As disciples pray God takes those burdens off their shoulders and infuses his peace into their troubled hearts. That God desires you to be anxiety-free is amazing, for he doesn't want you to collapse under the burdens of life, he wants you to be free from troubling burdens, so you can worship him and enjoy his presence—even in difficult circumstances like Paul's. This isn't to say that a believer will never experience a degree of anxiety, because we are still living in a fallen condition.

Peace is a translation of *eirēnē*, from a root meaning: to tie together, to join, or to tie together into a whole. Therefore, the word in context means having a tranquil mind, in distinction from one that is frazzled and toxic with emotional trauma. During difficult times God enables people to keep everything "tied together" and provides the ability to keep emotions stable. God's peace is the cure for anxiety, in fact, it is the ultimate coping mechanism for the burdens that disciples carry. But God's peace is more than just having a tranquil mind during trials, the word carries with it the idea of wholeness, much like the Hebrew equivalent *shalom* meaning: health, prosperity, wellness, and wholeness. God's peace ties everything together in wholeness, thus giving us serenity in the midst of trauma.

Because God is always present in believer's lives, trials that produce anxiety take on a different meaning in that anxiety is displaced with the knowledge that all things work together for good to those who love God (Rom 8:28). God is with his people in intimate ways during moments of suffering and pain to produce greater levels of trust, dependence on him, and elevate holiness to new heights. Living on this side of heaven means that anxiety will never disappear completely because everyone bears the corruption of sin, but in heaven anxiety will be a thing of the past.

The peace that God imparts to us is indescribable and beyond human comprehension because Paul says it **surpasses all understanding.** Surpasses translates *hyperéchō*, from *hyper* (which means "above" or "beyond"), *and echō,* (meaning "to have"). Therefore, the word means: to have beyond, to surpass, or transcend, and it is written as a present participle which means God's peace continuously surpasses our understanding. God's peace that we experience surpasses our ability to rationally understand it because it is other-worldly. All human attempts to bring peace into our lives will not come even remotely close to the potency of God's peace and understanding it will always elude us.

Paul makes it sound like God's peace has personal attributes for he says God's peace: **will guard your hearts and your thoughts in Christ Jesus. Will guard** is a military term: *phrouréō*, which refers to a sentinel guarding his post. This would be a powerful image to the retired soldiers in Philippi, who themselves have guarded their posts in service to the Empire. Philippi was a Roman garrison town, very secure, perhaps the most secure in Macedonia. The image is very colorful, God's peace stands at his post, vigilantly guarding the believer's mind against anxiety, fears, doubts, the enemy, and so forth. The verb is written in the future tense meaning that in response to people's prayers God's peace will stand watch over their thought-life. It is a promise God makes to his people regarding their prayers.

He guards: **your hearts and your thoughts**, so his protection is exhaustive. The heart is the core of a human being. Solomon advised us to guard our hearts, for it is the wellspring of life (Pro 4:23). God's peace also guards one's thoughts in that thinking that leads to fear and anxiety will be warded off by God's peace. All of this takes place **in Christ Jesus.** Believer's spiritual sphere of existence is "in Christ" which opens the reservoir to the unending stream of God's blessings—one of which is his peace. Joy and peace are byproducts of the Spirit-filled life, for both are in the list of the fruit of the Spirit (Gal 5:22-23), and Paul links peace and Joy to the Holy Spirit in his letter to the Romans (14:17). Paul commanded the Philippians twice in v. 4 to rejoice in the Lord, thus establishing a link with God's peace as the cure for anxious moments of life.

Insights, Applications, and Life Lessons

As Paul is writing this section of his letter, perhaps he's dictating it to Timothy, they take a break from writing and start talking about the struggles of ministry, which I'm sure they've done many times before. Maybe Timothy asked him how he copes with all the pressure. The Roman soldier who is chained to Paul is listening in on the conversation. Epaphroditus is weighing in on the talk as well, because he's been overly anxious about being away from his home in Philippi. He feels as though he is causing everybody trouble and may be feeling a little guilty about it. He seems to be obsessing on himself. He asks Paul how he can cope with his anxiety. He seems to be constantly thinking about getting home and seeing his friends. Paul can see the anxiety on Epaphroditus' face and hear it in his voice.

Paul's words provide him with comfort as he tells Epaphroditus to pray, rejoice in the Lord and receive God's peace. He asked Paul if he's feeling high anxiety over his court appearance—life or death are the outcomes. Paul's answer was probably, "I feel God's peace in my heart about it, the matter is in God's hands. The Lord Jesus has been strengthening me, so I can cope with the situation." The Praetorian is eavesdropping and says to Paul, "You mean to tell me that a man who was crucified for being an enemy of the state can give you peace, strength, and take your anxiety away." Paul says, "That's right." "How can this be," the Praetorian says with a look of bewilderment on his face. Then a conversation begins.

Paul, Timothy, along with Epaphroditus are probably feeling some anxiety about the church in Philippi, and they may be feeling a bit stressed about the preachers that are undermining Paul from the Roman church. Paul's rented quarters could be a high anxiety environment given the circumstances. Four guys trying to cope are having a conversation about handling the pressures of life: Timothy, Epaphroditus, the Praetorian, and Paul.

How many times have you had conversations like that with your friends? Probably more than you can remember. This passage provides us with some of the most useful and practical tools for developing good emotional health. Millions of people struggle with intense anxiety in our country, so this passage of Scripture can be a solace for hurting people. God wants us to be emotionally healthy people, part of which is learning to cope with anxiety.

I have learned in my own experience that it is necessary to monitor my thought-life to effectively cope with anxiety. When my thoughts start drifting into negativity, pessimism, with doom and gloom scenarios entering my mind I need to stop entertaining those thoughts. When I notice myself obsessing on my circumstances that's the time to stop thinking about what I don't have and rejoice in what I do have. When I focus on the needs of other people, who may be in far worse shape than I am, that gives me a mental break from my circumstances and helps me to feel thankful for what I have.

Additionally, we mustn't be naïve and miss the aspect of spiritual warfare in coping with anxiety. Satan doesn't want people to be mentally healthy individuals with stable emotions. He will do everything he can to rob you of joy, steal your peace, and make you miserable. After all, he is the thief that comes to steal, kill, and destroy (John 10:10). He's highly skilled at that and is very proficient! When our minds are filled with destructive thoughts and are plagued with worries it is appropriate to say, "Satan, I rebuke you in the name of Jesus." We must learn to discern when the enemy gets inside our heads and plays his evil games with us. Paul said we are to take every thought captive to Christ (2 Cor 10:5). We need to use our God-given authority over the demonic realm and resist the Devil when he attacks (Eph 6:10-18; Jam 4:7).

Did Paul Struggle With Anxiety?

Was Paul such a super-Christian that anxiety was beneath him, only for lesser Christians to struggle with? Paul absolutely struggled with anxiety—I'm certain of it. In fact, at times Paul must have been overwhelmed with anxiety. Put yourself in his shoes and try to imagine how it felt being imprisoned for over four years and running. Talk about people that carry burdens, Paul must be near the top of the list. His life was threatened many times, he was physically beaten on several occasions, one of which was at Philippi. He had the pressure of dealing with immature believers, like the Corinthians, and all their whining and complaining, which can be emotionally draining. Paul spoke of the pressure he felt about the hardships he and his entourage endured in Asia to the point where he despaired even of life and felt as though he had the sentence of death in his heart (2 Cor 1:8-9). Through persecutions, death threats, plots against his life, being stoned, beaten, betrayed, run out of town by antagonists, coming to Corinth in fear and trepidation (1 Cor 2:3) and more, he must have had anxious moments. Plus, he was concerned about the future of the Jesus movement. Who will take his place if he's executed?

Reading 2 Corinthians 11:26-28 reveals the anxiety producing situations Paul faced:

> I have been in *danger* from rivers, in *danger* from bandits, in *danger* from my own countrymen, in *danger* from Gentiles; in *danger* in the city, in *danger* in the country, in *danger* at sea; and in *danger* from false brothers. [27]I have labored and toiled and have often gone without sleep; I have known hunger and thirst and have often gone without food; I have been cold and naked. [28]Besides everything else, I face daily the pressure of my concern for all the churches. (Italics Mine)

It seems as though Paul never had a break. His life was filled with deadly perils almost daily. Of course, Paul felt anxious moments. How could he not? However, Paul learned how to cope with his stresses by knowing Christ (3:10). Throughout his life as a Christian he learned by personal experience how to cope with the pressures he faced and the suffering he endured. By going through the school of hard knocks, depending on Jesus, seeking comfort from him, finding strength in him when he was depleted, and praying without ceasing Paul discovered how to cope with anxiety. He gives us his own personal experience (4:6-7), not something theoretical that he read in a book from amazon.com. How did Paul know that the peace of God surpasses all understanding? He discovered that for himself through years of toil, hardship, prayer, and walking with Jesus and so can you! We are blessed to have him give us his personal experience to draw on in coping with our own anxiety. You can offload your anxiety to Jesus in prayer, let him carry your burdens and receive his peace.

Summary

In this section, Paul commands the Philippians to rejoice in the Lord, which seems to be his mantra in this letter. Christians are to be celebrators, rejoicers, who are filled with Joy because they are in relationship with Christ. One particular virtue that believers must display, to believer and nonbeliever alike, is gentleness because of the Lord's nearness.

The Philippians had a lot of stress to deal with so Paul offers a coping mechanism of offloading one's anxieties through prayer. He commands them to stop being filled with anxiety over their circumstances, because God wants his people to be free from crippling moments of worrying, so they can be at their best for him. As believers offload their concerns to God through prayer with a thankful heart, he takes our burdens from us and replaces them with his incomprehensible peace, that watches over our thoughts like a sentinel guarding his post. Truly, this is one of the most appealing features of the Christian life.

In the next section, Paul presents Christ-formed virtues that every believer should have instilled in their character, which will enable them to experience an elevated level of God's presence in their lives.

CHAPTER TWENTY ONE

* * *

"Think About These Things" Philippians 4:8-9

The thought-life of Christians has been a key theme in this letter, in fact, in the introduction the statement was made that Philippians is a thinking person's letter. Paul has challenged the Philippians to adopt the mindset of Christ (2:5), to be like-minded, and one in spirit (2:2; 3:15). He is going to list eight virtues that he commands the Philippians to *think about*. These are the thoughts that should occupy a Christian's mind, the result of which would be that the God of peace will be with them (4:9). With Paul's emphasis on peace in the last section and here, that certainly elevates peace as a primary emphasis of these two sections. As Christians think correctly, it will harvest more peace in their daily experience. The verb *logízomai*, which means "to think" or "to consider" is written as a command in the present tense, so Paul is telling the Philippians to keep on thinking about these things, and don't stop. This verb governs the eight virtues that he lists in v. 8. These are the things that should be the focus of the Christian's thought-life and will lead to more of God's peace in the believer's experience as well as assisting them in living as good citizens of heaven.

But there is more to it than just right thinking, because in v. 9 Paul tells them to "practice these things," which is a translation of *prássō*, written as a command in the present continuous tense, so Paul is telling them to keep on doing these things and don't stop. He's referring to behavior, therefore, right thinking should lead to right behavior, which will lead to the experience of more peace in the believer's life.

Virtuous behavior was a big deal in the Greco-Roman world, because their culture taught people to esteem the four cardinal virtues of justice, self-control, prudence, and courage. The question to ask is: do the virtues esteemed by the world have any common ground with the virtues held by Christians? The answer is yes. For instance, a believer and nonbeliever can both regard honesty, integrity, and faithfulness as virtues to be esteemed. There is a degree of common ground between the church and the world when it comes to morals and ethics. However, Paul isn't assimilating the world's value system and placing it in the church. Quite to the contrary, Paul takes values that were commonly held in the Greco-Roman world and reinterprets them through the filter of Christ and his teachings. In other words, Christ sets the agenda for virtues, ethics, and morals, not the world. This means that some of the world's virtues are given different meanings by Paul, so they line up with the teachings of Christ.

One example of this is the virtue of humility, which wasn't even considered a virtue in the Greco-Roman world, which would include Philippi. However, through Paul's lens, and the example of Christ, humility becomes a positive example for the Philippians and all Christians to emulate. It now becomes a virtue whereas in the First Century world humility was something to be scorned. Virtues are cultivated in Christians not by their human effort, but by the Holy Spirit. It is the work of God in the individual that brings life transformation, not just a matter of following good examples of people as their schools of philosophy taught. The Greek philosophers didn't believe that humans had a sinful nature and didn't believe that one had to have a religious experience to become a virtuous person.

The key virtue of the Greeks was *moral excellence* (*arétē*), but Paul differed with the philosophers about how that virtue is produced and what it means, so he reinterprets it through the teaching of Christ. For the Philippians, who were familiar with Greco-Roman teachings about virtues from their childhood, they would have to place them into Paul's matrix, and view them through the Christian paradigm of morals and virtuous behavior. Thus, he isn't asking the Philippians to renounce the virtues they were taught from childhood, he's asking them to reinterpret them through their experience with Christ.

"Each of these virtues and the sum total of them are what Greco-Romans prized as the best virtues a person could display. This sentence could easily have been found in Epictetus's *Discourses* or Seneca's *Moral Essays*, in the context of extolling the best of moral virtues. But the words also are found in the LXX (the Greek version of the Hebrew Bible). So it is not necessary to argue that Paul drew upon either source to the exclusion of the other. However, it should be noted that he used terms that were familiar to his Greek readers from the Philosophical moralists (particularly the Stoics)."[126]

Paul was a unique individual who understood culture. He was a master at applying theology into any cultural context, so that people could connect with what he's teaching. He understood that people are raised in a cultural context and see things through the lens of their culture. He had unique insights about how to speak to people theologically through the eye glasses of their culture, which is referred to as *contextualizing* the gospel. An example of this is when Paul was in Athens and gave his talk in the Areopagus (Acts 17:19-34), his gospel presentation connected with them through his insights into their culture. Paul could explain the gospel in ways that made it understandable to people in any cultural context, without ever compromising the content of the Good News. However, he knew a methodology that worked in one cultural context might not work in another culture, so Paul was fluid in the way he presented the gospel and taught theology. This is what Paul is doing here; he's trying to get the Philippians to elevate their thinking regarding virtues they've been taught from childhood, and see them through the life of Christ, and his example.

It is necessary to step into the Philippians' world as we read vv. 8-9 and comprehend how important virtues were to them. From our perspective they might not seem that important, but to them virtues surely were, which is why from a rhetorical perspective this is a key point in Paul's letter. In the *peroration*, (this section of the letter) the author holds nothing back to influence his audience in making the response he's been calling for. At this

---

[126] Comfort, p. 215

point in Paul's letter he is trying to persuade his readers to action, much like a trial lawyer is making his closing argument to win the hearts and minds of the jury, so his client gets a favorable verdict.

He wants to make a lasting impression on his readers here by summing up everything at this strategic point of his letter, like a lawyer summing up his case and trying to win over the jury. As we focus our attention on the eight virtues Paul will mention (v. 8), it should be obvious that one of the key emphases in the letter is character formation. Christians should be people of virtue, which is why Paul is commanding the Philippians to think about these eight virtues, for right thinking leads to right doing. Whatever a believer learns he must put into practice, hence, right belief must translate into right virtuous living as good citizen of heaven.

The first six virtues are plural, the last two are singular and summarize all the virtues mentioned. The first six virtues are connected with the word "whatever," the last two with "if there," and Paul is commanding the Philippians to keep on thinking about these things because it is written in the present continuous tense.

Finally, brothers (and sisters), whatever things are true, whatever things are honorable, whatever things are just, whatever things are pure, whatever things are lovely, whatever things are of good report; if there is any virtue, and if there is any praise, think about these things. 9The things which you learned, received, heard, and saw in me: do these things, and the God of peace will be with you. (4:8-9)

That Paul says **finally** (*to loipon*, same as 3:1), indicates that he is drawing his *peroration* to a close. As discussed in 3:1, the Greek word could also be translated "additionally" or "furthermore," which seems to be the better translation because it connects vv. 8-9 with the previous section. The link between the two sections is the "peace of God" (v. 7), and the "God of peace" (v. 9). Therefore, this section extends what Paul said about coping with anxiety and realizing the peace of God in one's experience.

This is the sixth time that Paul refers to the Philippians as **brothers (and sisters)**, which makes this another family matter, and Paul includes himself with them, not above them. The first virtue they are to focus on is: **whatever things are true.** To philosophical Greeks and Romans truth was of mammoth importance, such that it was a virtue to be esteemed in that day. Truth isn't just acquiring facts and racking up intellectual knowledge, it is about what is authentic, and reliable because it has been fully tested. When Christians think about truth, the Good News of Christ appears center stage under the spotlight. God is truth, there is no lie or deception in him and his word. In the quest for truth people should look to God and they will find it. Christians live out the truth of God's word in their daily behavior, thus truth is truth lived out, it goes beyond intellectual stimulation. Placing truth first on the list was deliberate because everything flows out of God's truth.

The second virtue to focus one's thought-life on is: **whatever things are honorable**, which translates the Greek word *semnós.* The word has the sense of something that is: sacred, to be held in awe, or to be revered. In this context it means something that is noble, worthy of respect, or honorable. Paul uses this word as a characteristic of deacons (1 Tim 3:8), older men (Titus 2:2), and godly living (1 Tim 2:2). People who are honorable and worthy of respect are those whom believers should want to be in relationship with, which can only benefit them. But it goes beyond that, disciples of Christ should *be* people that are honorable and of noble character, such that they provide a good witness to their community and conduct themselves respectably in the church as well.

The third virtue to dwell on is: **whatever things are just**, which translates the word *díkaios.* This word means righteous or justice, which was one of the cardinal virtues of the ancient world. "We are at the core of ancient values—the cry for justice was a constant in a world full of oppression."[127] Social justice is something that all Christians should be concerned with. In today's world looking out for the homeless, mentally ill, the poor, and those who are suffering should be a focus of Christ's disciples. Christians are to live righteously and act justly, which can be done by obeying God's word and following all the examples Paul has presented thus far.

---

[127] Witherington, Loc. 3928

The fourth virtue to think about is: **whatever things are pure**—a translation of *hagnós*, which can mean ritual or ceremonial purity for temple worship or moral purity, but it goes beyond that because it includes purity of motives, transparency, and integrity. The same word is used in 1:17, where Paul said his rivals didn't preach the gospel with *pure* motives. Essentially, Paul is calling for Christians to have a pure thought-life, which is done by thinking about the things that please the Lord. Pure thoughts will lead to behavior that honors the Lord.

The fifth virtue to contemplate is: **whatever things are lovely**, which is the only occurrence of this word in the New Testament, and translates *prosphiles*, which is a compound word consisting of *pros* (to extend toward) and *philéō* (one of the Greek words for "love"). Therefore, putting the two words together the meaning is: things that are loveable, or everything that a person loves. "Here is the word that throws the net broadly, so as to include conduct that has little to do with morality itself, but is recognized as admirable by the world at large. In common parlance, this word could refer to a Beethoven symphony, as well as to the work of Mother Teresa among the poor of Calcutta; the former is lovely and enjoyable, the latter is admirable as well as moral."[128] This shows that Paul had an appreciation for aesthetics, not just morality and truth. The mind should focus on things of beauty in God's creation—things that people find beautiful and pleasant. Paul is bringing morality and ascetics together in this list.

The sixth virtue to think about is: **whatever things are of good report.** This translates the word *euphémos*, which means: things spoken of in a respectable way, reputable, or a good report. This type of conduct is that which is well spoken of by people. Things that people generally find to be admirable and speak highly of is what this word refers to. When some people are brought up in a conversation comments that follow are positive such as: "he's a fine person, I have a lot of respect for that man." Or if people are talking about a business they may say: "those people really do good work, I highly recommend them." Christians should strive to be people that are worthy of good reports from those in their community and church.

---

[128] Fee, p. 418

The final two virtues that Paul mentions are collective singulars and serve as a summary of the preceding six. This brings us to the seventh quality: **if there is any virtue**, which translates *aretē*, the most commonly used Greek word to describe virtues, so his audience would connect with this word. It can also be translated praiseworthy, or moral excellence. This is an all-encompassing term referring to all that is good, even works of art, literature, architecture, etc. However, Paul uses this word to refer to moral virtues of Christians. Paul is talking about conduct that is praiseworthy and excellent in the sight of God.

The eighth and final virtue is: **and if there is any praise**, a translation of *épainos*, which refers to things that are praiseworthy. This word is generally used for people praising God, but here it is used to refer to things that people find to be praiseworthy. As a summary virtue, it indicates that Christians should conduct themselves in their community in such a way that people consider their behavior worthy of commendation. They are Christ's representatives, so they should want to cast him in a positive light through their conduct. It should be apparent that there is a degree of overlap in the meaning of these terms.

Notice that the last two virtues began with **and if there is**, (and there truly is) connects to **think about these things.** Paul gave his readers this list, so they could give these virtues a great deal of attention in their thought-life. **Think** is written in the present tense, so Paul is calling for these virtues to continually occupy a central place in the mind of Christians. They are to mull these over, and carefully examine each of these virtues to gain understanding of how they can be applied to their conduct, which was the whole point of this list. One's thoughts are the origin of their behavior. Right thinking leads to right living, which for Paul are always welded together, as the next verse suggests.

The things which you learned, received, heard, and saw in me: do these things, and the God of peace will be with you. (4:9)

The thoughts that are to govern Christians' minds (v. 8), must translate into action (v. 9), which is Paul's focus here. In a sense, Paul is saying read the list (v. 8) like you have your eye glasses fixed on me. It shouldn't be surprising that Paul is calling for imitation, which is a major theme running through his letter. He seems to be calling for exhaustive imitation for he says: **The things which you learned, received, heard, and saw in me: do these things, and the God of peace will be with you.** The things you have learned and received are Paul's teaching that he passed on to them. **Teaching** is the translation of *manthánō*, a form of the word disciple (*mathētēs*). Paul is referring to the things he taught them when he was at Philippi, which would include things he received from Jesus. **Received** is the word *paralambánō*, also translated "traditions." Both the above words (teaching and received) were used in the early church for the careful transmission and reception of the sacred tradition passed down by Jesus and the other apostles.[129]

Philippians 4:9 supports the idea that early Christianity had a sacred tradition, that involved ethics (including some sayings of Jesus) as well as theology and was disseminated widely in Jewish and Gentile churches."[130] In other words, before the New Testament was written there was a sacred tradition that was orally passed along from Jesus and the apostles. Here it refers to authoritative teaching. The Philippians received from Paul that which he received from Jesus, which would include the Christ hymn (2:5-11) and the rest of this letter. Jews spoke of receiving from their teacher and handing it down to others, which implies that the Philippians should also receive from Paul that which he taught, then hand it down to others (Mark 7:13; 2 Tim 2:2).

Paul mentions the things you have **heard**, which could also refer to Timothy, Epaphroditus, and other co-workers of Paul. The things that they **saw in me** refers to the time that Paul was there in person at Philippi (Acts 16:11-40), which provided a living example that they should remember about his life, teaching, and conduct that would prove to be invaluable to them in their spiritual formation. What they **saw** in Paul must refer to the virtues mentioned in v. 8, which he may have taught about when he was there in Philippi.

Paul lived these out in his experience, he modeled these virtues to them, so they could see them in living time, now he challenges them to do the same:

---

[129] See: 1 Cor 11:23; 15:3; 2 Thess 3:6
[130] Witherington, Loc. 3964

do these things. They are commanded to practice these things continually, for it is written in the present continuous tense, and is an imperative. He's telling them to scrupulously examine his life: his teaching, what he handed down to them, what they heard, and what they saw in him, and do likewise. Paul has already told them to follow his example (3:17), now he is challenging them to do so again, which will result in them being good examples to others.

As in 3:17, Paul isn't being arrogant, and boasting about how great a Christian he is, rather he is giving the Philippians an example of how discipleship works. Paul received things from Jesus that he passed along to the Philippians, who also learned things from some of Paul's colleagues. They saw what godly behavior should be through Paul's life, and others, now they are to do the same, and model Christian virtues to others. What you learn you pass on. Paul is humble, but he does have a sanctified sense of self-confidence in the Lord about his life (see 3:17).

Paul is speaking to the Philippians as their spiritual father, who led them to Christ. He presented the Good News of Jesus Christ to them and passed on the sacred traditions, while showing them how to live the gospel in their daily experience. Philippians is a friendship letter, but Paul hasn't stopped being an apostle, vested with authority from Christ, who became their spiritual father and continues to guide, instruct, and direct them in the ways of Christ. He ends the *peroration* with one last word of encouragement for them: **and the God of peace will be with you.** If they do as Paul has said: following his instruction and example, adjust their thinking to adopt the mindset of Christ (2:5), and occupy their thoughts on what he's taught in v. 8, he's certain the God of peace will be with them. Peace and more peace for believers to receive as they obey Christ.

We must see the peace of God (4:7), and its relationship to the God of peace (4:9). As we cast our burdens on God in prayer we receive God's peace in our heart, and as we seek to live a virtuous Christian life we experience the presence of God among us—the God of peace. Although the Holy Spirit isn't mentioned in the passage, peace is a fruit of the Spirit, the presence of the God of peace is through his Spirit. "It is an advance in thought over the promise provided in v. 7. There it was said that God's peace would be with them; now it is said that God himself, who gives peace, or who himself is peace, will be with them. God is both the author and giver of peace, and contention will have no hold over you."[131]

Through much of Paul's ministry he was in the line of fire and was wounded many times. If he was awarded a Purple Heart for every injury, beating, abuse, etc. he would have more metals than he could pin on his chest. That God is the God of peace, must have been a source of comfort for Paul who suffered so much for the gospel, constantly living in turmoil, persecution, and imprisonments. He spoke often of God as the "God of peace" to encourage his disciples and used it frequently as a benediction.[132] Perhaps, Paul had in mind Isaiah 26:3 when he penned the above passage: You will keep in perfect peace him whose mind is steadfast, because he trusts in you.

This brings Paul's *peroratio* to conclusion. Its purpose was to reiterate the themes in his narrative, while evoking the emotions of his audience so they embrace the appeals made to them. Therefore, the *peroratio* is the emotional climax of the discourse.

Insights, Applications, and Life Lessons

This passage challenges us to think about the common ground that exists between believers and nonbelievers, Christian culture and secular culture. Paul was acutely aware of the fact that people are the product of the culture they were raised in. Often Christians take the position that everything in the world is of the Devil to be steered clear of and must be renounced. But is everything in secular culture bad and to be avoided? For instance, take a nonbeliever that is an artist of some type: a musician, singer, writer, sculptor, or architect that is extremely talented and produces amazing work. Can a believer find enjoyment and appreciation in that work of art? Of course she can. Christians can find things that are good in the world and appreciate them. They must avoid being so inflexible that they regard everything as evil because it was the product of secular culture.

---

[131] Hawthorne and Martin, p. 254

[132] See: Rom 15:33; 16:20; 1 Cor 14:33; 2 Cor 13:11; 1 Thess 5:23; 2 Thess 3:16; Heb 13:20

When a believer and nonbeliever both appreciate something that they experience in the world, such as a song, a poem, or a mystery novel they have common ground—a point of intersection to begin a conversation. What about virtues? Are there things held in common with believers and nonbelievers in today's world when it comes to behavior? Yes, there is. For example, if you ask a Christian and a non-Christian if being a hard worker is a virtue, they would most likely say yes. If you ask them if being a good steward of one's resources is a virtue, they would probably both say yes. However, the Christian would have a different understanding of what it means to have a solid work ethic and be a good steward than the nonbeliever. The Christian does his work on to the Lord and understands he must be a wise steward of his God-given resources. The nonbeliever will not see it that way. If the nonbeliever becomes a disciple of Christ, he must reinterpret his understanding of a work ethic and stewardship through the teaching of God's word.

There are many points of disagreement between today's secular culture and Christian culture, where there is little or no common ground. For instance, start talking about truth, human sexuality, marriage, family, gender roles, etc. and you will find much disparity on these issues. Christians never compromise what God's word says to make Christianity more palatable, politically correct, or socially acceptable to get people to come in the doors of their church. When people become believers, they realign their values with God's word. Christians never realign the teaching of God's word to conform to secular culture. This means when people become disciples of Christ their understanding of things must be filtered through God's word. Things they've learned in the home growing up, things taught at school, or on the playground need to be reinterpreted through the matrix of Christ and his teaching. This is what Paul has done with the Philippians. He's challenging them to rethink what they've learned about virtuous behavior in view of Biblical teaching. This is how one develops the mindset of Christ (2:5).

Virtuous behavior and integrity in today's world seems to be in short supply, so Paul's teaching on virtues is apropos for today. Like the Israelites in Jeremiah's day America has become a nation that doesn't blush: "Are they ashamed of their loathsome conduct? No, they have no shame at all; they do not even know how to blush" (Jer 6:15). America seems to be heading in this direction.

This passage shows us that Paul had an appreciation for ascetics—things of beauty. When you consider the arts, there are many amazingly talented people. When I listen to music that is performed by a nonbeliever I can be absolutely amazed at his level of talent and be moved by his music. When I watch sports on TV, I'm watching world class athletes bring their best game and dazzle the spectators, but they aren't all Christians. Where did all their talent come from? We can point to God as the giver of the gifts he gave them and appreciate their abilities.

Can a Christian learn from a non-Christian? Why not? Some non-believers are incredibly smart, and teach in universities, write books, and have much to say about science, business, technology, and so forth. We should listen to them and glean what we can, but Christians must do so with a critical ear, so we know where to depart from their views.

Summary

Paul has made his concluding argument to the Philippians, similar to a trial lawyer making his closing argument to the jury to win their hearts and minds. He instructed them to dwell on eight virtues, which will lead to virtuous behavior that honors God. Therefore, he established a connection between how people think and how they live. Once more Paul tells the Philippians to imitate him as their spiritual leader, as he is offering them guidance in their spiritual development. The result of following Paul's instruction is that their experience of God will be greatly enhanced, because the God of peace will be with them, and ease their troubled minds during the trials they face.

In the next section, Paul will directly address one of the key issues for writing this letter, which is thanking them for their generous gift of money that Epaphroditus delivered to him.

CHAPTER TWENTY TWO

* * *

"Show Me the Money!"
Philippians 4:10-20

Any time the topic of money comes up between two people it can be a very sensitive, delicate, even a dicey issue to discuss. Such was the case here, with Paul acknowledging the Philippians for their generous monetary gift delivered by Epaphroditus. Strangely, Paul never uses the words "thank you." When it comes to understanding this passage, it is vitally important to understand the social conventions of the day regarding client and patron relationships, reciprocity, and Paul's rhetorical approach to breaching this delicate subject. Failure to do this will skew the understanding of the passage and cause one to read it with Western eyes, that are far removed from the social norms of Paul's day. Furthermore, it is necessary to understand what Paul's position was on taking money from churches while he was there ministering to them. All these factors make a correct understanding of this passage difficult, but certainly not impossible.

Wise rhetoricians knew it was best to establish rapport with their audience before bringing up delicate subjects. Paul seems to be bringing this subject up as an addendum, or as the Post Script of a modern-day letter. He has brought up all the major topics that were of importance to him, making his emotional appeal in the *peroratio*, (4:1-9), now he presents his *denouement,* which is the very last thing your audience hears, so it must be well-written or the story can end on a sour note. He has paved the way for this last topic to be breached, which is thanking them for the money they sent him.

We begin the discussion by considering Paul's policy on receiving financial support from other churches. Normally, wherever he was staying he didn't take money from that church. Paul was a skilled tent maker, so he could utilize his craft to make money and be self-sufficient. For instance, when he was staying in Corinth he didn't take any money from them. He worked as a tent maker, because for him to be able to preach the gospel free of charge was a great honor, and he didn't want to be a burden to them (1 Cor 9:1-18). He made it clear that he had the right to take support from the churches he was ministering to, but he chose not to. This put him in a difficult situation with the Corinthians because it was considered a normal practice to pay people for their services.

That Paul refused to take money from them caused some offense. There were many traveling philosophers and sages in those days who would charge for their speaking engagements. Paul would not do that, which seemed odd, even offensive to the Corinthians, which is why Paul asked for forgiveness from them (2 Cor 12:13). Most likely, Paul refused to take money from them because he wanted to distance himself from the philosophers and didn't want anybody to think he was preaching just for the money. One common theme of Paul is that he had the right to take support from churches, but often chose to suspend his God-given rights for the sake of the gospel, so that he could be more effective in advancing the Good News.

He had no problem asking all the Gentile churches to contribute to the collection he was taking for the impoverished church in Jerusalem, and even commended the Macedonian churches for their extreme generosity in giving to this cause (2 Cor 8:1-5). He saw the collection as a means of bringing unity between the Gentile and Jewish churches. However, there is no mention of this offering in Philippians. This collection was very important to Paul because he saw it as an expression of love that the Gentile believers would show to their Jewish believing counterparts. All efforts to bring Jew and Gentile Christians together was worth it for Paul, because he was a Jew who felt a deep concern for his countrymen, but he was the apostle to the Gentiles who saw an opportunity to extend Christ's love to the Jerusalem church, where the Jesus movement began. The important thing for Paul was to see unity between Jewish and Gentile Christians effected through this offering.

It's important to distinguish between several types of support that Paul took. When Paul visited churches, or traveled he stayed with people who provided food and shelter. He had no problem with this at all. Secondly, he took travel funds, so he could go from one place to another and get food and shelter as needed (1 Cor 16:6b). Thirdly, there was a relationship he referred to as *giving and receiving*, which was receiving money from a congregation when he was serving a church in a different location (4:15). It appears that the Philippians were among the churches who supported Paul when he stayed in Corinth. They also sent Paul money when he was under house arrest at Rome, which this letter points out.

Paul speaks to the issue of patron-client relations. He didn't want to become the client of an individual patron, or a congregation because he wanted to avoid the entanglement of such a relationship. To prevent becoming a client he supported himself as a tent maker.[133] If he became a client to some local patron, or church, under the social conventions of his day he would be obligated to them, but Paul didn't want to be in that position. He would rather put up with difficult circumstances to be free from obligation to others (2 Cor 6:4-10), which is why he spoke of not wanting to be a burden to anybody (1 Thess 2:9; 2 Cor 12:13). He wanted to avoid appearing as though he was owned by a patron and indebted to them. In some social settings these client patron relationships were extremely important, such as at Corinth, but Paul wanted to avoid the appearance of patronage so there would be no obstacles to preaching the gospel. He didn't want anybody to think that a patron owned him and had him in their wallet.

By preaching the gospel free of charge nobody could accuse him of having ulterior motives, being in it for the money, and he could provide a positive example by working hard as a tent maker so as not to be a burden to anyone.[134] He also chose to be free and indebted to no one, so as not to place an obstacle in the path of the gospel.

---

[133] See: 1 Cor 4:12; 2 Cor 11:7-11; 12:14-15

[134] See: 1 Thess 1:6; 9; 2 Thess 3:7-10

It appears that the Philippians were the only church that had an arrangement with Paul of *giving and receiving*. He took money from them while he was at Corinth, and Rome, but now he wants to change the financial relationship with them, which will be explained in this section. Only indirectly has Paul alluded to their financial support in this letter (1:4-5; 2:17; 30), now he addresses it head on.

It is best to avoid concluding that Paul is being ungrateful and saying something like: "thanks for the gift, but that's enough." If Paul were addressing them in this way, almost being rude and sarcastic, that would undermine all that he's said in his letter so far and damage his relationship with the Philippians. I could hear them saying to themselves, "This is the gratitude we get from Paul after all we've done for him over the years." This is surely not Paul's rhetorical tone to them. It is necessary to understand that he's trying to persuade them to make a change in their relationship with him regarding finances, not hurt them and damage the friendship that had been forged over the years.

At this juncture, it is necessary to firmly grasp the nature of ancient reciprocity conventions (giving and receiving) and understand what Paul is trying to accomplish. "What is going on here is that Paul is gently reminding the audience that he is not their client and does not require such kind gifts, and so is not in their debt really, precisely because he is the ambassador of their patron and benefactor Jesus, and what they are giving needs to be seen as the response to all that God in Christ has done for them. They should see it as a giving with no thought of return, not a giving that sets up a further reciprocity cycle. In such a setting it is the one who initiates the relationship that sets up its terms, and in this case that would be Christ and his apostle Paul. Paul, then, can bring that cycle to a proper conclusion if he chooses, without creating odium or shame and without violating or breaking his relationship with the audience and thus setting in motion the enmity conventions."[135]

Paul doesn't want them to give him any more money, which is why he tells them their gift is an acceptable offering to God, not himself (4:18). He wants

[135] Witherington, Loc. 4146

them to understand that they owe him nothing, and he owes them nothing, but they do have an ongoing debt to the Lord Jesus. This changes their relationship with Paul by breaking the cycle of reciprocity. He wants the Philippians to think of their giving as if it is to God and view it from the perspective of an investment in their eternal wellbeing, secondarily to Paul's ministry.

Accepting money and gifts from people can be difficult because there can be a feeling of obligation or indebtedness to the giver. Perhaps, Paul struggled with this as well. While ministering at Corinth he considered accepting the monetary gifts from the Macedonian churches as robbery (2 Cor 11:8-9). These churches were poor and needy, but they gave beyond the point of being generous, such that Paul, on one occasion considered their generosity an act of God's grace (2 Cor 8:1-5). Paul used the money, but one gets the sense he used it somewhat reluctantly, so he may have been conflicted about it.

We need to keep ourselves firmly anchored in Paul's world and understand the social conventions of his day. When someone returns a gift, refuses it, or doesn't give a gift of equal or greater value to the original giver there is a deep offense that occurs—one that could be extreme enough to harm the relationship. If the recipient of a gift didn't match or exceed the gift he received, the recipient of the gift could come under long-term obligation. Often the giving and receiving in a friendship became ugly and amounted to one-upmanship, which became an unhealthy situation that digressed into a client-patron relationship where one party held the upper hand."[136] The unique aspect to the partnership that Paul had with the Philippians regarding giving and receiving was that there was a third party—the Lord Jesus.

Here is Paul's dilemma: if he offers the Philippians a hearty: "Thank you so much for the gift, I really appreciate it, bravo." They may feel they should go ahead and send him another gift. This is what Paul wants to avoid. He doesn't want to be indebted in any way to them. On the other hand, he must acknowledge the gift without sounding ungrateful and damaging the relationship, but he must make it clear that he wants to change the

[136] Fee, p. 444

relationship of giving and receiving. He wants them to see their indebtedness as belonging to God, so their giving is done to him—not Paul. Therefore, Paul is on a slippery slope, and has to navigate his way through this mine field very carefully, which he will masterfully do.

Paul waits until the end of his letter to bring up the issue of money because it indicates where his priorities were. He feels it's more important to discuss their ability to stand firm in the Lord and be a unified congregation more so than their financial contributions to his ministry. He wants them to mature spiritually by living as good citizens of heaven, so he directs his attention to that primarily, and secondarily discusses their financial gifts at the end of the letter. Plus, this is how the letter ends, so they will remember this item as the last thing Paul says. This is what they will remember after the letter is read out loud in their worship service. Many of the Philippians contributed to the offering they took for Paul, so they would expect Paul to express some gratitude and acknowledge their gift.

Having discussed these preliminary issues, the path is cleared to make our expedition into vv. 10-20.

But I rejoice in the Lord greatly, that now at last you have revived your concern for me, in which you indeed were concerned, but you lacked opportunity to show it. 11Not that I speak in respect to lack, for I have learned in whatever state I am to be content. 12I know how to be humbled, and I know also how to abound. In everything and in all things I have learned the secret both to be filled and to be hungry, both to abound and to be in need. 13I can endure all things through Christ, who strengthens me.

14However you did well that you shared in my affliction. 15You yourselves also know, you Philippians, that in the beginning of the Good News, when I departed from Macedonia, no church partnered with me in the matter of giving and receiving but you only. 16For even when I was in Thessalonica you sent help more than once. 17Not that I seek a gift from you, but I seek the profit that increases in your account. 18But right now I have all I need and more. I am generously supplied, having received from Epaphroditus the gifts you sent me, they are a sweet-smelling fragrance, an acceptable and well-pleasing sacrifice to God. 19My God will supply every need of yours

according to his riches in glory in Christ Jesus. [20]Now to our God and Father be the glory forever and ever! Amen. (Author's Translation, 4:10-20)

The whole letter has been moving to this point. He begins with the repetitive theme of joy: **But I rejoice in the Lord greatly, that now at last you have revived your concern for me, in which you indeed were concerned, but you lacked opportunity to show it.** When Epaphroditus showed up with the gift of money from the Philippian church, Paul was filled with joy, but this was extreme joy for he rejoiced **greatly**, which is a translation of *megalós* and is the only occurrence of the word in the New Testament. This is overwhelming joy and is like saying "mega-joy." The reception of this gift and Epaphroditus showing up brought a sense of mega-joy to Paul, but **in the Lord.** Paul must have thought about the special friendship he had with that church and how they were progressing in the Lord, and it brought Paul a sense of joy to have a gift of money. However, it was hearing from them that brought Paul the greater joy, not receiving the money, although he surely appreciated that gesture, because he could pay the rent and buy food. Paul viewed the Lord's hand behind Epaphroditus' arrival and the generous gift they gave him.

It was the concern they showed for Paul, rather than the gift itself that caused Paul to rejoice because he says: **that now at last you have revived your concern for me.** The word **revived** is an interesting word. It is the Greek word *anathalló*, which can refer to flowers blooming in the spring time, or flourishing plants. This indicates that their reaching out to Paul was like plants and flowers coming to life like they do every spring. That the Philippians hadn't forgotten about Paul was like a fresh blooming flower for him to receive their gift. This is the ninth-time Paul has used the word *phroneō*, translated "thought" or "concern."

There appears to be a lapse in time where he didn't hear from the Philippians, which doesn't mean Paul thought they wrote him off and were done with him. He says: **in which you indeed were concerned, but you lacked opportunity to show it.** He acknowledges their concern but understands they didn't have the opportunity to show their concern for him. However, things changed, and they sent Epaphroditus to Paul with their financial gift. They heard from somebody, through the grapevine, that Paul was in Rome and they decided to reach out to him. We don't know how long this period of time was that Paul didn't hear from them, but when Paul's whereabouts became known they took action. The problem wasn't that they forgot about Paul, it was that they didn't have the opportunity to show their concern for him.

Paul isn't angry with them for he's not saying, "It's about time you showed up and helped me." "Did you forget about me?" Paul rejoices in the Lord that they reached out to him and hadn't forgotten him. Hearing from them and reconnecting with them was, for Paul, like a blooming flower in the spring time.

Not that I speak in respect to lack, for I have learned in whatever state I am to be content. (4:11)

Paul makes it clear that his joy isn't about the money they sent him, because he says: **Not that I speak in respect to lack.** He isn't lacking anything, he's not destitute, he's getting along just fine. His joy is over their concern for him. In other words, he's saying I didn't really need the funds **for I have learned in whatever state I am to be content.** Paul went through a learning process to find contentment in his travails. It was by going through the school of hard knocks that Paul gained this understanding about being content in whatever circumstances life presented to him. Paul was a well-to-do person who lived a life of privilege before he became a disciple of Christ. He received the finest education money could buy, and was making incredible progress in Judaism, even surpassing his contemporaries. He was on the fast-track for success, so he didn't go without in his life as a Pharisaic Jew, but when he became a follower of Christ that all changed rapidly. It was then that Paul was baptized into a life of hardship and suffering for the advancement of the gospel. It must have been a difficult learning curve for Paul, as it would for anybody to have that kind of abrupt change in life and become familiar with deprivation.

The term **content** is a translation of *autárkēs*, a term which literally means: self-sufficient, independent or satisfied. The Stoic philosophers and Cynics used this term to refer to the person who finds resources within himself to cope with his circumstances. A person was thought wise if he was sufficient in himself for a happy existence. By marshalling one's strength of will, reason, and self-control, it was thought that people could rise above their circumstances in life and find happiness. This type of self-sufficiency was considered a virtue by the philosophers of Paul's day.

Paul is using the above term, which was familiar to that culture, but he is assigning a new meaning to it. He is redefining the term and putting a Christian meaning to it. For Paul life isn't about being self-sufficient, it's about being Christ-sufficient. Therefore, Paul is saying: "I have learned to be Christ-sufficient in every set of circumstances that I may find myself in." This is written in the present tense, so Paul has learned to be continuously Christ-sufficient. Paul knew very well that his source of strength in life was Christ, and that Christ's strength was made evident through his weaknesses. There was no prideful self-sufficiency in Paul, for this is where he parted company with the philosophers regarding this term. Finding meaning and joy in life, for Paul, was all about being dependent on the resources that Christ provided him with.

I know how to be humbled, and I know also how to abound. In everything and in all things I have learned the secret both to be filled and to be hungry, both to abound and to be in need. (4:12)

Paul has experienced both the highs and lows of life regarding economics, but I don't think it should be limited to just money. When reading through Paul's list of hardships that he endured he suffered in every way imaginable, not just financially (2 Cor 11:23-33). Paul is intentionally distancing himself from the Stoics and Cynics of the day when he says: **I know how to be humbled**, because humility wasn't a virtue to them. In fact, humility was thought to be repulsive and was held in contempt in Greco-Roman culture. It was the Christian community that held humility as a virtue to be esteemed.

The Stoics may experience want, that is material shortages, and even basked in deprivation, but not in humility. They would have none of that. The word **humbled** is written as a present infinitive which denotes continuous action, thus pointing to the extent of the difficult times Paul faced in his ministry. He experienced shortages all the time. That Paul faced humility provides a link to Christ humbling himself and being obedient to death (2:7). Paul is emulating Christ and wants the Philippians to do the same. Of course, Paul's humiliation didn't come even remotely close to that which Christ experienced, but Paul is walking in his footsteps.

Paul isn't saying that he sought material deprivation, as the Stoics may have, he's saying when times of shortage (humiliation) came he accepted them and became familiar with those times of life. He certainly wasn't living out the lifestyles of the rich and famous—his lifestyle was more of a Spartan existence.

Paul was familiar with the other extreme for he says: **and I know also how to abound**, thus establishing a contrast between being humbled and being in prosperity. **Abound** is a present infinitive denoting continuous action, so Paul was well familiar with those times of life as well. It isn't entirely clear how Paul abounded and experienced prosperity. Perhaps, he's referring to when he initially came to Philippi and stayed in Lydia's house, and the times they reached out to him when he was in Corinth and Thessalonica with a monetary gift, and the present gift they gave Paul through Epaphroditus. One thing is clear from reading about Paul's life is that he wasn't living a hedonistic life filled with all kinds of perks and luxuries. Most likely, if Paul's needs were met he considered that living in abundance.

Paul didn't seek prosperity just as he didn't seek humiliation. Whatever came his way, deprivation or abundance, he was good to go and could cope with either extreme because he found his sufficiency in Christ. The circumstances didn't matter, Christ was the anchor in Paul's life. He makes this point by saying: **In everything and in all things I have learned the secret both to be filled and to be hungry, both to abound and to be in need.** Paul makes another reference to the learning curve he was on to find contentment: **I have learned the secret.** The word translated **learned** is *myéō*, a word that was associated with initiation rites of mystery religions, which involved secret knowledge only given to insiders. Paul is saying he has gained insider knowledge by being initiated into life in Christ where he experienced both plenty and want, but in either case it didn't matter for he was totally sufficient in Christ. To what extent did Paul feel this way: **In everything and in all things**. What Paul has learned is exhaustive, in that in all circumstances of life he can cope, because he is content in Christ. This includes **both to be filled and to be hungry, both to abound and to be in need.** In times where

Paul was well fed or had stomach pains because he was hungry (1 Cor 4:11), and in times where he was in prosperity or was suffering need Paul had learned the secret of contentment.

Whatever hand life dealt him, good or bad, he could rise above it through his relationship with Christ. It appears that Paul is implying that his earthly conditions were irrelevant because of what he learned about walking with Jesus. For a man who has been off the grid for over four years: two years detained at Caesarea, shipwrecked on his way to Rome, then under house arrest for two years at the capital city Paul has grown deeper in his knowledge of Christ (3:10), and is still running the race to gain more of his Lord. It was probably through his imprisonments that his learning curve about contentment skyrocketed. He learned the secret of being content through his perils. Absolutely amazing! What is the secret that Paul has learned?

I can endure all things through Christ, who strengthens me. (4:13)

This is one of the most often quoted and beloved passages of Scripture that has brought much comfort and hope to God's people. It is rich in meaning and deeply personal to each believer, however translating this verse presents challenges. In Greek the verse literally reads: All things I can ________ in the one strengthening me. Something must be added after the word "can" for it to make sense in English, so translators most often fill in the blank by adding the word ***do*** so it reads like this:

All things I can ***do*** through the one strengthening me.

To smooth it out most translations write it this way: I can ***do*** all things through the one strengthening me. Adding the word ***do*** doesn't even remotely fit the context of the passage and lends itself to a litany of misapplications. This verse is often taken out of context to mean one can do just about anything if he relies on God, such as scoring the game-winning touchdown, getting an A on a test, starting a successful business, and so on. This verse is often applied to what the individual does for his own personal successes in life, but that is a far cry from what Paul intends. He is referring to his ability to *endure* or *cope with* any set of circumstances that come into his life through Christ's strength. Therefore, a better translation is:

I can ***endure*** all things through the one strengthening me.

Or

I can ***cope with*** all things through the one strengthening me.

These translations fit the context of the passage, which the NIV agrees with: I can do all ***this*** through him who gives me strength. *This* referring back to coping with the things he mentioned in vv. 11-12. With the correct understanding of the passage all should see that it is still a powerful verse that is deeply personal and rich in meaning for God's people. Now that the translation issue is cleared up we can move forward in our analysis of the passage.

This verse has two power words that are worthy of comment. **I can** is a translation of the Greek word *ischyō*, which means: I am strong, I have power, or I am able. Therefore, Paul is saying "I have power to endure all things," but it isn't his power, it's God's power channeled to the apostle.

The second power word is **strengthens**, which is a translation of *endynamóō*. The word means: to fill with power, make strong, or make able, and is written as a present participle which means the Lord continuously imparts his divine strength to Paul, so he can cope with life's difficult moments. The Lord Jesus never takes a break from strengthening his people. He is at work 24 7 on Paul's behalf to help him cope with life's challenges. Therefore, *Paul has power to endure all things through the one who continuously strengthens him.* These two power words in the Greek language underscore God's power that is active in the lives of his people helping them cope in life's difficult moments.

In contrast to the Stoics, Paul doesn't draw on his inner resources to cope with life's challenges, he draws on God's power to sustain him through difficulties. There is nothing about Paul that caused him to boast about his own strength, because he learned from the school of life that trying to marshal his own strength in difficult circumstances was ineffective. It is far better to depend on the One who imparts power to his disciples. Paul went through a substantial learning curve throughout his life to grasp this wonderful truth. The only way believers can understand this great passage is through personal experiences of life—the school of hard knocks. Reading about other people's experiences are helpful, but one can never grasp the meaning of it unless he is in a situation where he must totally rely on Christ for strength to cope with life.

However you did well that you shared in my affliction. (4:14)

Paul doesn't want the Philippians to think that he is in any minimizing the unsolicited gift they sent him. He wants them to avoid the conclusion that he didn't really need the money and come across as ungrateful, because he could endure all situations in life through Christ (v. 13). In v. 10 Paul stated his joyful disposition that their concern for him had flourished, and this is what Paul is primarily thankful for, secondarily he is thankful for the financial gift. He returns to that idea in v. 14 and speaks to their relationship: **However you did well that you shared in my affliction. Shared** is a translation of *synkoinōneō*, another use of the Greek word for fellowship. This is the term Paul has already used several times to describe the relationship that he has with this church (1:5; 7). They were partners with Paul in his imprisonment as he defended the gospel, and they were partners with Paul in his **affliction**, which is a word that is often used to describe the tribulation that people suffer because of their relationship with Christ. They fellowshipped with Paul's affliction by sending him the financial gift through Epaphroditus, and they endured their own afflictions as mentioned in 1:29-30. Their relationship was one of partnership, as they bonded together for the purpose of advancing the Good News. They sent money to Paul on several occasions, prayed for him, and were always concerned about his welfare. They truly had forged a very special relationship with him. Paul is complimenting them and giving them a pat on the back by saying: **However you did well...**they were partners in the gospel so they were in this together, they shared a common bond with Christ and the mission to advance the gospel.

It is essential to understand the partnership they had in the gospel is expressed in Greco-Roman friendship language in vv. 15-16. The primary expression of friendship in that culture was giving and receiving, of which reciprocity was an enormous part.

You yourselves also know, you Philippians, that in the beginning of the Good News, when I departed from Macedonia, no church partnered with me in the matter of giving and receiving but you only. (4: 15)

Paul recaps the history they share together from the time he arrived in Philippi and founded the church. **You yourselves also know**, indicates that Paul hasn't forgotten their kindness, or anything they have done for him. He wants to remind them of their stellar performance of partnership with him. This is Paul's way of saying I haven't forgotten anything you've done in our relationship, for I know the sacrifices you have made in our partnership, and you know the sacrifices I have made for the gospel. This is mutual care and concern that Paul is expressing to them. He uses the Latin form of **Philippians**, rather than the Greek form to bring to their minds their special status of living in a Roman colony as Roman citizens.

In **the beginning of the Good News**, refers to the time Paul was in Philippi on his second missionary journey, preached the gospel to them, then left Macedonia to continue planting other churches. The most likely reconstruction of Paul's itinerary after leaving Philippi is that he went to Thessalonica and planted a church there. However, after being there a short time, troublemakers persecuted the new believers and things got ugly. Because of the volatile situation they thought it best for Paul to leave so he went to Berea (Acts 17:11). His reception there was much better because they were of far more noble character, which was reflected in their scrupulous examination of the Scriptures. But the Jews from Thessalonica showed up in Berea, stirred up the crowds and ran Paul out of town (Acts 17:13-14). From there he went to Athens where he had his famous talks in the Aeropagus (Acts 17:15-34) and several people became followers of Christ. After that Paul traveled south in the region of Achaia and arrived in Corinth.

Paul says **when I departed from Macedonia**, he is most likely referring to the time when he left Berea and headed to Athens, then Corinth, which are both out of Macedonia. From that moment on **no church partnered with me in the matter of giving and receiving but you only.** This is when they entered into partnership with him which included giving and receiving. No other church had this relationship with Paul—it was only the Philippians, which in Paul's way of thinking made them very special. The **giving and receiving,** *doseōs kai lēmpseōs*, is business language referring to credits and debits, and buying and selling goods. Their partnership in the gospel involved mutual giving and receiving. This is the principle by which they partnered with Paul, which is according to the social customs of the day. It is crucial to understand the social convention of reciprocity in the ancient world in that when someone gave you a gift, it was expected that you would reciprocate with a gift at least of equal value, if not of greater value, especially when the gift was unsolicited.

It is necessary to grasp the metaphorical business language that Paul is using here. "He portrays the financial support from Philippi as the means of distributing a life-saving commodity from heaven, the gospel. This arrangement is described as an exchange between friends and partners. The relationship between Paul and the church was cemented by the gift, yet they were drawn together by sharing not just the financial transaction but also the gospel itself. Only the Philippians had this kind of partnership with Paul, and that made them very special to him. The emphasis is on the reciprocity in their sharing: They had sent gifts and services (Epaphroditus) to Paul, and he had given them a share in his ministry of spreading the gospel—an enterprise in which they had participated with him. Each party had given the other friendship, affectionate care and support, and partnership in the work of the gospel."[137]

Their partnership wasn't just about money, it included friendship, and mutual care, so it wasn't strictly business—it went well beyond money. There is no evidence to suggest that Paul was under contract with the Philippians and they were paying him to preach the gospel. Paul wasn't their client such that they owned him. Paul wanted to avoid being entangled in that type of relationship.

For even when I was in Thessalonica you sent help more than once. (4:16)

Thessalonica was in Macedonia, which means that the Philippians started sending Paul financial support almost immediately after he left Philippi, more than once. This is amazing when you consider that the Philippians weren't a

[137] Osborne, Loc. 3099

well-to-do church rolling in piles of cash. Paul mentioned the extreme poverty of the Macedonian churches, one of which was Philippi, and how they gave generously above and beyond the call of duty. God had poured out his grace on them inspiring their generous gift for the church in Jerusalem (2 Cor 8:1-5).

When Paul was in Corinth he worked as a tentmaker until Silas and Timothy came from Macedonia, then Paul devoted himself full-time to the preaching of the Good News. Most scholars think the Philippians had given Silas and Timothy money they raised for Paul (Acts 18:3-5). He mentions the gift from the Macedonian churches he utilized so that he wouldn't be a burden to the Corinthians (2 Cor 11:8-9). This makes it clear that Paul didn't have a partnership relationship with the Corinthians as he did with the Philippians. How often they sent Paul money after Corinth is unknown.

This points out that it isn't always the rich who are generous with their funds in supporting the work of the gospel, it is often those who are living in poverty that are the most generous and faithful supporters of their church and missionaries. The Macedonian churches, more specifically Philippi, leave us with a rich legacy of giving, one that the Western church can learn from.

Not that I seek a gift from you, but I seek the profit that increases in your account. (4:17)

Paul has already expressed his joy over the renewed flourishing relationship he has with the Philippians, and how much he appreciated them sharing in his afflictions. Now he expresses another aspect of how he looks at their financial gift to him. **Not that I seek a gift from you**, which means Paul is trying to break the cycle of reciprocity and remind them that their gift was unsolicited. Certainly, Paul benefited from their gift because being under house arrest in Rome he had to pay for his room and board, so their financial gift enabled him to eat. What Paul is happy about is how their giving has increased their stock portfolio in God's economy: **but I seek for the profit that increases in your account.** He is still using commercial language because **profit** (*karpós*), also has the sense of interest that would accrue in an account. This metaphor indicates that Paul is primarily concerned, not with the financial gift they sent him, but with the heavenly dividends they will receive from investing in his ministry. God is keeping track and the interest is piling up in the Philippians' account, which means that they will be richly rewarded.

I seek, is a translation of *epizētéō*, often translated "I search for" or "I pursue." It is an intensified version of the same word Jesus used in the Sermon on the Mount where he said: "But ***seek*** first his kingdom and his righteousness, and all these things will be given to you as well (Mat 6:33, Italics Mine). Paul is always seeking for the good of the Philippians, because **I seek** is written in the present continuous tense. They have invested in Paul's ministry, so he could eat and travel, and their investment is paying them a spiritual dividend. It is this that Paul is excited about for the Philippians, because their financial support is further proof of their spiritual progress in the gospel (1:25).

Rewards are part of the Christian experience. Jesus spoke about rewards in the Sermon on the Mount (Mat 5-7), as did Paul (1 Cor 3:14), and Peter spoke of our inheritance (1 Pet 1:4) so rewards are coming to believers in heaven when Jesus returns. However, this isn't to say that the Philippians aren't realizing any interest from their investment in the present. They have the privilege of seeing people come to know Jesus, new churches planted, and the long-term fruit of Paul's ministry would cause them to be amazed if they saw the scope to which the Christian faith extended globally as it has today. If some of the Philippians, let's say Lydia and Clement, visited one of today's Christian book stores, grabbed a Bible off the shelf, opened it up to the New Testament and found "Philippians" they would be flabbergasted. Their partnership with Paul in the gospel ministry contributed to the writing of this letter and the expansion of Christianity.

The Philippians share in the rewards of Paul's ministry—they partnered with him. At the return of Jesus, they will receive their blessings in full, but they do not escape the Philippians in their present circumstances. Believers don't do good deeds because they are on the heavenly rewards program, they serve the Lord out of love and gratitude.

But right now I have all I need and more. I am generously supplied, having received from Epaphroditus the gifts that you sent me, they are a sweet-smelling fragrance, an acceptable and well-pleasing sacrifice to God. [19]My God will supply every need of yours according to his riches in glory in Christ

Jesus. [20]Now to our God and Father be the glory forever and ever! Amen. (4:18-20)

Regarding the matter of giving and receiving, Paul says: **But right now I have all I need and more.** The verb used here was commonly used in business transactions for writing a receipt, which is why the NIV translates the phrase: **I have received full payment and have more than enough.** Paul is acknowledging receipt of their gift, they have paid in full, and his letter, in a sense, serves as their receipt. He adds that his needs are well provided for because he has more than enough. Their financial gift was well appreciated by Paul, because it put him in a position where he was in plenty. **I am generously supplied, having received from Epaphroditus the gifts you sent me.** He is amply supplied and has an abundance, having been given the money by Epaphroditus that they raised for him. It must have been a sizable amount because a couple of months after Epaphroditus arrived with the gift, Paul is still overflowing with gratitude and living in abundance.

In the normal conventions of friendship in Paul's day regarding giving and receiving, the ball is now in Paul's court. He must reciprocate, but Paul doesn't want to do that. His intention is to change the relationship he has with them and break the cycle of giving and receiving. He doesn't want to be indebted to them, he doesn't want them to think that they should continue to raise money for him. Therefore, he will point out that the money the Philippians had raised for him, delivered by Epaphroditus, was more about giving to God than to him.

Paul is going to shift metaphors now and introduce the priestly language of sacrifice. Paul has described how he feels about their gift, but how does God regard their giving? Paul describes how God views their gift in three ways, the first of which is their gift is **a sweet-smelling fragrance.** This is a reference to animal sacrifices that were burnt at the altar, causing smoke to rise to the heavens and was regarded as a sweet-smelling aroma to God (Lev 1:9; 13). Earlier Paul used sacrificial language to describe himself being poured out like a drink offering on the sacrifice and service of their faith (2:17), so the present verse builds on this imagery.

The second way God views the Philippians giving to Paul is: **an acceptable sacrifice.** Paul was pleased with the gift, but from God's perspective it was an acceptable sacrifice to him. The Israelites were supposed to offer animals for sacrifice that met certain criteria. When someone presented an animal for sacrifice to the priest, he was only to accept it if it met the requirements set forth in Scripture. The prophet Malachi spoke harshly against the priests on this issue (Mal 1:7-9). The Israelites knew what God's standards were, but deliberately withheld their best animals from God and offered him animals that were old and sickly, thereby insulting him. The Philippians' gift of money to Paul wasn't in that category, it was an acceptable sacrifice to God. In the same way that God was honored when the best animals in the flock were offered to him, so God was honored by the money they gave Paul. It was an acceptable sacrifice to God, which Paul benefited from. Quite often Paul spiritualizes the sacrificial system in his writings, which is what he's doing here.[138]

The Philippians gift was thirdly: **well-pleasing to God.** Christians should always focus their behavior on what pleases God (Eph 5:10). Living a life that pleases God is the primary ethical focus for believers. Romans 12:1-2 instructs the believer to be a living sacrifice holy and *pleasing* to God, and to demonstrate through their life that God's will is good, *pleasing* and perfect. This priestly language implies that the Philippians were in fact, acting as priests as they made this offering to God for the benefit of Paul.

This gift did more than just meet Paul's physical needs, it was an act of worship to God described in priestly language: a sweet-smelling fragrance, an acceptable sacrifice, and pleasing to God. This was a sacred gift given to Paul, but it was really a gift given to God. The ramifications of this are enormous when it comes to the stewardship of our resources. The interest keeps piling up in the Philippians' heavenly account because this was an act of worship—an offering given to God primarily, secondarily to Paul, and God is keeping a running tally of their account.

My God will supply every need of yours according to his riches in glory in Christ Jesus. (4:19)

---

[138] See: Rom 12:1-2; Eph 5:2; Heb 13:15-16; 1 Pet 2:5

The normal thing would be for Paul to reciprocate in a giving and receiving friendship. But Paul just said that their gift was to God, so the onus of reciprocity lies with God not Paul, which is why he says: **My God will supply every need of yours according to his riches in glory in Christ Jesus.** The ball was in Paul's court, but God will hit it back to the Philippians. God is the real benefactor. It is God who initiated the relationship through Paul with the Philippians, making it a unique three-way relationship. The Philippians are not the benefactor or patron of Paul, and Paul isn't a client of the Philippians. Both Paul and the Philippians have God as their benefactor and have a continuing debt owed to him. Every gift they sent Paul was ultimately given to God, but Paul received the gift. Every gift given to the Philippians by Paul: the gospel, partnership, friendship, teaching, and more, were also ultimately from God, but received by the Philippians. Therefore, it is God who is the benefactor of Paul and the Philippians.

Now that he has received full payment from the Philippians, his letter serves as the receipt, but it is God who will reciprocate. Paul says **my God** meaning that God will on Paul's behalf assume responsibility to reciprocate in a grand way by supplying every need they have, which can go way beyond any gift that Paul could have sent them, whether it be writing a letter, praying for them, visiting them, sending one of his coworkers, etc. They can rest in the assurance that they are in good hands through God's provision in Christ. God will meet all their needs, which refers to the basics of life, not extravagant wants. This would include the material necessities of life, as well as the ability to be content in every situation.

God's provision is exhaustive to meet every need the Philippians may have because it is: **according to his riches.** The earth is the Lord's and everything in it (Ps 24:1), he is the owner of all that exists, so his riches exceed even those of Solomon's. God's treasure chest is deep, it is never empty, the well never runs dry because God's resources are always without limit, such that he can meet every human need. This verse is often misapplied by teachers of the prosperity gospel, to indicate that God's provision goes way beyond just fulfilling basic needs, rather he provides belivers with the finer things of life because it is done according to his riches in glory. However, this is a gross misunderstanding of what Paul is saying.

The Philippians should understand that the gift they gave Paul was an offering to God, and he takes care of his people through the kindness of others. The Philippians will have their needs met most likely through other people as well, but ultimately it is God who is the giver.

That his riches are **in glory** indicates that God's riches are found in the realm of his glory, for nothing is outside of God's sovereign domain and all the resources of the world are his. God's glory is that unapproachable place that he lives that is totally *transcendent,* being beyond people's reach. However, God shares his riches from the transcendent realm of glory by meeting people in the everyday grind of life. Thus, displaying his *imminence*—his nearness to us. God is both transcendent and imminent.

All this is done **in Christ Jesus.** All of God's incomprehensible riches are received through Christ (Eph 1:3; 7-8; 18), he is the person that paves the way to reconciliation with God (John 14:6), and all God's blessings are given to people through Christ. Therefore, Jesus is the door that opens God's resources that meet the Philippians needs, whatever they may be. God is sharing his inexhaustible resources with his people as they draw near him in faith, and work to spread the gospel. That he supplies every need out of his inexhaustible storehouse should be a source of comfort and encouragement to believers of all eras of history. God is truly involved in the lives of his people in providing for their needs.

This letter really is all about Christ. Paul began the letter by identifying himself and Timothy as slaves of Jesus Christ, and it is addressed to all the saints in Christ at Philippi (1:1). The last word in the main body of the letter is about God's glorious riches that he gives in Christ Jesus. Even in the concluding verse Paul mentions Jesus again. For Paul, it's all about him: to know him (3:10), and to live is Christ (1:21).

Now to our God and Father be the glory forever and ever! Amen. (4:20)

Paul offers this doxology as he concludes his letter. A doxology comes from two Greek words: *doxa*, meaning "glory", and *logos*, meaning "word", so a doxology is basically a word about glory. They are a sudden outburst of praise to God in response to something wonderful that he has done for us."[139]

After describing God's willingness to supply the Philippians needs through God's vast storehouse of resources and considering how God took care of his own needs through the Philippians' generosity, how could Paul not break out into a doxology of praise.

The doxology is addressed to **our God**, which emphasizes the personal relationship that believers have with him through Christ. But there is more to it than that because God is also our **Father**, so this is even more personal and intimate. God isn't just a distant impersonal deity, he is the Father of every believer, which means that he has a vested interest in each of his children's wellbeing and provides for their needs through Christ. **Father** brings out the family dimension of the church, in that the church at Philippi is the family of God, and all the believers are God's adopted children for the rest of eternity. Therefore, his children will ascribe to him **glory forever and ever!** God's people will spend eternity worshiping him, acknowledging his glory and ascribing to him glory (Ps 29:1-2; 96:7-8). It will never end, no one will ever get tired of giving glory to God, it won't become boring and lifeless, because worshiping God in the New Jerusalem will be an exhilarating experience that will occupy the people of God forever. **Amen** is a word of affirmation which means "so be it."

God has been glorified in the relationship Paul had with the church at Philippi. Paul has brought up many things to the Philippians, his most beloved church, and there is nothing more that he has to say except: to God be the glory forever and ever. Amen! The goal of all believers should be to bring glory to God in all that they do.

---

[139] See: Rom 11:33-36; 16:25-27; Eph 3:20-21; Gal 1:5; 1 Tim 1:17; 2 Tim 4:18; Jude 24-25

Insights, Applications, and Life Lessons

This passage has much to teach about giving and overall stewardship. Christians must recognize that all they have has been given to them by God, to be used wisely for his glory. They are entrusted with resources and will one day give an account to God for the way they have practiced their stewardship (Mat 25:14-30; 2 Cor 5:10).

The way Paul described the monetary gift of the Philippians in sacrificial priestly language challenges believers to think seriously about their giving. Most people that go to church are encouraged to support their church financially, which every believer should do. Some churches may encourage the practice of tithing—giving 10% of their income to the church. Some people give more than others, some people give willingly, some people give in a resentful way because they think they could put their money to better use elsewhere by paying some bills or going on a nice vacation.

Paul considered the money the Philippians gave him to be a fragrant aroma, an acceptable sacrifice, and pleasing to God. When giving to one's church the check is made out to the church, but that offering is made to God, at least that's how he views the offering. Giving is first and foremost to God. If someone supports his church with a begrudging attitude he needs to remember who it is that he is giving to. If he writes his check thinking, "I don't want to contribute to my pastor's salary because his sermons bore me to death," he not only has a bad attitude, he isn't understanding that the giving is to God—not to the pastor. If he refrains from giving because the elders of the church made a decision that he disagreed with, he must consider that the offering is withheld from God, not the elders.

One member of a church I pastored could be a bit abrasive at times. He once told me that he votes with his checkbook or his feet. What he meant by that was if he doesn't get his way in a congregational meeting, or if the leadership of the church goes in a direction he disagrees with, he won't write his check to the church any more. If he really doesn't like the direction they are going, then he votes with his feet and walks out the door to find a new church to attend. This is precisely the wrong kind of attitude in giving, because it doesn't consider to whom the offering is made. God never said only support your church when you get your way.

The Legacy of the Macedonian Churches

It might be assumed that those who are well off and have a lot of money are the biggest contributors to their church, but that isn't always the case. One of the things we learn from the Macedonian churches, which included Philippi, is that they were very poor, but their generosity exceeded their poverty. Paul describes the churches as giving way beyond their ability, in that they gave not out of the depth of their riches, but out of the depth of their poverty. He understood their extreme generosity as a work of God's Spirit in them. We don't know how much money they raised for the Jerusalem church, but Paul thought it was amazing considering their financial position (2 Cor 8:1-5).

Sometimes when people have a lot of money they hold on to it tightly, they are overly protective of it, even becoming hoarders of their resources. This is unfortunate, because if someone has been blessed with an abundance by God, he should be mindful of where those blessings came from, and realize God is honored when his blessings are shared generously to help other people in need and contribute to the advancement of the gospel. Many people could give thousands of dollars every month to their church and it wouldn't faze them. Some people may be able to give much more than that, and it wouldn't affect their lifestyle one bit. It isn't how much you give, it's how much you give in proportion to how much you make (Luke 21:1-4).

True Contentment

This passage provides one of the most valuable lessons that all people should learn about life. One question that people have been asking themselves throughout history is, "How do I find contentment?" In my own experience, as a teenager and in my early 20s, I sought contentment but could never pin it down. Contentment was slippery, evasive, and stealthy such that I never could seize it. As hard as I tried to find contentment, it kept flying under my radar. In fact, my lack of contentment was one of the issues in my life that caused me to become a follower of Christ. Even after becoming a Christian I still struggled with being content in all circumstances of life and still do today.

I have concluded that contentment is a spiritual discipline that one must learn. Part of maturing as a disciple of Christ is developing the fruit of contentment. The great apostle Paul had to learn the secret of being content, so even he struggled with it. Contentment doesn't come over night it is a process that involves a learning curve. This is a valuable lesson that everybody needs to learn.

There will be seasons of life where one might be making good money and there may be times that are leaner. There will be seasons of life that are tough emotionally because of challenging circumstances: a failed business, loss of a job, a law suit, etc. The challenge we all face in any of these circumstances is whether we go through them while being content? Paul figured it out! He learned how to be content through the Lord's help and so can you.

Most people are under the illusion that if they had more things: a new car every year, a 5,000 square foot home, wore designer jeans, and high-end suits contentment would naturally follow, but that it not the case. People who have a lot are not always content individuals. Times of prosperity can lead one away from focusing his attention on God, depending on him, and being humble before him. Living in times of abundance can lead to complacency, such that people lose their spiritual edge. It is a myth, a falsehood, a deception to think that having more stuff with bring people into the land of contentment. Wherever you are in life learn to be content with what you have, by making Jesus your source of contentment. Life is always fluid because things can change overnight. The stock market may crash, a fatal illness may be contracted, World War III might start, and no one has control over those variables in life. However, Jesus isn't a variable, he's a constant, and he is the source of true contentment.

Summary

Paul is filled with joy because his relationship with the Philippians is flourishing. He hasn't heard from them for a while not because they stopped caring about him, rather it was that they didn't have the opportunity to show their concern for him and establish contact. He is grateful for the money they gave him, but Paul wants to make sure that they understand he didn't need this unsolicited gift, because with or without it he is content. Through the school of hard knocks Paul has learned to be content living in abundance or in deprivation, being well fed or hungry, but only through his relationship with Christ he is content. Paul has learned to cope with whatever circumstances he finds himself in through the strength that Christ supplies him with.

He acknowledges their stellar performance in supporting him and sharing in his afflictions. They stand heads above the other churches in this regard, because from the very beginning when Paul founded the church they immediately partnered with him by sending him financial support. No other church had a relationship of giving and receiving with Paul as the Philippians did, and Paul acknowledges their generosity when they sent him funds when he was in Thessalonica and is deeply grateful. Paul hasn't forgotten their kindness to him.

But he makes it clear that he isn't wanting them to send him more money, he's more concerned about how they are growing spiritually and how God views their financial contributions to his ministry. According to the normal social conventions of the day, giving and receiving, Paul would have to reciprocate by sending them something, such as a visit, more prayers, etc. but Paul wanted to change the relationship. He informs them that he has all he needs because of their gift, which is really given to God not him, even though Paul is the beneficiary of that gift. He describes the gift as an offering to God that is totally pleasing and acceptable to him. God will supply all the Philippians' needs, thus the cycle of giving and receiving is broken. He wants the Philippians to break the normal social conventions of the day and understand that there are three parties in the relationship: Paul, the Philippians, and God. God is the benefactor to the Philippians through Paul's apostolic ministry. They need to view their giving as to God primarily, secondarily to Paul. As the Philippians give to Paul's ministry, God will supply their needs, and richly reward them for their sacrifices in partnering with him. This is all to the glory of God.

In the next section, Paul will sign off and say good bye to his beloved Philippians.

CHAPTER TWENTY THREE

* * *

"Final Thoughts" Philippians 4:21-23

When we come to the end of Paul's letters we don't want to gloss over them thinking there is nothing of theological substance to be found. We may conclude this is boring stuff in that Paul often talks about his travel plans, say hello to so-and-so for me, greet one another with a holy kiss, etc. There are some things in the closing that we should take note of. Benedictions are not a feature of ancient letters, they reflect a unique practice of Paul meant to have a cumulative effect on his audience. As Paul wrote Philippians he crafted his letter from the perspective of it being read out loud in a worship service. Therefore, he has built up to this point and like a modern-day service this is his closing.

Greet every saint in Christ Jesus. The brothers who are with me greet you.
22All the saints greet you, especially those who are of Caesar's household.
23The grace of the Lord Jesus Christ be with your spirit. Amen. (Author's Translation, 4:21-23)

Greet is the translation of *aspazomai*, which is a warm affectionate way of greeting someone, which Paul says three times. This is one more reason why many scholars think that Philippians is a friendship letter, for Paul has expressed his affection and deep feelings throughout the entire narrative. Paul began his letter by addressing "all the saints in Philippi" then mentions the leaders, but in his ending he doesn't mention the leaders, nor does he offer a list of names as he does at the conclusion of some of his other letters, such as Romans.

He says **Greet every saint in Christ Jesus**, thus he means every person. This could be because Paul had special feelings for all the believers and didn't want to single out anybody by name. He wants them to know that they are all important to him and he felt a special bond with each one of them. Usually Paul says greet all the saints (plural), but here it is singular, most likely to express the unity of *one body* of believers, which Paul has stressed throughout his letter. That they are **in Christ** indicates the union that they all share with Jesus, which should serve as a reminder to them that they need to be of the same mind and be a unified body of believers. To whom is Paul addressing this command? Could it be to the leaders, as if Paul was saying to them: "greet each one on my behalf." Could this be to Euodia and Syntyche to greet everyone on Paul's behalf as a way of getting them to assist in bringing unity to the church? We don't know, it is mere speculation. It is better to see this as Paul's way of saying: "everybody give each other a warm greeting in Christ from me as an expression of your unity."

Next Paul says: **The brothers who are with me greet you.** This would include Timothy, and other co-workers of Paul, but we can't know for certain who was with him at the writing of this letter beside Epaphroditus. These are the people that labored with Paul in spreading the gospel, they were his close associates, and they offer their greeting to the Philippians.

Next Paul says: **All the saints greet you, especially those who are of Caesar's household.** All the saints would be the wider circle of Christians at Rome that Paul knew. He was able to receive visitors, so some of the people from the Roman church would have visited with Paul, and one of the topics of discussion was how the church at Philippi was doing. They may have told Paul to say hello to them from their brothers and sisters in Rome. That Paul mentions those of Caesar's household would suggest that the gospel had made significant inroads and was coming very close to Caesar. His household included many people including slaves, freemen, and other servants of the Emperor, civil servants, and probably include the Praetorian Guard. Some of the people that became Christians may have been within arm's reach of Caesar.

The gospel was advancing in Rome, even to the halls of power in the Roman Empire, which is something that the Philippians would want to know. Perhaps Lord Caesar would become a believer in Lord Jesus, through the testimony of someone in his household. One would think that being a Christian in Caesar's household was a dangerous place to be, requiring a great deal of courage if he was working near the Emperor. At the end of Paul's letter to the Romans he has a long list of names, some of which could be members of the Imperial household. It isn't unlikely that Paul would have had contact with some of these people, since he was under house arrest and could receive visitors.

What an amazing thought it would be to see Caesar become a follower of Christ. One must see the contrast of two Kingdoms here: first, the Roman Empire which is the most powerful Kingdom on earth ruled by Lord Caesar. The second is the Kingdom of heaven ruled by the Lord Jesus Christ, whose Kingdom is not of this world. The Good News of Jesus Christ is knocking at Caesar's door. Will Caesar bow the knee to Jesus as Paul has said will happen in time (2:10)? We know that Nero did not, but eventually Constantine was converted to Christianity around AD 300 and bowed the knee to Jesus.

To conclude that Paul's ministry in Rome was ineffective because he was under house arrest for two years is the wrong conclusion to draw. Members of the Praetorian Guard and some in Caesar's household have come to know Jesus. The word is being preached with great boldness by some of the Roman Christians, who were highly motivated because of Paul's example. The gospel is reaching people in power, so there was a great evangelistic thrust with Paul's presence in Rome.

The grace of the Lord Jesus Christ be with your spirit. Amen. (4:23)

Paul offered grace and peace to the Philippians (1:2) from God our Father and the Lord Jesus Christ in the beginning of the letter, now he closes the letter with a wish that the grace of the Lord Jesus Christ be with them all. Grace became a greeting as well as a farewell in the Christian community and is the usual way Paul closes his letters. He has come full circle and signs off with grace to be with the entire church.

Grace (*charis*) is the unearned favor that God displays to sinners. All that we have is by the grace of God in Christ. All the gifts of God given to the church are through **the Lord Jesus Christ**, which focuses on his exalted position in heaven at the right hand of God. The grace of the Lord Jesus Christ, who is mentioned almost forty times in this letter, is what sustains believers through difficult trials of life, such as what Paul endured. His grace to the believer is sufficient for any set of circumstances in life. For the Philippians, who were at times persecuted, having some conflicts in their fellowship and were very poor, the river of grace was flowing their way and could sustain them.

Paul wishes each Philippian to experience grace, but he writes this in an unusual way: The grace of the Lord Jesus Christ be with **your (plural) spirit (singular)**. Why doesn't he write both in the plural since he's talking to the entire church? Most likely Paul is stressing that within the diverse (plural) composition of the church, believers must be unified in one spirit (singular). Everybody is unique, having different skills, life experiences, personalities, and so on, but as everyone gathers in the church they must be one unified body of believers. Paul has been driving home the point of unity throughout his letter, so this is his final way of making that point—the church is a diverse body but must function in unity.

The Christian community was comprised of a mixture of people: rich, poor, slaves, freemen, women, men, soldiers, civilians, Jews, and Gentiles so it was certainly a diverse group of worshipers. The one thing they all share in common is the experience of God's grace received in Christ. He is the channel of every spiritual blessing in the heavenly realm. The Philippians need to stand firm in the grace of the Lord Jesus Christ and they will be able to overcome the pressures they face. Paul ends with **Amen**, which is another way of saying "Let it be so."

Summary

As Paul wraps up his letter he once again makes an appeal for unity. He reminds the Philippians that they are "all" God's people "in Christ." The brothers that are with Paul send their warm greeting to Philippi. "All" the believers in Caesar's household greet you, and the grace of the Lord Jesus Christ be with you "all."

This is Paul's way of saying: "we're all in this together as the one family of God, and partakers of grace." Whether in Philippi or in Rome, wherever Christians live they are one body of believers living in unity focused on accomplishing Christ's objectives, and living as good citizens of heaven (1:27). Paul opened his letter referencing grace now he has come full circle and closes with the mention of grace. The Philippian narrative is one of grace received through the Lord Jesus Christ, so God's people live out of a sense of appreciation for all he has graciously given.

CHAPTER TWENTY FOUR

* * *

"Philippians For Today's Christian"

Studying any book of the Bible must involve reflection, meditation, and drawing conclusions about what this book means for each person. This is the final step in journeying through any book of the Bible. You have been escorted back into the world of Paul's day to understand his horizon and the Philippians' horizon. Now it's time to focus attention on today by addressing *our horizon.* What does Philippians have to do with life today since this letter was written over 2,000 years ago?

This is where the harvest of divine wisdom from Philippians begins. The question each person needs to ask herself is: "How can I apply Philippians to my life and make it my story?" After going on this journey through the Philippian narrative you have been challenged from cover to cover in many ways. As you reflect on this letter and pray that the Holy Spirit will give understanding and enlightenment, divine wisdom will come and show you how to make Philippians your own story.

In analyzing Philippians there are several things that stand out to me that have impacted my life significantly, but there is one main idea that keeps lingering in my thoughts, which is my big takeaway from this letter:

We must develop a Christ-formed mind through which we view our circumstances.

When things happen to people, whether good or bad, they process those events and draw conclusions that will shape their outlook on life and influence their mental health. Paul seems to be drawing the right conclusions about the things that took place in his life, which enabled him to have a remarkable experience of joy, peace, and contentment despite his dire circumstances.

Spending time reflecting on Philippians will improve one's mental hygiene. The data indicates that Paul was a healthy individual emotionally, spiritually, and relationally. He offers profound insights about how people can cope with issues that hit them right where they live, while ramping up their *joy, contentment, and peace.* These can replace the unhappiness, dissatisfaction, and anxiety that so many people struggle with. Who wouldn't enjoy an elevated presence of these three virtues in their life? These are the trinity of mental wellness that Philippians opens a door to and can help improve the quality of one's emotional well-being. Paul seems to have mastered this.

Whatever dire circumstances Paul faced he always found God working in them for good. He understood his life was about something far greater than himself. There was a higher purpose in life that always occupied Paul's thinking. His Christ-given mission as apostle to the Gentiles dominated his life, because he was completely dedicated to that purpose. There lies one aspect to discovering joy, contentment, and peace: when believers walk in what God has for them, while focusing away from themselves, joy will enter their lives and be accompanied by contentment and peace. God will supply each person with the resources to fulfill whatever it is that he calls them to do.

Paul had been in prison for over four years and has demonstrated how he coped with life and rose triumphantly above his circumstances, which is nothing short of amazing. Many people today live in a prison of sorts. Some people might feel chained in a bad relationship. Others may be locked up in an addiction, some folks are in the prison of depression. Many people hate their job, so going to work is like going to jail. Lots of people are in debt up to their eyeballs, so it feels being in a maximum-security prison. Whatever prison people are in they can cope with it by developing the mindset of Christ (2:5; 3:10; 4:8-9). Look for God in the things that happen, identify what he's doing, draw the right conclusions which will enable you to be emotionally and spiritually healthy.

It was mentioned in the introduction that Philippians is a thinking person's letter. It's time to start thinking things over and reflecting on the many topics Paul brought up in his letter, so that a Christ-formed mind can be developed, which will give everyone a fresh outlook on life.

What New Insights Have You Acquired About Philippians?

After going through this commentary and reading through the analysis of each passage and the applications that followed, how has it impacted you? It's always good to write down your thoughts so you can review them from time-to-time. It's time to grab a notebook or the computer and start jotting things down that the Holy Spirit may reveal to you. Going through this study in Philippians challenges you to answer the following questions:

- What fresh insights do you have about Paul?
- What have you learned about Paul's circumstances?
- What have you learned about Joy?
- What have you learned about contentment?
- What have you learned about receiving God's peace?
- What have you learned about coping with anxious moments of life?
- What have you learned about processing things that happen to you in a healthy way?
- What fresh insights do you have about sanctification?
- What new discoveries have you made about fellowship?

- What have you learned about stewardship?
- What have you learned about conflict resolution?
- What have you learned about the need for unity in church?
- What have you learned about witnessing to your community?
- What new discoveries have you made about the end times?
- What other insights have you acquired through this journey in Philippians?

Did Paul Visit the Philippians Again?

Paul was released from prison and continued his ministry. He must have been thrilled to be a free man and continue to do what he loved—travel to different cities and plant churches. Paul stated his intentions to visit the Philippians when released (1:25-27; 2:24) and it appears that he made good on his promise. In 1 Timothy 1:3 Paul mentions his trip to Macedonia, where he presumably visited Philippi. It is difficult to reconstruct Paul's travel itinerary after he was released from Rome, but it would seem likely that he paid his beloved Philippians a visit. He wrote 1 Timothy around AD 62-64, however the precise date eludes us, but what a visit that must have been!

I can see Paul showing up at Lydia's house and giving her a big hug, since she was the first convert in Macedonia (and Europe), and the church met in her home. Epaphroditus, Paul's fellow-soldier in the faith, must have been overjoyed to see Paul. Hopefully, Euodia and Syntyche reconciled and gave Paul a big hug as well. Clement and the true partner have helped the two women work things out, and they feel happy to see Paul and tell him all about it.

It would have been a big celebration in Philippi when Paul showed up. I can hear Paul in a gathering of the church doing some teaching, explaining what it was like to be detained for over four years, and I'm sure they had multiple questions for him to answer. Paul got to see his beloved Philippians, who were his most faithful supporters, and his sense of gratitude to these precious friends would have been off the charts. Paul wrote about joy throughout his letter and when he saw his Philippian friends, he must have been flooded with joy as they celebrated their life in Christ together.

It's my prayer that going through this commentary has enriched your soul and brought you closer to the Lord Jesus Christ! After 2,000 years Philippians is still a big hit. Paul has left us with some of the most often quoted and treasured passages of Scripture in the entire Bible. I hope this study has deepened your insights and appreciation of these powerful passages:

Being confident of this very thing, that he who began a good work in you will complete it until the day of Jesus Christ. (1:6)

For to me to live is Christ, and to die is gain. (1:21)

That at the name of Jesus every knee should bow, of those in heaven, those on earth, and those under the earth, [11]and that every tongue should confess that Jesus Christ is Lord, to the glory of God the Father. (2:10-11)

So then, my beloved, even as you have always obeyed, not only in my presence, but now much more in my absence, work out your own salvation with fear and trembling. [13]For it is God who works in you both to will and to work, for his good pleasure. (2:12-13)

Yes most certainly, and I count all things to be a loss for the excellency of the knowledge of Christ Jesus, my Lord, for whom I suffered the loss of all things, and count them nothing but refuse, that I may gain Christ. (3:8)

That I may know him, and the power of his resurrection, and the fellowship of his sufferings, becoming conformed to his death; [11]if by any means I may attain to the resurrection from the dead. (3:10-11)

For our citizenship is in heaven, from where we also wait for a Savior, the Lord Jesus Christ; [21]who will change the body of our humiliation to be conformed to the body of his glory, according to the working by which he is able even to subject all things to himself. (3:20-21)

In nothing be anxious, but in everything, by prayer and petition with thanksgiving, let your requests be made known to God. [7]And the peace of God, which surpasses all understanding, will guard your hearts and your thoughts in Christ Jesus. (4:6-7)

I can do all things through Christ, who strengthens me. (4:13)

My God will supply every need of yours according to his riches in glory in Christ Jesus. (4:19)

BIBLIOGRAPHY

Barclay, William, *Letters to the Philippians, Colossians, and Thessalonians: The Daily Study Bible*. Philadelphia: Westminster Press: 1975.

Bockmuehl, Marcus, *The Epistle to the Philippians.* Black's New Testament Commentaries. London: A & C Black, 1997.

Caird, G. B., *Paul's Letters From Prison.* London: Oxford University Press, 1977.

Cohick, Lynn, *Philippians.* The Story of God Bible Commentary. Grand Rapids: Zondervan, EPub Edition, 2013.

Comfort, Philip, *Philippians.* Cornerstone Biblical Commentary. Carol Stream: Tyndale, 2008.

Fee, Gordon, *Paul's Letter to the Philippians*. The New International Commentary on the New Testament. Grand Rapids: Eerdmans, 1995.

Flemming, Dean, *Philippians: A Commentary in the Wesleyan Tradition.* New Beacon Bible Commentary. Kansas City: Beacon Hill Press, 2009.

Guckelberg, Bruce, *Get Out of Jail Free: Breaking Out of Legalism.* Kindle Edition, 2017.

Grudem, Wayne, *Systematic Theology: An Introduction to Biblical Doctrine*. Grand Rapids: Zondervan, 1994.

MacArthur, John, *Philippians.* The MacArthur New Testament Commentary. Chicago: Moody Publishers, 2001.

Martin, Ralph, *Philippians.* The Tyndale New Testament Commentaries. Downers Grove: Intervarsity Press, 1987.

Martin, Ralph, & Hawthorne, Gerald. *Philippians.* Word Biblical Commentary. Colombia: Thomas Nelson, Inc, 2004.

Osborne, Grant, *Philippians: Verse by Verse.* Osborne New Testament Commentaries. Bellingham: Lexham Press, Kindle Edition, 2017.

Osiek, Carolyn, *Philippians.* The Abingdon New Testament Commentaries. Nashville: Abingdon Press, Kindle Edition, 2011

Silva, Moises, *Philippians, Second Edition.* Baker Exegetical Commentary on the New Testament. Grand Rapids: Baker Publishing Group, 2005.

Thielman, Frank, *Philippians.* The NIV Application Commentary. Grand Rapids: Zondervan, 1995.

Wall, Joe, *Going For The Gold: Reward and Loss at the Judgment of Believers.* Chicago: Moody Bible Institute, 1991.

Witherington, Ben, III, *Philippians: A Socio-Rhetorical Commentary.* Grand Rapids: Eerdmans, Kindle Edition, 2011.

Made in the USA
Middletown, DE
13 September 2018